'This engaging text provides students with b[...] nal sources... The new edition includes e[...] Berlusconi era in its full historical context.' [...] *Newcastle University, UK*

'The new edition of Modern Italy remains an excellent survey of key issues and the relevant literature.' – **Geoff Haywood**, *Arcadia University, USA*

This new edition of an innovative textbook places Italy at the heart of modern European history, tracing the often difficult relationship between Italians, the State and the Nation. Thoroughly revised and updated to take into account the latest scholarship and recent events, *Modern Italy, second edition*:

- features broad thematic chapters ('The Nation', 'The State', 'Economy and Society', 'Politics'), which introduce students to the main debates and controversies
- includes maps, tables, original sources and boxed material to assist teaching and learning
- adopts a multi-disciplinary approach making it ideal for teachers and students of European politics, European Studies, Italian Studies and anyone studying modern Italian history
- now contains new sections on the Risorgimento, the 2011 national celebrations, Beppe Grillo and the Five Star Movement, and the Silvio Berlusconi era.

Clear, concise and well-organized, this established book remains an invaluable introductory guide, helping readers to understand the complex nature of Italian history and politics over the last 150 years.

John Foot is Chair of Italian in the Department of Italian at the University of Bristol, UK. His previous publications include *Italy's Divided Memory* (2009) and *Pedalare! Pedalare! A History of Italian Cycling* (2011).

Modern Italy

Second Edition

JOHN FOOT

palgrave
macmillan

First edition published 2003
Second edition published 2014 by
PALGRAVE MACMILLAN

Palgrave Macmillan in the UK is an imprint of Macmillan Publishers Limited, registered in England, company number 785998, of Houndmills, Basingstoke, Hampshire RG21 6XS.

Palgrave Macmillan in the US is a division of St Martin's Press LLC, 175 Fifth Avenue, New York, NY 10010.

Palgrave Macmillan is the global academic imprint of the above companies and has companies and representatives throughout the world.

Palgrave® and Macmillan® are registered trademarks in the United States, the United Kingdom, Europe and other countries.

ISBN 978–0–230–36032–7 hardback
ISBN 978–0–230–36033–4 paperback

This book is printed on paper suitable for recycling and made from fully managed and sustained forest sources. Logging, pulping and manufacturing processes are expected to conform to the environmental regulations of the country of origin.

A catalogue record for this book is available from the British Library.

A catalog record for this book is available from the Library of Congress.

Typeset by MPS Limited, Chennai, India.

Printed in China

Contents

List of Boxes

Acknowledgements

Literally hundreds of people have helped me over the many years it has taken for this book to be written and extensively revised for this second edition. To cite some would inevitably leave far too many out. However, I feel I must prioritize my gratitude to the students and colleagues in the series of universities where I have taught Italian politics, Italian history and courses on the Italian city throughout the tumultuous (for Italy, and for myself) decades of the 1990s and early 2000s; at Churchill College and King's College, Cambridge, the Department of Social and Political Sciences also at Cambridge, the Department of History at Keele University, the Department of Government at Strathclyde University and the Department of Italian at UCL. This book is, in one sense, the text I would have liked to have had in trying to understand Italy, and make Italy understood, in all these places. I would also like to thank various editors at Palgrave Macmillan, for their patience, and Monica Foot, who prepared the original index for *Modern Italy*.

Preface to Second Edition

This new edition was written and updated in 2013, at a time of deep economic and political crisis. Inevitably, I have tried to take account of the new tendencies and movements that have arisen in Italy since 2003, when the first edition of *Modern Italy* was published. At the beginning of the twenty-first century, Silvio Berlusconi might have appeared as an eccentric, short-term politician, a mere blip in Italy's history. However, it is clear, today, that we now need to talk about a 'Berlusconi era'. This is one of the key changes to this edition, which takes a deeper look at the long-term cultural and political changes introduced during a period dominated by this businessman-politician-showman. The last decade or so has been a dramatic time for Italy, and this is also reflected in the new material in this volume. The present helps us to understand the past, and Italy's present has been invaluable in re-evaluating an understanding of her many histories. I would also like to thank the anonymous readers of the manuscript for their full and extremely useful reports on an earlier version of this text, and Sonya Barker at Palgrave Macmillan for her help with this new edition.

List of Abbreviations

AN	*Alleanza Nazionale*/National Alliance (Italian right-wing political party)
ANI	*Associazione nazionalista italiana*/Italian Nationalist Association
CdC	*Corte di Cassazione*/Cassation Court
CdL	*Casa delle Libertà*/House of Liberties
CdLi	*Casa della Libertà*/House of Liberty
CDU	*Cristiani Democratici Uniti*/United Christian Democrats
CGIL	*Confederazione Generale Italiano dei Lavoratori*/Left Italian Trade Union Federation
CISL	*Confederazione italiana sindacati lavoratori*/Catholic Trade Union Federation
CSM	*Consiglio Superiore della Magistratura*/Superior Council of the Judiciary
DC	*Democrazia Cristiana*/Christian Democratic Party
DL	*Democrazia di Lavoro* (left grouping from the 1940s)
DS	*Democratici di Sinistra*/Italian Left Party (formerly PDS)
ENEL	*Ente Nazionale per l'Energia Elettrica*/Italian State Electricity Company
ENI	*Ente Nazionale Idrocarburi*/Italian State Oil and Gas Company
FI	*Forza Italia!*/'Go for it Italy!' (Italian centre–right party)
IMI	*Istituto Mobiliare Italiano*/Institute of Construction
INPS	*Istituto Nazionale di Previdenza Sociale*/Italian State Insurance and Pension Organisation
IRI	*Istituto per la Ricostruzione Industriale*/Institute for Industrial Reconstruction (State Holding)
IRPEF	*Imposta sui Redditi delle Persone Fisiche* (Italian income tax)
IVA	*Imposta sul valore aggiunto* (Italian sales tax)
M5S	*MoVimento Cinque Stelle*/Five Star MoVement)
MSI	*Movimento Sociale Italiano*/Italian Social Movement
NATO	North Atlantic Treaty Organization
PCI	*Partito Comunista Italiano*/Italian Communist Party
PdL	*Popolo della libertà*/People of Freedom
PdLi	*Polo delle libertà*/Pole of Freedoms
PD	*Partito Democratico*/Democratic Party

PdA	*Partito D'Azione*/Action Party
PDS	*Partito Democratico della Sinistra* (Democratic left party, formerly PCI)
PLI	*Partito Liberale Italiano*/Italian Liberal Party
PM	*Pubblico Ministero*/Public Minister
PNF	*Partito Nazionale Fascista*/Italian Fascist Party
PPI	*Partito Popolare Italiano*/Italian Catholic Party
PR	proportional representation
PRI	*Partito Repubblicano Italiano*/Italian Republican Party
PSDI	*Partito Socialdemocratico Italiano*/Italian Social Democratic Party
PSI	*Partito Socialista Italiano*/Italian Socialist Party
PSIUP	*Partito Socialista d'Unita Proletaria*/Italian Socialist Party of Proletarian Unity
RAI	*Radio Televisione Italiana*/Italian State Television Company
SEL	*Sinistra Ecologia Libertà*
SPD	*Sozialdemokratische Partei Deutschland*/German Social Democratic Party
TAR	*Tribunale Amministrativo Regionale*/Regional Administrative Courts
Udeur	*Unione Democratici per l'Europa*/Democratic Union for Europe

MAP 1 ITALY IN 1861

Source: Adapted from John A. Davis (ed.), *Italy in the Nineteenth Century*
(Oxford: Oxford University Press, 2000), p. 292, Map 4.
Reproduced by permission of Oxford University Press.

MAP 2 ITALY IN 1870

Source: Adapted from John A. Davis (ed.), *Italy in the Nineteenth Century*
(Oxford: Oxford University Press, 2000), p. 293, Map 5.
Reproduced by permission of Oxford University Press.

MAP 3 ITALY SINCE 1919*

* There were some small changes to the French border after World War II. In 1954, Trieste came back into the Italian fold (see Chapter 1, Box 1.6, for details).

Source: Adapted from C. Duggan, *A Short History of Italy*
(Cambridge: Cambridge University Press, 2000), p. 197.
Reproduced by permission of Cambridge University Press.

Introduction: Studying Italy

Like all textbooks, this book aims to fill a 'gap'. In this case, the gap is a precise one. For teachers and students of Italian politics, history and culture, the material available in English has mushroomed over the last twenty years. In terms of history texts, the choice is now particularly rich.[1] In political science, the increasing interest in Italian politics has also produced a number of sophisticated volumes.[2] The vast majority of these texts take a *chronological* approach towards history and politics. Most do not use source material. These authors usually *narrate* the history of Italy, usually over the same period or periods (most frequently either from 1860 to the present day or since 1945). With relation to specific events of great importance – unification, fascism, 1968 – the analysis may differ (but it often does not) – yet the facts laid out tend to remain the same, and are repeated from volume to volume. As textbooks, these volumes can only be starting points for students of history, since they encourage similar styles of history-study and historical analysis. In many cases, the idea of debate is itself marginalized. The same sets of 'facts' are filtered through different political ideologies, writing styles and editorial decisions, and in the same chronological order. Other sets of 'facts' are left out altogether.

This book is trying to do something different – it is a textbook organized *thematically*, using various kinds of material both as part of the historical account of Italy and (above all) as stimuli to further reflection on and study of

1

these themes: as texts for *use* in classes and seminars. This volume also encourages readings of Italy which draw from different disciplines. Too often, whole crucial areas of Italian history have been studied in compartments – the law by legal students, the economy by economists, the political system by political scientists. All of these areas, and others, should be taken on board by all historians, from students to professors. In escaping from stale and oft-repeated versions of Italy's historical progress, *Modern Italy* takes nothing for granted, and tries to pose as many questions as it answers.[3] The use of source material in this book, often collected in 'boxes' laid out throughout the volume, is aimed at provoking discussion and debate, not at backing up rigid arguments. As a result of this choice, much of the narrative history of Italy is missing from this book – it can be found elsewhere. Here, students will find ways to study and criticize those narratives, to understand the ways in which history is continually subject to revision and debate, and the ways in which 'the facts' are not, by any means, the whole story. Just as important as 'the facts' are the *experiences* of events: how they were lived, narrated, remembered or forgotten.

One other task of this book will be to integrate subjective or personal experiences of history with more so-called 'objective' historical accounts. For example, the Nazi massacre of 115 civilians in the village of Civitella Val di Chiana in Tuscany in June 1944 is an objective fact from Italian history (albeit a little-known one). The different experiences of that event (in 1944, and over time) make up the raw material of that history: German soldiers, victims' families and anti-fascist partisans all carried forward various versions of the massacre, the events which immediately preceded it and the responsibility of various actors. These stories were part of the lived experience of the massacre, and found historical form in memoirs, judicial investigations, public debates, monuments, anniversary 'celebrations', films, photographs and, finally, the work of historians. The tiny centre of Civitella itself is now covered in a patchwork of plaques, statues and other references to the 1944 massacre and its aftermath. All this was and is history, not just the event itself (whose 'facts' are in any case disputed). The task of the historian, and of the student of history, is to interpret these different experiences of historical moments, trends and epochs – to bridge what oral historian Giovanni Contini has called 'the continual gap between History and the history of every individual … it is clear that the events of grand history do not take place in the abstract, but only in relation to real people'.[4] Finally, history almost always uses implicit models (of the nation, of the state, of what Italy should have been and has never managed to be), which are rarely made explicit. This book will also draw out some of these models and discuss whether they are appropriate in the Italian case.

THEMES AND CHRONOLOGIES

Most current histories of Italy take a chronological approach. They move forward from one specific date to another through a series of periods, moments and key 'turning points'. This book aims to use a different method of study. By taking a thematic approach the book will draw out the key questions concerning Italian history, which stretch across these dates, turning points and moments. As such, it will look in more detail at certain processes and will also allow for the continuities and discontinuities of history.

These thematic chapters are not a replacement for thorough historical background reading, but aim to complement study of contemporary Italy. *Modern Italy* does not intend to tell the whole story, but more of the story, and from a number of different viewpoints. Readers will come across laws, constitutional clauses, speeches, maps, newspaper articles and debates, on their journey through this book, as well as references to the rich and varied historical research that has looked at Italy since unification. For reasons of clarity, broad themes have been adopted for each chapter. A longer study would have included separate chapters on the south, or the north, or on Italian culture. Here the categories have been reduced to four: the nation, the state, the economy and society, and politics.

Modern Italy inevitably reflects personal research interests, foibles and eccentricities – an interest in social history and anthropology, in periods of revolution, in the economic boom, in divided memory, in communities and classes, in the relationship between city and countryside. Inevitably again, much has been omitted which should have been here, or material has been placed within one themed chapter instead of another.

These pages are dedicated to all those students and teachers of Italy who have grappled over the years with the complexities and contradictions of a place – a country – which has exercised its 'fatal charm' (Luigi Barzini) on so many of us.[5]

DATES AND EPOCHS

Modern Italy concentrates on the history of twentieth-century Italy, with a strong basis in post-unification and Liberal Italy.[6] However, history rarely works within neat patterns of dates. The nationalist elites who pushed Italy into the Great War began to shape themselves in the Liberal period and before. The cold war continued even after it had formally ended. The accepted dates of the 'short' twentieth century (1914–89) must be breached in order to understand many events and trends of contemporary Italy, but the main focus will remain within this period. Various other periodizations will also be taken into consideration, beyond that of the 'numerical' twentieth century (1900–2000) that is used by some historians and journalists.[7] Nobody has yet attempted to periodize the 2000s, or the twenty-first century. Classic texts divide Italian history into the Liberal period (1861–1915), Fascism (1922–43) and (most markedly) the Republic (1945 to the present day). Other periods cut across these largely *politically* inspired time divisions – such as those which underline the importance of the second economic boom,[8] or the first industrial revolution (1880 onwards), or the collapse in 1992–3 of the political parties which had governed Italy after 1945, ushering in what many commentators described as the 'Second Republic'. More recently, there has been premature talk of a 'Third Republic' beginning with the fall of Silvio Berlusconi's government in 2011. A technical administration made up of non-elected 'experts' was in charge from late 2011 onwards, and a 'grand coalition' government was formed in 2013. Yet, there has been little agreement about the timing or boundaries of this 'Third Republic'. This book will refer to an ongoing 'Berlusconi era', which could be dated as running from 1994 to 2013, but has its roots in the 1970s and 1980s.

Good arguments can also be made for introducing further mini-periods within these broader moments – the epoch of political struggle and violence from 1967 to 1980, or the importance of 1969, or the turning points of 1898 or 1920, or 1947–8, or 1992. Above all, the time-scale used here is a flexible one, not adhering to the rigid structures imposed by various historiographical schools whose work moves forward inexorably along pre-ordained tracks, always stopping at the same fixed points, and beginning again. Traditional historical start and finish lines have been dictated above all by political considerations (the rise and fall of fascism) and by war. The continuities of the Italian economy and its state structures have thereby been downplayed in favour of other areas. These continuities are none the less crucial to any understanding of Italian history.

METHODS OF ANALYSIS

No one methodological school underpins *Modern Italy*. There is no overarching master key explaining all that appears in the volume. The economy is not seen as 'in the last instance' the most important factor in Italian history, although in many cases it has been the most powerful guiding force. Neither is there a primacy of politics here, nor a privileging of the role of the nation, or society, or the Church. This book does not look at Italy exclusively from above, nor from below.

Modern Italy moves between *micro-* and *macro*-levels of analysis. It is now widely accepted that one of the most effective ways of understanding the history of a country, a city or a people is to look at apparently minor stories in detail. The particular, the everyday and the ordinary are used to try and explain the general, the extraordinary and the exceptional. These micro-histories do not aim to replace the big picture or a wider analysis, but are part of a more complete story. Nor is this an automatic process – a series of micro-histories does not necessarily make a macro-history. Smaller stories need to be interpreted, drawn together and compared. Some of this work is descriptive, but no less historical for that. The historian often benefits from playing the role of reporter, or that of detective. Clues, small signs and traces can be as important as broad trends and big set-piece moments. Non-events can mean as much as real ones. An extended period of social peace can tell us as much as ten years of street demonstrations.

Narration and description have always played a key role in historical explanation and these techniques have recently begun to take on more credibility in conjunction with other methods and alternative sources. Yet, 'no description is neutral' and 'the reporting of concrete facts is a way of understanding the real functioning of society ... which otherwise would end up as simplified or distorted by quantitative calculations or excessive generalisation' (Luca Pes).[9] This micro-approach has been inspired by the work of many historians and researchers, in Italy (where micro-history was born, and first flourished) and elsewhere.[10]

READINGS

A Century of War and Violence

Italy's history can be read as a history of war. For much of its lifetime, Italy has been involved in wars of various kinds. Some of these were colonial adventures (Abyssinia/Ethiopia, Libya, Somalia); some were world wars (1915–18; 1940–5); others were 'wars' of a different kind, but wars none the less: above all, the cold war, which was played out most viciously, within Europe (apart from in Berlin), in Italy with its huge Communist Party and front-line status. Italy was invaded by the Austrians and Germans (in 1917) and by the Allies and the German army (in 1943–4). After 1945, Italy managed to stay faithful to its 'pacifist' Constitution, whose Article 11 declares that she 'repudiates war as an instrument offending the liberty of the peoples and as a means for settling international disputes'. Italian troops played no part in the Korean or Vietnamese conflicts. However, after the end of the cold war, Italy did participate in the Gulf War, the Iraq War, the bombing of Serbia (or Kosovo War) and the Afghanistan War and occupation. All of these conflicts were extremely unpopular domestically.

Italy has also experienced a series of high- and low-level civil wars over the past century. Italians fought Italians in either organized military battles or highly violent 'unorganized' events during the upheavals after World War I (1919–22), in the Spanish Civil War (1936–9), during World War II (1943–5) and in the 1960s and 1970s. Strikes, riots and protests were often resolved at gunpoint, not at the negotiating table, although the peninsula never degenerated into the full-scale autonomous civil wars (outside of world wars) which marked Spain in the 1930s and Greece in the 1940s. These wars had a profound influence on Italy's own history, providing the ideological and material basis for the anti-fascist resistance (in the case of Spain) and serving as a warning to the Left in cold war Europe (in the case of Greece).[11] Italy's civil wars have contributed to a strong *politicization* of historical practice in Italy, limiting real, open debate over what happened and how history was experienced in the real world. Historians of Italy have often felt the need to line up behind set versions of history, dictated by political considerations.

Italy and Stereotypes

Italy and its histories have been dogged by various common-sense interpretations, which have dominated academic discourse. The most important of these concern Italy's 'weak' national identity and her inefficient and corrupt political system and state bureaucracy. Most of these concepts are seen as both effects and causes, in a form of circular reasoning: her national identity is weak because she is a young country, not united until 1861; Italy was not united until 1861 because her national identity was so weak. The south was underdeveloped because it did not identify with the new Italian state; the south did not identify with the new Italian state because it was poor and underdeveloped. Italy arrived 'late' onto the industrial scene because her industrial and political elites were corrupt and 'backward'; Italy's elites were and are corrupt and backward because of the lack of a modern industrial society. These interpretations will be avoided in this book. Italy's supposedly 'weak' national identity did not prevent it participating in two world wars (unlike Spain, Portugal or Switzerland, for example) or producing the world's first fascist movement based on an ultra-nationalist ideological world-view, or a series of nationalist political movements in the 1990s as hostility to new immigrants in Italy intensified. Italy's history can also be read through the master key of a *surfeit* of national identity in the twentieth century.

Underpinning many of these clichés are many others that rely on notions concerning a common Italian national 'character'. Often, commentators on Italy will go no further than the explanation, 'after all, we are in Italy'. It is often assumed that there is an *Italian* way of doing things, which seems to consist of a kind of crafty muddling through and a healthy disrespect for the law and institutions in general. None of these ideas will be knowingly employed in this book as explanations, although the ideas themselves are part of Italian history. These stereotypes are often employed most powerfully in popular film and fiction.

One illuminating example of this tendency can be illustrated with reference to the huge international success of Louis de Bernières's novel *Captain Corelli's Mandolin*. This book is a love story set in the Greek island of Cephalonia around the events of 1943 with its main source being another fictionalized account, Marcello Venturi's *Bandiera Bianca a Cefalonia* (*The White Flag*, 1966). In May 1941 Italian troops occupied the Greek island of Cephalonia, along with a smaller German contingent. After 8 September 1943, following a vote amongst the Italian troops at which they decided *not* to surrender their arms to the Nazis, a battle took place between Italians and Germans which saw the Germans crush the Italians after days of fighting. In the aftermath of the battle, the Germans executed up to 5,000 Italian troops, who they refused to consider as prisoners of war (instead they were dubbed 'traitors'). The whole officer corps was summarily executed. Other Italians died during transportation to prisoner camps in Germany. Cephalonia represented one of the few instances where Italians fought back as an army against the Germans after 8 September 1943. Explanations for this decision range from links to the Greek resistance, to the strategic position of Cephalonia in the Mediterranean basin. Revisionist accounts claim that the Italian decision was a rebellion against military authority – a kind of mutiny. The war crime committed by the German army was dealt with at Nuremberg. Cephalonia was not part of the Italian Resistance, in the sense of the movement which grew up within Italy after September 1943, but did represent an early act of resistance. On a visit to the island in 2001, Italian President Ciampi called the events of Cephalonia a moment when the Italian nation 'was re-born', in response to a historical debate which presented September 1943 as 'the death of the nation'.

De Bernières's book fits into a genre that dramatizes disaster and war whilst trying to 'see' such events through intimate stories (such as Sebastian Faulks's World War I novel *Birdsong*, or Roberto Benigni's holocaust comedy *La vita è bella*). Both the book and subsequent film rely heavily on a series of stereotypes which represent Italians as music-loving, pacifist romantics, forced against their will to occupy 'this beautiful island'. The film in particular has problems dealing with the difficult historical period around July and September 1943, and finesses the question by collapsing the two dates together. The massacre itself is not explained adequately and is described as 'an ambush' in some of the film promotion literature. Some of this also ties up with traditional Italian-inspired stereotypes which strip Italians of any responsibility for the events or disasters of the war, and present them mainly as victims. Here the comparison with Nazi Germany can always be relied upon to let the Italians off the hook, historically, and has prevented much serious analysis of Italian policies abroad and at home. The myth of the 'Good Italian' remains powerful, and survives to this day, although historical research over the last decade or so has done much to undermine it.[12]

Italy and the World: Comparisons and Models

One of the most important interpretative questions regarding Italy is that of comparison. Who do we compare Italy with? Is she a south European or a north European country? Has Italy always been a 'Mediterranean' country, with all that this entails?[13] Italy seems to be lumped in with southern Europe when the subject-matter is her economy, or her society, and with Western Europe when the political system is under discussion. One problem here is the unit of comparison. Parts of Italy (and not necessarily the geographical 'south') have always been closer to south European models, others much more at home in northern Europe, some areas (Trieste, for example) nearer to Mitteleurope. Milan was always influenced by Switzerland, Germany and Austria, Turin by France. Italy was 'late' industrially in comparison with Germany, but not with Spain, or Greece. Italy's clientelist history looks strange when compared with the United Kingdom, but perfectly explicable in the context of Spanish political cultures; her history of civil wars pales in comparison with that of Greece and Spain. It is important not to be hemmed in by Italy's real boundaries and by broad and not particularly useful categories. Italy has both south and north European characteristics, she is at times European, and at times non-European. Italy has been 'backward' and highly advanced at the same time, and often in the same region. One of the fascinating features of Italian history lies in its flexible character and the difficulties historians have in placing it into easy categories. A systematic comparative analysis is beyond the scope of this book, but comparisons will be made throughout *Modern Italy*.

Italian historians, and historians of Italy, often seem to adopt very stringent models to which Italy, inevitably, has failed to adhere. For example, the model of 'the nation' used is one where everyone speaks the same language and where there is near-unanimity at crucial historical moments. Italy has never come close to this model. However, we also need to question these implicit models, and not just the failures of Italy in comparison with them. Why not use other models of nations (multi-lingual, regionalist, federalist, for example), and compare Italy with those – models taking into account Italy's long history as a series of separate states with different governments, languages, laws and cultures within its territorial 'borders'? The Risorgimento generation took power with a far more radical vision of the nation than that held by many of their subjects – and this led to constant attempts to force through a particularly rigid and monocultural form of national identity from above. If we remove, or tone down, some of the models employed (often without argument) by traditional historical analysts, Italy's history becomes much more than a series of spectacular failures and disasters. By looking at Italy as a nation fitting into neither a south European nor a north European model, then she can be seen as the 'least of the great powers', but also as the 'greatest of the lesser powers'.[14] Narratives of (relative) failure depend largely on where borders and historical lines are drawn.

And, a long way from 'semi-peripheral' status, Italy's history, at least in the twentieth century, can be read in very different ways. Far from being at the margins of Europe, Italy has often been right at her centre. Fascism was born in Milan in 1919, and first took power in Rome in 1922. Italy's anti-fascist resistance (1943–5) was a movement of extraordinary depth and power. Later, the Italian Republic produced a mass party system unrivalled in world history, with political sub-cultures that spread their tentacles deep into civil society, the economy and cultural spheres. Italy's 'long May' was quite easily the most radical, interesting and, in the end, violent of all the world's '1968s'. The Italian economy – with the 'flexible specialization' of the 'third Italy' and its industrial districts – provided a way out of Fordism that is now a model for economists and politicians. Politically, in the 1980s, Bettino Craxi prefigured Tony Blair by crafting a new, strongman social-democratic politics that broke with both the symbols (the hammer and sickle) and the material interests (indexed wage-rises) linked to the industrial working class. Italy has not always followed others, and it has often set trends. Silvio Berlusconi was a precursor of trends towards highly personalized, business-model political strategies that triumphed without any need for mass parties on the twentieth-century model.

Democracy or Dictatorship?

Italy has been a formal democracy for over a hundred years, yet full suffrage was only achieved in 1945. Democracy has always been a problematic concept in Italian society. In Liberal Italy only a tiny minority of Italians were allowed to vote and this period has been described as a 'soft' or 'benign dictatorship' (Paolo Pombeni). After World War I, many on the Left and the Right rejected the formal aspects of the democratic process and called for revolution. Those defending liberal democratic institutions were reduced to a minority. The result was the collapse of those institutions and the installation of a fascist dictatorship. Yet, even after the restoration of full democratic rights for men and the vote for women in 1945, Italy remained a strange democracy. One group, the Communists, were not allowed to win. This system has been given a number of labels over the years – blocked democracy, imperfect bi-polarism, polarized pluralism. Even within the formal rights of a democratic system, many Italians were not free to vote for whom they chose. Clientelism, organized crime, corruption, patronage and intimidation sullied the Italian democratic process for long periods, before and after fascism. The concentration of media control and the conflict of interests that marked Silvio Berlusconi's political project and his use of power were often seen as profoundly undemocratic. Berlusconi's governments were described as a kind of 'regime' or a 'videocracy'. Berlusconi presided over governments where 'Institutional power attacks the institutions themselves'.[15]

However, in other ways, Italy was an extremely democratic country, more than many other so-called democracies. If we measure 'democracy' beyond its formal aspects, then Italians have participated in huge numbers in political and civil organizations. The mass parties of the post-war period were models of democratic participation and debate (although clearly with many negative features), which penetrated into all levels of cultural and civil life. The Church provided broad avenues of participation for many. Civil and political society created powerful networks of unions, local councils, neighbourhood councils, immigrant organizations and student bodies – all these types of organization proliferated in Italy. The collapse of this kind of mobilization after the 1980s did not lead to greater democracy; on the contrary, the 1990s and 2000s were a time when politics and democracy in Italy reached a new low point, and public interest in the political process collapsed. More generally, one feature which marked Italy out in the south European context was the survival of parliamentary democracy in a period when other nations – Greece, Portugal, Spain above all – were frequently governed by dictators.[16] It was precisely those groups so often accused of wanting to subvert Italian democracy – above all the Communists – who became the staunchest defenders of the legal framework represented by the Republican Constitution.

In 2011 an elected government was replaced by a technical administration that was supported by the two main political coalitions. This development led some to claim that Italy was now a 'post-democracy'.[17] The difficulties in forming a political government after 2013's elections seemed to confirm this trend, as did the new government itself, a 'grand coalition' that united centre-left and centre-right in an uneasy truce. The strength of anti-political movements revealed just how low the legitimacy of Italy's political system had become. The 1990s and 2000s were accompanied by frequent claims (from both left and right) that Italian democracy was dead, that 'coups' had taken place, and that the Constitution had lost its meaning. Had Italy become a post-democracy, where institutions had lost all legitimation, the decline of mass parties and falling voter turnout?

Fascism and the Consensus Debate

For the first thirty years or so of the Italian Republic, the history of the fascist period was more or less taboo. The anti-fascist coalition that produced the 1948 Constitution agreed on an overwhelmingly negative view of Mussolini's regime. Mussolini had kept power by repression alone, and had remained highly unpopular throughout his twenty years in power. This 'consensus' over a lack of consensus was only challenged by self-proclaimed neo-fascist historians, or mavericks such as Giovanni Guareschi.

Cracks began to emerge in this version of fascism with new historical work in the 1970s and 1980s. Scholars began to investigate fascism's relatively successful attempts to build support through cultural policies, propaganda, welfare policies, public works projects and the cult of the leader – Mussolini had not ruled through repression alone. Renzo De Felice's monumental biography of *Il Duce* argued that consensus had been achieved by the regime in the 1930s, in particular in the wake of the victorious colonial wars in Ethiopia and Somalia. De Felice claimed that this popularity was maintained right up to the beginning of World War II. Viciously attacked at the time the biography first appeared, many of De Felice's ideas are now accepted by most historians of fascism. Of course, many of these arguments are difficult to prove or disprove either way. The very suppression of dissent by fascism blacked out the opinions of those who opposed the regime. Other historians, following on from the work of De Felice, began to examine the ways in which fascism developed into a kind of civil religion in the 1920s and 1930s.

In the late 1970s the oral historian Luisa Passerini's work took on, from the Left, some of the deepest-held ideas about fascism. Her study of Turin showed how individual workers and their families came to a kind of arrangement with fascism, in part because this was the only way to survive, but in part because their 'anti-fascism' was not as crucial to their daily lives as it had been painted by traditional historians. Later, Passerini's work on the image of Mussolini revealed the myriad ways in which *Il Duce* maintained and built consensus and the avenues through which his image filtered down into society. However, Passerini also opened up the debate around forms of resistance to fascism, a resistance that was expressed not only through open, political dissent, but also in other realms such as the refusal to obey norms concerning childbirth and abortion.[18]

Debates in the 1990s and 2000s re-evaluated the meaning of the terms 'fascism' and 'anti-fascism', especially in the wake of the presence in power of the heirs of Italy's post-war neo-fascist parties. On the one hand there was a rich and historical debate about the real power of fascism and the support for the Mussolini regime. Meanwhile, 'nostalgic' interest in the period of the regime seemed to be on the increase. Finally, debates over the memory of those years, over *what* to remember and *how* to remember it, were translated into a series of initiatives at a local and national level. Previously 'forgotten' episodes, such as wartime Allied bombings, were given more visibility than before. *Divided* memories gave way to *fragmented* memories, as the state and local administrations adopted an ad hoc policy of pluralism in terms of commemoration and 'days of memory' (see Box 1.17). This also led to historical confusion, as different versions of the past were increasingly displayed in the public sphere without explanation. A battle over victim status took place that mirrored similar trends in other nations such as Germany and Spain. By allowing all sides to portray themselves as victims, the Italian authorities were able to broker an uneasy truce in its memory wars. But the price of this unwritten agreement was historical confusion. The past was reduced to a catalogue of different forms of suffering. Remembrance was universalized. Politics and history itself became secondary.

The 'Roman Question' Yesterday and Today

Traditional histories of Italy tend to play down the role and importance of the Catholic Church. From the very beginning, the hostility of the Church to the project behind Italian unification, and the anti-clerical nature of many protagonists of the Risorgimento, hampered any kind of conciliation between the political system and Catholic institutions and believers. The king was, after all, excommunicated in 1871 after Italian troops had attacked Rome itself. The Pope remained in 'internal exile' in the Vatican for over fifty years. This fracture within Italian society was a key feature of Italy's early history, with Catholics being ordered to boycott the new state, while the massive cultural, economic and temporal power of the Church only highlighted the weaknesses of the new state. At various times, this fracture was healed, often in response to the presumed threat of anti-clerical socialist revolution. Various secret and formal pacts preceded the 'resolution' of the Roman question with Mussolini's Lateran Treaty in 1929. After the war the Church entered politics with a vengeance, through the Christian Democratic Party, and managed to control the country politically for over fifty cold war years. Yet this period was also one of enormous decline in Catholic ideological power, as Italians broke from the constraints of religious teachings. Issues such as assisted suicide and the application of the abortion law still tended to divide Italians along religious lines, but these divisions were increasingly blurred. None the less, in Italy more than in any other European country, the Church remains a centre of debate, ideology and economic hegemony. This is partly thanks to the weight of Rome as site of the Papal-state, but also a result of the absences and failures of the Italian state in so many areas of civil life, from the school system to the welfare state.

It has been argued that the Catholicism of Italy is a key factor, perhaps the key factor, in explaining a series of problems which have beset the country since unification. Giovanni Levi has written that 'Catholicism is ... pervasive, part of our character: it is intrinsic for us, in the air that we breathe; it is everywhere, but invisible'. The anthropological relationship with Catholicism has led, it could be argued, to a state of 'Catholic anarchism' where 'the state is widely seen as extraneous, an institution which almost everyone has the right (almost a duty) to defraud'. 'Beneath the surface of an apparently secular society and state', Levi continues, 'four centuries of co-habitation between church and state have shaped politics and created a sense of justice that is dominated by this dualism'. The Church is not just an institution, it has created a way of being, over a long period of time.[19]

Family, Civil Society and State

At an everyday level, the contradictions in Italian society are played out between the family, civil society and the state. The strength of the family in Italian society has often been the subject of historical debate, although it has far too rarely been the subject of historical research. Once again, we find ourselves in a series of circular arguments. The south remained poor because people privileged their family interests, some claimed. Others argued that, on the contrary, people privileged their family interests *because* the south was so poor and the state so hostile. Civil society was weak because the family was so strong. The family was strong because civil society was weak. There is no easy way out of these dualisms – it would be pointless (and wrong) to 'choose' one explanation against another. Both aspects are part of the complete picture – the family was strong, in part, because civil society was weak, and civil society was weak, in part, because the family was strong. The history of Italy can *also* be read as a complicated series of relationships between family, kin and other institutions, including the state and the Church.

The state has done little, over a century, to encourage an attachment to it and the lack of enthusiasm of many Italians for Italy's military adventures has been perhaps the most obvious example of this rejection of state authority. Yet many Italians at many moments in their country's history have chosen the state and/or the nation rather than their families. Both the partisans and the volunteer fascists of the 1943–5 period gave up family life to fight for ideals. The moral judgement may well be a different one, but both experiences deserve study as examples of attachments beyond those of the immediate family unit. Often, the interests of family and state have coincided. At many other moments, the return to civil society has been part of an attempt to put pressure on the state to carry out reforms. The inability or unwillingness of the state to reform itself or society over the past century has been a key component of these difficult relationships. The state has usually been unable to respond to legitimate requests for change, and this has pushed movements into extreme positions. On other occasions, the family has provided a series of services where the state has been found wanting – childcare, housing, emotional support, economic unity, financial backing for the period of a university education. Moreover, the family itself has been a key economic unit, and the links between business, family ethics and profit are important ones for understanding Italian economic progress. Families have provided a basis for economic transition and growth across the peninsula, from the sharecroppers of Tuscany to the small businesses of Prato, from the landowners of the Veneto in the 1950s to the north-east economic miracle of the 1980s.

Territories: South and North, City and Country

Broad territorial divisions have usually been adopted in attempting to understand the history of Italy. The most obvious of these has revolved around the so-called 'southern question' – the historic inability of the Italian state to bring progress to the south as well as the north. Certain recurrent aspects of southern society are usually included in traditional analyses of the 'southern question' – organized crime, 'backwardness', familism, and ethnic differences. In recent years, however, the whole basis on which the 'southern question' has been studied has been called into question. Historians began to ask themselves very simple questions, the answers to which had previously been taken for granted. Where is the south? Is it, or has it ever been, a unified entity? When did the southern economy begin to diverge from that of the north? Where is the north? All of these questions have led to a reassessment of the 'southern question' as a far more complicated set of issues involving ideology, the creation of national identities (with southerners often playing the role of 'foreigners' within Italy) and a detailed analysis of the history of the southern economy. In addition, the history of 'southern' areas in the north, such as the Veneto, has been used to draw out the relationship between richer and poorer zones of Italy. Institutional changes have also affected regional identities, especially with the increasing powers handed over to regional governments in the 1980s, 1990s and 2000s. Macro-regions became states within the state, and forged alliances with other regions or internationally.

The speed of change in some areas (in particular the north-east but also parts of the south) should also lead to a reassessment of the historic nature of the 'southern question' in the light of a century of development – and of uneven development. Italy, of course, was not alone in the world in having marked regional economic and political imbalances, although the particular nature of the *mezzogiorno* has often been seen as central to any real understanding of her history, and above all of her failures.

A further set of relationships includes those between city and country. Italy developed industrially in very different ways from other European countries. Often, as with Lombardy, there was a kind of slow industrialization, where the countryside was industrialized and cities were not necessarily the centre of production. Even the boom of the 1960s, the closest Italy came to a 'real' industrial revolution, did not lead to mega-cities but brought a kind of dispersed urbanization which saw many smaller businesses located in more rural areas. Urban sprawl has marked the landscape of Italy in such a way as to transform both the city and the countryside. Much of the Italian landscape now consists of a connected series of conurbations where both the urban and the rural are never far away. So vast have these areas become that they now stretch across national borders into France, Switzerland, Germany and Austria. In general, the importance of place cannot be underestimated in attempting to understand the shape of Italian politics and society.[20] Geography can often be as important, if not more so, than more traditional explanatory tools such as class, in the mapping of cultures and histories.

Italians on the Move

Another master-key for the reading of Italian history over the twentieth century lies with the propensity of Italians to move across both vast and small tracts of land and ocean to find work elsewhere. The first mass movements took place from the Veneto and Lombardy in the 1870s. Later, Italians from the south travelled thousands of miles to build new lives in the United States or Argentina. In the 1950s and 1960s, the main destinations became Italian ones – Turin, Milan and Rome. Finally, Italians developed into some of the most avid mass tourists in Europe, visiting other European and international destinations in their millions. These movements had deep effects on those who moved, on those who remained, on those who came back and on the societies who hosted the Italians. Yet rarely has this history been incorporated in an organic way into Italy's history. The memory of those millions of Italians who left their villages to work in foreign cities, be they Italian or non-Italian, has usually been relegated to a footnote from the past. In recent years, there has been a new 'exodus' of Italians, many of them highly qualified, as a response to the economic crisis and the lack of openings for young people at home. Some have dubbed Italy a 'gerontocracy' where young people are excluded due to the persistence of clientelistic and patronage networks of power. This new diaspora has proved to be a powerful lobby for change within Italy itself, and the new voting law of 2006, which gave Italian emigrants their own constituencies, also allowed Italians abroad to play a vital if controversial role in the electoral process.

Since the mid-1970s, Italy has begun to attract its own immigrants from abroad. By 2010, there were over four million foreign immigrants in Italy. These immigrants were from a variety of nations, and from both within and outside of the EU (whose borders have been changing in any case). This trend has led to intense debates over Italian identity, citizenship, racism and the role of the Other in Italian society. Little mention was made in these debates of Italy's long history of emigration both outside Italy and within the peninsula. The arrival of *outsiders* seemed to reinforce, or reflect, a sense of national or localistic identity amongst many Italians, but this process needs to be placed firmly in the historical context of migration involving Italians over the last 150 years. A new Italy was being created (for economic reasons) which spoke other languages, sometimes prayed to other gods and had little democratic stake in the Italian state.

The Berlusconi Era

In 1974 an entrepreneur called Silvio Berlusconi set up his first TV channels inside a modern, middle-class housing estate he had built just outside Milan. The neighbourhood was known as *Milano 2*, and the TV station was called *TeleMilano*. Quickly, Berlusconi built up a vast media empire, based on a diet of game shows, US soap opera imports and football. It was glamorous and popular at the same time, and it transformed the Italian media scene. After a long legal battle Berlusconi's powerful political allies finally managed to sanction and protect his virtual monopoly of the private television sector in the early 1990s. By then, Berlusconi had tapped into (and helped create) an increasingly consumerist and individualist society, a 'new common sense' (Luigi Manconi). Berlusconi's networks 'furnished Italians with a new set of values and aspirations' (Gundle and O'Sullivan).[21] In addition, Berlusconi expanded his business interests, buying, for example, the major Serie A football club AC Milan in 1987. AC Milan went on to become one of the most successful clubs in the world in the 1990s and 2000s.

In 1994, in the wake of the collapse of the old political system, Berlusconi 'took the field', forming a 'party' that was able to win the elections only months later. This extraordinary political moment was the beginning of the 'Berlusconi era'. For the next twenty years or so, Berlusconi would dominate Italy's political scene. His use of his own media was modern and all-encompassing. He transfixed Italians, rewriting the language and style of the entire political system. The clear conflict of interests between his public duties and powers and his vast private wealth and influence was never resolved. Each election became a referendum about *him* – Berlusconi himself. His body, his hair, his 'lack of shame', his private life, his carefully constructed gaffes – in short *everything* about him – became the subject of public debate. He used straightforward, non-political language and symbols, he constructed enemies and preyed on fear, he built alliances (above all with the Northern League) and he frequently contradicted himself. But it didn't matter. He knew that the electorate had a short memory. In this way, he won elections (1994, 2001, 2008) and he lost them (1996, 2006, 2013), but reports of his imminent demise were usually mistaken. Meanwhile, he had a series of complicated run-ins with the Italian justice system (which he accused of orchestrating a political conspiracy against him) and passed a number of 'personal' laws to protect himself against various trials and investigations. By the end of the first decade of the 2000s, Berlusconi had become part of Italian history, an object of study, a phenomenon about which numerous books, documentaries and journalistic enquiries have been written and produced.

Anti-Nation, Anti-Risorgimento

In the 1980s and 1990s, and then in the 2000s, two separate but connected trends have seen a sustained political and historical attack on the Risorgimento (the movement which led to the unification of the country in the nineteenth century) and on Italy itself. In the north, ever since the late 1980s, the regionalist *Lega Nord* movement has propagated an anti-Risorgimento version of the past from within and outside of government. This idea of past was accompanied, in the present, by the symbols of a 'new (imagined) northern nation' (with its own history): *Padania*. *Lega* strategy gave *Padania* a flag, a history, an anthem, a set of regular events and anniversaries, a football team, a cycling race and an institutional base. Although never hegemonic nationally, as the 2011 national celebrations would show, the *Lega* nonetheless planted the idea of an alternative *to* Italy in people's minds, or reinforced that alternative when it was already there. This was a nation-building strategy, and an extremely flexible one. It was riven through with contradictions, but this was part of the point. It also pushed a powerful critique of the Risorgimento itself, its symbols, and its history, while imitating its methodology.

Anti-Risorgimento attitudes in the South had never gone away, and the most serious challenges to the nation-state had always come from the *mezzogiorno*, from banditry in the 1860s onwards. But in the 1990s and in particular the early twenty-first century, these hostilities began to crystallize around popular forms of counter-history that seemed to reflect those of the *Lega Nord*. The south, it was argued, had been the *victim* of the Risorgimento, whose leaders had murdered its citizens and put them in 'concentration camps'. Popular books about the 'horrors' of the Risorgimento, usually written by journalists or amateur historians, became best-sellers. The journalist and writer Pino Aprile, for example, compared the activities of the Risorgimento armies and government to the Nazis, the US army in Iraq and to Pinochet's regime in Chile. The fate of southerners after unification was, according to Aprile, similar to that of the Jews who died in the Holocaust. The south, according to this version of history, had been systematically exploited and ravaged economically and politically within the new Italian state.[22]

These books (which were often based on stories which had strong roots in local popular cultures, such as those linked to the history of banditry) were usually accompanied by a powerful rhetorical device. This version of history, these events themselves, it was argued, had been *hidden, covered up, forgotten, distorted*. It did not really matter that this claim itself was often untrue, because the work of professional historians rarely reached the same public or had the same impact in the media as these popular histories. A similar strategy has been adopted by the journalist Giampaolo Pansa, who published a series of best-sellers in the 2000s documenting the 'crimes' of the anti-fascist Resistance during the 'settling of accounts' after the end of the war in 1945.[23] Despite the fact that many of these events had been documented and discussed by historians, and often by those from the anti-fascist tradition, Pansa's book reached a much wider public both because of the way it was written, and because of its message that all of this had been kept secret and covered up in some way. This 'rhetoric of forgetting' also applied to other historical areas, and was not confined to the right of the political spectrum. The fact that school students rarely studied the twentieth century also helped create a gap within which this kind of historical production could work.

Progress? Italy One Hundred Years Ago and Italy Today

Looking back over the last century or so, we see that Italy has gone through a bewildering series of social and political revolutions. From a rural-based society, Italy became an industrial and then a post-industrial country with a speed unmatched in other European countries. This speed alone has been used as an explanation for a number of negative aspects of Italian society – the lack of planning, the destruction of the environment, the power of consumerism. Italy's second, post-war industrial revolution was concentrated in a few years, and there was no time for the 'virtuous' aspects of industrial society to develop fully. In a brief period of time Italy moved through its own, historically specific, industrial/big factory phase and became a dynamic post-industrial economy with a vast network of small, quality industries. This transformation has led to the virtual disappearance of peasant society, and of working-class urban traditions, but not of the cultures and ways-of-being associated with these social groups.

These transformations have also led to vast increases in wealth for many Italian families. From a situation where consumerism was a luxury available to a tiny minority, Italy today is a country where large sums are spent on consumer goods and services not linked to basic survival. Often, the traces of these changes have been wiped out – as if the past had never happened. The images of the 1951 Polesine floods in the Veneto, with peasants fleeing from the Po flood plains in boats or with their farm animals, remain a strong testimony to a world that has disappeared. In the Veneto today, these memories have faded as the region has become one of the richest and most productive zones in the world. In the twenty-first century there were strong signs that this rush to wealth was slowing down. Yet, despite this history of deep transformation there are some constant features of Italian society. The state has often been way behind economic and cultural developments, and certain features of the way the state works remain locked in ancient rituals and bureaucratic traditions. Similar conclusions can be drawn for the role of the family, which has modernized within traditional structures, adapting itself to change and producing change over time. It is in the complicated nexus between tradition and innovation where the originality of Italy is perhaps best understood. Italy's history is also Europe's history.

Italy invented fascism, and was the first country to bring down a fascist regime; political changes elsewhere have often been experimented with in Italy, from euro-communism to the postmodern 'personal' politics of Silvio Berlusconi. Beppe Grillo's Five Star MoVement has been seen as a prototype for post-political and anti-political movements in the twenty-first century. As with many other countries, Italy's economic and financial crisis has been deep and traumatic since 2008. Despite an overall sense of progress, there was a strong sense of a long-term decline, and the idea of Italy in decline has been around since before the country was unified.[24] For some time, the fate of the European Union itself, and the single currency eurozone, has been tied in with that of Italy. Italy, it is argued, is one of the sick men of Europe (in the company of Greece, Spain, Ireland and Portugal with their own economic and political crises). The battle between 'Good' and 'Bad' Italy, between 'virtuous minorities' and 'immoral majorities', is an ongoing one – and these categories were never clear-cut nor unambiguous. As the twenty-first century moved into its second decade, it was unclear which of these forces was in the ascendency.

What is clear is that Italy, and its history, matters. Far from being on the periphery of Europe, Italy has often been at its very heart. Far from merely following other countries, Italy has often been a leader, an innovator – of both positive and negative trends in the political, economic and cultural spheres. *Modern Italy* is also an attempt to relocate this centrality within the international system.

The Nation

CONTENTS

DEFINING THE NATION

Debates and Contexts

Nations, nationalisms and national identities have been the subject of extensive academic, political and cultural debate since the revival of interest in studies of nationalism in the late 1980s and the 'new Risorgimento history' movement of the 1990s and 2000s. This 'revival' coincided both with a crisis of the traditional nation-state in the world system with the collapse of the Soviet Empire and the end of the cold war, and with the assault on traditional historical approaches from postmodernism, discourse analysis and the concentration on identity and language in approaches to history. The resurgence of smaller, often ethnic-based, nationalisms – seen most horrifically during the Yugoslavian civil war in the 1990s – also led to increased interest in the questions of national fragmentation and regionalist identity.

For Italy, groups of historians began to rediscuss the traditional interpretations of the 'southern question', Italian national identities and regionalist politics. Whole categories, which had been used to explain a series of processes and historical moments, were called into question: the south itself, the 'southern question', the backwardness/development divide. The very existence of any kind of coherent southern region (and a north) was problematized. The south had not always been backward, historians claimed. Moreover, there were many souths, and many norths, and there always had been.[1] Finally, the Otherness of the south had been crucial to the nation-building of

Italy. The anti-nation, represented by the *mezzogiorno*, had been a central part of the creation of various Italian national myths. This rich vein of studies revolutionized the ways in which Italian history was being written, and provided scholars with new and exciting interpretations to apply to well-worn historical moments, institutions and movements – the Risorgimento, fascism, the Church. At the risk of simplification, we can draw out two main ways of defining the nation and national identity that have characterized these debates and can be applied to Italian historical development.

The Nation as an Entity

The first, most traditional approach sees nations as defined entities, which exist outside of the subjective experience of them. This approach continues to inform the bulk of historical work on Italian national identity, as well as mainstream theoretical approaches to the nation.[2] For example, if we take the definition given in a modern Italian Dictionary of Sociology, a nation must contain these aspects:

> a population which has experienced, over many generations, a common land, economic life, culture, language, and a common sense of its historical events so that the greater part of the individuals within the nation has formed a precise conception of this common ground and has developed a high level of emotional attachment towards the nation.[3]

On the basis of this kind of definition, Italy has failed to develop into a nation. If such a definition is taken as a basis for studying the history of the nation, Italy's history is invariably seen as a series of attempts to 'create' Italians. History is written as a series of 'lacks' and omissions. *Nation-building* is defined mainly through state-based strategies to construct a unified Italian nation, from the Risorgimento project to Liberalism, through fascism and on to the smaller nationalist strategies adopted by regionalist movements or the Christian Democrats. Historians using this approach have looked at the various tactics adopted to *build* Italy (usually from above), from monument-construction, to language, to the education system, to colonialism and war.

Although many of these studies are extremely useful as indicators of the state of play within Italy as a nation, they suffer from a number of serious drawbacks. For example, the idea of a given national model has dominated (either explicitly or implicitly) this way of looking at Italy. Italy has failed to measure up to the national model of, say, Germany or the UK. The moral imperative here is often that a strong sense of national identity is a 'good thing', necessarily. This type of approach also tends to confuse nationalism in a strong sense, in terms of aggressive feelings about Italy (often organized in nationalist movements), with a much more complicated and weaker sense of national belonging. It might be argued, for example, that nationalism has been an extremely damaging ideology over the last two hundred years. If we calculate the number of Europeans killed in war in the twentieth century, Italy is far down the list. This ideal has also led to the prioritization of state-based strategies for creating Italians. Many 'Italians' have steadfastly refused to be 'created', as Italians (in a strong sense), in the face of such policies. In addition, ideas concerning Italy's 'weak' sense of national identity are often combined with disdain for the majority of the population. 'Italians' had to be forced to become Italians. They would not do so of their own free will. In such a situation, the radical nature of the crises produced within Italy by voluntarist approaches to politics and policy has produced a series of civil wars where 'the nation' was at stake – from the Risorgimento wars, to brigandage, through to the violence after World War I, to the struggles between 1943 and 1945 and then again after 1968.

The nation-as-(incomplete)-entity and 'nation-building' approach tends to ignore complicated questions of shifting individual identities, which cannot just be lumped in with collective identities. The sheer variety of sentiments of national identity forces us to adopt a more flexible and less deterministic methodology which takes on board the mosaic-like nature of Italy and the contradictory history of *la patria italiana*. Finally, a very strong model of what a nation should be tends to dominate these debates. It is taken as read that a nation must speak the same language, have the same school programmes, act in the same way at certain moments. This model excludes all nationalisms that have adopted different roads towards national identity, and often with more 'success'. More recent elaborations of the idea of nationalism with regard to Italy have adopted a more sophisticated approach, allowing for more flexible ideas of the nation. Rusconi's influential analysis, for example, allows for diversity within the nation and privileges the importance of an ethical–political component within the nation, and the failure of this component in Italian history. For Rusconi 'the democratic nation ... is a delicate and complicated social construction, made up of shared cultures and histories, of obvious and reciprocal consensus, based on reciprocity between citizens'.[4] Where the political system is corrupt and inefficient (as in Italy), it does not produce loyalty, or create a national-based community. Finally, identities (national, regional, ethnic) are also political resources, which can be 'modified, manipulated, functionalised'.[5] Rusconi's account tries to bridge the gap between traditional ideas of the nation as a fixed entity and more modern analyses that take into account the complicated nature of this question, and the importance of myths, memories and discourse within concepts of national identity.

Imaginary Nations

For the alternative way of looking at the nation, nations 'are best thought of as social fictions rather than real entities'.[6] A nation is 'an imagined political community'.[7] Ideas about the nation combine elements of narrative, ideology, and concepts of geographical space. Central to this discourse is the importance of the Other – 'defining the nation by what it is not'.[8] The nation defines itself against impurities and weaknesses, traces of the foreign, which can be projected onto phenomena both inside and outside of the real boundaries of the state.[9] If we adopt this kind of methodology, then our focus is on different *narratives* concerning the nation, which shift and adapt over time, and the use of stereotypes. In the Italian context, the key Others have been the south, and political ideologies/movements – anarchism, socialism, communism. The south was constructed as an anti-nation through the medium of the press and propaganda and through virtual civil war (especially the brigandage wars after 1860) and then reappeared as an Other at various moments in Italian history, right up to the anti-southernism of regionalist parties in the 1980s, 1990s and 2000s. Also important here were the disrespect and fear of the south within the official socialist movement in the north, the scientific theories adopted by criminologists in the 1890s to link southerners to crime, the absence of the south in the Resistance, and the racism towards southerners which arose following mass internal migrations in the 1950s and 1960s.[10] This construction of a foreign south cannot simply be collapsed within various political and strategic discussions of the 'southern question' that dominated certain phases of political debate from unification onwards. This way of looking at the south also had origins in post-colonial theory, which examined the relationship between imperial powers and their colonies.

Other 'Others' have also become important at certain moments in Italian history, from foreign enemies in colonial wars (Abyssinian, Libyan, Yugoslavian, Austrian, German, Albanian, Greek, Ethiopian and Somalian, English and American) to those who opposed war within Italy. The fascists defined certain socialists and pacifists as 'the anti-nation' after 1915. These disputes exploded again during World War II, where the idea of what the Italian nation was, and who represented it, entered into a deep crisis. Alternatively, for the nationalists who came from the Risorgimento tradition, the Church often played the role of the anti-nation, and the Italian nation was often constructed, willingly, in opposition to the institutions of the Church. A kind of 'civil religion' was encouraged to rival that of the Church. Later, socialists in the Po Valley built alternative worlds that often used religious symbols but were in opposition to the official institutions of the Catholic Church. Thus, various Others, various boundaries and borders, various competing 'anti-nations' have existed, disappeared and reappeared at different moments in Italy's history.

New ways of looking at the present and the past have also been applied to the very formation of the Italian nation-state, and the movements that were behind the creation of Italy itself.

The Risorgimento and its histories

The Risorgimento itself had been a long and complex process, involving wars, plebiscites, secessions and treaties, with changing capital cities (Turin, Florence, Rome) and numerous setbacks. Historians still disagree over its beginning, and its end. In 1999, for example, Gilles Pécout published a book called *The Long Risorgimento* which covered the period from 1770 right up to 1922. A central genre or trope in historical work on Italy has been the discourse of failure. Italy itself, it is often argued, was a project that had simply *not worked*. This idea of a failed Italy has a long tradition, stretching back to

Antonio Gramsci and remaining popular today, as in, for example, David Gilmour's recent volume, *The Pursuit of Italy*. It also runs through Christopher Duggan's monumental work, *The Force of Destiny*. Moreover, aspects of this discourse of failure had been internalized by the Risorgimento generation and those who came afterwards. In many ways, the new cultural history of the Risorgimento is in direct opposition to these historical narratives.

Historical research into the Risorgimento has exploded into life in recent years, after a long period in the doldrums.[11] It would not be an exaggeration to call this a historical and historiographical revolution. New methodologies have been brought to bear on old material (which was often approached afresh) as well as on newly uncovered sources of all kinds. Cultural activities ranging from opera to art to poetry have been analysed as part of a 'Risorgimento canon' that inspired an emotional attachment to ideas and movements. These 'deep' emotions, it is argued, created shared communities, and a group of people who were willing to live and die for these ideals. The imaginary was central to this community, which has also been recast as a 'mass movement', in open opposition to previous representations of the Risorgimento (from both right and left) as a 'passive revolution' or a move-ment restricted to elites.[12] According to Lucy Riall in her discussion of the work of Alberto Banti, it was through this 'Risorgimento canon' that 'the future young patriots of Italy "discovered" the nation'.[13] The nation was imagined as 'a voluntary pact amongst a free and equal fraternity; an organic community; an extended family; and a shared historical identity' it was a 'community established by the bonds of affection, nature, kinship and his-tory'. Italy was also tied together by blood and sacrifice – by martyrdom.[14]

The collective volume *Il Risorgimento* edited by Banti and Paul Ginsborg, which was published by Einaudi in 2007, became a kind of manifesto for this new approach, a touchstone around which further debate took place and new research was launched. As the editors wrote in their introduction, they were trying to 'bring to life the deep-rooted culture of the Risorgimento, and look at the mentalities, the sentiments, the emotions, the life stories and the politi-cal and personal projects of the men and women who took part in it'.[15] Lucy Riall's study of the Giuseppe Garibaldi was another key text for the under-standing of how the Risorgimento had really worked. Riall analysed the original creation of a Garibaldi myth by Giuseppe Mazzini and the increasing power of the press and publishing industries. The idea of Garibaldi as hero, Riall shows, was disseminated through pamphlets, newspapers, novels, art work, music and political propaganda, and was a powerful tool in the Risorgimento itself, *as well as* in the way that history was written and its mem-ories utilized in post-Risorgimento Italy. 'Garibaldi' was a malleable figure, fought over and exploited by the left and the right, Communists and Fascists. His statue stands in most Italian cities and towns and his retreat in Sardinia became a place of pilgrimage when he was still alive. He pressed all the but-tons as a national hero, but very little of this process had been spontaneous and unplanned. For the first time, historians were looking critically at the beating heart of the Risorgimento. As they unravelled its myths, they gave that period new weight and importance (see Box 1.1). Recent debates have

---

Box 1.1 New Risorgimento histories

The work of historians such as Alberto Maria Banti, Paul Ginsborg and Lucy Riall has recast and revitalized the understanding of the Risorgimento in recent years. As the extracts below demonstrate, by concentrating on emotions, narratives and rituals, and analysing the communicative strategies used by the leaders of the movement, these studies have created a 'new Risorgimento history' that challenged stale orthodoxies. At the same time, old anti-Risorgimento narratives were given new life and found a mass audience through the work of journalists such as Pino Aprile, who saw the unification of Italy through a lens where the South was a victim of the new Italian state and the movement to create it.

National discourses were constructed through extremely seductive communicative means … [and] were able to provoke strong emotional reactions. They reached an increasing number of people [and] could transform a basic hypothesis (the existence of a nation) from a remote and abstract idea into something which seemed to have a role and weight in an effective reality. (Alberto Maria Banti, *Sublime madre nostra*, p. vi)

The (narrative or ritual) practices of nationalism during the Risorgimento attempted to understand the nation as a community of fighters, who had signed up to a common sentimental pact in the name of a para-metaphysical entity – the nation/fatherland. And the key point which sanctified political activity, which made it sacred and beyond debate, something to be believed in, was the ultimate figure of sacrifice – the martyr. (Alberto Maria Banti and Paul Ginsborg, *Il Risorgimento*, p. xxxiii)

Modern political heroes, like the nationalist movements with which they are identified, are often treated as political inventions imposed from above on a passive population. I will suggest instead that, while there was a great deal about Garibaldi's appeal which was planned by political leaders, his definition and creation as a political hero was still largely a collaborative effort, involving audience participation as well as directions from the stage. The public's enthusiasm for Garibaldi reflected a broader contemporary appetite for romantic heroes and adventure stories, and Garibaldi modified his political image to fit this popular demand. The task of Garibaldi was not only to make Italy, he also had to make Italy convincing. (Lucy Riall, *Garibaldi*, p. 18)

I had no idea that the Piedmontese did what the Nazis did at Marzabotto. But many times over, and for years. And they wiped out many villages, forever, like the marines in Iraq. I had no idea that, for the purposes of revenge, southern women were raped as were women in the Balkans, during the civil war there … I hadn't realized that in the name of national unity … torture was used like … the French in Algeria, or Pinochet in Chile … I didn't want to believe that the first death camps in Europe were set up by northern Italians in order to torment and kill thousands, perhaps tens of thousands of southern Italians … as had happened in the Soviet Union under Stalin … I had always believed the history books, and in the legend of Garibaldi. (Pino Aprile, *Terroni*, pp. 23, 26, 35, 40, 72) concentrated on the continuities, or otherwise, between the Risorgimento and fascism. Some historians have drawn strong links between the ideas (and to some extent the practice) of Risorgimento thinkers (and in particular Mazzini) and the theory and practice of fascism. Others see discontinuities rather than parallels between the two movements. These are crucial issues, which are explicitly political and provoke strong emotions. The Risorgimento itself (its symbols, its texts, its martyrs) was utilized and exploited by all sides of the political spectrum, from the fascists to the far left.

Creating the Nation: Models and Debates from the Risorgimento – Persistent Myths

The Risorgimento military model of nationalism and war was a persistent myth in twentieth-century Italy. The idea that a small, ragbag army of volunteers, moved by nationalist zeal, could win conflicts and unite peoples continued to inform state policies and military adventures for much of the post-unification period. This was due in part to a continuity of men and ideas (from Crispi onwards), and in part to the all-encompassing myth of the Risorgimento (a narrative of *re-awakening*, as the name itself implies) which dominated Italy's view of its own history (and many foreign views of Italy's history) and created a thousand statues of Garibaldi, Victor Emmanuel II, Mazzini and Cavour. This idea of nation-building (the active minority had to pull along a reluctant majority) led directly to the farcical attempts to create Italian colonies in the 1890s, and then informed many of the foreign policy initiatives of fascism, which attempted to militarize and nationalize Italy from above. Common to all these ideas and informing all these practices was a heroic idea of the nation, and a voluntarist ideal of nationalism. The nation was to be created by deeds. It was not simply *there*. In fact, many nationalists combined a zealous nationalism with an intense disrespect for *Italians*. It was just because of the laziness, the weakness, and the provincialism of the vast majority of Italians that they had to be pushed, cajoled and bullied into becoming part of a nation. The only way this could be achieved was through action, either from above or in conflict with other nations and/or those who opposed nationalism from the inside – the enemy within. A nation was a nation only when it acted as one. Recent historical research has contested this view of what the Risorgimeto was about, arguing that it was a 'mass' movement, an analysis which has led to fierce debate.

Nonetheless, 'mass' movement or not, the Risorgimento foot-soldiers and ideologues were always in a minority, and they were rarely united in terms of what kind of Italy they wanted. There were bitter disagreements about the form the nation should take, the means with which it should be made, and remade, and the role of various institutions within that possible nation. A crucial choice remained that between a republic and the monarchy, with many nationalists (most importantly Mazzini) lining up on the Republican side. This question was only resolved with the referendum of 1946, which abolished the monarchy and created the Italian Republic. Italy was not alone in Southern Europe in having a problematic relationship with its royal families – republicanism was extremely strong amongst the Spanish, Portuguese and Greek Left throughout the twentieth century. Within nationalist movements the role of the king remained a controversial one, dividing fascists, nationalists and even socialists throughout the first part of the century. The demise of the monarchy also created problems for memory and commemorations. Looking back, what was to be done with an institution which the Italian people had subsequently voted to abolish altogether? A second key point of disagreement amongst nationalists centred on the question of democracy, and the centrality of the democratic ideal to that of the nation. Other divisive concepts and institutions included the role of the Church, international alliances and the relationship with foreign cultures both inside and outside Italy.

The study of Others and minorities is crucial to an understanding of national identities because all imagined nations are partial, reflecting particular world-views. They are all also ideals, utopias: models of a different kind of society. Thus, all imagined nations leave some people out, even when they claim to represent the 'whole nation'. All these models implicitly or explicitly exclude – sometimes in the strong sense of the creation of Others, sometimes in weaker ways – and this exclusion is a key part of the creation of national identities. By looking at what is excluded, and what is included, we can understand a great deal about the nature of the particular nation that is being imagined and translated into reality. The following section will analyse some of the components of Italian ideals of national identity.

COMPONENTS OF THE NATION

Languages and Dialects

It is a well-known fact that united Italy was divided by hundreds of local dialects and languages. Italian itself did not become a truly national language until the 1950s, although massive linguistic Italianization took place during World War I and then again under fascism and with the spread of radio. Tullio De Mauro's thesis that the decision to teach Italian in schools after unification set back the spread of the language for years (by creating too big a leap for dialect-speakers) is tied to the idea that it was the spread of television which really united Italy linguistically in the 1950s and 1960s.[16] Such an analysis plays down the enormous impact of World War I (1915–18), when millions of troops were called up from all over Italy to fight together and follow orders *in Italian*. The melting pot of the trenches had a substantial impact on the unification of the language. Later, fascism used other mass media to communicate with its subjects. The spread of radio and cinema clearly led to a leap in the understanding if not the speaking of Italian.

However, it should be noted that this historical debate around linguistic unification relies on a very selective idea of what a nation should be, and on an exaggeration of the role of a single language in 'creating a nation'. In many modern 'nations' a number of languages are spoken. The idea that the Italian nation was only 'complete' when all its subjects spoke one, national, language highlighted a particularly restricted and mono-cultural view of the nation. And, quite apart from the rich tradition of dialects within Italy (with their own dictionaries, cultural forms, literatures and music), Italy had never been a country where only one language was spoken, rather than many dialects. In fact, the very distinction between a language (deemed to be *Italian*) and dialects (Milanese, Sardinian etc.) was a false one. But, in addition, other languages were spoken by many Italians or by foreigners living in Italy (see Box 1.2). The numerical weight of these languages depended on the shifting borders of the Italian state. Thus, there were large pockets of German-speaking populations in Alto Adige and Trentino, brought into 'Italy' after 1919–20 (see Map 3). Other languages were spoken in many parts of the north-west, and especially in the Aosta Valley. One town in Sardinia has a Catalan language. Many English tourists visited and lived in Italy during and after the golden age of the Grand Tour. There were Slovenians in the north-east, who changed nation as the borders moved, traumatically, around them.

Box 1.2   Language variety, Italy and national identity

Historically, Italian was imposed upon Italians after unification, but a number of zones remained where not just dialects, but different languages were spoken within Italy. It should also be noted that those zones which became part of Italy in 1918 had been under Austrian administration and the official language there had clearly not been Italian. This dual-linguistic situation remained after 1918 until the suppression of other languages by fascism (which did not mean that the use of these languages was effectively suppressed, it was just outlawed).

Many minority languages survived through to the post-1945 period, so that in the 1990s and 2000s there were a number of zones in Italy where Italian was not spoken, or where other languages rivalled Italian: Albanian was spoken by 100,000 Italians in certain parts of Basilicata, Apulia and Sicily; Greek in parts of Calabria and Apulia; German in large sectors of the north, particularly the Alto Adige; Slovene by some 53,000 Slovenians in the north, French by many close to the French border and in Valle d'Aosta. Sardinian was still spoken by 1.3 million people in 1990, Friuliano by 700,000 Italians, and Ladino delle dolomiti by 400,000 in the Alto Adige region. Article 6 of the Constitution sanctioned the official use of French in the Aosta Valley, of German and Ladino in Alto Adige, and of Slovene in the provinces of Gorizia and Trieste. The autonomist struggles of the 1960s in Alto Adige led to protection and greater rights for Germans in that zone. Italians abroad usually spoke (or understood) at least two languages and this was often transmitted back to their home towns if they returned there, or through other linguistic devices, letters in particular. Finally, and perhaps most importantly, more than four million foreign immigrants arrived in Italy in the 1980s, 1990s and early 2000s. Most of these people spoke their own language plus Italian, which they either learnt in Italy or had picked up already (as in the case of many Albanians). This linguistic revolution is often overlooked and the effects of this ongoing transformation are still being felt within Italy.

Pockets of Greek and Albanian were to be (and can still be) found in the south of Italy. Yet, language mosaics of this kind were features of almost all European countries, and in some cases (as with Catalan) these languages formed the basis for regionalist movements that dwarfed those of Italy.

The experience of occupation, settlement and successive kingdoms left traces of Spanish, French and Austrian within the languages and dialects of various parts of the peninsula. Finally, dialects were often the only 'Italian' spoken by Italy's other nation, that of the emigrants in South America, North America and elsewhere across the world. Amongst these diasporas, Italian was rare, and dialects far more common. But these emigrants were no less 'Italian' than many left behind, and historians have recently argued that, in fact, and in many ways, Italians abroad were more *Italian* than those at home.[17]

The restricted definition of the link between national language and 'nation' entered into a new crisis with the multicultural thrust that followed mass foreign immigration into Italy from the mid-1970s onwards. By the end of the first decade of the twenty-first century, Italy was coming to terms with over four million foreign immigrants who spoke a huge variety of languages, along with Italian. The school system, public bureaucracies, mass media and industrialists were having to adapt to a new kind of linguistic mosaic which demanded the adoption of more flexible linguistic approaches.

The crisis of the nation-state that intensified in the 1990s and 2000s saw the rediscovery of dialects. Speaking dialect was a question of identity, and could also be intensely political. In some macro-areas in both north and south (the Veneto, Campania, Calabria), dialects remained or became more popular than Italian, at least on an everyday level. A survey carried out in 2006 found that less than half of Italians (45 per cent) spoke Italian in the home, although this figure increased to 48 per cent when talking with friends and to 73 per cent when conversing with others. Only 20 per cent of Calabrians, 25 per cent of people in Campania and 23 per cent of Veneto residents spoke 'mainly' Italian. Fifty-five per cent of Italian families used dialect on a daily basis.[18]

Pulling in the other direction were questions linked to Europe and the increasing hegemony of English, which invaded the Italian language at a whole series of levels.[19] Finally, slang and the impact of social media also transformed language use, creating shorthand and new phrases and vocabularies as well as entirely new forms of communication.

The richness and diversity of Italy's dialects was also played down in post-unification Italy within the prevailing view that everyone should speak exclusively Italian (although later a strong sense of nostalgia pervaded discussions over the decline of dialect). Italian itself had always developed and had borrowed from other languages, above all English (with regard to both spoken and written Italian), throughout the century, despite fascism's attempts to re-Italianize the language in the 1920s and 1930s. Fascism's Italianization programme forced non-Italians in Italy to use Italian and attempted to eliminate 'foreign' words (and habits, such as the handshake) from Italian life. Like all languages, Italian underwent considerable development throughout the twentieth century, both as a written and as a spoken language. Certain key texts provided a kind of official version of the Italian language, from Dante to Leopardi to Carducci and Manzoni, to De Amicis, Silone and Vittorini. Even within Italian itself, various forms of language evolved, as elsewhere. Italy created particularly impenetrable bureaucratic and legal languages, designed to exclude rather than spread understanding. Other language forms were adopted by journalists, political commentators, singers, poets and teachers, political groups or youth-based cultural movements. The Internet altered language use at all levels.

Finally, language has often provided a significant basis for political mobilization within Italy. The existence of Italian speakers in Trentino and Yugoslavia formed the basis for nationalist claims to the so-called unredeemed lands, which led directly to Italy's participation in World War I. German speakers in Alto Adige later led a bitter campaign for autonomist rights, which created its own terrorist movement in the 1960s. Slovenians also struggled long and hard for nationalist and language rights within Italy, often in the face of hostility from first the fascists and later the democratic state and right-wing parties. These rights were only finally secured with a law passed in 2001. Other dialects formed part of the resources used by nationalist and autonomist movements ranging from Sicily and Sardinia in the 1940s and 1960s, respectively, to the use of dialect employed by regionalist movements in the Veneto and Lombardy in the 1980s, 1990s and 2000s. Lega Nord posters and other propaganda often used dialect as a means of inclusion and exclusion. All of these language-based strategies had a dual purpose: the creation of a community and the marginalization of Others from that community.

Borders: The Limits of the Nation

A modern nation is partly defined by its borders. Italy's borders have shifted significantly since the 'definitive' creation of a bordered Italian nation in 1870 (see Maps 1, 2 and 3). Some of these borders are geographical (the sea around the peninsula, and the islands, mountain ranges and rivers which mark various frontiers); others are political (to the east and west). World War I saw the addition of Trentino–Alto Adige and the post-war period was dominated by debates over the 'lack' of territories acquired by Italy in the peace settlement. During the conflict itself, Italy's borders were breached by invasion after Caporetto and, for a time, a new border was held along the Piave River in the north-east. The post-war settlement failed to satisfy the nationalist ideals of many of those who had supported intervention, and D'Annunzio's invasion of Fiume in 1919 (see Box 1.3) set the scene for fascism in the 1920s and an aggressive foreign policy in the 1930s.

Many nationalists thus defined the Italian nation as stretching beyond its political borders. Claims were made on various lands as intrinsically 'Italian', either through historical arguments or with reference to the peoples currently inhabiting them, and the languages spoken. These claims originally took the form of a movement – *irredentism* – with regards to the Trentino region in particular in the late nineteenth and early twentieth centuries. The question of Rome (still not under Italian control) was also central to debates between

---

Box 1.3   Nationalist mobilization: the Fiume affair, 1919–20

Fiume, a small port town on the Dalmatian coast, became for many nationalists the symbol of the 'mutilated victory' after World War I. Italy's failure to secure more territory in Yugoslavia at the Paris Peace Conference in 1919, thanks to the Allies' refusal to honour the terms of the London Pact of 1915 (especially in Albania) left space for nationalist mobilization. The fact that many of the terms were later honoured was overtaken by claims on Fiume.

The poet and nationalist Gabriele D'Annunzio, at the head of a ragbag militia of 2,500 men, occupied Fiume in September 1919 and declared it part of Italy. Many of the soldiers involved were regular troops who had been withdrawn from Fiume after the final peace agreement. The D'Annunzio operation was a mixture of overblown rhetoric (*Fiume or death!*) and brilliant use of propaganda, often against the democratic wishes of the people of Fiume themselves, particularly after a plebiscite in the city in December 1919. The inertia of the Italian government in the face of this open, armed, challenge to its authority was indicative of the power of the nationalist ideal, the dissatisfaction of many Italians with the peace settlement, and the overconfidence of the liberal elites in their own ability to manipulate the nationalist movement.

The 'Fiume question' dominated the headlines for more than a year, as D'Annunzio kept interest alive by such stunts as a semi-socialist constitution, the occupation of nearby Zara, and other military/political manoeuvres. It was only with the Rapallo Treaty of November 1920 that a workable solution was found, as Fiume was declared a free city within Yugoslavia and citizens there were left free to opt for Italian citizenship. In the wake of this agreement, the Italian government finally acted to remove D'Annunzio from Fiume by force in an operation that began on Christmas Eve, 1920. After four days of fighting, D'Annunzio negotiated his withdrawal from Fiume in January 1921. This episode ('the Christmas of blood') was later rewritten as a heroic defence of Fiume.

Fiume continued to be a powerful symbol of nationalist desires and liberal failures linked to the Great War. In March 1922, Fiume was the scene of a mini-insurrection organized by nationalists and fascists, who proclaimed, once again, the annexation of the city to Italy. Under fascism, the city was assigned to Italy under the Treaty of Rome (1924), signed as part of a peace pact with Yugoslavia. In September 1943, the Germans declared Fiume part of the Third Reich. Fiume was later assigned to Yugoslavia under the 1945 peace agreements. Following the Yugoslav civil war (1992–6) Fiume became part of Croatia.

1860 and 1870. It was claimed that the Risorgimento would have to be completed with a so-called 'fourth war of independence' to capture (back) these regions. Fascism also made claims on Corsica, various parts of what was then Yugoslavia, Nice, Corfu and other zones. These were seen by fascism as part of 'Italy'. Other areas were coveted as imperial prizes, which would extend the borders of Italy but had no real claim, historical or otherwise, to be part of a traditional *Italian* state. None the less, every imperialist adventure, victory and defeat altered the borders of Italy as nations, islands, cities and towns were either brought into or taken out of the nation. Fascism set about increasing Italy's territory and widening her borders through a series of colonial conquests (see Boxes 1.4 and 1.5), from Corfu to Albania to Abyssinia and Somalia to Libya. A series of treaties and negotiations over treaties also altered international frontiers. The nation and its borders have thus been in continual flux. In 1939, after an invasion by Italian troops, King Victor Emmanuel III was 'crowned' King of Albania. The difficult relationship with Albania epitomizes the ways in which Italy has expanded or shrunk in line with specific historical, military and cultural movements (see Box 1.6).

Some new lands were taken after Mussolini's decision to enter the war in alliance with Germany in June 1940, but defeat in 1941–2 and the dissolution of the army on 8 September 1943 led to the collapse of these colonial dreams, and the colonial empire, forever. Italy lost Libya, Ethiopia and Somalia, and was invaded by Germany *and* the Allies, as well as by Tito's armies from the east. For two years, new mobile internal borders criss-crossed Italy as the Allied army moved up from the south, 'liberating' cities as it went, and the so-called Republic of Salò governed in the north, with Italians and Germans in charge. The king and the legitimate Italian government, meanwhile, set up a Southern Kingdom (*Il Regno del Sud*). This chaotic situation continued until the end of the war, and the liberation of the entire country. In the post-war settlement, Italy's borders were again modified, with the loss of much of the Yugoslavian coast (Fiume, for example, became part of Yugoslavia again), and of some territory to France.

Even in the post-1945 period, the situation has not been a stable one. First, and most importantly, there was the difficult dispute over Trieste, which was partly resolved in 1954 and finally settled in 1975–77 (see Box 1.6). The eastern frontier represented a number of different borders for the new Italian state. First, it was a reminder of the legacy of World War II, and the continuing hegemony of the Allied armies. Secondly, it was the edge of Europe itself. Thirdly, it was a key cold war boundary, dividing liberal democracies from the communist powers (and Communists and Christian Democrats within Italy). For Italy, and for Europe, the iron curtain began at (or after) Trieste (and to some extent Gorizia). Trieste was so important that Italy even risked military struggle with Yugoslavia over the city. In addition, other borders were constructed or dissolved, over time. The European Union (from its origins as the Iron and Steel Federation in the 1940s to the enlarged EU of the 1990s) included and excluded various nations, and redrew borders whilst continually redefining their functions and meanings (as did the Schengen agreement in the 1980s and other international treaties). The cold war created its own borders, and Italy was on the front line for fifty years. In Gorizia the border ran right through the town. Other populations have always experienced the border issue in different ways. The Slovenians saw the borders of Italy and Yugoslavia (and Slovenia) move around them, leading to changes in citizenship and democratic rights. The end of the Cold War opened up borders to the east, creating new economic cooperation and cultural exchange, as well as new conflict.

> **Box 1.4** Colonialism and the Italian nation: the Liberal period
>
> The 'lack' of an Italian Empire was deeply felt by Italy's post-unification govern-
> ments. Colonialism was seen as a way of gaining prestige in Europe and of
> creating a 'place in the sun' to which Italians could emigrate. In addition, the
> Italians used similar justifications to other colonialists – talking of their 'civilizing
> mission' and thus creating the basis for a racist discourse that exalted Italian
> culture. There were also, of course, economic interests at stake, including the
> control of key ports and pressure from the iron and arms industries.
>
> The quest for empire was also a consequence of Liberal Italy's militarized
> society and the ambitions of the monarchy. The obvious site for this empire was
> East Africa (one of the few uncolonized parts of the continent), and large tracts
> of the Eritrean and Abyssinian coasts were occupied in 1885. An army of some
> 18,000 troops was sent to Ethiopia in 1894 after long and tortuous negotiations
> with various African leaders. This expensive campaign ended in the unmitigated
> disaster of Adowa (March 1896), where the Italian army was routed by far greater
> numbers of Ethiopian troops. The war divided Italians at home. The brutal meth-
> ods used by the Italian army were kept secret for years and never affected public
> opinion at home. Although Adowa put a stop to colonial expansion for over ten
> years, the ways in which the defeat was narrated by intellectuals and nationalists
> meant that 'a military disaster passed into memory not as a lesson to be learned,
> but as a moment of shame to be wiped away by great victories to come' (John
> Dickie, 'Introduction', John Dickie *et al.* (eds), *Disastro!*, p. 20).
>
> After Adowa, Italy's attentions switched to Libya. Negotiations dragged on
> throughout the early part of the twentieth century, but the Italian government
> was only pushed into action in 1911. The Libyan campaign gained more support
> than that in East Africa – from sections of the Catholic Church, from economic
> interests led by the *Banca Romana*, and from parts of the Left who saw a pos-
> sible solution to the continued pressures of mass emigration. Libya brought
> together many of the same nationalist elements who were to push for interven-
> tion in World War I, from D'Annunzio, to the (growing) nationalist movement
> itself, to the reformist Right. In addition, Libya divided the Socialist Party, leading
> to the expulsion of a number of pro-war reformists, who were later to become
> part of the interventionist movement in 1915. The Libyan campaign was
> extremely expensive (costing more than half the annual state budget) and the
> army never really penetrated beyond the coastal zones of the country. The
> Italians were pushed out by the Turks during World War I, before re-taking the
> colony in the 1920s. Parts of Libya remained Italian until 1943, when British
> troops entered Tripoli.

Internally, borders also shifted, with the creation of regions, provinces and
new metropolitan areas, and the construction of airports, mountain passes,
motorways, ports and frontier tunnels, thus continually redefining the spatial
moment when people entered or left 'Italy'. Other areas were not marked by
clear borders on maps, but remained powerful indicators of difference and

Box 1.5 Colonialism and the Italian nation: fascism and the Republic

Fascism adopted, from the outset, an aggressive policy of colonization and conquest, accompanied by nostalgic ideological claims to continuity with the Roman Empire and Italy's right to 'greatness'. Mussolini inherited 'the poorest colonies in the world' from Liberal Italy, but soon set about preparing for expansion. The positions in Somalia and Libya were reinforced after long and costly campaigns that lasted until 1928 and 1932 respectively. After a huge propaganda effort, Italy invaded Ethiopia from its bases in Eritrea in October 1935. A rapid campaign saw quick victories and the symbolic 're-taking' of Adowa and occupation of the capital, Addis Ababa, in May 1936. Italy had gained control of a rich country consisting of 3.5 million square kilometres and 13 million inhabitants. The war led to widespread international protest and sanctions were imposed against Italy, but the conquest was popular at home, coinciding with the peak of consensus achieved by the fascist regime. The campaign was accompanied by racist propaganda at home and in the army and brutality by the Italian troops, including the use of poison gas. The king was appointed Emperor of Ethiopia, which was united to Somalia to create Italian East Africa. None the less, the dream of mass emigration to Ethiopia proved a chimera, not least because of the high costs involved. In the end, only 31,000 farmers and administrators settled in Ethiopia instead of the planned 2 million. Yet many Italians had some sort of dealings with the empire between 1935 and 1941 (Del Boca estimates that a million Italians visited at least one of the countries of the Italian empire in that period) for a whole series of military and commercial reasons. A huge road network was built using 100,000 Italian and local workers. Fascist racist ideology was troubled by the widespread practice of 'madamism' whereby Italian men lived with Ethiopian women. A system of semi-apartheid was introduced to try and stamp this practice out. In 1941, the Italians were forced out of all their African colonies after the 'desert war'. In 1950, Somalia was handed back to Italy as a kind of UN protectorate. This situation lasted until 1960, when the Somalian Republic was set up. None the less, post-war Italy maintained strong trade and cultural ties with its ex-colonies. In 1970, 20,000 Italians were expelled from Libya following orders from Colonel Gaddafi. Later in the 1970s Italy accepted a number of refugees from Somalia and Ethiopia in the wake of the civil war there. Italian troops briefly re-entered Somalia in 1992 as part of the disastrous 'Restore Hope' mission organized by the UN and the USA. Modern Italy's short-lived imperial history had much less effect upon the nation than the much deeper experiences of other European countries.

nationhood. Most crucial here was the idea of the south (and the north, and the centre, and the north-east). No two historians (or Italians) agree about where the south begins or ends (or began and ended) but the ideas of the south and the 'southern question' have dominated much political and historical thought about the Italian nation during the past century. Similar claims can be made about the power of regionalist movements, with their claims to

---

Box 1.6   The nation and its borders: the question of Trieste

One of the most consistent areas of dispute over borders and nationality was that of Trieste. A key city within the so-called 'unredeemed' lands after unification, Trieste became part of Italy after 1919, as part of the post-war settlement. A city of rich cultural exchange, it attracted writers and intellectuals in the early twentieth century – from Joyce to Svevo. Trieste was host to many different peoples, from Slovenes to Austrians to Slavs. The city was the site of national and ethnic conflict, and the Italian community erected a monument to Dante there, which was destroyed in 1915 with the outbreak of the war. The Italians took Trieste in 1918 and fascism was active in the city from 1919 onwards. In addition, the city had an important Jewish community, and was the only part of Italy to host a death-camp during World War II. The 'question of Trieste' was also strategic, symbolizing the shifting allegiances of an Italy torn between Austria, France and Germany.

The tragic events of 1943–5 saw Trieste occupied by the Nazis, and then by the victorious Yugoslav armies (on 1 May 1945), who beat the Allies to the city by a matter of days. Tito's troops repressed dissent in the city in brutal fashion. Reprisals took place against fascists but also against many whose only crime was to be Italian, as well as some of those on the Left opposed to Tito. These massacres – known as the *foibe* massacres thanks to the deep pits into which the bodies were thrown – remain the subject of bitter debate. The *foibe* events were used as propaganda during the cold war, and the number of those killed was exaggerated. On the other side of the divide, either the massacres were ignored, or the victims were dismissed as fascists or collaborators.

Trieste was a front-line state in the cold war. The border region was divided into two zones in 1947 and the city remained high on the political agenda until the mid-1950s. Zone A, including Trieste, was governed by the USA and the UK; Zone B by Yugoslavia. The Right called for the city to be given entirely to Italy, and organized nationalist demonstrations within Trieste, some of which were suppressed by the Allies. The Left prevaricated (although the Italian communists pledged their support to Italy in the event of a Yugoslav invasion). Meanwhile, the Slovenes demanded their own nation and Tito claimed Trieste as Yugoslavian. Tensions in 1953 reached such levels that war between Italy and Yugoslavia seemed a possibility. It was only with the 'Memorandum of Understanding' of October 1954 that the 'Trieste question' was partially resolved, with the city being handed 'back' to Italy and other land going to Yugoslavia. A final agreement on Italy's borders to the East was only signed in 1975 (The Treaty of Osimo) and became effective in 1977. After the Yugoslavian civil war in the early 1990s Slovenia finally gained independence, taking in the former Zone B of the 1940s and 1950s. EU borders continued to shift outwards, altering the geo-political geography of Italy's frontiers.

---

territorial difference (the 'nation' of 'Padania', for example) and the economic, cultural or social bases for such border-drawing.

Since the partial resolution of the Trieste issue in 1954, ratified in 1975–77, Italy's external borders have remained unchanged *on the map*, although there have been numerous changes in the political and symbolic function of those borders. European integration has led to shifting political boundaries around the changing member states, and various historical events have threatened Italy from the outside – for example, the Yugoslav Civil War (1992–5) and the Kosovo War in 1999. The end of the cold war in the 1990s led to significant increases in attempts to migrate into Italy from the east, particularly across the Otranto strait from Albania. This boundary was defended almost as if war had been declared, and there were constant battles between traffickers in immigrants and the Italian coastguards and navy. Later, this battle shifted to the Straits of Sicily to the South, where thousands of potential migrants drowned in their attempts to reach European soil. The tiny island of Lampedusa to the south of Sicily was often the first port of call for these potential migrants. Agreements were made with Colonel Gadaffi's Libya to control migration from Africa, but these broke down during the Libyan civil war/revolution in 2011.[20]

Italy became a symbolic defender of European identity, and its supposedly 'porous' borders and 'long' coastline marked the boundary between 'good' and 'bad' Europeans. Nightly news broadcasts quoted figures of those who had been picked up, found abandoned on beaches or had simply disappeared. Even in the age of supposed transnationalism, Italy's border was being defended as never before. Yet, even here, policy on the border veered widely according to political imperatives. At crisis points, Italian troops were sent to Albania to try and prevent the total breakdown of law and order. The army was also sent to Lampedusa in 2011 to 'deal' with the arrival of hundreds of immigrants by boat, the so-called 'sbarchi'. Later 'moral panics' were linked to different national and ethnic groups, in particular those from Romania and 'Rom' communities.[21] Common to all these events was the idea (with the brief exception of the very first refugees after 1990) of Albania and Africa as an enemy, a threat, or a land of conquest (see also Box 1.7). These 'enemies' shifted over time, with developments linked to geo-politics and the European Union.

Internal Borders and Boundaries: Regionalism, Separatism, Municipalism

Italy has always been host from the inside to various regionalist and separatist movements, which have rejected the idea of a central state and of the political boundaries of that state. The most important of these movements, historically, have been those located in the edge regions of Italy – Valle d'Aosta, Trentino–Alto Adige, Sicily and Sardinia. In Alto Adige there were historical tensions between the German-speaking and Italian-speaking communities and the 1960s saw the emergence of a terrorist movement in the region, dedicated to the promotion of German-speaking rights and independence. All of these regions obtained special statute rights at various times which granted them special governments with differing powers, often with tax collection and local administration laws. These distinctive regional

Box 1.7   Italy and Albania

Italy's relations with Albania have been marked by imperial ambitions, hostility and reciprocal claims over territory. There are also a number of historical settlements of Albanians in southern Italy. In 1901 there were at least 200,000 people of Albanian origin in Italy and a 1921 inquiry found 80,000 Albanian-speakers in Italy. During World War I Albania was put on the negotiating table by both Italy and Austria. Italy occupied Valona in December 1914, imposing Italian schools and legal codes. In December 1915, Italian troops landed in Durazzo, where they were attacked by Austrian troops in February 1916. Towards the end of the war, 70,000 Italian troops occupied Albania, where they came into conflict with a strong independence movement. Heavy fighting took place around Valona in June 1920, and the Left in Italy called for an Italian withdrawal. In June 1920 a mutiny amongst soldiers in Ancona, who refused to go to Albania, sparked off rioting and strikes. Giolitti announced an end to new troop deployments in Albania in the same month. In August the Italians left.

In 1926 King Zog of Albania signed an agreement with Italy which provided financial aid and set up military alliances against Yugoslavia. During the 1930s, this relationship began to look increasingly like colonialism. In 1933 the Italian language was made obligatory in Albanian schools. In 1939, before Italy's entry into World War II, Mussolini invaded Albania, following the refusal of the Albanian authorities to accept more control over their affairs and territory. King Zog escaped to Greece and the King of Italy was crowned King of Albania. In October 1940 Mussolini's ill-fated attack on Greece began from within Albania, as did the invasion of March 1941, this time with German help. In the same month, the invasion of Yugoslavia also began from Albanian positions. After 1945 Albania became an independent state within the communist bloc. Little population movement or cultural exchange took place between the two countries for the next forty years.

The collapse of the communist bloc in 1989 thrust Albania dramatically back into the Adriatic world. Thousands of impoverished Albanians crowded onto makeshift craft and headed for Italy, in a dramatic exodus towards the wealth they had seen only on their TV screens. Almost 25,000 Albanians arrived in Italy in March, to be followed by another 20,000 in August 1991. The first arrivals were given jobs and refugee status. Yet, the Italian government soon began to repel craft and send back Albanians. The Albanians themselves began to be seen as 'white–blacks', the lowest immigrants on a long social and cultural scale. Very few accounts understood this historical legacy of imperialism, invasions and exploitation and real debate was only provoked by Gianni Amelio's extraordinary film *Lamerica* (1994). After that period of crisis, the Albanians 'integrated' with speed into Italian society, and the role of the lowest of the low was taken up by Romanians (for a time) and especially by Rom communities, who were subjected to political and judicial discrimination.

governments were installed well before the generalized formation of regional governments in 1970, institutions provided for in the Republican Constitution of 1948 (for details of regional powers see Chapter 2).

Regionalism exploded again in the 1980s, in the face of increasing central government corruption, high taxation and state spending and the decline of 'old' mass party structures. This time, the movement had its epicentre in the north and the richer areas of Italy – specifically in the north-east and areas to the north of Milan (Bergamo, Varese, Brescia). Politically, this neo-regionalism used unconventional organizational forms – which became known as Leagues – and mobilized its supporters through the use of a combination of negative propaganda (*against* Rome, against southerners and the south, against foreign immigrants, against high taxation and corrupt politicians) and proposals for radical decentralization. Italy's regionalism can be fruitfully compared with that of other European countries, from Scotland to Spain, and should not be seen in isolation from globalization processes involving threats to local identities and demands for 'less state'.

The Leagues went through various shifts of policy that ranged from relatively mild forms of regionalism right up to separatism and the formation of a separate state known as 'Padania'. For a time, the Leagues even set up their own puppet Northern Parliament in opposition to that in Rome (in Mantua). This regionalist movement began to lose its anti-national character in the face of mass immigration in the 1990s and 2000s. The League's prioritization of anti-immigrant propaganda reinforced Italian national identity against foreign Others, and at the same time undermined regionalist identities held in contrast with other Italian regions. Only a very small minority of League supporters (let alone Italians in general) ever expressed support for the total separation of northern and southern Italy. Many more called for radical federalist reforms and an end to the redistribution of taxes from north to south. This radical federalism began to be seen as the only way to keep the Italian nation together, and to satisfy the discontent expressed by the richer regions of the north with their high taxes and poor public services. In the early twenty-first century regionalist movements began to re-emerge in the south, and especially in Sicily. Thus, Italy was being pulled apart at both ends. Decentralization and federalist reforms were passed by the centre-left government in 2000–1 and confirmed by a referendum in 2001.[22] In 2006 further and more radical changes were rejected by the Italian people following a constitutional referendum.

The Italian Diaspora: Italians Abroad

These debates over the borders marking the Italian nation leave out questions regarding the identities of 'Italians' abroad – the vast Italian diaspora. 'Italy' has also included those millions of Italians who left their nation – crossing various borders – to seek their fortune in other countries in Europe, North America and hundreds of other countries across the world. Any serious analysis of the Italian nation and national identity must take these populations into account. Electoral reform in 2006 gave Italian emigrants their own 'foreign' constituencies (12 in the Camera and 6 in the Senate) from which they elected deputies and senators who stood in the Italian Parliament in Rome. An analysis of the diaspora raises crucial questions about identity and what being Italian means and meant, from generation to generation down through the various levels of the emigrant experience.

Italians exported national identities and nationalisms during the period of the Great Emigration (before World War I) and to a lesser extent after 1945. Emigration created thousands of 'Little Italies' outside the traditional boundaries of the nation-state. National identities were subject to continual renegotiation in the face of other cultures, languages and territories. These identities then changed again for the many emigrants who returned, temporarily or permanently, to their homeland (at least half returned permanently, and many more for briefer periods). Cultures and identities were also exported and imported through letters, songs and other cultural products, which travelled back and forth between emigrant and home-based communities.[23] For some historians, these Italians abroad became 'more Italian' than those in Italy itself.[24] Their role *as* foreigners led to an exaggeration of their Italianness and they took on features of 'being Italian' which were weaker, or even absent, amongst Italians based in Italy. This *italianità* was, clearly, a hybrid identity (as are all national identities) thanks to its territorial base in a foreign land and the daily bartering with foreign cultures (defined in a very broad sense) (see Box 1.8). The Otherness of these emigrants was sometimes brought into sharp focus by periods of crisis, such as World War II when many Italian-Americans were interned in the USA as 'aliens', whilst others joined the US army and some were later involved in the invasion of Italy itself in 1943–4.

There are two common stereotypes of Italian emigrants. First, there is the idea of the poor Italian, lost and disorientated by his or her new surroundings. Here the poor-Italian stereotype looks very similar to that of many other immigrants arriving at Ellis Island around the turn of the century. This image holds true for many early immigrants, bracketed amongst the poorest arrivees – in the US, Italians were at first classified as 'black' for the purposes of segregation laws; Italians were sometimes the victims of lynchings in the deep south.[25] However, this image does not capture a number of features of Italian emigration. Most emigrants were neither lost nor helpless. Most had contacts, family and often housing in their new country of residence. Many had a clear idea of what they would do and where they would go. At an even higher level there were those who seemed more like colonizers than emigrants. In Brazil in the later nineteenth century, Italian emigrants from the Trentino region carried out frequent hunting missions against forest Indians, capturing *indios* children for 'conversion' to Catholicism, murdering their parents and stealing their possessions.[26] The dividing line between colonization and emigration was not always clear-cut.

Italian emigration was an extremely complicated phenomenon, which cannot be summarized within the histories of the USA's 'Little Italies'. Italians settled everywhere, from Ireland to Australia. They went to rural as well as urban zones. Their economic activity was neither fixed over time nor limited to certain professions, and many, perhaps half of those who went,

Box 1.8   Italians abroad: portrait of a 'Little Italy'

The classic experience of Italians abroad has been linked to the creation of numerous 'ethnic' neighbourhoods in North American cities in the early twentieth century. Italians settled all over the USA and Canada (as well as in Argentina, Brazil and numerous other countries) but the most influential communities developed in Chicago and New York. New York's 'Little Italy' on the Lower East Side was the most famous and well documented of these neighbourhoods. Most Italians came to the Lower East Side in the late nineteenth century, and the majority settled between Mulberry, Mott and Elizabeth Streets (although many others went to Brooklyn or Queens). By 1910 there were over half a million Italians in New York – most were from the south.

Immigrant housing was overcrowded and based around the tenement model. Streets teemed with life, day and night, with 'people meeting, idling, arguing, playing, courting, going to work and wearily returning home' (Mario Maffi, *Gateway to the Promised Land*, p. 75). Most Italians worked at first in the sweatshop garment industries, or in small-time trading, but others set up their own businesses and moved into commerce or the service sector. Italian banks were formed, and linked to them there often developed a kind of semi-criminal underworld. The language of the Italians also began to change and adapt to their new country, with a kind of pidgin English or 'Italglish' developing (Elizabeth Street was known, for example, as *Elizabetta stretta*). Unions were set up, as well as political organizations, including anarchist movements. Major strikes of garment workers took place in 1909 and again in 1910. Religious festivals were organized, with the *festa* of San Gennaro (19 September) being the most important. But although Little Italy was an Italian neighbourhood, 'the Lower East Side was also a place where, in a complex interplay, different cultures came together, influencing each other and America' (Maffi, *Gateway*, p. 133).

Later the Lower East Side and Little Italy were created, invoked and re-created by numerous journalistic and photographic inquests, novels, and above all films. The movies of Scorsese and Coppola, in particular, were central to the mythical re-creation of the Italian-American world of Little Italy (*Mean Streets, Italianamerican, Taxi Driver, The Godfather II, Raging Bull* – the latter set in the Bronx). Little Italy began its long decline as an Italian neighbourhood in the 1920s and 1930s, as Italians left (to Brooklyn and Queens, or back to Italy) and the area began to gentrify. Today, the zone is almost entirely a zone of Italian restaurants and tacky shops selling pictures of famous Italian-Americans, a parody of the extraordinary world of immigrants from the early part of the century.

came back. And this is to omit the frequent temporary migrations, often within Europe, undertaken by Italians right up to the 1970s. It is also inaccurate to tell the history of Italian emigration with a full stop around the 1970s. Italians have continued to travel abroad in vast numbers to live and work since the end of 'traditional' forms of migration. For example, large numbers of young Italians spent time in London in the 1990s and 2000s, often working in fast-food outlets whilst they learnt English. Others have taken up jobs abroad in a series of professions, from the university sector to fashion and design, within a globalized world economy. A sense of unease about the lack of opportunities for young and talented (and often highly educated) Italians spread with the global financial crisis after 2008. It was a widely held view that these Italians were being forced abroad in order to find work.

The second stereotype has an extremely powerful hold over the international image of Italians abroad – the Italian as *mafioso*. This image, already present in popular literature and political debate during the phase of the great emigration, was reinforced and glamorized by the huge popularity of mafia-cinema and TV over the last 30 years. *The Godfather, Goodfellas, Casino, The Sopranos*, all presented Italians above all as *mafiosi* and told the story of Italians abroad through the history of the Mafia and organized crime. This stereotype dominates media presentations of the Italian-American experience and 'character', whilst its constant use inspires protests from leaders in that same community. Spin-offs from this stereotype include the description of the Italian family as a closed, hierarchical and conspiratorial organization, ready to use any means to protect itself from outsiders.

Finally, the identity–migration relationship was also transformed by mass internal migration throughout the twentieth century (but especially during the period of the economic miracle, in the 1950s and 1960s), and then again by mass foreign immigration into Italy after the mid-1970s. The former process radically altered whole regions of Italy, creating 'southern' zones in the north (Turin became the third 'southern' city in Italy by 1975, after Palermo and Naples) and emptying many southern regions. At least 9 million Italians changed their place of residence over a mere 10 years (above all from the mid-1950s to the mid-1960s, but movement continued right up to the 1970s). The effects of this demographic and social revolution transformed the urban and cultural landscape of both northern and southern Italy (see Box 1.9). Italy's migratory history was not a unique one in southern Europe (although the *extent* of Italian migration was particularly impressive). Greece, Portugal, Spain and Turkey, in particular, have always exported workers in much the same way as Italy has.[27]

Citizenship, Exclusion and the Nation: Defining Italians

How have Italians become Italians, or lost that right? What rights do Italians have and what rights have they had over the last century? The answers to these questions depend on how *citizenship* has been defined, which in turn depends on how different groups define the 'nation' and national identity. Are we talking about the right to vote, or the right to a passport, or the right to work, or the right/duty to serve in the army? Many of these rights were taken away under fascism, and women did not get the vote in Italy until 1945. The question of citizenship also concerns Italians abroad and foreigners in Italy. At certain times, the state decided that some Italians were to be placed outside of the nation, most notoriously with the anti-Semitic laws of 1938. Other moments have seen the extension of 'being Italian', by force (as with

Box 1.9 Internal migration in Italy: Milan, the 1950s and 1960s

Some statistics
From 1951 to 1961, 300,000 people moved to Milan in search of work. Industrial employees in Italy rose by 1,379,000 over the same period and more than 20 per cent of these jobs (279,000 posts) were in the province of Milan alone. Most are still there, or have moved to the vast urban hinterland. During the heady years of the boom (1958–63) internal migration to the 'capital of the miracle' reached huge proportions: 32,619 came in 1955; 36,970 in 1956; 41,416 in 1957; 55,860 in 1958; 59,856 in 1959; 66,930 in 1960; 87,000 in 1961. In 1962, 105,448 immigrants arrived. The city took in nearly 400,000 residents in 15 years. Certain peripheral areas saw their population increase fivefold.

Myth and reality
A considerable mythology has built up about those years, and the migration of workers to Milan. This mythology is based around three main clichés. First, that the migration was overwhelmingly from the 'deep' south of Italy to the north. In fact, most immigrants were from Lombardy, whereas those from the south and islands only made up 24 per cent of the total immigrants to Milan in 1958. Many came from the Veneto region, especially in the early 1950s.

Secondly, there has been a tendency to concentrate the effects of migration into the five 'peak' years of the 'miracle' (1958–63). Mass migration to Milan had been a fact of life from the early 1950s onwards, and the city's demographic decline, accompanied by rapid deindustrialization, did not begin until the 1980s. In addition, Milan had been a centre for migration in the past, particularly in the 1890s and during World War I, but also right through the 1930s.

In some ways these 'myths' served a purpose – reinforcing the depiction of the early southern immigrants both as 'backward' and as 'helpless' on arrival in the big city – as passive victims/recipients of poor conditions and economic and social repression. In fact, there was another side to these migrants and their lives in Milan. Many came already armed with contacts – family, regional or otherwise. Many already had a house or a job to go to, or both. Many were not politically naive, but had participated in the last great rural struggles (and defeats) in the south (1944, 1950–1), centre and north of the country.

There is also a third, unwritten, cliché. This is the assumption that, somehow, the whole problem of what was called the 'integration' of these immigrants had been solved almost immediately, or even *before* the migrants had arrived. In reality, the experience of this immigration was an extremely complicated one, which saw instances of positive integration as well as many examples of exclusion.

colonialism) or by legislative reform. Other groups have defined themselves as 'outside of the nation' in some way, from pledging their loyalty to a foreign power and not to Italy, as did many Italians during the cold war, to desertion from the army, or defeatism, to a more ideological rejection of the supposed 'values' represented by Italy, however these have been defined.

The first hint at an answer to these complicated questions lies with the laws passed by the Italian state concerning citizenship: these defined who was to be *officially* Italian. The 1912 law (n. 555) adopted a basic blood definition of citizenship, with exceptions for some people born on Italian soil. You were Italian if your parents were Italian, wherever you were born. But, of course, this right was not an automatic one. Other duties and complications could delay this citizenship, from military service to the need to 'ask' for such rights in certain cases. Further complications were introduced by various international treaties, by agreements with the Catholic Church and by the need in some cases for citizens to swear allegiance to the state, the monarchy and the Republic (after 1946). Citizenship could also be taken away in various cases, such as treachery (however this was variously defined). The most famous case of this removal of citizenship involved the Italian royal family, deposed by a referendum in 1946, and banned from Italy by a constitutional clause. The various debates over their possible return to Italy in the 1990s partly depended on the refusal of the ex-king to swear allegiance to the Italian Republic. In 2002 Parliament decided to rewrite the constitutional clause banning the royal family from Italian territory.

The family duly applied for and received Italian passports, and they returned to Italy in December 2002 (for a day trip, but instead of meeting the President of Italy, the ex-royal family were received by the Pope). In 2005, on the 'Day of Memory' in January, the son of the last king of Italy, who was often called Vittorio Emanuele di Savoia, finally apologized for the signing of the anti-Semitic laws in 1938. However, in 2006 Vittorio Emanuele was arrested after an investigation into fraud and a prostitution racket. He was cleared in 2010 before the case came to trial. The ex-royal family also made a claim for damages against the Italian state, which was rejected.

For a long time, citizenship was also a gender issue. A further general anomaly, removed in 1948, allowed only the father to 'impart' nationality to his children. In certain cases, such as when the father was 'unknown', citizenship could be passed through the mother. Many of the more anachronistic clauses of the 1912 law were updated in 1992 by a new law (L. 91), which brought Italy into line with some of the requirements of European legislation. For the first time, Italians could be dual nationals, although at a certain point, usually at the age of 18, they had to choose between the nationalities they possessed. Key rights (the vote, for example) forced dual nationals to choose which citizenship they preferred. The new legislation also introduced a new form of citizenship – European Union citizenship, and new European passports.[28] Other citizenship rights were linked to adoption procedures (an increasingly important phenomenon in contemporary Italy). Citizenship rights were also extended to Italians living abroad – to the diaspora – but the attempts to give Italian emigrants a vote in Italian national elections were blocked time and again by bureaucratic and procedural debates, and were still not in place by the time of the 2001 national elections. This was changed with the 2006 law, as we have seen.[29]

More difficult questions emerged with foreign immigration after the 1970s. Although there had always been foreigners in Italy, the numbers arriving in the late twentieth century were far greater than ever before, and presented Italian society and the legal system with a series of problems that were not dealt with in a systematic way. The intermediate categories between those without any rights or the correct papers (so-called *clandestini* or undocu- mented immigrants) and those with full citizenship – Italians – became crucial to the lives and rights of these immigrants. 'Residence', confirmed by a visit of a public official to a house or flat and documented by an identity card – giving access to a whole series of services – was a crucial right. In the 1930s and 1940s, the Fascist government had passed laws (abolished in 1961) that denied residence to Italians migrating within Italy under certain circum- stances. Until 1961, many of these Italian immigrants were also known as *clandestini*.

Foreign immigrants also required a so-called *permesso di soggiorno*, issued by the police, to obtain residence rights. Immigrants could easily slip out of semi-citizenship through loss of their papers, or if the same papers were not renewed in time. This 'loss' was not just a question of formality for many of these immigrants, but could easily lead to arrest and even expulsion from Italian territory. Successive immigration laws (1990, 1998, 2002) clarified mat- ters somewhat after the chaos of the legislative gap of the 1980s. A series of regularizations also brought many immigrants out of undocumented status and into legality. None the less, these laws also carried heavy sanctions for those found without documents, or with out-of-date papers. The 1998 law set up a series of detention centres across Italy for those awaiting deportation or who were stopped and found to be without regular papers. Here the boundary between semi-citizen and non-citizen (without any rights) was made very clear (as clear as the iron bars and barbed wire around Milan's immigrant detention centre, see Box 1.10). A new law in 2002 made life for immigrants even harder, linking residence rights to job contracts and forcing non-European Union resi- dents to leave their fingerprints with the police. Yet even the 2002 law was accompanied by a huge amnesty limited to carers and domestic workers.

The new immigration into Italy created a series of intermediate categories that complicated previously clear distinctions between citizens and non- citizens. Over a million residents of Italy veered between legality and illegal- ity, and their status ranged from those awaiting expulsion to those who gained full citizenship through marriage or other means. A further set of citi- zenship and national barriers were drawn around membership of the European Union. The distinction between *comunitari* and *extra-comunitari* was much over-used in Italy in the 1980s but it did indicate the differences in citi- zenship rights of various kinds between those originating from EU countries and those from outside 'Fortress Europe'. For example, EU residents were given the right to vote in local elections in the 1990s in Italy, whereas non-EU residents were denied this right.

As more and more immigrants had children in Italy, the absurdities of the law became increasingly obvious. Take, for example, the case of Mario Balotelli, whose parents migrated to Italy from Ghana. Born in Palermo, Balotelli was adopted by a Brescian family when he was just two years old. He grew up as an Italian (which was his first language). But Balotelli was not able to apply

Box 1.10 Foreign immigration to Italy since the 1970s

By the early twenty-first century there were over four million foreign immigrants in Italy (7.5 per cent of the population). The majority worked in the low-level service sector (restaurant workers, cleaners, maids, domestic workers) or in factories and building sites, while many others had started up their own businesses. These immigrants came from a whole series of countries, with the most important groups originating in North Africa (Morocco, Senegal, Egypt), the Philippines, China, the East (Albania, Romania, Bulgaria, Ukraine) and South America (Ecuador, Peru). These arrivals began to take shape in the mid-1970s and increased throughout the 1980s, 1990s and 2000s, and were linked to various historical moments and world events, such as wars, economic change and the end of the cold war. The country of origin of the immigrant population in Italy has changed over time. It should be noted that some foreign immigrant communities had already begun to settle in Italy in the 1920s and 1930s (such as the Chinese in Milan). By 2009 nearly 600,000 children had been born in Italy of immigrant parents. These were the second generation about which so much has been written. These figures do not include illegal or unregular or undocumented people, for which only estimates can be provided. The biggest immigrant populations were to be found in the cities of Milan and Rome and Turin. Some smaller cities like Brescia and Reggio Emilia had big immigrant communities in percentage terms.

In many areas these immigrants were essential to the functioning of the economic system. Immigrants were generally younger and had more children than Italians, and were more likely to work and pay taxes. In the north-east (especially around Brescia) many of the workers in the steel furnaces were (cheap and often non-unionized) African immigrants. This integration at an economic level is necessary to keep the northern economy alive, as the 'Italian' population ages at an alarming rate. None the less, it is clear that these immigrants are, to cite Aristide Zolberg, 'needed but not welcome ... there is a contradiction between their presence as economic actors and the undesirability of their social presence'. The increasing fear and tension linked to deindustrialization, rises in criminality and the spatial segregation of the major cities have created tensions that Italy appears to be unready and unwilling to confront. Yet the immigrants of the 1950s and 1960s were also 'wanted but not welcome' – in different ways. This phrase is not enough to encapsulate the differences and the similarities between the two mass immigrations experienced by Italy over the last fifty years. The reaction to this mass immigration can tell us much about Italian identities and the Italian nation. Second and third generation immigrants have now grown up in Italy, testing the very definition of the word 'immigrant'. Outdated laws excluded many of those born in Italy from citizenship until they reached their 18th birthday, an anomaly which was the subject of intense political debate. Some 2.4 million of these immigrants were classified as Christians (with nearly 900,000 Catholics) while there were 1.5 million Muslims.

for Italian citizenship until he reached the age of 18. This anomaly affected many similar people, and left them in a limbo state, unable to leave Italy for fear of losing their right to Italian citizenship. Despite this, no changes were made to citizenship laws to accommodate a changing Italy, although there were calls for easier roads to Italian nationality. The centre-right opposed such measures and this meant that nothing was done. Balotelli went on to become a famous footballer in Italy and abroad, and was the first black player to score for the Italian national team. He became officially Italian on his 18th birthday, after a special ceremony near Brescia in August 2008. Mass immigration had led to a bizarre situation whereby people who had never seen Italy had more rights than those born and brought up entirely within her borders (see Box 1.11).

Voting is a key subject of any analysis of membership of a national community. Some historians have doubted the real existence of 'normal' democracy in Italy since unification. (The details of the voting process can be found in Chapter 4.) The post-Risorgimento state was based on an extremely limited form of suffrage. Semi-full suffrage, for most men, introduced in 1913, only really lasted for two 'free' national elections (1913, 1919) before fascist violence began to impact upon the liberty of the ballot box.[30] Fascism abolished this limited form of democracy, replacing it with showpiece plebiscites and a one-party state. In the post-war period, voting was extended to women, and to other categories denied the vote in other liberal democracies, such as prisoners. However, once again, certain barriers existed (age, for example) and the 'blocked' nature of the cold war system meant that, effectively, many of those who voted for the Italian Communist Party (*Partito Comunista Italiano* – PCI) at a national level were disenfranchised. The PCI would never have been allowed to govern, even if it had won. It was only after the end of the cold war, in the early 1990s, that the system was freed of these barriers. Yet that period coincided with a significant decline in voting turnout as Italians turned away from political participation. In other ways, however, Italy was an extremely democratic country, with guarantees set up in the 1970s for workplace democratic bodies, the right to use referenda against unpopular laws, and the central role of mass-based political parties.

THE CONTESTED NATION

Redefining the Nation, Redefining Citizens: Anti-Semitism and the Laws of 1938

The Jews are not part of the Italian race.

MANIFESTO DEL RAZZISMO ITALIANO, 14 JULY 1938

The best-known case of redefinition of what it was to be 'Italian' occurred with the anti-Semitic laws of 1938. These laws, based on the German legislation but with significant differences, removed Jews from the Italian nation. This was done both through a race/blood definition of what it meant to be Italian, and Jewish, and through the placing of Jews outside of this new

Box 1.11   Mario Balotelli and the New Italy

When Mario Balotelli smashed the ball into the corner of the net against Germany in the semi-final of the European Championships in June 2012, Italians all over the world jumped up from their seats and began to party. The *festa* went on deep into the night across Italy, with the usual chaotic cacophony of car horns, fireworks, flares, chants and scary car driving. But who was the two-goal Italian hero? Could some of those celebrating so wildly have been the same fans who, for years, had given Balotelli such a hard time in stadiums across the peninsula? The most infamous chant of all implied that the striker was not what he claimed to be: 'Balotelli you are not an Italian/you are a black African'. Another version of this chant was even more explicit: 'There is no such thing as a black Italian'.

Mario Balotelli was born in 1990 in Palermo to Ghanaian parents. He was adopted by an Italian family in the north of Italy when he was just two. Under Italian law, however, he was not able to obtain Italian citizenship until he reached the age of 18, despite having been born in Italy and having always lived there. Meanwhile, others born elsewhere had a near-automatic right to Italian citizenship as they had Italian relatives, even if they had never resided in Italy.

But Balotelli has always been Italian. He speaks the language with a broad Brescian accent, attended local Italian schools and learnt his football there. His 'blackness' is there-fore the issue, something which has marked him out in a country that has experienced mass foreign immigration since the mid-1980s. And SuperMario is not one to hide from publicity. He is not humble, but extremely sure of himself. He does not bow and scrape, but seems almost to enjoy the notoriety he has received from fans and players alike. He is black and extremely good at football, and he is a winner.

Balotelli's goals for the national team expose the contradictions of the racist chants against him. Those goals took on immense symbolic power. They are a sign that black Italians are here to stay, and this is something that a strong minority of Italians find very difficult to accept. Balotelli encapsulates the stark reality of a multicultural society. Immigrants are usually accepted as long as they are invisible and they don't have rights. Life in Italy, for many immigrants, is back-breaking and dangerous. They are not supposed to be *seen*, to be rich and famous, or to be good at anything, or to be 'one of us'.

Reactions to Balotelli's success with the national team have also been illuminating. After one game, *La Gazzetta dello Sport* published a bizarre cartoon depicting Mario as King Kong. At best this was in very bad taste, especially as Croatia had been fined for monkey chants towards Balotelli after an earlier game in the tournament. Yet, *La Gazzetta* didn't seem to think that they had made a mistake at all. They didn't get it. Their apology, when it finally came, was grudging. They simply didn't understand that depicting Balotelli as a large monkey could have been seen as a problem. In 2013 Balotelli threatened to leave the field altogether if he was abused again, after monkey chants from Roma fans had led the referee to stop the game for 90 seconds.

Racism itself is a contested idea in Italy, and this problem has dogged Balotelli's career. On many occasions, it has been said that the insults against him were his own fault. People blamed the victim, arguing that his 'attitude' was provocative, and that he wasn't a 'real champion'. This is why life in Italy, for Mario, will always be difficult. Mario Balotelli was a powerful symbol of change, and as such he was able to catalyse (often without wanting to) a series of discomforts and negotiations about where Italy was going, and where it had come from. April 2013 saw the appointment of Italy's first black cabinet minister, Cécile Kyenge, who was born in Congo in 1964. Kyenge became Minister of Integration, and her rise to public office was accompanied by a series of racist insults of an extreme kind. For example, in 2013 the vice-president of the Senate, Roberto Calderoli, said this: 'I love animals, but when I see her [Kyenge] I can't help but think of an orangutan'. Calderoli apologized, but refused to resign. Kyenge herself arrived in Italy in 1983, and is a qualified ophthalmologist. She married an Italian man in 1994 and her two daughters were born and have grown up in Italy. She is Italian, and black, and she has promised to try to reform Italy's citizenship laws, a change which the Italian centre–right is violently opposed to. The exclusion of immigrants from the political system and from any sense of power makes them vulnerable to attack and exploitation, even if they are Cabinet Ministers.

definition of Italianness. A series of measures then removed Jews from the arenas that also define citizens – work, property, the army and public education. After 1943 and the Nazi occupation, many Italian Jews had their lives threatened by the actions of the German army and the Italian fascist authorities. Some Jews were stripped of Italian citizenship, while others maintained formal rights whilst having all the other aspects relating to this 'citizenship' taken away (see Box 1.12). But even here, a number of exceptions were made to this exclusion, such as the families of those Jews who had fought in World War I and the 'families of fascist squad members'. Strangely, a further clause allowed for the 'free [*sic*] expression and practice of the Jewish faith' and for the institution of Jewish schools. None the less, a fuzzy dividing line was maintained (within the law) between 'foreign Jews' (who were now doubly 'foreign') and Italian Jews, despite the fact that the law itself substantially placed Italian Jews outside of the legal and cultural category of Italians, redefined as 'Aryans'. This was an extreme case, and a shameful one, of the redefinition of the nation for political purposes, and its outcome was tragic, especially after 1943.

Testing the Nation: The Italian Nation at War

The Italian population has gone through various stringent tests of their attachment to the state and the nation over the last century, and these episodes have divided Italians over the role of the state and their conception of the role of their nation. Most important of all have been the two world wars and various imperialist military struggles. War called on Italian citizens to give up their lives, their homes and their families for struggles that might be thousands of miles away from their home villages and towns, and for imprecise and distant objectives.

The relative military failures of Italy during these conflicts have traditionally been seen as further proof of the 'weak' national identity possessed by Italians. Yet, such interpretations undervalue both the commitment to the war-effort of many Italians, on the battlefield and on the home front, in various national struggles, and the power of the nationalist and fascist movements, and nationalist rhetoric and ideology, to mobilize a significant part of Italian society. In addition, these were also struggles, within and outside Italy, over how to define a nation. In some important cases, the civil aspects of wars brought these different conceptions into direct military conflict. Italians fought Italians at various points throughout the century, from the street battles after World War I, to Fiume, to the military clashes during the Spanish Civil War (such as at Guadalajara in March 1937, where Italians fought Italians under the various flags of the Republic and the Franchist forces), to the Resistance and finally during the 'years of lead', marked by terrorism and political violence, during the 1960s and 1970s. Wars did not simply divide Italians into those with 'strong' and 'weak' levels of national identity.[31] On the contrary, wars have been central moments when different ideas concerning the nation, its aims, its activities and its legitimacy (and who should decide what the nation does) have come into conflict. Sometimes, these conflicts remained at the level

Box 1.12 The anti-Semitic legislation, 1938: a selection

Italians and Racism: Extracts from Anti-Semitic Laws and Decrees, 7 September to 17 November 1938.

(a) Decree: 7 September 1938

Article 2 A Jew is considered, for the purposes of this decree-law, any person whose parents were both Jewish, even if they practise a religion different from Judaism.

(b) Decree: 5 September 1938

Article 2 No students from the Jewish race can attend school of any type or level.

Article 3 From 16 October 1938 all teachers belonging to the Jewish race who teach in state schools are suspended from service. This also applies to head-masters, university assistants and professors and other employees in elementary schools.

(c) Decree: 17 November 1938

Article 1 Marriages between Italian citizens of an Aryan race with people belonging to other races are prohibited.

Article 9 Membership of the Jewish race must be communicated and noted in the register of *Stato Civile* and Populations.

Article 10 Italian citizens from the Jewish race cannot:

a. perform military services in peacetime or wartime; [...] d. own land superior in value to 5,000 lire; e. own properties that are superior in value to 20,000 lire.

Article 12 Members of the Jewish race cannot employ Italian citizens from the Aryan race as domestic servants.

Article 13 The following institutions cannot employ people belonging to the Jewish race:

a. civil and military state administrations; [...] c. provincial, local administrations, health services, etc.; d. bank administrations; e. private insurance administrations.

Article 17 Foreign Jews are forbidden from living permanently in Italy, Libya or the colonies.

Article 19 All those who find themselves in the situation stipulated by Articles 8 and 9 must inform public registration offices in their local area within 90 days of the signing of this decree.

Article 24 Any concessions of Italian citizenship made to foreign Jews after 1 January 1919 are revoked.

of academic debate. Other times, at moments of great tension and deep crisis, these battles actually led to different armies, all containing Italians, confronting each other on battlefields across Europe, with each side defending its own ideal of the nation and the community. Each side also tried to classify the other as the *anti-nation*, as acting against the interests of Italy, as traitors. Divided and fragmented memories emerged from all of these conflicts. Memory wars decided which versions of the past would be carried forward and passed down, and which would be excluded. The Church usually provided its own memories and interpretations, which did not always coincide with those of the state. The next section will examine some of these moments in detail: World War I, the Fiume crisis, colonialism in the 1930s, World War II.

A Nation in Crisis: The 'Radiant May' and Intervention in World War I

Italy declared itself neutral when war broke out in 1914. In the meantime, Italian politicians negotiated with the two warring blocs. The main issues at stake, for the interventionists, were the so-called 'unredeemed' lands and Italy's strategic position in the Adriatic. Most historians agree that the vast majority of Italians were opposed to any change to this neutral position. The Left ran a vehement campaign against the war in this period. Many ordinary Italians, peasants and workers, socialists and non-socialists, were fiercely opposed to the war from the outset, understanding little of the reasoning behind a conflict which brought them little but hardship, death and suffering and forced them into a hostile and semi-foreign army. The enormous numbers of military tribunals held during and after the war for numerous acts of disobedience (ranging from anti-war slogans to mutiny) provide some proof of this attitude within the army itself.[32]

In addition, the neutral front in Italy extended across vast sectors of middle-class and intellectual opinion, and to the Catholic Church, which was divided but generally opposed to the war. Pope Benedetto XV's powerful pronouncements against the 'horrific massacre' (1915) and the 'useless slaughter' (1917) of the war were hardly ambiguous in their criticism of the conflict. Catholics, unlike many socialists, generally did not rebel against the state in an open fashion and many priests actively helped the war effort, holding services at the front and taking part in propaganda efforts. Finally, the liberals favoured negotiating around the question of Trentino and the Adriatic and judged Italy ill-prepared for a conflict on a vast scale. The Liberal front, however, was also divided and unable to mobilize any kind of concerted anti-war movement.

None the less, this majority of Italians was unable to prevent Italy entering the war in 1915 after the nationalists had taken control of the streets in a series of violent demonstrations in favour of Italy's participation. The nationalist front was also a variegated one. Some militant nationalists were organized in nationalist groupings, such as the Italian Nationalist Association (ANI), but there were also more maverick tendencies such as the futurists, many revolutionary syndicalists, some leading socialists and the unique personality of the poet, aesthete and nationalist Gabriele D'Annunzio. Nationalists generally saw war both as a revolutionary act and as necessary for the dignity and

defence of a Great Italy. Nationalist rhetoric combined elements of social-
ist-style propaganda (such as anti-parliamentarianism and radical reform
proposals) with violence and disrespect for the law. D'Annunzio's speech at
Quarto, near Genoa, on the anniversary of the sailing of Garibaldi's 'thousand' from there on 5 May 1915, was the spark for further demonstrations and
protests across Italy in the rest of that month, a period later to be baptized by
the nationalists as the 'radiant days of May' (see Box 1.13). Other pro-inter-
ventionists, such as Salvemini and Bissolati, placed the war within the
Risorgimento tradition: Italy's participation would complete the work of
Garibaldi, and a 'fourth war of independence' would lead to a further democ-
ratization of Italy. Other establishment groups were less interested in these
aspects, and more concerned about the damage to Italy's international role by
the adoption of a neutral position. These conservatives were able to mobilize
public opinion at certain levels through the support of the press and in particular the *Corriere della Sera*, Italy's leading daily paper.

Under pressure, the government's emissaries made an agreement with the
Alliance powers to enter the war on their side, against Austria-Hungary and
Germany. The so-called London Pact (signed secretly by the king and the
government in April 1915) guaranteed Italy Trentino–Alto Adige, Trieste,
Istria, Valona in Albania and the Dalmatian region (without Fiume). However,
the pact was held up by Parliament, whose majority was neutralist. Here, the
violence on the streets began to overwhelm the liberal elites. The anti-
democratic nature of these events, encouraged by the conservatives and the
government in order to force neutral parliamentary deputies to change sides,
was once again a dress rehearsal for the collapse of Italian democracy after
1919. The police held back from suppressing the violent nationalist demonstrations, just as they would with the fascists after the war. Giolitti, the symbol
of the neutralist position, and the hate-figure for the nationalist campaign,
gave in and war was declared against Austria on 24 May. The decision to
enter the war was made in secret at the highest levels of power, but the pressure from the streets had been one factor behind these negotiations.

A Nation in Conflict: The War, Caporetto, the Defeatists and the Fiume Crisis

World War I divided Italians in profound and long-lasting ways. Many saw
the war as an unnecessary disaster, and lived through that disaster as
reluctant soldiers, drafted from their remote villages to hear orders barked in
a language (Italian) that very few of them understood. Six million Italians
were called to arms, 571,000 died, 451,645 returned with serious injuries.
Others, however, viewed the conflict as an opportunity to reinvent Italy's
image in the world and restore (or create) nationalist aspirations and identities. These deep fissures ran right through society. The war also transformed
the Italian landscape as vast swathes of the countryside and mountain zones
were turned into mud or covered in trenches for the benefit of the war effort.
Yet the impact of the war only really took hold with the Italian defeat *par
excellence* – Caporetto. The breaching of Italy's lines on 24 October 1917 at the

---

Box 1.13   Speech by Gabriele D'Annunzio: the 'Radiant May', 1915

If it is considered a crime to incite citizens to violence, I am proud to have committed this crime ... every excess of force is permissible, if it stops the loss of the nation ... we are about to be sold like infected sheep. Our human dignity, that of every one of us, of mine, yours, your children, those who are not yet born is threatened with a servile branding. To call yourself Italian will be an embarrassment, something to be ashamed of, a title which will burn your lips, something to hide from. Is that clear?

This lot want to turn you into another breathless licker of sweaty Prussian feet ... they want to turn you into a rabble. They will not succeed.

We have had enough! Turn over the tables! Destroy the false scales! ... organise yourselves into platoons, organise civic squads and hunt them, catch them. You are not a baying crowd, but a vigilant militia.

(Gabriele D'Annunzio, 'Arringa al popolo di Roma in tumulto' (13 May 1915),
in *Per la più grande Italia*, Milan, 1920)

---

town of Caporetto was a traumatic event for both sides. Italy was invaded for the first time since unification, and the threat of defeat in the whole conflict seemed very close, as foreign troops occupied much of the Friuli-Venezia Giulia region. Hundreds of thousands of troops were captured and whole villages razed to the ground. Refugees flooded out of the occupied zones and fled from cities close to the new front line, from Treviso to Venice.

The military elites and nationalists blamed the Left for the disaster. For them, Caporetto was a deliberate act of cowardice and sabotage. Soldiers and socialists had worked together to bring about defeat – they had planned a 'military strike', as General Cadorna put it. They were not merely shirkers – *imboscati* – but defeatists – *disfattisti*. Thus some Italians, it was claimed, had actively sought military defeat, just as Lenin had organized 'revolutionary defeatism' in Russia during the war. These 'defeatists' became, for the fascists and many who had fought in the war, the symbol of the anti-nation (see Box 1.14). This case of blame for defeat – that a disaster had been organized for political reasons – was to return later in the century, with the bitter debates around 8 September (and 25 July) 1943.[33]

Some took pride in this label – happy to call themselves *disfattisti*. They rejoiced at the news from Caporetto, or looked to recapture that event as an active revolt against authority. Yet, the reality of Caporetto was that a poorly motivated, badly led and ill-provisioned army, tired of a largely futile conflict, had ceded to a rapid and well-planned attack. The separation of Italians into those who had 'run away' and those who had 'stood and fought' – into the courageous and the *vigliacchi* – was a constant one in the post-war period, when these wounds were ever-present and as the Caporetto Inquest raged on throughout 1919. Mussolini and the fascists presented themselves as the *anti-disfattisti*, brave, nationalist and willing to defend Italy at all costs.

Box 1.14 Nation and anti-nation: Francesco Misiano, 'The Deserter'

The most potent 'defeatist' symbol of all for the fascists during and after World War I was socialist Francesco Misiano. Misiano made no secret of his hatred of war, and when he was conscripted in 1915 he carried out anti-war agitation amongst the troops. For this, he suffered harassment and torture, and was even locked up in a mental asylum for a while. He was soon accused of desertion, after leaving the barracks to say goodbye to his family before leaving for the front. None of the other soldiers who acted in the same way were similarly accused. As a consequence, Misiano fled to Switzerland (he faced execution) and only returned to Italy in 1919, to be elected to Parliament in Socialist Party (PSI – Partito Socialista Italiano) lists in Naples and Milan. After 1919, Misiano was able to take up his seat, but the fascists picked him out as a hate-figure – the 'anti-nation' – and he was threatened with violence on numerous occasions. Mussolini declared in 1921 that Italy should have been 'ashamed to have elected in two cities that ignoble deserter who I don't even want to name (applause: Death to Misiano!)'.

The Socialist Party relaunched its anti-war campaign in the post-war period and made it very difficult for the Italian flag to be flown, or for war memorials to be constructed. The nationalists tried to fly the flag at every occasion and commemorate the war, but this was almost impossible in such Socialist strongholds as Milan. Forceful cartoons in *Avanti!* depicted mountains of dead and laid the blame firmly at the government's door. Wounds were paraded as political weapons. Uniforms were seen as a sign of pride (for the nationalists) or a provocation (for many on the Left).

Misiano and the fascist leader Roberto Farinacci were the protagonists of one of the most serious episodes of violence in post-war Italy, a moment which signalled the beginning of the end of parliamentary democracy. In 1920 Misiano had returned to Parliament, after a series of court cases and parliamentary procedures, and had cried out 'Down with the war!' during a debate. D'Annunzio, from Fiume, dubbed him a 'miserable deserter' and called on nationalists to 'hunt him down'. In June 1921, on the opening day of the new Parliament, Farinacci and others attacked Misiano, threatened him with a pistol, took away his gun and threw him out of Parliament. Farinacci displayed Misiano's pistol in the debating chamber as a trophy. This unprecedented attack on democratic rights caused protests from many not close to Misiano's ideas, including the reformists Modigliani and Turati. In any case, with the confirmation of Misiano's sentence, he was forced to give up his seat and to leave Italy for his own safety.

Mussolini's first words to the king on taking power in October 1922 were 'I bring you the Italy of Vittorio Veneto.' By definition, the Italies of 'Caporetto' were excluded from this historic moment. They were the anti-nation. The fascists used war metaphors well into the post-war period, and painted themselves as those who 'were not tired of fighting ... and were ready to restart the war and to dig ... trenches in Italian cities' as Benito Mussolini said in 1932.[34] A memory war after 1918 saw socialist and fascist versions create different versions of the past. Liberals and Catholics also pushed other ways of

---

Box 1.15   Divided memories: World War I – a selection of inscriptions

a) Anti-war monument
This plaque with its anti-war message was put up in 1919 in a small village called
Cardano da Campo, near Varese, which was destroyed by fascists in 1920.

> Forced to leave the fields and the factories
> to fight in a four-year long fratricidal war
> the best of Cardano's youth died
> on the cursed battlefields of
> Trentino, the Carso and the Piave
> May 1915 – November 1918

(b) Liberal Inscription (The Tomb of the Unknown Soldier, 1921, Rome)

Ignoto militi

MCMXV (1915) – MCMXVIII (1918)

(c) Fascist plaque (Turin)

On 25 October 1932 this ossuary was inaugurated, in the Presence of
Benito Mussolini, in order to glorify the heroic sons of Turin who fell in the
Great War of 1915–1918

*

PRESENTE, PRESENTE, PRESENTE, PRESENTE (repeated 748 times),
Redipuglia war monument, 1938

(d) Soldiers' monument *Associazione Nazionale Alpini*

1915–1917

Per non dimenticare

National Mountain Soldiers Association

1915–1917

Do not Forget

(Truncated column, Monte Ortigara, 1920)

---

understanding the conflict. Fascism was the victor in this memory war, and
imposed its own ideological vision of the past and the future on Italy.

This experience was not unique in Europe – much greater defeats were
experienced by Russia, Germany and Austro-Hungary. Yet the divisions in
Italian society, despite eventual war victory, did lead to intense conflicts that
the Liberal state was unable to heal in the post-war period. Even the victory
at Vittorio Veneto could not unite Italy. The horrors of war remained
ever-present in many people's minds. There was a strong desire to punish
those responsible for the conflict, and also to gain reward for the suffering and
sacrifice of the war: hence the rapid growth of ex-combatant movements,

of land occupations and of socialist organizations during the *biennio rosso* (the 'two red years', 1919–20). For many on the Left, the war had been a criminal act of folly and violence. All symbols of the war became targets. Milan found it impossible to organize annual celebrations of the war in 1919 and 1920. Many people were vehemently opposed to war memorials. Anti-war counter memorials were erected in many places, which denounced the horrors of the conflict, depicted the war as an international class conspiracy and claimed that soldiers had been 'murdered'. The Italian flag was frequently torn down and burnt. People in uniforms were attacked in the street, as during the 'hunt of the officers' in December 1919. Pro-war groups and individuals also used violence, which had often been honed on the battlefield. War militarized a whole generation.[35] Nationalists exhibited their wounds as trophies, as examples of their heroism and national pride. The greatest symbol of all was a one-legged soldier, Enrico Toti, who had apparently carried on fighting despite his disability and had even thrown his crutch at the enemy. Toti's funeral in San Lorenzo (Rome) in May 1922 was the scene of violent clashes between Left and Right. Yet the Right had not been placated by victory, and the defeat at the bargaining table had helped to produce the myth of a 'mutilated victory', a phrase first coined by D'Annunzio, which enthused the fascist movement.[36] D'Annunzio's own occupation of Fiume was an inspiration for nationalists and fascists in the post-war upheavals (see Box 1.3).

Concepts of the Nation: Fascism and the Nation

Fascism was an ultra-nationalist movement that argued that only a voluntarist minority could create a great Italy. For Mussolini 'the Risorgimento was only the beginning'. Italy was unfinished, unmade, incomplete. The first steps towards the voluntarist 'completion' of Italy had been taken during World War I, which had created a new generation of extreme nationalists – united by their hatred of socialism (and its 'anti-national' character) and their ideals of the nation, war, Italy's lost colonial empire and her past glories. However, this strong, extreme nationalism, which used violence to impose its will, along with its symbols and its songs and uniforms, was combined with an intense disdain for the majority of the Italian people.

Fascism tended to view Italians as a fundamentally weak people, who needed to be continually forced and 'tested' from above in order to become part of an Italian nation. As Benito Mussolini (1915) said:

> This is Italy's first war. As a nation, as a people, united in a solid united structure from the Alps to Sicily ... it will be a great test. The war is an exam for populations ... the war must reveal Italy to the Italians. It must destroy the despicable legend that the Italians do not fight, it must wipe out the shame of Lissa and Custoza [two famous Italian military defeats in 1866], it must show the world that Italy is able to make war, a great war ... only in this way, can Italians be proud to be Italian, only the war can make the 'Italians' which D'Azeglio wrote about. Or the Revolution.[37]

A heroic minority would show the way, and the state would create, by force as necessary, a new, glorious, Italian empire (for details see Box 1.5). For fascism, it was the state, controlled by the fascists, which created the nation, and not vice versa. Democracy played no part in this conception of the nation, although fascists often employed populist and sometimes class rhetoric borrowed from the Left and embellished with syndicalist and populist slogans. The nation was never completely 'made', but subject to continual 're-making' through the actions of the state and the ideas of 'The Leader'. This nation would not include everyone within Italy, and in fact much of fascism's early period of growth consisted in violent struggle against those groups which the fascists defined as outside of the Italian: the anti-nation, the defeatists and the socialists.

As Giovanni Gentile, philosopher and ideologue of fascism's idea of the nation, put it in 1919:

> Here we are at a crossroads ... on one side, the easy Italy, the lazy Italy, sceptical and superficial with a culture without religion and without character, the old Italy. On the other side, the Italy which, when she arrived at Piave and on the Grappa, refused to budge, and threw out the attackers from Montello, before reaching them, on the other side of the river, and destroying them. This was an Italy which won only because it wanted to win, and shocked the world and even some Italians with this stupendous example of its tenacity and its ability to resist: the new Italy. Which of the two will survive? The old type is not dead, he deceives us and entices us and crosses our path. We have to fight and destroy him; and the struggle is a bitter one, because this man is part of us.[38]

Fascism, as we have seen, attempted to create (or re-create) a particular kind of Italy through the use of the state, from above. There were a number of important aspects to this strategy. First, the Italian nation was to be unified around a common party, ideology and leader – Mussolini. The cult of personality and the state were as one. This 'civic religion' looked to gain hegemony amongst Italians. Secondly, Italy was to expand abroad. It was finally to have an empire worthy of the name and Italians were to have their 'place in the sun'. In addition, Italy would take back those territories that fascism claimed were Italian – from Corfu to Nice to Corsica. Imperial wars would help further to unite Italians, as Italians, on the field of battle. Thirdly, class struggle, which had divided the country, was to be replaced by inter-class unity within a corporative state. Finally, the historic breach with the Church, which had marked the first sixty years of Italian history, was to be resolved. This was done through the Lateran Pacts of 1929. The anti-clerical nature of the Italian state was also toned down considerably. In 1930 the national holiday celebrating the final battle of the Risorgimento of 1870 (20 September) was replaced with a holiday on the anniversary of the signing of the Lateran Pacts (11 February).

How successful were these strategies, and what kind of Italy did they produce? Most debates over the consent or otherwise displayed by the Italian people towards the regime under fascism touch on the answer to this question. Clearly, individual Italians related to the regime in different ways, and through their own particular vision of the nation and fascist ideals. Many did support the colonial wars of the 1920s and 1930s, many did idolize Mussolini, and were willing to fight and die for him in a series of wars throughout the world. However, many others were less enthusiastic about the whole fascist project, and compromised on a daily basis with the regime because there was little alternative. Others openly rebelled, either from exile or within Italy itself. Forms of rebellion ranged from opposition to the regime's maternity drives, to the stubborn silence of the Fiat workers in the face of Mussolini himself in 1939.[39] Some would wear red ties on May Day, or refuse to take part in fascist parades. The ultra-nationalism of Italian fascism certainly won over a minority of Italians, many of whom ended up in the ill-fated Republic of Salò after 1943, but its autocratic nature prevented wider consensus. Fascism's state-based idea of nationhood, and its connection to a transient political movement and an ephemeral political personality, meant that with the disappearance of these components, the fascist nation collapsed. The voluntarism of Gentile's fascist nation required a kind of continual 'revolution', a daily re-making of the nation, its symbols and its 'grandeur'. As soon as the fascist juggernaut went into reverse, there was nothing to hold the fascist nation together. *That* nation died in July (and not September) 1943, with the arrest of Mussolini and the dissolution of the institutions of fascism.

The Nation and World War II

An extensive historical debate has taken place in Italy concerning the relationship between the Italian nation, World War II and the Resistance. The drastic language of this debate – with its claims that the nation 'died' in September 1943, or was 're-born' at the very same time, reveal the deep-rooted divisions created by fascism and by intervention in the war. In many cases these divisions went right back to the bitter social struggles of the later nineteenth century in areas as diverse as the Po Valley or the great estates of Apulia and Sicily.

World War II was presented to the Italians as a heroic moment, and opposition to Italy's entry into the war (late, as with World War I) was muted, not least because the country had been under a dictatorship for the previous twenty years.[40] Yet, after an initial sense of 'victory', defeat and disaster came rapidly – first in Greece, then in Africa, then in Russia. The catastrophic Russian campaign (1941–3) involved over 230,000 men. Thousands of Italian troops were more or less abandoned (and surrounded) on the freezing banks of the Don River without backup or proper equipment, subject to constant bombardment from Russian tanks and planes. As with the high mountain 'battles' of World War I (the so-called 'white war'), more soldiers died from the cold than in actual combat. Nuto Revelli's memories reveal his own personal odyssey, from convinced fascist to anti-fascist, via the terrible experience of the retreat from Russia. 'And my country?' he writes: 'The only country I believed in was that of the poor beasts who paid with their lives the mistakes of the "others" … the 8th September moved me, and my choice was immediate, instinctive. As soon as the Germans arrived in Cuneo I ran home, gathered up my three automatic weapons … and put them in a rucksack. Then I went to my first partisan base.'[41]

The war itself rapidly became unpopular at home as news filtered back of death, imprisonment and defeat abroad, and the economic and social effects of the conflict began to hit hard. Military hubris led to the desperate decision by the king and the Fascist Grand Council to arrest Mussolini, replace his administration and dissolve the Fascist Party. Wartime defeats had brought down the regime, just as Caporetto had indirectly led to the collapse of Liberal Italy. The forty-five days that followed have been analysed and re-analysed by historians, politicians and others ever since. Italy veered between its allies and the Allies, as the Pact of Steel came apart. Finally, as the army itself was dissolving before his eyes, and the situation was becoming ungovernable on the home front, Badoglio (a veteran of the World War I, like Pétain – the 'victor of Verdun') was forced to sign an armistice with the Allies.

This was on 8 September 1943 – a date overloaded with meaning that has pivotal importance for the history of modern Italy. The Italians had changed sides, mid-conflict. Many soldiers deserted, and were faced with a series of acute choices.[42] Should they take to the hills, becoming partisans and forming what was to become known as 'the Resistance', should they join the Fascist armies in the Republic of Salò, or should they try to avoid the conflict altogether? Many other ex-POWs from various armies tried to escape into Italy, often finding help amongst peasant families.[43] Many units were left without orders, others were ordered not to resist the Germans. Radically different conceptions of the nation, duties and obligations, and the state came into play. The response to this choice cannot be reduced to simple fascist/anti-fascist, nationalist/anti-nationalist or left/right dualisms. Many monarchists (who had backed fascism) supported the Resistance, as did many Catholics. The rhetoric of the nation and of national liberation formed a strong part of the ideology behind the partisan groups, even those organized by the Communist or Socialist Parties. Within the broad alliance that made up the Resistance, there was little agreement about the shape of a future Italian nation, and a (fragile) unity was achieved only through the common struggle against a common enemy – the Nazis and the Italian (fascist) army.

The main effect of 8 September on the official Italian army – another key component of certain national myths, particularly that of fascism – was one of collapse. Official orders called on Italian troops only to respond *if* attacked. Some (a small minority) disobeyed, and fought the Germans in open battle, refusing to surrender – as in Rome or, most famously, at Cephalonia in Greece where over 5,000 Italian soldiers were wiped out by the Nazi forces. In short, 'on the 8 September, everything that could have happened, happened'.[44] The major representatives of the state and the nation hardly provided an example of resistance, as the king and the prime minister fled to the south, leaving the capital in the hands of an invading army.

The events of 8 September have inspired considerable discussion as representing a singular moment in Italian history, with particular focus on the role of ideas of national identity before and after that date. Galli della Loggia has interpreted the armistice and the dissolution of the Italian army rather grandly as *The Death of the Nation*. The whole idea of the nation, he argues, collapsed in the shame and collapse of the Italian army (and state). Whilst this intelligent polemic carries a certain force in its depiction of the extremity of the events of 1943, the argument is based on an extremely specific idea of 'the nation' and on a series of hypotheses that bear little relation to history. *If* the Resistance had combined with the Italian state, *if* the king had resisted, etc., etc., *then* the nation would have been preserved. Above all, however, such extreme conclusions rest upon a highly controversial idea of what national identity should be and, in this specific case, on a gross exaggeration of the 'consent' achieved by fascism at the moment of entry into war.[45]

Others have traditionally viewed this moment in positive terms, as a moment when Italy (and the nation) was *re-born* through armed resistance to the Germans and the fascists. Thus 8 September is presented in ways that cannot be reconciled – as death and birth at the same time – as 'symbolic of disintegration and at the same time a prelude to a revival'.[46] The fascists also saw 8 September as a moment of possible revival, with the origins of the Republic of Salò and the decision to fight on with the Germans against the Americans and the 'Italian' army. For nearly everyone, 8 September was a complicated and confused moment – a time of defeat, of new allies and of momentous *choices*, which were to have life-changing consequences. For the Communists, the choice between the Red Army and Mussolini's (or Badoglio's) Italian army was no choice at all. Togliatti, the leader of the PCI, was still in Russia when it was invaded by Mussolini. Many Italian nationals simply did not identify with the Italian army, as it was constituted. As Pavone noted in 1991, 'even today, to look on September 8 as a tragedy or the beginning of a liberation process is a line which separates interpretations by opposing schools'.[47]

Italy's World War II was a complicated set of experiences which were difficult to categorize under terms such as 'victory' or 'defeat'. Italians fought and died in a whole series of countries for the Italian army, and then for the Resistance in all its various forms. Many were deported, numerous others became prisoners of war. Others took part in what has been defined as a 'civil resistance' on the home front. A large number simply did their best to survive, as they were bombed from above and attacked from below, and as food supplies ran out. A vast 'grey zone' waited for the war to end. Not surprisingly, this set of experiences (which included a fair amount of changing of sides) was impossible to summarize in a coherent national narrative after the war. Much was left out, forgotten or pushed to one side. Historians also struggled with the multi-faceted nature of events. Memories came and went, history discovered trends, and ignored others. The war itself was a powerful creator of myths and trauma. It took fifty years or so for a fuller picture to emerge.

The Monarchy and the Nation

For the first 82 years of Italy's history, the idea of the nation was embodied, for many Italians, by the monarchy. The failure of the Republican ideal, held most importantly by Mazzini, set in place a state with a monarch not just as constitutional leader, but also as symbol of the unity and greatness of the Italian nation (see Chapter 2). At moments of national crisis, the monarchy

Box 1.16   Divided memories: World War II – parallel plaques

San Miniato (Tuscany). These two plaques, which are fixed side-by-side on the façade of the town hall, relate to the deaths of over 50 people in a church in San Miniato in 1944. Originally attributed to the Nazis, it was later confirmed that these deaths were probably caused by a US shell accidentally hitting the building. This change led to a new plaque, although the original was left in place.

1954 (first plaque)

Through the centuries this plaque will commemorate
the cold-blooded killing by the Germans
on 22 July 1944
of sixty unarmed, aged, innocent victims
perfidiously encouraged to take refuge in the cathedral
This allowed the evil deed
dictated not by any necessity of war, but by pure ferocity
to be carried out with greater speed and arrogance
As befitted an army that was denied victory
because it was the enemy of all liberty, the murderers were driven
to launch a lethal shell into the cathedral
Italians who read this, forgive but do not forget!
Remember that only through peace and work is civilization eternal
The Town Council on the 10th anniversary

2008 (second plaque)

More than sixty years have passed
since the terrifying massacre of 22 July 1944
which was attributed to the Germans
Historical research has now shown
that the Allied forces were responsible for those deaths
The truth demands respect and must always be declared
It is also true that the Germans
were responsible for the war, for shameful and unjust reprisals
and that in this area,
with the complicity of Italian Fascists,
they sowed death, destruction and tragedy
This is what happens in war
For this reason the Italian Constitution
proclaims in Article 11:
'Italy repudiates war'
The Town Council on the 64th anniversary

played a key role – such as during the 1908 earthquake in Messina.[48] History was written exalting the role of the monarch during the Risorgimento, and statues and monuments were erected across the peninsula in his name. Republicanism, none the less, remained extremely popular throughout Italy.

The Socialist Party and, obviously, the Republican Party were convinced anti-monarchists. Any support for, or even contact with, the monarchy was taken as treachery within the socialist movement. The anarchists were also radically republican, and individual anarchists continued to carry out assassination attempts – succeeding only once, when anarchist Gaetano Bresci shot King Umberto I dead at Monza in 1900.

The monarchy also played a key role at crucial moments in Italy's history – most notably with the invitation to Mussolini to form a government after the march on Rome in October 1922, despite fascism's contempt for the law, its use of extreme violence and its small parliamentary representation. Throughout fascism, the king limited himself to accepting various proclamations of his greatness throughout the world (Emperor of Ethiopia, May 1936; King of Albania, April 1939). These titles did nothing to change the fact that Mussolini had far more power and was more popular in the country than the supposed head of state, the king. Only with complete disaster looming did the king finally act. In July 1943, he sacked Mussolini (with the help of a number of leading fascists) and pulled Italy out of the war.

With the war over, the monarchy attempted to re-impose itself as a major power in the land and as representative of the nation. Yet many Italians blamed the king for fascism and for the disasters of the war – and the passing of powers to a new, younger, monarch in May 1946 was a desperate gamble. The Italian Republic was created, by referendum, in June 1946 (see also Chapters 2, 3 and 4). When Umberto II was voted out in the first full and free elections in the history of a united Italy he had been king for a mere 34 days. The head of state became the president of the Republic, who took on many of the functions formerly performed by the monarchy and, at times, rivalled the former monarchs in terms of national popularity. After 1946, the Italian ex-royal family was in exile, important more for the gossip magazines than for any historical debates or significance. Their return in 2002 changed very little. They remained an ex-royal family.

THE REPUBLIC AND THE NATION, 1946–2014

The Italian Nation and the Cold War

After 1945, the borders of Italy were all but fixed (with the exception of Trieste and the eastern border, whose limits were finally decided in 1975), but debates over national identity remained highly charged. One indication of this was the regionalism that spread through the edges of Italy after 1945, leading to the creation of semi-autonomous regional governments. Another sign was the uncertainty over the role of 'Italy' in a divided post-war Europe. Italy was on the front line of the cold war, and the divisions in Europe were reproduced within the nation itself, with loyalties being divided between the USA and the USSR. The model of what a nation should be, with the decline of the fascist model, went through a radical rethink. Italy was no longer to take part in war or to aspire to possess an empire. The disappearance of this 'strong' model of the nation (except amongst minority groups, from the neo-fascists to the monarchists) certainly led to a less aggressive conception of the role of Italy and of the state on the international stage. In fact, Italy was a prime mover in the creation of the European Community and did not take part directly in any kind of world conflict until the Gulf War in 1991 and the Kosovo War of 1999, followed by the Afghanistan invasion in 2001 and the Iraq War in 2003. Italy also participated in the Libyan War in 2011. Italy's participation in these wars did mark a turning point of sorts, although the large pacifist majority in Italy was a significant factor in limiting the extent of all these operations.

Regions and Regionalism

The crisis brought on by the war, and the legacy of fascist centralization (as well as the crushing of localist traditions), encouraged regionalist movements across Italy after World War II. The strongest movements were organized in Sicily, Sardinia, Alto Adige and Trentino and in the Aosta Valley. These movements varied greatly in their ideological outlook and origins. Some were inspired by right-wing ideologies, and were manipulated by powerful interest groups in order to put down peasant movements or to win concessions from the state. This was certainly the case in Sicily. Other movements had a strong left-tinge and called for liberation from the centralized powers of the state. The Sardinian Action Party developed from democratic and anti-fascist traditions and combined support for the protection of Sardinian interests and cultural traditions with federalist ideals. This organization maintained strong support throughout the post-war period. Meanwhile, the autonomist and regionalist movements in the Alto Adige and Aosta Valley regions were more concerned with linguistic issues, which often masked much wider problems of discrimination and identity. These regions were all awarded 'special region' status in the 1940s (Sicily in 1946; Trentino, Alto Adige and Sud Tyrol, Sardinia and the Aosta Valley in 1948; and Friuli-Venezia–Giulia followed in 1963). All were given elected regional assemblies, access to state funds to finance regional development, and various other powers which varied from the ability to raise taxes locally (as with Sicily) to support for linguistic minorities (Alto Adige, Aosta Valley). In reality, although this regional status diffused regionalist movements (most successfully in Sicily, where the regionalists had all but disappeared by the 1950s, after gaining 10 per cent of the vote in the first regional elections in Sicily in 1947) it also set up a further level of bureaucracy which, in some areas, was used as a powerful tool of clientelism and patronage. This was particularly true of Sicily's regional government organization.[49]

In 1970, after much delay, the regional governments called for by the Constitution were installed, and all Italian regions were given their own elected councils. With time, more and more powers were transferred to the regions including the management of health services after 1977. Other areas administered by the regions, and not centrally, now include tourism, trade fairs, the environment and many educational services. Regional presidents became more and more powerful vis-à-vis the central government, and the move to the direct election of presidents in 2000 gave these politicians a legitimacy that surpassed that of many Rome-based politicians. This shift away from Rome was cemented by the explosive growth of new regionalist movements in the 1980s, 1990s and 2000s in the north of Italy. The regionalists of the Northern League, who originated in the Veneto and Lombard regions, utilized a mixture of radical anti-state rhetoric with calls for drastic tax cuts, an end to state corruption and cuts to state funding for the south. This propaganda won over vast swathes of middle- and working-class opinion for a time, contributing to the collapse of the major political parties after the corruption scandals of 1992. The Leagues were able to tap into the frustration of those entrepreneurs who had contributed to massive economic growth in the north and north-east in the 1980s and 1990s, often through the use of high-density, small, family-run firms producing quality export goods. This new entrepreneurial class was frustrated by continuing high taxation and poor state services, as well as the policies and behaviour of a corrupt and inefficient political class.

The *Lega* first stood in elections in 1983 and two local government councillors were elected in Varese in 1985. In 1987 *Lega* leader Umberto Bossi was elected to the Senate and in 1990 the movement won 8 per cent of the vote in the European Elections in Lombardy, electing two MEPs. Similar results were obtained in the north-east. Using simple language ('Rome the thief'), authoritarian and charismatic leadership (in the extraordinary shape of Bossi, a figure radically different in every way from those politicians who had dominated the 'first republic') and building upon local traditions, prejudices (against the south and southerners, and also new immigrants from outside Italy) and discontent with the political system and above all *politics in general*, the *Lega* quickly won over supporters from other parties. In 1992, the *Lega* won 34 per cent of the vote in local elections in Mantua and a similar result was obtained in Brescia. The movement exploded with the corruption scandals of that year and the *Lega* was part of the victorious national centre–right political alliance in 1994. That short-lived experience in government led to a shift towards independentist positions, which called not just for federalism but also for the division of Italy and the creation of a maxi-region known as 'Padania'. For a time, this strategy gained widespread national attention, culminating in huge demonstrations surrounding the so-called 'declaration of independence' of the north in 1995.

The *Lega* continued to propose tax cuts, tax federalism and privatization, mixed with euro-scepticism and a call for a block on foreign immigration. This programme was not without its contradictions: for example, the north-east miracle relies heavily on cheap foreign labour. The basis of *Lega* support, despite momentary victories in Milan (in 1994) and other cities, remains the industrial provinces of Lombardy and the Veneto and, to a lesser extent, Piedmont. This support has traditionally come from the so-called 'productive middle class' with a strong element of working-class 'leghism'. The alliance with Silvio Berlusconi (which had its ups and downs, but was pretty solid after 2000) brought *Lega* representatives into power at a national, regional and local level. But the payback from Berlusconi was meagre. Only the centre-left passed any serious federalist reforms, while the constitutional changes proposed by the centre-right was defeated in a referendum. Power led to corruption and clientelism, and the *Lega* was increasingly similar to other parties. A massive scandal erupted in 2012, which exposed mis-use of public and party funds at all levels of the party. The *Lega* remains, however, the only serious social movement to emerge from within Italian society over the past three decades, and cannot be dismissed as a short-lived protest movement.

Only a small minority of northern Italians have ever supported the division of Italy, and the *Lega* slowly moved back to more moderate, federalist positions, which called for a radical transfer of powers to the regions and an end to the redistribution of state funds from north to south. The racist aspects of *Lega* propaganda began to concentrate on new immigrants, making it difficult to distinguish them from other right-wing parties, such as *Alleanza Nazionale* or Berlusconi's various groupings. In fact, these racist discourses have a strong nationalist (and not regionalist) tinge. This more realist strategy culminated in a new centre–right alliance with Berlusconi and Fini in 2000, which triumphed in the 2001 national elections at great cost electorally to the *Lega*, which saw much of its 'softer' support transfer to other centre-right forces. Alone, the *Lega* was stronger, but it was usually only through alliances that it could gain access to power. The *Lega* was torn between a desire for independence and 'anti-politics', and the deadly embrace of Silvio Berlusconi. Roberto Maroni's leadership after the demise of Umberto Bossi's clique in 2011–13 promised a more independent attitude to the more objectionable aspects of Berlusconian politics. The *Lega* also saw its anti-system clothes stolen by Beppe Grillo's Five Star MoVement.

Regarding 'the nation', the *Lega* has attempted to create an alternative nation, with its own language, symbols, festivals, places, leaders and histories. This attempt has been relatively unsuccessful in the short run. None the less, the long-term effects of the continual anti-national propaganda of the *Lega* are still being felt, and the transfer of powers to the regions, begun under pressure by the centre–left governments (1996–2001) and continued (with little success) by the centre–right (2001–6, 2008–11), will alter the structure of the Italian state in a permanent way. A significant proportion of Italian citizens took up the banner, however superficially, of this *other* nation in the 1980s, 1990s and 2000s, rejecting 'Italy' in favour of Lombardy, the Veneto or 'Padania'. The national state survived this period (though the main national political parties did not), but not without the emergence of a different idea of nation and state amongst significant sectors of the population, and not just those linked directly to the *Lega*. However, it also appears that Italian national symbols were destined to survive, despite everything, as the reaction to the elaborate 2011 commemorations showed.

Italy and the Nation since 1945: Four Themes, Many Debates

Since 1945, the question of national identities and the Italian nation has been the subject of continual debate. We can divide these debates into four broad themes. First, there was the constant problem of regionalism and 'minorities'.

A second theme developed around the role of the Italian nation on the world stage. The fissures opened up within Italian society by the cold war led to identifications which went way beyond the Italian nation itself – and spread on to the divisions between the communist and non-communist blocs (or to other institutions, above all the Church). Within Italy this set of divisions expressed itself most obviously in the membership of or sympathy with the Communist Party or the Christian Democrats. But the issues at stake went far beyond the possession of a party card. What was up for grabs was the type of nation itself and the national identities of all Italians. Both Communism and Christian Democracy looked to defend or create a particular kind of nation, partly drawn from international models. Yet, neither movement was anti-national in a strict sense. Moreover, the cross-contamination between Soviet ideologies, Americanization and the Church created a series of overlapping ideologies and identities.

The events of 1968 led to a further muddying of the waters, with the PCI no longer seen as the undeniable defender of the Soviet model, and a strong Catholic Left emerging to challenge the hierarchies and conservatisms of the official Church. These questions were never really put to the test given Italy's non-participation in international wars between 1945 and 1990. The role of Italy within Europe can also be placed broadly within this theme, from the pioneer position of the 1940s and 1950s to the enthusiastic acceptance of European Unity in the 1980s and 1990s (and relatively painless transition to the euro). The support for Europe within Italy has often been read as yet another indicator of the dissatisfaction of Italians with their own nation-state. Euroscepticism only really began to emerge within political discourse after the centre–right victory in 2001. The financial crisis after 2008 and the subsequent difficulties in the eurozone provided strong arguments for Italian Eurosceptics, who began to make headway in the major centre–right groupings. Beppe Grillo's Five Star MoVement railed against the euro and the hegemony of financial power. Analysts differed in the way they understood this movement, with some placing it within the left tradition, others saw it as drawing on right-wing populist narratives. It appeared as if traditional categories of left and right were not particularly useful here. Grillo's movement was post-political and post-ideological, and as such could not simply be slotted into twentieth-century ideological slots. Its support came from across the spectrum.

By the time of the 2013 elections, many Italians had begun to doubt the wisdom of so much sacrifice, given the austerity packages being forced upon them. Support for Europe seemed more a reflection of the low levels of legitimation enjoyed by 'the system' rather than any positive evaluation of the EU, its institutions, or the single currency. The crisis was threatening the future of one of the most pro-European countries of all. Italy stood at a crossroads.

A further set of debates concerns the 'public use of history' and the divisions of the past left unresolved over time. The phrase *una storia all'italiana* ('an Italian story') is often used to indicate a mess or a mystery without a guilty party. Italian history is full of such stories. This continuing conflict over the past has translated itself into bitter struggles over responsibilities, testimonies, memories, and over who has the right to testify, to hold someone else responsible, to remember and forget. The politicization of Italian society and Italian institutions, from the civil service to the legal system, was both a result of the cold war and clientelistic networks, and a contributor to the widespread distrust of the state and its legitimation. Divided and fragmented memories have prevented the emergence of a strong, unitary version of the past. However, these divisions have also been an indication of democracy, where debate and scepticism were common and there was a refusal to simply toe the line. People often carried forward their own versions of the past, usually in some sort of local or collective form, and often with the legitimation of public memorials and commemorations. The national state, however, was rarely seen as an institution that represented all Italians, but appeared to reflect the needs of only certain Italians at certain times. This politicization of history often prevented a real critical examination of many of the most important events in Italian history – the support for fascism, the sectarianism of the Resistance, the 'patriotism' of those who fought for Mussolini and Hitler. Similar debates over an uncomfortable past took place in other countries, above all in France, Germany and Spain, but also in Russia and South Africa.[50]

A third theme is structured around the tensions and opportunities opened up by continuing emigration, return immigration, massive internal migration (all involving *Italians*, the latter above all between 1950 and 1973) and then, during the 1980s, 1990s and 2000s, foreign immigration into Italy on a large scale. All of these movements called into question identities and national ideas, however defined. Languages, cultures, families and customs came into contact with each other across Italy, as millions of Italians moved up or across the peninsula and then, later, millions of non-Italians chose Italy as their final destination. The effects of these extraordinary movements are still being felt (and, as we have seen, identities are often at their most potent when created in the face of Others, be those Others from the Veneto, or southerners, or Moroccans, Albanians, Romanians or Pakistanis). Political mobilization for or against this kind of movement also contributed to the debates over national identity and to the creation of certain kinds of national identity.

A final strand of debates relating to national identities since 1945 concerns the much more slippery subject of Italian self-assessment. The widespread anti-national sentiments present in Italy have been commented on already. This tendency, along with the problems introduced by the three previously noted themes, has led to a wide-ranging academic and public debate over national identity. This debate took its cue from the growth of regionalism in the 1980s and 1990s but went way beyond that narrow subject-matter. There are a number of different strands to this debate, but the crux of the question can be summarized as follows: there are those who argue that it has been the failings of the Italian state (in a whole series of areas, from services to public order) which has created weak national identification. Civic pride has never been easy in the face of a corrupt and inefficient state machine. Secondly, there is the key role of the family. These debates first originated with the work of the American anthropologist Edward Banfield in the 1950s. Banfield, drawing on a study of a small southern village, came to the conclusion that

Box 1.17 Days of memory and remembrance: a selection

A series of days of memory were set up in Italy in the twenty-first century to cover a range of events, from the Shoah, to the reprisals and mass arrests and exodus which were linked to the war with Yugoslavia and the cold war, to the 'years of lead' linked to political violence in the 1960s, 1970s and 1980s. These official days had the effect of raising awareness of these issues and of recognizing the 'victim' status of various groups within Italian society, and in terms of history itself. They also seemed to confirm a situation where no one version of history was imposed by the state from above. Italy was marked by *divided* or *fragmented* memories.

1. The Day of Memory. Law 211, 20.7.2000. The Shoah.

'Institution of a "Day of Memory" in memory of the extermination and persecution of the Jewish people and of Italian military and political deportees to Nazi camps.'

Art. 1. 1. The Italian Republic recognizes 27 January, date of the removal of the gates of Auschwitz, as a 'Day of Memory' in order to remember the Shoah (the extermination of the Jewish people), the racial laws, Italian persecution of Jewish citizens, the Italians who experienced deportation, imprisonment or who were killed as well as those who, in the camps and in different organizations, opposed the extermination plans, and risked their own lives in order to save others and protect those who were being persecuted.

Art. 2. 1. During the day of memory as outlined in article 1, ceremonies, initiatives and collective moments for the narration of the facts and for analysis will be organized, especially in schools of all levels, in terms of the fate of the Jewish people and of political and military deportees who ended up in Nazi camps. The aim is to preserve the memory of this tragic and dark period for Europe and for Italy so that similar events can never happen again.

2. The Day of Remembrance (Law 92, 30.3.2004)

'The institution of a "Day of Remembrance" in memory of the victims of the *foibe*, of the exodus from the Giuliano-Dalmatian region, of events around the Eastern border and recognition of the status of the relatives of the *infoibati'*.

Art. 1.

1. The Republic recognizes 10 February as a 'Day of Remembrance' in order to conserve and strengthen the memory of the tragedy of Italians and all victims of the *foibe* and the exodus from their lands of the Istriani, Fiumani and Dalmatians after World War II as well as the complex events linked to the Eastern border.

2. On that day lectures and meetings will be held in order to spread information about these tragic events in all kinds of schools. Institutions and organizations are also encouraged to carry out research, organize conferences and debates in order to conserve memory linked to those events.

3. The Day of Memory for the Victims of Terrorism

'Institution of a Day of Memory dedicated to the victims of terrorism and massacres [a word usually linked to bomb attacks which killed numerous people from 1969 to 1984]', Law 56, 4.5.2007.

Art. 1.1. The Republic recognizes 9 May, anniversary of the murder of Aldo Moro, as a Day of Memory in order to remember the victims of domestic and international terrorism and of massacres/outrages linked to this activity.

2. On this Day of Memory, public initiatives, ceremonies, meetings and collective moments for remembering facts and for reflection can be organized, in schools of all levels and elsewhere, in order to conserve, renew and construct a shared historic memory which will be able to defend our democratic institutions.

the extreme poverty and backwardness of the village was 'largely (but not entirely) due to the inability of the villagers to act together for the common good, or indeed for any good transcending the immediate, material interest of the nuclear family'.[51] This familism prevented collective action, the only way that things could be improved. Clearly, according to Banfield, as an explanation of southern backwardness, such a concept is simplistic and ahistorical. But as a portrayer of a key feature of Italian ideology and social life, Banfield remains important. Familism, however, needs to be seen as both cause and consequence of a weak attachment to the state and the nation, in historical and anthropological terms.[52] In the face of an inefficient and faceless state unable to meet the basic needs of its citizens, familism was one obvious and logical response. Clearly, however, it was not the only possible response. There is also evidence to show that the equation 'familism = the south' is a mistaken one. Familism also marked social relations in the north, especially in the wake of the individualist mass cultural revolution brought about by the economic miracle in the 1950s and 1960s.[53] Sport had always been an important factor in terms of national and regional identity in Italy, but with the boom and the increased use of television, the Italian love affair with football became even more of an obsession. The 1982 World Cup victory against West Germany captured the interest of the entire nation, and had an emotional impact that had not been seen since the war.

Robert Putnam's important and influential research feeds into these debates. Putnam found strong evidence of much higher levels of regional government 'performance' in the north of Italy since the regional governments were set up in 1970, when compared with those in the south. The explanation for this trend, however, has caused great controversy. Putnam argues that the north (and centre) has greater levels of 'civic traditions', stretching back hundreds of years to the city-states of the past. This tradition was more or less absent in the south. Two different 'patterns of governance' were produced by Italy: 'in the north, people were citizens, in the south they were subjects … In the north the crucial social, political and even religious allegiances and alignments were horizontal, while those in the south were vertical.'[54] This type of analysis reproduces what has been called the 'southern question discourse' whereby 'Italy appears dragged down by its southern half'.[55] The important school of 'new southern historians' have been at pains to reject and problematize this approach to the south. They have questioned the common use of simplistic categories of explanation with regard to the south, and even the category of 'the south' itself. These new approaches to the question have opened up whole areas of study and forced scholars to rethink the way the south has been depicted (see also Box 2.18). The increasing penetration of criminal organizations into the north of Italy has undermined some of these conclusions, as have corruption scandals which seem to be as prevalent in the north as they have been in the south. In Italy's twenty-first century, it was becoming difficult to argue that northern elites and political institutions enjoyed any kind of civic primacy. An idea of an all-encompassing political 'caste', separated from society and local territories, began to take hold.

Box 1.18   Sport and national identity

1. Football: The National Team (*La Nazionale*)

The *azzurri* – the blues – the national football team, was one of the few institutions which united most Italians. In 1982, Italy won its first post-1945 World Cup, against West Germany. This victory was an extraordinary moment of national emotion after the bitter divisions of the 1970s:

> The party that followed the 1982 World Cup victory is remembered as a joyous moment of collective celebration. That match still holds a record for an Italian TV transmission, with 32 million viewers, while seventeen million Italians watched the celebrated 1970 semi-final ... this support has rarely been seen as a political issue, and has seldom divided Italians into left and right factions. It is quite normal for extreme left- and extreme right-wing factions to be united in their backing of *la nazionale*. (John Foot, *Calcio*, p. 438)

2. Cycling

The Giro d'Italia cycling race began in 1909, and was seen as a creator of national identity. It has run ever since apart from during the World Wars I and II:

> Many women were on their knees, with their children by their side ... the wide road was packed with people who were crying I-T-A-L-Y, I-T-A-L-Y, I-T-A-L-Y ... Sport, at that moment was a flame which lit up the nation. (The journalist Bruno Roghi describing cyclists entering the city of Trieste (still under Allied control) in 1946.)

Fausto Coppi

The 1946 Milan–San Remo, commencing on 19 March, was the first post-war classic and the first big race in Italy since 1940. The great cyclist Fausto Coppi broke from the pack just outside Milan and emerged from the Turchino mountain pass tunnel on his own. This is what the French journalist Pierre Chany later wrote about that moment – a quote which underlined the strong links between national and sporting history:

> The tunnel was of modest dimensions, just 50 metres long, but on 19 March 1946 it assumed exceptional proportions in the eyes of the world. That day it was six years in length and lost in the gloom of the war ... A rumbling was heard from the depths of those six years and suddenly there appeared in the light of day an olive-greenish car stirring up a cloud of dust. '*Arriva Coppi*' the messenger announced, a revelation only the initiated had foreseen.

Coppi won the race by 14 minutes.

Coppi and Italy became one. They were fused together. A myth of endurance, of a superman in peasant's clothing, had come into being, and for many it wiped out, if only briefly, bad memories of the war. (Foot, *Pedalare!, Pedalare!*, p. 111)

****

In September 1947 the Pope made speech from the balcony of St Peter's, 'To the men of Catholic Action'. It was a call to arms. A huge crowd packed the wide square below him. 'The time of reflection and of projects has passed. Are you ready? In the religious and moral camps, the opposing fronts are becoming more and more clearly defined. It is time to put ourselves to the test.' In this 'hour of action', the moment to act decisively against the Communist threat, the Pope employed a cycling metaphor. 'This difficult competition, which St Paul spoke about, has begun. It is a time for intense effort.' He then did something extremely unusual. He named an individual, a sportsman, a cycling star. 'The winner can be decided in an instant. Look at Gino Bartali, member of Catholic Action. Often he has earned the right to wear the much-sought-after "jersey". You should also participate in a championship of ideas, so you can conquer a much more noble form of victory'. (Foot, *Pedalare!, Pedalare!*, p. 128)

The Giro d'Italia was much more than an annual sporting event:

> Cyclists taking part in the Giro were not just riding in an annual race; they were taking part in the creation and recreation of historical, national and regional narratives. These stories were embellished and transformed every year, becoming compelling myths, reinforced by nostalgia, commemoration and constant retelling. (Foot, *Pedalare!, Pedalare!*, p. 305)

Generic forms of anti-politics were increasingly hegemonic. Grillo's Five Star MoVement was the most important twenty-first-century example of this trend.

A final, and perhaps least useful, strand of explanation blames the Italians themselves for their own lack of national sentiment. Italian identity has often been linked to a strong sense of 'Italian vices'. This tradition of self-criticism has a long tradition, from Croce to D'Annunzio to Mussolini to Montanelli to De Felice. Although often little more than prejudice, this rhetorical tendency has dominated much of the public debate over the Italian nation. The Italians could not be trusted to support their nation in a crisis, and therefore had to be forced into war (1915); the Italians had to be pushed into a new kind of relationship with the state (fascism); the Italians had failed to respond to the defence of the nation in a time of crisis (1943). Only the nationalist minority, a small group of heroes, could be trusted to defend the integrity of Italy. The consequence of this world-view has often been violence, rhetoric and voluntarism. The key problem has been that underlying many of these analyses has always been a very strong model of what a nation should be, a model that is rarely acknowledged, let only justified. If we adopt a more flexible idea of the nation, less packed with morality, then we can escape from a quantitative measure of 'amounts' of national identity and move towards a more measured analysis of the complicated historical roles of the nation and the state.

chapter

2

The State

A PERMANENT LEGITIMATION CRISIS?

This chapter will examine the history and structure of the Italian state from two viewpoints. First, the state is viewed as a *collection of institutions*, with varying levels of continuity, change and development over the course of more than a century and a half of a nation's history. The key institutions to be examined will be the armed forces, the legal system, tax collection (the ways the state has financed itself), and government organizations including the state bureaucracy (the ways the state has been administered, governed, reformed and reorganized).[1] However, this analysis will not ignore the ideological construction of what the state is or has been. The state, like the nation, is also a product of stories, narratives and anthropological structures. The rhetoric surrounding the supposed failures of the Italian state has been particularly strong. Crimes, massacres or disasters are often accompanied by a call for 'the state to be present'. 'The state is not here' has been the frequent accusation when things go wrong. And when the state has been 'present', its actions have often been inefficient, corrupt or tardy.

The 'building-block' view of the state, as a collection of institutions and procedures, is complemented by a discussion of the *relationship* between Italian citizens and the state over time. Institutions cannot govern, survive or function properly without significant degrees of legitimacy amongst the citizens of any one country. All states require considerable levels of legitimation if they are not to govern mainly through the use of or threat of force. A political system 'requires an input of mass loyalty that is as diffuse as possible' (Habermas).[2] Citizens must have certain levels of faith in the right of the state to govern, collect taxes, enforce law and order, fight wars and educate their children in order for these institutions to work with any efficiency. *The Italian state has found legitimation extremely difficult to obtain since unification.* It has never been, in any real sense, hegemonic.[3] In fact, this chapter will argue that the Italian state has been in the throes of a semi-permanent *legitimation* crisis ever since its inception. The basic 'rules of the game' have never been accepted by most Italians in terms of a 'rational' management of the state and the political system. They have, instead, been partly replaced by other, unwritten 'rules' that have institutionalized patronage, clientelism, inefficiency and informal modes of behaviour and exchange.

In Italy, one of the key prerequisites for the 'normal' functioning of the state – the independence (whether real or imagined) of the administrative and legal systems from political control – has never been in place. 'Mass loyalty' has never been achieved. The evidence for such a state of affairs is easy to obtain. At an extreme level, legitimation crises are at their most evident when citizens refuse to vote, pay taxes, fight 'for their country' or obey basic laws, or when the state resorts to violence to regulate 'normal' economic or social conflicts – but this crisis can also be seen every day in the normal set of relationships between the citizens and the state at a local and national level, and in common attitudes amongst Italians towards the state. This legitimation crisis has deepened at certain key moments, where the consent given towards state institutions has been particularly low and protest especially violent and widespread. The crisis has always been there – it has never come close to being resolved – but its intensity has risen and fallen, in various ways, through historical time. At times, the citizen–state relationship has been close to total collapse, leading to mass legitimation crises. In the 2000s a series of movements emerged who defined themselves by their anti-political nature. At times it even appeared as if the entire system was unravelling, and that the state itself was no longer sustainable. Without doubt, Italy had reached a crossroads.

Italy has lived through mass legitimation crises on a number of occasions after unification – with brigandage in the south (1861–3) and the tax riots against the grist tax (after 1869), and again with the political crisis of the 1890s leading to the traumatic events of 1898. Later, mass disobedience during World War I (1915–18) revealed deep fractures between many Italians, the state and the nation. This crisis exploded during the civil war period of 1919–22, when state institutions lost complete control of whole areas of society, from public order to the use of violence. The state, by 1922, was so deep in crisis that it was absent from vast sectors of its normal activity. Armed bands were free to roam the country, murdering and terrorizing Italian citizens, while the state stood back and watched, or even encouraged the violence. Twenty years later, in September 1943, the state came near to total collapse. Italy's army was disbanded, and its government was divided in two, with both 'parts' essentially under the control of (different) foreign powers. A bitter civil war followed whose consequences were still being felt through to the next century. Normal state functions, across the whole of Italy, were only resumed in April 1945. A mass legitimation crisis reappeared in the late 1960s (1969–80) and again during the corruption scandals of the 1990s (1992–4). It could be argued that this legitimation crisis dragged on through-out the 2000s and was caught up in the financial and eurozone emergency at the end of the first decade of the twenty-first century. By that time, the crisis appeared endemic and ongoing, with no end in sight.

The Italian state has frequently resorted to violence and repression to impose its laws and collect its taxes – sending troops to disband strikes and put down land occupations. This use of violence in itself is an indicator of the lack of legit-imation enjoyed by state institutions (and also a contributor to further delegiti-mization). Even periods of 'high' legitimation have been marked by mass protest and confusion, from the 1930s, when consent was tempered by repression and the absence of democracy, to the post-war period (from 1945) when support for the new state was conditioned by the impending cold war and a sudden break-down in law and order. With hindsight, however, the post-war period appears increasingly as a period of high legitimation. Democracy survived, despite everything, and put down deep cultural roots through the mass party system and its sub-cultures. From the 1980s onward, however, things went downhill.

At a more everyday level, the ramifications of this semi-permanent crisis have been felt in every corner of Italy. As Piero Calamandrei said:

in the most perfect European democracies, in England, in Switzerland, in Scandinavia, people respect the law because they have participated in its construc-tion and are proud of it. Every citizen obeys the law because they know that all will do so. There is no dual interpretation of the law, one for the rich and one for the poor! But this is the ancient curse that weighs upon Italy. The people have no faith in the law, because they are convinced that these laws do not belong to them. They have always seen the state as an enemy. ('In difesa di Danilo Dolci', 1956)

Mass illegality has always been a fact of life in the peninsula, from tax evasion to illegal construction to political and civil corruption to regular football-related violence. This is not to place the state on one (good) side of the fence and illegal citizens on the other. Often, the very illegality of the state, and its representatives, has contributed to this crisis of legitimation over time. The lack of legitimation has also been seen within the state, and on occasions elements inside the state have worked to destroy legitimacy from within – such as dur-ing the 1960s and 1970s, with the 'strategy of tension' (see Box 2.1) – or in con-junction with the Mafia and other criminal organizations. Italian citizens have frequently preferred to be loyal to other institutions within society – the Church, the family, the various Mafias, foreign governments – in preference to their state. In addition, the state has been blamed for many of the problems that have plagued Italian society – from poverty to inefficiency to disasters of all kinds. The over-reliance on the state by various governments, from the post-Risorgimento administrations to Giolitti to fascism through to the Christian Democrats, has created high expectations, and contradictions. The state has been charged with being absent, and, often at the same time, over-present.

Box 2.1 The 'strategy of tension'

Elements from within the state were working to undermine democracy and subvert state institutions from the 1960s onwards. The 'strategy of tension' itself
evolved out of the social and political struggles of 1967–8. Right-wing elements
within the security forces, working with NATO agents and Italian neo-fascists,
began to implement a strategy based on events in Greece. Disorder would be
created, and blamed on the Left, in order to create the conditions for a military
coup. The key event of the 'strategy of tension' was the bomb in the Piazza
Fontana in Milan in December 1969, left in a bank crowded with middle-aged
farmers, 16 of whom were killed and 88 injured. This outrage was blamed, by the
police, on an anarchist group, infiltrated with informers and neo-fascists. One
anarchist, Pietro Valpreda, spent three years in prison awaiting trial and was only
absolved of the crime in 1981. Another anarchist, Giuseppe Pinelli, 'fell' to his
death from a fourth-floor window of Milan's police station, days after the bomb.
The circumstances of his death have never been fully clarified. The Pinelli and
Valpreda 'cases' galvanized opinion across Italy, with massive campaigns in the
press and on the streets. Meanwhile, the strategy of tension continued. Other
bombs were set off, causing a series of massacres, from Peteano in 1972 (where
three *carabinieri* were killed), to Milan again in 1973 (four killed), to Brescia in
1974 (where eight anti-fascists died) to the worst massacre of all, a bomb left in
a crowded second-class waiting room in Bologna station on 2 August 1980,
which killed 80 people and left over 200 injured.

However, a military coup never happened. There were moments when it
appeared likely, such as with the so-called *Tora Tora* coup attempt, led by ex-fascist
Junio Valerio Borghese, in December 1970. A number of troops occupied the
Interior Ministry for some hours and tanks rumbled through Rome but, mysteri-
ously, the coup was called off. Democracy survived in Italy despite the persistence
of dictatorships in Greece, Spain and Portugal until the 1970s. By the mid-1970s,
judges had begun to indict those involved in the strategy of tension, and even
called to task leading members of the governments of the 1960s and 1970s.
Meanwhile, the Left was dividing into a myriad of small, sectarian organizations
and many of its militants were recruited to terrorist groups. This was probably the
most lasting legacy of the strategy of tension: the destruction of the democratic
and peaceful aims and methods adopted by the movements that grew out of
1968. Slowly, the truth about this period has emerged, although the interest in that
truth has waned. In 2001 the eighth trial relating to the Piazza Fontana bomb
convicted three neo-fascists of having organized, financed and planted the device
in the bank. However, various appeals and further trials eventually cleared
everyone of responsibility. *Nobody* was guilty of this hideous crime, according to
the Italian justice system. Meanwhile, divided memories and complicated versions
of history created a legacy of confusion, misinformation and ignorance
(see Box 2.2). Closure had not been achieved. Justice had not been done.
Forgetting was, perhaps, the only option available.

This strange, schizophrenic attitude to the state and many of its institutions has been mirrored within the state by an inability or unwillingness to reform itself. As Paul Ginsborg has written, with reference to the post-1945 period, 'if there is a single, recurrent, almost obsessive theme in the political history of post-war Italy, it is that of the need for reform and the failure to achieve it'.[4] Italian governments have veered between inclusive and repressive strategies towards demands for change, never succeeding in either.[5] Even minimal reform has proved problematic. As Gaetano Salvemini wrote in 1900, 'In Italy today our aim is not to create a socialist state, but a state which is simply less bestial than the current one.'[6]

It has proved impossible to break the vicious circles created by legitimation crises and low loyalty. Serious attempts at reform have been made at various times, most notably in the early twentieth century, during the constitutional reforms of the 1940s and with the centre–left of the early 1960s, but they have been short-lived, contradictory and suffocated by compromise, lack of ambition and the power of corporate and vested interests. Fascism attempted to reform Italy from above, without any reference to democratic control – by-passing the question of mass loyalty by creating structures that could ignore dissent. State- and nation-building strategies have usually been based upon co-option through clientelism, and on short-term solutions to long-term problems. The state has been used instrumentally by both rulers and the ruled. Illegitimacy has produced further illegitimacy, leading to further and deeper crises. The real reformists never took power, and left us only with blueprints of what might have been.[7] This lack of reform can be seen everywhere in Italian history, and will be one of the main themes of this chapter.

Explaining Italy's Legitimation Crises: Historical Answers

How can we explain this lack of legitimacy? The answer to this simple question is a long and complicated one, to which only partial answers can be given here. The first answer lies in the relative weakness of the state and its institutions after unification. This was in part a result of the elite nature of the Risorgimento itself (both in the way unification was achieved and in its interpretation by Risorgimento leaders, as well as in the mythical qualities assumed by this period after unification). Italy's problems, it is often argued, were there right from the moment of its birth. The nation was marked by a kind of original sin. New historical research has challenged this idea, opening up debates in a whole series of areas.[8] Yet, the southern peasant masses, in particular, were neither transformed by nor won over to the new Italian state. Italy's elites showed little interest in changing things in the *mezzogiorno*. Real agrarian reform did not follow unification, or the agrarian movements of the 1890s. Reform was attempted after the land occupation movements of 1944–5 and 1949–50, but its results were partial and problematic, and out of step with social change. Without rural justice, without the division of the huge landed estates of the south, it was unlikely that southern peasants would willingly join an Italian army, speak Italian or pay taxes to an Italian state which appeared most frequently (when it bothered to make an appearance) in the

Box 2.2   Divided memories: the 1960s and 1970s

Two almost identical plaques, whose inscriptions are listed below, stand side-by-side in Piazza Fontana in the centre of Milan. Their histories are linked to the death of an anarchist railway-worker, Giuseppe Pinelli, who 'fell' from a police station window in Milan in 1969. Pinelli was in custody at the time having been wrongly arrested in connection with a bomb that had exploded in a bank in the Piazza on 12 December, killing 17 people and injuring 88. The left blamed the police for Pinelli's death, and argued that he had been murdered. Others called his death an accident, or suicide. The militant first plaque was put up in the Piazza in 1977. In 2006 it was removed by the local council and replaced with a second plaque with a different inscription. Radicals then put the original plaque up again, leaving the second one in place. The two plaques were still there in 2013.

1977
To
Giuseppe Pinelli
Anarchist railway-worker
An innocent man
Murdered in the rooms of the Central Police Station of Milan
On 16.12.1969
The students and democrats of Milan

2006
Milan: Milan City Council
To
Giuseppe Pinelli
Anarchist railway worker
An innocent man who died tragically
in the rooms of Milan's Central Police Station on 15.12.1969

guise of a tax collector, a *carabiniere*, a soldier or a corrupt politician. Millions simply left Italy altogether, to seek fame and fortune, or just a job, elsewhere in the world. Many preferred the certainties provided by their own families,[9] or local bandit gangs, or the Church, or the Mafia, to a state that spoke in a foreign language and arrived in uniform, or to force people *into* uniform. This relationship was always a dialectic one – a two-way set of relationships where legitimation was never 'given' forever and loyalty had to be won over, time and time again, in the face of recurrent crises, mobilizations and (rare) moments of unity.

A second answer, linked to the first, concerns the Catholic Church (see Box 2.3). The Church was hostile to the unification of Italy, and the leaders of the Risorgimento were unsympathetic to the Church, both before and after 1860. In 1848 the Pope had been forced out of Rome and the Risorgimento was completed with a military attack against the capital of Catholicism. Once the

Italian capital was in Rome, the new state set out to build a civil state religion in the 'eternal city', seizing Church buildings and building monuments to heretics. Many leading politicians were anti-clerical Masons, including Crispi (prime minister in the 1890s) and Nathan, the mayor of Rome for a time in the early twentieth century. In sensitive areas, such as agrarian property and education, the new Italy challenged Church power. The Church maintained an intractable hostility towards the new state, excommunicating the king of Italy and ordering its followers not to participate in any national political processes (through the 1874 *non expedit* ruling, only lifted in 1919). Thus this vast social and cultural organization, with its organizational networks spread across Italy, and especially in the north, not only opposed the formation of an Italian state, but actively organized against that state, first through military struggle, and then through appeals to its followers, not just in Italy but throughout the world. Italy's status as an independent power was undermined by Catholic propaganda. Over time, compromise was inevitable, as co-habitation was necessary. The long history of the slow rapprochement in Italy between Church and state, with its various key historical moments (1848–9, 1870–1, 1874, 1891, 1904, 1914, 1915–18, 1929, 1945, 1984, see Box 2.3), is one of mutual mistrust, and of negotiations between two organizations which behaved like sovereign states – understandable in the case of Italy; more difficult to justify in the case of the Catholic Church. Yet, at the level of everyday life, 'Italians' and Catholics were often at one, and the role of the Church within Italian society, the economy and later political life was always important, even at the moments of greatest official distance in the late nineteenth century. Individual Italians had to balance these twin loyalties (which were not always in conflict), and were usually able to mediate between spiritual needs, political obligations and civil codes of practice.

A third answer points the finger at the state itself, and the failures of nation-building strategies, its endemic inefficiencies, the inability to reform itself or to respond to protest with anything but repression, the widespread and deep-rooted corruption added to high taxation, the continual call on its citizens to fight obscure wars, and the political plots and conspiracies which have dogged Italian history. It would be very easy to write a complete history of Italy from this point of view, with the state as the sinner and the Italians as the sinned against. Such an account ignores the symbiotic relationship between citizens and any state, and the ways in which state organizations and legitimacy are created and re-created over time, not just through administrative practice but also in the key spheres of ideology, legitimation and identity. The state never stood apart from the Italian people, but was a *reflection* of those people, and any explanation of the failures of the state must also take into account the world-views and histories of Italians over time. The Italian state was, as Gobetti wrote of fascism, the 'autobiography of a nation'.

The strength of criminal, anti-state, institutions is thus both a reflection of the particular weakness of the Italian state, *and* a phenomenon that helped to reproduce a weak and corrupt state. The Mafia spread its tentacles deep into the state machine from the very beginning and many within the state responded by pledging their own loyalties to the Mafia, above those to the

Box 2.3   Church and state: extracts from agreements between the Catholic Church/the Vatican and the Italian state and from Italian Constitutions and statutes regarding the Church

a. The Albertine Statute (1848)

Article 1   The Roman Catholic religion is the only state religion. Other existing cults are tolerated as long as they stay within the law.

b. The Lateran Pacts. Treaty and Concordato between the Holy Seat and Italy, Law 810, 27 May 1929

1. Italy recognizes and reaffirms the principle consecrated in Article 1 of the Albertine Statute by which the Roman Catholic (and apostolic) religion is the only religion of the state.
2. Italy recognizes that the Holy Father has full property over and exclusive legal and political power over the Vatican, as it is constructed today.
   The Italian state will pay compensation for the Church's loss of property of 750 million lire following the events of 1870.
   Ten religious holidays are recognized by the Italian state plus all Sundays.

c. The Republican Constitution (1948)

Article 7 [Relations between State and Church]
(1) The state and the Catholic Church shall be, each within its own order, independent and sovereign.
(2) Their relations shall be regulated by the Lateran Pacts. Such amendments to these Pacts as are accepted by both parties shall not require the procedure for Constitutional amendment.

Article 8 [Religion]
(1) All religious denominations shall be equally free before the law.
(2) Religious denominations other than Catholic shall have the right to organize themselves according to their own by-laws provided they are not in conflict with the Italian legal system.
(3) Their relations with the state shall be regulated by law on the basis of agreements with their respective representatives.

d. The New Church–State Agreements (1984) and changes to the 1929 agreements (converted into Italian law in March 1985) [extracts]

The Vatican and the Italian Republic:

Taking into account the processes of social and political transformation over the last few decades and the developments within the Church after the Second Vatican Council,

Have recognized the need to introduce the following changes to the Lateran Pacts:

1. The Italian Republic and the Vatican re-affirm that the state and the Church are ... independent and sovereign, and both will endeavour to respect this principle and to collaborate for the good of humanity and the nation.
2. The Italian Republic ... will continue to provide, within schools, Catholic religious education in state schools of every level. With respect for the freedom of conscience and educational responsibility of parents, every child has the right to choose to follow or opt out of this teaching.

e. Additional Protocol (direct modifications to the 1929 agreements)

1. With relation to Article 1 (1929)

The principle, originally laid out in the Lateran Pacts, which states that the Catholic religion is the sole religion of the Italian state, is no longer valid.

nation or the state. In a social and political situation where protection and trust were rare commodities (as in Sicily in the late nineteenth century) the Mafia provided these 'goods', but at a very heavy price.[10] The state not only failed to protect its citizens from crime and criminals, but also co-habited with the Mafia in a system of business extortion which controlled large parts of Sicilian territory. This relationship changed over time, and many within the state (and society) refused to bow down to the Mafia, but the process of identifying the Mafia, prosecuting its leaders and restoring 'normal' economic and social relationships in Sicily and elsewhere was painfully slow. A series of politicians used the Mafia to gain power, influence, wealth, and the exclusion of political opponents. For years, opponents of the Mafia were treated with scorn, or simply disappeared. The word 'Mafia' was not even used in official legislation until the 1965 'Measures against the Mafia' (Law 575, 31.5.1965), and the concept of 'association with the Mafia' was only introduced in 1982. It was only when the Mafia decided to confront the state head on (particularly in the 1980s and 1990s), in a violent war that claimed hundreds of victims on both sides, that the state was able to get the upper hand. The emergence of supergrasses from within the organization proved invaluable in tracing the structure of the Mafia and its inner logic. Yet the old myths concerning the Mafia, its laws of honour and silence, its 'character', its 'Sicilian nature' were of a strength that surprised even Mafia-watchers. In addition, the Mafia 'fish' continued to swim in a social-cultural sea – Sicily (and much of the rest of the south, especially with the Camorra in and around Naples and the 'Ndrangheta in Calabria), where illegality was the norm, not the exception, and where civil society never gathered enough strength to deal a final blow to mass criminality.[11]

One response to the failures of the state has been the creation of movements dedicated to overthrowing that state. Italy has always produced strong revolutionary movements as a challenge to the existing social and political order, which have attracted far greater numbers of supporters than in other, comparable countries, with the possible exception of Spain in the 1930s or Greece in the 1940s. In turn, these movements, with their rhetoric and their organization, have contributed to the further delegitimization of the existing state apparatus. The much-heralded socialist revolution, however, never arrived, and reaction buried in blood the dreams of change. Italy was host to revolutions of various kinds, and to mass revolutionary movements, in 1848–9, in 1860, in the 1890s (and particularly in 1898), in 1904, in 1914, in 1919–20, in 1943–5, in 1948 and during the Italian 'long (or 'drawn-out') May', 1968–80.[12] The protagonists of these movements were very different, over time, and each 'moment' failed for different reasons. Often, revolutions were simply repressed (1848–9, 1898, 1904, 1919–20 to some extent), but all too often the revolutionaries failed to understand Italy, and to elaborate successful tactics for overthrowing the Italian state. One key 'lack' was in the area of alliances – between workers and peasants, between north and south, between the middle classes and the working classes, between Catholics and socialists. Historically, these alliances never materialized. In addition, revolutionaries were often hopelessly divided amongst themselves, over doctrines

Box 2.4 Criminal organizations in Italy

Historical research allied to far-reaching judicial investigations in recent years has outlined the long-lasting histories of Italian criminal organizations. For years, politicians, *mafiosi* and many researchers argued that these organizations did not really exist, and that the mafias were more an expression of a state of mind or a culture than anything else. Yet it is now clear that the Sicilian Mafia (or *Cosa Nostra*) was born around the time of Italian unification, and created a powerful set of institutions, rituals and networks of crime that have, to some extent, survived to this day. The Sicilian Mafia works through the forced provision of protection in a situation where such protection and trust is lacking. It has sub-committees and centralized leaderships, although these various bodies have gone to war with each other at various times.

The Mafia has made its money in different ways over the years, from the control of the fruit export market, to the black market during the war, to the lucrative drugs trade from the 1980s onwards, as well as classic illegal activities linked to building contracts and speculation and simple, day-to-day extortion (the *pizzo*). Naples and its surrounding regions gave birth to the Camorra, which originated in the prison system. The Camorra has a much looser organizational structure than Cosa Nostra. Calabria's main criminal organization is known as the *'Ndrangheta*, and was born in the 1880s as a loose coalition of small criminal gangs. The *'Ndrangheta* later developed into a centralized organization with its own structures, rituals and memberships.

(such as between anarchism, revolutionary syndicalism and socialism), over tactics, over leaders, over timing, over international loyalties. Finally, revolutionaries have frequently been attracted by terrorist ideals, as a substitute for serious revolutionary preparation and thinking – from the anarchist assassinations of the 1890s and the attempts on Mussolini's life in the 1920s, to the military-type socialism which came out of the Resistance, to the tragic turn to terrorism in the wake of state repression and defeat in the 1970s.

Illegality has been a constant feature of Italian society – the most obvious indicator of the semi-permanent legitimation crisis of the Italian state. This is not simply a reworking of the well-worn distinction between 'real Italy' and 'legal Italy'. In reality, the situation was a far more complicated one. The state's own illegality undermined its illegitimacy. Corruption produced corruption. Failed reforms reinforced a belief that any future reforms were doomed. The law was not there to be obeyed, but to be used, for private, political or instrumental purposes. Thus, 'real Italy' and 'legal Italy' could not be separated. The laws themselves were also part of the problem. This is not only an anthropological argument, but a historical one. Cycles of illegitimacy produced and reproduced themselves. But this was not the whole story. Minorities within and outside the state worked for change – and at certain moments in Italian history were able to influence events. Socialist reformists built extraordinary networks of educational and mutual-aid institutions from the 1890s onwards; the Church worked deep within Italian society, forming communities and senses of belonging. Heroic struggles took place, every day, against the power of organized crime. The state was not a monolith, but it often acted like one. These 'virtuous minorities', in the long run, could never succeed in the face of the inert power of the Italian state – its ability to co-opt and block change, to create continuity, to protect itself from reform. This remained as true at the end of the twentieth century as it had been at the beginning.

INSTITUTIONS, RULES AND ORGANIZATIONS: THE ARCHITECTURE AND STRUCTURE OF THE ITALIAN STATE

Overarching Rules: The Albertine Statute and the 1948 Constitution

The overarching rules that have governed the functioning of the state and the legal system have been enshrined in two documents, which governed the administration and governments of Italy from 1848 to 1948, and since 1948, respectively. These rules were the frameworks for the system, and in particular the political sector of the state. The details were left to ordinary laws, statutes and other systems of rules. The Albertine Statute (*Statuto Albertino*) was drawn up and issued in March 1848 in the wake of European revolutionary movements that had shaken the rulers of the continent. As a document it drew on various other statutes, including those of France (1814), Spain (1812) and Belgium (1831). Piedmont was organized as a *Parliamentary Monarchy*, extending its systems to the rest of Italy after 1860 and 1870. The head of state (and the justice system) was the monarch, who transmitted his or her powers to his or her heirs on death or abdication. All the crucial powers of the government and the state were held by the monarch, including the appointment of the president of the Council of Ministers, and of individual ministers (who had to be approved by Parliament), the dissolution of Parliament, the signing and promulgation of laws and the declaration of war (for a selection of specific Articles see Box 2.5). The monarch was responsible to nobody but himself or herself, and was most powerful in the areas of foreign policy and military strategy. The Albertine Statute, unlike the 1948 Constitution, was a *flexible* document that could be modified by ordinary laws. This made the Statute adaptable to the social and economic changes over a century of development and political change, but also allowed fascism to empty the Statute of its mild liberal and democratic elements during the 1920s and 1930s. A two-house Parliament was instituted with the upper house (the Senate) entirely appointed by the monarch, and an elected lower house (although the electoral law itself was not part of the Statute).

The 'revolutionary' push behind the Statute was clear in the Articles that guaranteed (in theory) the right to free speech, equal legal rights, press freedom, the right to collect petitions and the right to peaceful assembly. Meanwhile, the conservative aspects of the Statute were to be found in the explicit protection of private property and the definition of Catholicism as 'the only religion of the state' (Article 1). Even here, however, the Statute also

Box 2.5   The Albertine Statute 1848: extracts

Article 2   The state is governed by a representative monarchical government. The throne is hereditary.

Article 3   The legislative power shall be exercised collectively by the King and the two houses, the Senate and the House of Deputies.

Article 4   The person of the King is sacred and inviolable.

Article 5   To the King alone belongs the executive power. He is the supreme head of the state; commands all land and naval forces; declares war; makes treaties of peace, alliance, commerce, and other treaties, communicating them to the Houses as soon as the interest and security of the state permit, accompanying such notice with opportune explanations. Treaties involving financial obligations or alterations of the territory of the state shall not take effect until after they have received the approval of the Houses.

Article 6   The King appoints to all the offices of the state, and makes the necessary decrees and regulations for the exclusion of the laws, without suspending their execution or granting exemptions from the law.

Article 7   The King alone approves and promulgates the laws.

The Rights and Duties of Citizens

Article 24   All inhabitants of the kingdom, whatever their rank or title, are equal before the law. All shall enjoy civil and political rights, and shall be eligible to civil and military office, except as otherwise provided by law.

Article 26   Individual liberty is guaranteed. None shall be arrested or brought to trial except in the cases provided for and according to the forms prescribed in law.

Article 29   Property of all kinds whatsoever is inviolable. In all cases, however, where the public welfare, legally ascertained, requires it, property may be taken and transferred in whole or in part, upon payment of a just indemnity in accordance with law.

Article 32   The right to assemble peaceably and without arms is recognized, subject, however, to the laws that may regulate the exercise of this privilege in the interest of the public welfare.

Article 39   The elective house shall be composed of deputies chosen by the electoral districts as provided by the law.

Ministers

Article 65   The King appoints and dismisses his ministers.

proved itself to be a liberalizing document, with a 'toleration' of other religions. After 1848, most ghettos were opened across Italy, freeing the Jews from a number of rules and regulations (an event known as 'the emancipation') that had severely limited their economic activities and movements. Fascism made radical changes to the 'Albertine' political system, but left the overarching framework more or less untouched, creating an ambiguous situation where 'nobody could claim to have changed the rules of the game while everyone knew that the rules were absolutely different' (Paolo Pombeni).[13]

The 1948 Constitution

The 1946 referendum removed the monarchy and instituted a Republic (more information can be found in Box 4.2). This set the scene for the drawing up of a new Constitution, and at the same time a *Constituent Assembly* was elected (using proportional representation). After two years of debate, compromise and political wheeler-dealing, the new Constitution was passed in 1948 (see Box 2.6) – replacing the Albertine Statute, which had been modified by various decrees between 1943 and 1947 (for the Constituent Assembly see Box 2.7). The 1948 Constitution contains 139 Articles. It can be changed only by special constitutional laws and processes, unlike the Albertine Statute. All ordinary laws must conform to the Constitution. Yet, the Constitution did not wipe the slate clean of laws. Many laws remained on the statute book from fascism and earlier, including the Rocco penal code (1930), which governed a whole series of crimes and punishments and was only reformed in a piecemeal fashion and with great sluggishness after 1948. Thus, there was no legal 'year zero'. Many of the Articles from the Rocco code are still in force today (see also the section on the law, below). In fact, strong elements of legal continuity with fascism remained despite the reintroduction of democracy and the rights and liberties contained in the Constitution.

Many of the safeguards and reformist aspects enshrined in the Constitution took years to be implemented. Most importantly, the Constitutional Court, the legal guardian of the Constitution (see Box 2.8), was only set up in 1956. This body set about reforming and modernizing the legal framework of Italy, especially in the wake of the mass student movements after 1967–8, but this process itself was also extremely lengthy, bureaucratic and fragmentary. Wholesale legal reform was never attempted, which left many old structures more or less intact. Other measures took even longer – the CSM (Superior Council of the Magistracy/*Consiglio Superiore della Magistratura*, an independent body for the administration of justice, see Box 2.7) was only instituted in 1958. The right to hold referendums to quash certain laws was activated as late as 1970. The 'anti-fascist' and libertarian aspects of the Constitution were often forgotten, especially during the early years of the cold war, and 'fascist' laws were used against anti-fascists by the Christian Democrat governments of the 1950s. The central state only reluctantly gave up its powers to decentralized bodies. Regional governments (apart from the special regions) were set up in 1970. And these 'decentralized' institutions often merely re-created the problems of central bodies. Decentralization

---

Box 2.6   The Republican Constitution, 1948: extracts
[Adopted: 22 December 1947; effective from 1 January 1948]

Article 1   Italy is a democratic republic based on labour.

Article 3   All citizens possess an equal social status and are equal before the law, without distinction as to sex, race, language, religion, political opinions, and personal or social conditions.

Article 5   The Republic, one and indivisible, recognizes and promotes local autonomy; it shall apply the fullest measure of administrative decentralization … and adjust the principles and methods of its legislation to the requirements of autonomy and decentralization.

Article 13   (1)   Personal freedom shall be inviolable.
               (2)   No one shall be detained, inspected, or searched nor otherwise restricted on one's personal liberty save by order of the judiciary, for which the reason must be stated, and then only in such cases and in such manner as the law provides for.

Article 17   (1)   Citizens shall have the right to assemble peaceably and unarmed.

Article 21   (2)   The press shall not be subjected to any authorization or censorship.

Article 36   Workers shall be entitled to a weekly day of rest and to annual paid holidays; they cannot relinquish this right.

Article 39   The organization of trade unions is free.

Article 40   The right to strike shall be exercised according to the laws which regulate it.

Article 49   All citizens shall have the right to associate freely in political parties in order to contribute by democratic means to the determination of national policy.

Part II   Organization of the Republic
Title I   Parliament   Section I: The Two Chambers

Article 55   (1)   Parliament shall consist of the Chamber of Deputies and the Senate of the Republic.

Article 70   Legislative power shall be exercised jointly by the two Chambers.

Article 72   Every bill introduced to one of the Chambers shall be, according to its Standing Orders, examined by a committee and then by the Chamber itself, which shall approve it Article by Article, and with a final vote.

Article 74   (1)   The President of the Republic, before promulgating a law, may request a new deliberation by means of a message to the Chambers stating the reasons for such a request.

               (2)   If the Chambers adopt the bill once again, the law shall be promulgated.

Article 78   The Chambers shall resolve upon the state of war and confer the necessary powers on the Government.

---

without reform re-created 'little states' with less power, at least until the end of the 1990s. Federalist reforms altered the constitution in the early twenty-first century, although these became caught up in bitter political struggles between left and right, and failed to achieve wide consensus amongst the Italian people.

Box 2.7 The Constituent Assembly, 1946–8: building a new framework

In 1944 the king, under pressure from the re-formed democratic parties in the south, issued a decree-law which stated that 'after the liberation of the national territories the institutional forms would be chosen by the Italian people' and that after direct elections a 'Constituent Assembly would be elected to deliberate the new constitution'. Defeat for the monarchy in the June 1946 referendum left the Assembly with more room for manoeuvre – 'the sky was empty' (G. C. Floridia, 'La costituzione', p. 8). Some of this power had, however, already been limited by De Gasperi's first government (which replaced the much more radical Parri administration in late 1945) to purely constitutional matters. Italy's Constituent Assembly was never to be a revolutionary, legislating assembly like that of the French Revolution. Laws were still made elsewhere. However, this concentration on the formal Constitution allowed for collaboration and helped to produce a 'refined' and 'high-level' debate, which was not present in other, more 'political' spheres.

The never-to-be-repeated moment represented by the Constituent Assembly, which discussed the new Constitution from 1946 to 1947 (18 months in all, with over 170 sittings), created the institutional and political framework for the new Republic. The Assembly was elected in 1946 by proportional representation, via the first free and full elections in Italian history. The results of the election set up a balance between the Left and centre who had fought together (loosely) within the anti-fascist Resistance (the Christian Democrats won 35 per cent of the vote; the Italian Socialist Party (PSI) 21 per cent and the Italian Communist Party (PCI) 19 per cent). There were bitter debates, but the whole process was under-pinned by a desire to compromise and to create workable and democratic institutions for a new Italy. Particularly important remained the decision of Togliatti and the Communists to give way over Article 7, which confirmed the Church–State accords of 1929. Only 21 of the 556 elected constituent members were women and some of the debates on women's rights – such as the admission of women as magistrates – were lost.

Many of the members of the Constituent Assembly were constitutional experts, and the names from the debates read like a roll-call of the best minds and political expertise that Italy has produced – from Croce to Lussu to La Pira to Di Vittorio. In December 1947 the Constitution was approved by 453 votes to 62. Generally, the Constitution has been seen as a success in guaranteeing certain rights and freedoms, and a failure in terms of the organization of the state and the government apparatus. The Christian Democrats narrowly failed to overturn many of these checks and balances in 1953, when an attempt to introduce a new type of electoral law was defeated. After that, the Constitution survived more or less unchanged until the 2000s, despite numerous attempts at reform and interminable debates. By 2013, only one original member of the Constituent Assembly was still alive.

Box 2.8   The Constitutional Court

In an influential series of articles in the 1950s, Piero Calamandrei argued that the DC was using a kind of 'majority obstructionism' that was blocking progress on the laws needed to put the Constitution into practice. One key institution here was the Constitutional Court, which was only set up in 1956, following a 1953 constitutional law. This delay was due in part to the decision of the Court of Cassation of February 1948, which divided the Constitution into those parts that were immediately operational and other norms that could wait. This 12-year hold-up deferred long-awaited legal reform, especially of fascist laws. The court has the power to declare laws unconstitutional (without appeal) – and is made up of 15 judges, lawyers or university law professors, three of whom are elected by senior judges on the Cassation Court, one by the Council of State and one by the Court of Accounts. Five others are appointed by the president of the Republic and a further five are elected by both Houses of Parliament. There is thus some scope for a politicization of the court although the terms of service (one term of nine years) have led to a certain continuity of behaviour in the court itself. At its first sitting, the court decided that it had the power to judge *previous* laws and not just future laws. In the wake of the 1968 movements, a number of archaic fascist and pre-fascist laws were abolished. The Constitutional Court also decides on the constitutional status of referendum proposals. The first woman to serve on the court was appointed in 1996.

The civil and penal codes are now full of minor and major amendments to laws and norms, imposed over time by Constitutional Court decisions. Many laws thus read as fragmentary histories of various discussions, debates and judgements. Between 1956 and 2002, the court made over 7,000 decisions. In 1967 alone 41 national laws and 9 sections of the legal codes ran afoul of court decisions. Far more laws and regulations have been examined in Italy than by similar bodies in France (whose constitutional court examined only 44 laws between 1958 and 1980), Germany (190 national laws between 1951 and 1990) and the US Supreme Court (152 from 1803 to 1997). The changes introduced by the Italian court have been an important source of democratic and constitutional reform, but this fragmentary approach has not led to organic and planned change, but rather to piecemeal and often incomprehensible changes to existing laws and regulations – to reform by *removal*.

In extreme circumstances, the court may be called to judge the president of the Republic, if he or she has acted unconstitutionally. The Constitutional Court is thus also the supreme guarantee against misbehaviour by the head of state.

In the 1990s and 2000s the Court sat on numerous occasions in order to adjudicate about a series of 'personal laws' passed by governments led by Silvio Berlusconi. All of these laws were judged to be unconstitutional and thrown out. On two occasions these included attempts to make the higher levels of the political and state system immune from prosecution while in office (see Box 2.11).

The Constitution is a mixture of abstract rights and concrete institutional measures. The former have been important in the modification of many laws (as *unconstitutional*) – where they have discriminated against women, for example. Moreover, the Constitution was a result of a compromise between anti-fascists of all kinds, and above all between the communists and socialists, on the one hand, and the Christian Democrats on the other. One price the Left had to pay for unity was to leave the 1929 Church–state agreements more or less intact, maintaining the privileged role within society obtained by the Catholic Church through those pacts (see Box 2.3). None the less, the Constitution remains an elegant and worthy document, even today. It set up a system full of safeguards, checks and balances, in reaction to the immense concentration of power (and the abuse of that power) that had existed under fascism.[14] As the mass party system broke down in the 1990s and 2000s, the defence of the Constitution became a value in itself. A sense of 'constitutional patriotism' developed, with a focus on the role of the Italian president. The Constitution was praised as 'the most beautiful in the world' and enjoyed something or a renaissance, with public readings and the study of articles. In a world where anti-politics had become the norm, the Constitution represented a set of overarching rules, regulations and principles to which Italy as a whole could aspire, in opposition to a corrupt 'caste' of career politicians.

The Italian Republic was constructed as a *parliamentary democracy*. Laws must be passed by both elected chambers (the House of Deputies and the Senate). The electoral system chosen was the most democratic of all – proportional representation (PR; although this was reformed in 1993 and again in 2006, see Chapter 4). The head of state is the president of the Republic, elected by Parliament. The Italian president is less powerful than heads of state in most other constitutional nations. Head of the *government* is the president of the Council of Ministers, appointed by the president. This duopoly has left most of the real power with Parliament itself, and hence with the political parties (of which there have been many, thanks in part to the very low thresholds adopted by the type of proportional representation system that was used). Secret voting on a number of issues reinforced the power of Parliament over the executive. At moments of crisis, however, the president of the Republic (and to a much lesser extent the president of the Council of Ministers) held a number of important powers. As the party system lost legitimacy in the 1990s and 2000s, presidents took on a central role. Giorgio Napolitano was the first president to be re-elected for a second term (in 2013). He was the architect of Mario Monti's emergency 'technical' government in 2011, and of the so-called presidential government, a grand coalition formed in 2013. With support for parties at an all-time low, the president appeared as the only guarantee of the integrity of the state and the Constitution.

This was the architecture of the First Republic, and remains the architecture, apart from the new electoral system, of the so-called 'Second Republic', even after the upheavals of the 1990s and 2000s. In reaction to twenty years of fascism, a system was set up which prevented single individuals from governing for long, and dispersed political power in a number of directions. The downsides of this system were governments that lacked stability, and huge

Box 2.9   Judicial independence and the CSM

Article 101   1948 Constitution: Judges shall be subject only to the law.

Article 104   The judiciary is an independent branch of government and shall not be subject to any other.

Until 1948, under the Liberal state and fascism, the Italian judiciary was answerable to the minister of justice. There was no formal independence from the political system. Political control was particularly strong for investigating magistrates. However, a number of reforms had set up systems of independence over time. In the 1890s measures were passed which ensured that judges were recruited by public competition, while the justice minister could appoint members of the Appeal Court and the Cassation Court (a power which was rarely used). In 1907 the Superior Council of the Magistracy (CSM) was created as a consultative body that gave advice on the promotion and transfer of magistrates. CSM members were in part elected by Cassation Court judges and in part by government appointees. In general, most ministers accepted CSM advice. In 1921, the CSM was made more democratic – its members were elected by *all* magistrates. Fascism overturned this reform in 1923. Magistrates formally took on the trappings of fascism, but the 'fascistization' of the judiciary itself was not total, although fascist laws were applied with some zeal.

The Constituent Assembly set out to ensure judicial independence. Investigating magistrates were freed from direct political influence. The most important institution was a new type of CSM. Not set up until 1958, the CSM runs the justice system. It has 33 members and is chaired, formally, by the president of the Republic. The rest of the CSM consists of 20 magistrates elected by the judiciary (via a PR list system from 1975 to 2002; eight members appointed by the Court of Cassation, four by the Appeal Courts and eight by the Tribunal Courts). Ten further members are elected by Parliament, and can be law professors or lawyers as well as magistrates. The CSM is renewed completely every four years and its members cannot be immediately re-elected. The CSM appoints, assigns, moves and promotes members of the judiciary although, over time, promotion has become more or less automatic, dependent only on age. Normally members of the judiciary are appointed through the public competition system. Powers exercised by the CSM include the possibility to discipline and warn judges, and to impose sanctions ranging from the loss of pension to dismissal. Disciplinary action can also be initiated by the justice minister. Judges in Italy are thus protected from direct political influence (but not from politics) by the CSM – and *govern themselves*. However, this *formal* independence has always been heavily conditioned by informal and/or explicit political pressure, the cultural *milieu* of the judiciary (and its continuity over time) and forms of corruption. The judiciary was drawn right into day-to-day politics in the 1990s and 2000s, with frequent accusations of political bias directed against magistrates. Increasingly, magistrates left their profession to enter politics. These debates and actions undermined the legitimacy of the rule of law in the eyes of many.

Box 2.10 Silvio Berlusconi: outcomes of a selection of trials*

1. Innocent verdicts (these fall into two main categories)
   a. Cleared because the facts contested were 'no longer a crime'.
      • False accounting (All Iberian 2: 2000–2005; and Processo SME: 2001–2008). Berlusconi cleared because his actions were 'no longer a crime' after reforms passed by his second government in 2002.
   b. Cleared (lack of evidence or various other reasons).
      • Fiscal fraud, false accounting, embezzlement. Land purchased in Macherio (1999).
      • Judicial corruption (Processo SME: 2000–2008).
      • Bribes to tax officials (2001).
      • Violation of anti-trust law, tax fraud, other crimes, including money laundering (Telecinco, Spain) (2008).
      • False accounting. Medusa cinematografica (2001).
      • Embezzling and tax fraud. Mediatrade (2013).
2. Statute of Limitations. In the following cases Berlusconi was cleared because the trials took so long that they fell under the Statute of Limitations.
      • Lodo Mondadori. Corruption (2000–2001).
      • All Iberian 1. Illegal political funding (1996–2000).
      • Consolidato Fininvest. False accounting (Trial never began, legal process ended in 2004).
      • Fininvest. False accounting and embezzling (1988–1992).
      • Lentini. False accounting (2000–2002).
      • Corruption. David Mills (2007–2012).
3. Guilty verdicts (all legal levels).
      • TV rights. Fiscal fraud, false accounting, embezzlement. Four-year sentence (2006–2013). The consequences of this verdict were the subject of bitter debate in 2013, but included the fact that Berlusconi could no longer stand for office, the confiscation of his passport, house arrest (or socially useful work) and his expulsion from Parliament (ratified by the Senate; 27.11.2013).
4. Ongoing trials (selection, September 2013).
      • 'Ruby' trial concerning alleged sexual relationships with an underage woman (Kharima el Marhoug, or 'Ruby') between February and May 2010 and aggravated corruption. Berlusconi is accused of abusing his position as prime minister to influence the functionaries of Milano's police station in May 2010 to release el Marhoug, who was accused of theft (2011–). Guilty (first trial). Seven-year sentence. Appeal pending (2013).
      • Unipol. For making public illegal wiretap material. Guilty verdict. First level of justice. One-year sentence (2012–2013). Appeal pending (2013).

* In Italy there are three grades of justice. Usually the third level (the *Cassazione*) is seen as definitive in terms of a guilty or innocent verdict. But the lengthy nature of the whole process often brings the Statute of Limitations into play. There is often confusion (in the public mind) between an innocent verdict and the role of the Statute of Limitations. In many of the cases cited here a 'final' guilty or innocent verdict followed different verdicts earlier on in the legal process.

> **Box 2.11** Silvio Berlusconi: laws passed by governments led by Berlusconi that affected his own private business interests or the legal processes involving Berlusconi himself or his companies (selection)
>
> - 4.8.2001 (operational from 2002). Changes to false accounting laws including shorter sentences and shorter periods for the Statute of Limitations to take effect. This law cancelled all trials involving Berlusconi and false accounting.
> - 24.12.2002. The 'Save-Football' decree (which later became law) allowing football clubs special privileges in paying tax debts, included Berlusconi's own AC Milan.
> - 22.6.2003. Lodo Schifani. Under this measure, the five most important institutions of the state were made immune from prosecution (President, President of the Council of Ministers, President of the Lower House, President of the Senate, President of the Constitutional Court). In 2004 the Constitutional Court threw out this law. But in the meantime, Berlusconi's trials were suspended.
> - 5.12.2005. 'Salva-Previti' (or ex-Cirielli). Here the time needed for the Statute of Limitations to come into play was reduced, along with other changes for older people. This measure was often linked to the fate of Cesare Previti, a close associate of Berlusconi, who was on trial for judicial corruption, hence its nickname as the 'Previti-saving' law.
> - 22.7.2008. Lodo Alfano. This was another attempt to bring in immunity for the higher echelons of the state (this time just the first four) with the suspension of trials for those holding high office. Once again (as with the Lodo Schifani) this measure was thrown out by the Constitutional Court as unconstitutional (in 2009).

institutional obstacles to any attempts at organic reform of the state. Compromise was built into the system. The vicious circles of incomplete and failed reform of the state itself have dogged Italian governments since 1945 (and, it might be argued, this was also the *leitmotiv* of the Liberal period). However, this is to assume that serious attempts at institutional reform were ever part of the plans of Italy's political oligarchies. In the real world, ruling elites have mainly concentrated on the simple 'management of power'.[15] Yet, on those rare occasions when society and governments have pushed in the same direction for reform (1945–8, the early 1960s, the early 1970s, 1992–4), wholesale reform has not been forthcoming, except for the unrepeatable moment of the Constituent Assembly. Moreover, these state 'architectures' – the rules and frameworks that governed the Italian state system – were always pliable ones, contingent on historical, political and cultural changes and flexible within the international context of the cold war, European integration and world wars.

JUSTICE, LAWS AND THE LEGAL SYSTEM

Producing Laws

How has the Italian state produced laws within these frameworks? The first and most clear-cut process has been through Parliament. Laws have always been drawn up by ministers and discussed in the Council of Ministers before being put before Parliament. In Parliament, these proposals are then discussed in the Senate and the Chamber of Deputies. Amendments are proposed and debated (without limits) by both the lower and upper houses. In order to become law a proposal needed to get a majority of votes in both houses, and then to be signed by the king (before 1946) and by the president of the Republic (since 1946). Heads of state have always had the power to refuse to sign laws and decrees, and to send this material back to Parliament for further discussion or amendment. These veto powers have been used fairly frequently throughout Italian history. However, if the same law is re-approved by both houses, the president is obliged to sign it. Thus, the king and then the president have represented one part of the system of controls and balances set up by the Albertine Statute and the 1948 Constitution. Governments have also used the device of 'confidence voting' to get through controversial or difficult legislation. When a confidence vote has been announced, a defeat entails a government crisis. Unsure deputies who do not wish to provoke the fall of their government are thus pushed to support particular laws or budget packages. Finally, the opposition, individual deputies and senators, and regional councils can also propose laws for Parliament to ratify, or not. This process of law-making has not necessarily been linked to democracy. Fascism maintained many of the formal aspects of the legislation process set out under the Albertine Statute, while the deputies themselves were not elected, after 1924.

These processes are not the only means by which laws are made and changed in Italy. Governments have the possibility to shorten this process through the use of decrees.

Decrees

Decrees (also known as decree-laws) can be issued by the Council of Ministers at any time. They are subject to debate and a vote in Parliament and can be rejected by the president. If not converted into laws, decrees disappear as law after 60 days, under the terms of the 1948 Constitution (Article 77). Although the Constitution provided for the use of decrees only 'in extraordinary cases of need or urgency', governments have increasingly used decrees for more 'normal' legislation, as a way of by-passing divided parliaments or responding quickly to demands for reform: 459 decrees were issued between 1987 and 1992, and 718 between April 1994 and May 1996 (see Box 2.12). Emergency and technical governments in the 1990s and 2000s also made frequent use of decrees. All decrees have to be declared 'constitutional' by the Constitutional Affairs Committee. The 1988 reforms, however, limited the use of decrees to specific questions in order to avoid further use of 'omnibus decrees', which had become commonplace during the First Republic. Decrees were often ill-thought-out reactions to 'emergencies', or to local pressure. For example, decrees passed after disasters have often unlocked funds, with little control over their use or distribution. Other decrees have reacted too strongly to events. The immigration decree of November 1995 was a reaction to small-scale immigration-linked violence in one zone in Turin. It set in place extremely stringent, and unworkable, immigration policies, which were toned down during later debates and in a subsequent immigration law. Constant use of decrees undermined the legitimacy of Parliament and the parliamentary system, and were a sign of an ongoing political and systemic crisis.

Committees and 'little laws'

Other modifications to laws are created by decisions taken by parliamentary committees, who, in any case, oversee most legislation. The permanent committees can also legislate following a four-fifths majority, under Article 72 of the Constitution. This system has been the source of much horse-trading since 1945, especially with regard to 'little laws' (*leggine*), leading to local spending which has often been utilized for clientelistic reasons. Decisions about which laws are passed by commissions and which by Parliament itself are taken by the presidents of the Lower House and the Senate. Parliamentary committees constitute the 'clearing-houses' for all laws, and are often where real power lies and real decisions are taken, away from the rhetoric and debates of the chamber itself.[16]

Checks and balances

All these laws, as we have seen, have been passed within the general frameworks imposed by the Albertine Statute and the Constitution. Parliament has historically provided the greatest source of control over law-making, apart from the period of the Fascist Parliament (1926–43). At times, in the face of particularly controversial measures, parliamentary oppositions have adopted obstructionist tactics to block or alter laws. In June 1899, Camillo Prampolini, a Socialist deputy, overturned parliamentary ballot boxes to delay discussion of repressive laws. Another Socialist deputy, De Felice, physically blocked the way to the ballot boxes. The abandonment of Parliament by a number of opposition deputies in 1924 (the so-called *aventine secession*) was a form of protest against fascist violence and the decline of democracy. Later, during the 1950s, the opposition used a series of measures to block a proposed new electoral law (1953), including filibustering. Given the time constraints and bureaucratic procedures adopted by the Italian Parliament, these tactics were often relatively successful. In 2013 the anti-political Five Star MoVement occupied Parliament as a protest against the 'system', and set up live streaming of their activities there, including readings from the Constitution.

The Constitutional Court has decided on the constitutional nature of laws since 1956. After the signing of the Treaty of Rome in 1957, European law and European institutions of various kinds have imposed legal limits and regulations on Italy, as in all member states. Italian law must now conform to European law, and the Italian government has often been taken before the European Court of Justice or the European Court of Human Rights. Slow but steady progress has been made in bringing Italian law in line with European legislation. Another control has been the possibility of calling referendums to abolish certain laws, a widely used tactic after 1970 (see Chapter 3).

Box 2.12   Making laws: decree-laws

The Constitution (1948)

Art. 77:   (1) The Government shall not, unless properly delegated by the Chambers, issue decrees having the value of law.

(2) When, in exceptional cases of necessity and urgency, the Government issues, on its own responsibility, provisional measures having the force of law, it shall on the same day submit them for conversion into law to the Chambers, which, even if they have been dissolved, shall be expressly summoned for that purpose and meet within five days.

(3) Law-decrees shall lose effect as of the date of issue if they are not converted into law within sixty days of their publication. The Chambers may, however, approve laws to regulate rights and obligations arising out of decrees that have not been converted into law.

Numbers of decrees

Legislature (period between elections)	Period	Ordinary laws approved	Constitutional laws approved	Decrees issued	Decrees converted into law	Not converted	Total number of laws approved
1	8.5.1948– 24.6.1953	2,316	1	29	28	1	2,317
2	25.6.1953– 11.6.1958	1,896	1	60	60	0	1,897
3	12.6.1958– 15.51963	1,793	3	28	28	2	1,796
4	16.5.1963– 5.6.1968	1,765	3	94	89	5	1,768
5	5.6.1968– 24.5.1972	839	2	69	66	3	841
6	25.5.1972– 4.7.1976	1,128	0	124	108	16	1,128
7	5.7.1976– 19.6.1979	666	0	167	136	31	666
8	20.6.1979– 11.7.1983	963	0	274	171	101	963
9	12.7.1983– 1.7.1987	795	1	302	136	129	796
10	2.7.1987– 22.4.1992	1,061	5	459	187	264	1,066
11	23.4.1992– 14.4.1994	311	3	493	123	315	314
12	15.4.1994– 8.5.1996	295	0	718	122	556	295
13	9.5.1996– 13.5.2001	706	4	149	146	3	710
14	2001–2006	481	5	226	200	26	686
15	2006–2008	79	1	51	32	19	112
16	2008–2013	281	4	123	107	17	391

The Shape of the Law: Civil and Penal Codes

Italian law has been shaped around two broad legal codes: the *penal code*, and the *civil code*.

The penal code

The penal code is a set of articles that lays out crimes and punishments. Following unification, no national penal code was introduced, and penal matters remained under regional codes. Only in 1865 was the Piedmontese criminal code extended by decree to the rest of Italy, although Tuscany kept its own penal code. Piedmont's code had, in turn, been largely drawn up from the Napoleonic model. A national penal code was drafted in 1889 – the *Zanardelli code*. The 1889 code was a product of liberal and classical traditions. Importantly, it abolished the death penalty by firing squad, which was only reintroduced in 1926 under fascism (for serious political crimes, and then extended in 1931 to certain types of murder and 'massacres'). The death penalty was repealed by Royal Decree in the Allied occupied areas of Italy in October 1944 (and reinstated for 'fascist crimes' and collaborationism), before being finally abolished in 1948 (it remained in force only within the military code, until 1994). Zanardelli's code was extremely conservative in a number of areas, especially in family law and moral issues. Its 'Liberal' reputation has been overstated in comparison with the 'fascist' code of 1930.

Fascism restructured the whole legal system. The Rocco penal code (named after the Fascist justice minister between 1925 and 1932, Alfredo Rocco), drafted in 1930 and in operation from 1931 onwards, remains (in 2001) the basis of that system.[17] This code is a mixture of 'classical' and 'positivist' law. Put very simply the 'classical' ideal assumes that crimes can only be punished if performed under 'free will'. Positivist ideas, on the other hand, assume that there are 'criminal' or 'dangerous' types of people, who must be punished, sometimes in advance of having committed any crime, and that society must be protected from such people. Put very simply, positivism concentrates on the criminal, and not the crime. In the Rocco code, most crimes were only punishable if the criminal was able to 'understand and to will' at the time of the criminal act in question, or punishment was far weaker if this was not the case. However, the Rocco code also contained traces of the positivism that had been made popular in Italy by the criminologists Lombroso and Niceforo, especially in terms of 'political' crimes and those defined as 'against the nation'.

If we look in detail at the code, and its changes over time, we get a sense of the shape of this fundamental set of laws and measures. In terms of positivist ideas, Article 202 read that 'Security measures may only be applied to *socially dangerous* persons who have committed an act designated by law as an offence' [my emphasis].[18] Other political crimes were also at the centre of the code: the crime of 'inciting civil war' (Article 286); 'the vilification of the monarchy [later replaced by the Republic], the nation and the armed forces', the 'national flag' and the 'religion of the state' [also later removed], as well as 'seditious assembly' (these crimes became known as the 'opinion laws').

Rocco's code was very harsh on women, as had been Zanardelli's. But, in many areas, Rocco toned down or 'modernized' clauses from the 1889 code. Rape was still defined as a 'crime against public morality and decency' (until the reforms of 1996) and not against 'the person', an extremely old-fashioned way of dealing with sexual violence. The concept of 'honour' was still important, leading to a reduction of punishment if it could be proved that a crime was committed 'to save one's own honour' – this applied to the murder of an unfaithful wife by her husband, and even to infanticide. Italy's legal system gave discounts to male murderers in line with this ancient conception of marriage – sentences were lower in cases where 'honour' was involved.[19] Abortion was illegal. Only women could be punished for adultery (Article 587): 'an adulterous wife shall be punished by imprisonment for up to one year. Her accomplice in adultery shall be punished by the same punishment ... the crime shall be punishable on complaint of the husband.' This law continued to be applied after 1945, for example to the lover of the famous cyclist Fausto Coppi, and was only removed (thanks to the Constitutional Court) in 1968, after being re-confirmed by the court in 1961.

No wholesale reform of the Rocco code was undertaken after the fall of fascism, despite the new Constitution. As a result, many outdated and clearly fascist clauses remained on the statute book for years.[20] Attempts at serious and radical reform of the penal code all failed. A committee was set up in 1945, but did not report back until 1950; drafts for reform were put forward in 1956, 1960 and 1968. The Constitutional Court started to reform the penal code after 1956, in the wake of the modernization of society and protest from below, but only in a piecemeal and 'negative' fashion, quashing certain clauses within laws and codes. The court had no power to propose new clauses or laws. Wholesale reform of certain key areas, such as prison law or family law, did not take place until the 1970s. This applied to the above-mentioned 'honour' clauses (1981), abortion (1980) and divorce (1970, 1974). As a result of this piecemeal and slow process of change, many 'crimes', such as those involving 'vilification of the flag' and 'the nation', are still on the statute book (Penal code, 2001, Articles 290, 291, 292, 293). Other Articles also remained active, or were only slightly modified, such as some of those dealing with the defence of the state, or the crime of plagio ('whoever subjects a person to their own power, in such a way as to reduce them to a total state of subjection, will be punished by from 5 to 15 years in prison'), which was used to intimidate gay men in the 1960s (as in the famous Braibanti case in 1968, when a teacher was given a nine-year sentence for plagio involving his ex-student) and was only declared illegitimate by the Constitutional Court in 1981.

Parts of the Rocco code were utilized as weapons against protest movements throughout the democratic period of the Republic. Many of Italy's politicians were in no hurry to eliminate such powers from the armoury of the state. In addition, the recourse to emergency legislation has been a frequent feature of Italian history. From the anti-banditry 'Pica laws' in the 1860s through to the 'anti-anarchist' laws in the 1890s, the Fascist public order and political laws (1926–8) and the anti-terrorist laws of the 1970s, the Italian state has adopted exceptional powers to deal with public order problems and political protest. All too often, these laws have remained active long after the 'emergency' was over. Italy's forces of law and order have thus been able to call on a formidable body of repressive legislation in the face of protest and political organization, way beyond the normal clauses of the penal codes and security laws. One aspect of this 'permanent emergency' has been the recourse to various forms of imprisonment beyond that of the classic prison, such as internment (see Box 2.13). Every Italian courtroom contained the phrase 'The law is equal for all', but in reality the system afforded privileges to those with the means to afford decent legal protection.

The civil code

The civil code regulates relationships between private persons and the state, as well as commercial rules. An Italian civil and commercial code was adopted in 1865, based on that used in the Kingdom of Sardinia (1837), which had its origins in turn in the French *code civil* of 1804, extended to Italy in 1806. Many articles were simply translated from the French original. This code was contained in three volumes – dealing with people, goods and property, and commerce. Much of the code concentrated on property, and its defence. People were essentially seen as legal entities in terms of their relationship to property, and its transfer and inheritance. A new civil code was then adopted during wartime, in 1942. The six books which made up this code covered people, family, hereditary rules, work, obligations and rights. This code attempted to modernize the 1865 system and was 'fascist' in the sense of attempting to regulate all aspects of people's private lives. European Union law now takes precedence over the measures included in the civil code, which has been extensively reformed in line with general legal changes, such as the introduction of divorce in 1970, the new family law of 1975 and the adoption law of 1983.

Specific Aspects of Italian Law: Law Inflation and Bureaucratic Language

Two areas regarding Italian law have been particularly important for the history of Italy and the difficult relationship between citizens, state bureaucrats and law-makers. The first regards the *number* of laws. Italy continued to produce laws at a rapid rate throughout the twentieth century. This law-expansion has been exacerbated by federalist reforms, which have given greater legislative powers to the regions since 1970. Nobody really knows how many laws there are in total, but estimates run to some 150,000. Officially, however, there are 13,000 state laws and 18,000 regional laws in operation. The civil code is now a series of huge volumes (in some editions), running to thousands of Articles. Many of these laws are, in fact, obsolete. In the early 1990s, there were 1,850 laws relating to the state budget alone. Reformers during the 1990s attempted to rationalize this system and slim down these codes, but with little success. In addition, laws always referred back to other laws, which in turn referred back to other laws, and so on. Law 662 (1996) ran to some

---

Box 2.13   Other kinds of imprisonment: internment

Overview

The Italian state has often resorted to alternative forms of incarceration, or limitation of movement, to those of the classic 'prison'. The most important of these systems has been internal exile (*confino*), introduced in the 1860s (for 'bandits' in the south) and widely used against Mafia and *camorra* suspects, 'anarchists' and those involved in the Sicilian peasant movements (in 1894) and, after the rise of fascism to power, anti-fascists. Giolitti also used internment for petty criminals, and for Libyan oppositionists deported from Libya during the 1911–12 war. Pacifists and militants were sent to *confino* during World War I. Between 1926 (following law n. 1848, 6.11.1926) and 1943, large numbers of anti-fascists (around 13,000) were 'confined' in various camps around Italy (mainly in the south), such as those in Lipari, Civitavecchia (which was somewhere between a prison and a confinement camp) and Ustica. Some internees had been through the political tribunals; others had been interned without trial. Among those sent to confinement were gay men, gypsies, Albanians, Slavs, dissident fascists and Jehovah's Witnesses.

The experience in these camps was often a brutal one (see the story of Giuseppe Massarenti, recounted in Chapter 3) but the decision to place anti-fascists together helped them to organize and prepare resistance. A whole generation of Resistance leaders and politicians developed their ideas in *confino* – Pertini (future President of Italy), Parri (prime minister in 1945), Foa, Terracini, Secchia, Ernesto Rossi. Gramsci wrote his Prison Notebooks in confinement. Carlo Rosselli composed his seminal *Liberal Socialism* in *confino* at Lipari, before escaping to France with Emilio Lussu and Francesco Fausto Nitti (son of the ex-prime minister) in 1929. Carlo Levi left a memorable account of his own confinement in the south in *Christ Stopped at Eboli* (1945). Internal exile also had other, unintended, effects: the moving of *mafiosi* (under the anti-Mafia laws of 1965) aided the spread of Mafia organization to the north and centre of Italy. The widespread use of internal exile also reflected the failures of the prison system, and the generally repressive nature of the Italian state before and after fascism, as well as during Mussolini's reign. The Fascist internment laws were not abolished until 1956, but the obligation to live outside of a certain area, or *in* a certain area, could still be imposed by a judge after trial.

---

129 pages of the *Gazzetta Ufficiale*. Since the 1950s and 1960s, there have also been thousands of changes to the legal system, introduced by the Constitutional Court (over 11,000 sentences between 1956 and the end of the 1990s), the European Court of Justice (nearly 4,000) and the European Court of Human Rights (also around 4,000). All these judgments affected national legislation and the legal codes. The system was incomprehensible to the vast majority of citizens. The legalistic and technical training of many state bureaucrats (see the section on the bureaucracy, below), who often possessed law degrees, intensified the

elitist nature of these laws and only a small group of specialists understood the system. Their power was thus augmented in terms of information and legal processes, to the detriment of the common citizen. The sheer number of laws was a sign of weakness of public institutions, not of their strength.

Box 2.14   The language of Italian law: an 'ordinary' example

Italian laws are marked by their clauses and sub-clauses, and frequent references to other laws and decisions. Here is an example.

Civil Code. L. 2109.[a] *Period of Rest*

General rules on the application of a weekly rest for workers:

An employee has the right every week to a day of rest that coincides with Sunday.

They also have the right (after a year of uninterrupted work)[b] to an annual period of paid leave, at a time decided upon by the employer, taking into account the needs of the company and the interests of the employee. The length of this period is decided by law (by the corporative regulations/norms),[c] by social customs and according to the principle of equality.

Sub-clauses and Constitutional Court decisions:

- Article 36, 3 from the Constitutional Court recognizes that all workers have a 'perfect' right, which cannot be suppressed or renounced, to a weekly rest which guarantees – in social and human terms – that the employee can renew his or her psycho-physical energy in order to ensure a certain amount of time is dedicated to recreation for himself/herself and his/her family (Constitutional Court decisions, 7.7.1962, n. 76, Fl. 1962, I, 1222; RGL 1962, II, 385 – Constitutional Court, 15.12.1967, n. 150, GI 1968, I, 1, 1302, etc., etc. for another 7 lines).
- Article 1, 2, n. 6, 22.2.1934, n. 370 is constitutionally illegitimate in that, for the category of those working in the rearing of wild animals, it excludes the right to a 24-hour weekly rest following every legislative and collective initiative in this area (unlike other areas regulated by this law, which allow for a specific use of collective contracts to sort out the rules regarding the real use of the weekly rest day) (Constitutional Court, 7.7.1962).

[a] The Constitutional Court, with its decision of 22 December 1980, declared constitutionally illegitimate Article 2109 of the civil code in the part in which it declares that there is no right to paid holidays for those who are laid off during a period of training.
  The Constitutional Court, with its decision of 30 December 1987, declared constitutionally illegitimate Article 2109 of the civil code in the part where it does not provide for the fact that an illness which arises during a holiday period should suspend the time defined as holiday.
[b] The Constitutional Court, with its decision of 30 December 1987, declared constitutionally illegitimate Article 2109 of the civil code in the part in the second column where it states that the right to holidays is only acquired after 'a year of uninterrupted service'.
[c] The corporative norms were suppressed by the decree-law of 23 November 1944, n. 369. Thus this clause refers to collective contracts within common law.

A second, connected, problem concerns the language of legislation. Always technical, usually clear only to specialists and often long-winded, 'opaque and obscure',[21] Italian law is invariably a mystery to those who try and follow the various clauses, sub-clauses and references to previous measures. (For an example, chosen at random, see Box 2.14.) This legal labyrinth excludes the common citizen from whole systems of power and regulation.

ENFORCING THE LAW, PROTECTING THE STATE, KEEPING ORDER, MAKING WAR

As we have seen, the production of laws is one area where the Italian state has been a world leader. Enforcing these laws, however, has been a different matter. In theory, in a liberal democracy, the enforcement of the law is the work of, primarily, a wide system of consensus. Most people, in theory, abide by the law and frown upon illegality. This type of consensus, in many cases, has been singularly lacking in Italian history, especially in periods of deep legitimation crisis. Thus, the traditional institutions associated with law enforcement have had to be deployed by the Italian state at frequent intervals. This very deployment, however, has also been a contributing factor to delegitimation. The key law-and-order institution which we will examine in this chapter is the army.

The Army: Continual War and Constant Defeat

The Italian army has played a pivotal role in Italian history. The two main institutional responsibilities of the army have been (a) to fight wars and defend the nation against foreign aggressors, and (b) to keep order within Italy itself and, at times, in her colonies.[22] The other responsibility of the army has been a more ideological one, signifying practical participation by Italians in the performance of these national functions and the solidifying of certain forms of national identity. Within this broad outline of military tasks, the Italian army has taken on specific features.

First, Italy was an exceptionally militarized society until 1945. War lay at the heart of the Risorgimento and the military histories of many of Italy's leaders (above all Garibaldi) helped to create a military-type society, where the army was omnipresent; 12 per cent of the members of Piedmont's Chamber of Deputies and nearly a third of the Senate were members of the military in 1849. Various military 'myths' surrounding the Risorgimento, from the 'Roman Republic' to the heroic feats of Garibaldi's 'thousand' and the military 'prowess' of Victor Emanuel II, reinforced a military model of change. War ministers were always military officers until 1907 when a non-military politician held the post until 1909. There were usually one or more military men within the cabinet. In 1920 a civilian defence minister was again appointed, but Mussolini brought in General Diaz to the post in 1922. Under fascism, *Il Duce* reserved this position for himself between 1925 and 1929 and from 1933 to 1943. The key role of certain generals in Italian history is testimony to this reliance on military leaders (above all Badoglio, from Somalia to Libya to World War I to Ethiopia to World War II). In a crisis, Italy resorted time and again to generals.

Militarization was kept alive by almost continual war, sometimes in the form of internal conflict (the southern brigandage wars of 1861–5, which involved two-thirds of the entire Italian army – 120,000 men) but more usually through 'real' war. Italy was almost permanently 'at war', somewhere, between 1848 and 1945 (Box 2.15). Continual war brought extremely high costs, and state spending was geared towards the maintenance of a permanent expensive army. Italy saw itself as a great military power, which needed an army to match. In 1882 the Italian army consisted of 12 army corps plus the alpine forces, as compared with 16 in France and 18 in Germany. However, these conflicts, apart from the Ethiopian colonization of the 1930s, were never particularly popular at home and did not create wide consensus around the institutions of the army or the state. There were frequent and traumatic defeats, from Lissa and Custoza (1866) to Adowa (1896) to Caporetto (1917) to Greece and Russia (1940–3). Each defeat had its own history, but a pattern emerged of weak motivation, poor organization and poor leadership. The failures of the Italian state were also reflected in the doubtful efficiency of the army. Moreover, the army failed to defend Italy itself when called upon to do so, allowing foreign powers to occupy large parts of the north-east in 1917–18, and the whole country in 1943–5. Militarization, however, did not necessarily imply an increase in loyalty or legitimation in the eyes of the Italian people.

The Italian army: structure and history

The fragmentation of the armed forces has been a specific trait of Italian history. The Risorgimento governments struggled to incorporate numerous armies into an 'Italian army' after 1860. Following World War I, private, armed, uniformed militia groups – organized above all by the fascists but also on the Left – were formed all over Italy and in many cases usurped the functions of the official armed forces. Often, those involved were ex-soldiers. Italians have fought Italians in many civil wars – from the brigandage wars of the 1860s, through to the struggles in 1919–22, to Spain in 1936–9 where Italian Republicans fought the Italian fascist army, to 1943–5. The cold war was perhaps at its most bitter within Italy. These civil wars left a bitter legacy, and the wounds were not quick to heal. After 8 September 1943, the army itself dissolved and separated, creating at least two different and mosaic-like armies, one broadly fighting alongside the Allies, and one with the Germans. It was only after 1945 that a unified set of armed forces was created again, but the post-war period was marked, unlike that before, by a lack of Italian participation in war. The army changed again, concentrating almost exclusively on domestic law-and-order operations, but also in the realms of civil protection and disaster relief. With the end of the cold war (despite some isolated incidents, such as the participation in the Lebanon

Box 2.15 Italy at war

Declarations of war and armed conflicts involving the Italian army, 1860–2001

17.6.1866	Austria
22.9.1870	Vatican (France)
1887	Ethiopia
1896	Abyssinia
1900	Italian troops form part of the international military expedition to Peking to put down the Boxer rebellion in China.
29.9.1911	Turkey
1911–12	Libya
1911–35	Dodecaneso Islands occupied

World War I

24.5.1915	Austria–Hungary
21.8.1915	Turkey
19.10.1915	Bulgaria
27.8.1916	Germany
1935–6	Ethiopia (war not declared)
1936–9	Spanish Republic (war not declared)
6.4.1939	Albania

World War II

10.6.1940	France/Great Britain
28.10.1940	Greece
April 1941	Yugoslavia
3.5.1941	Slovenia occupied
June 1941	USSR
11.12.1941	United States of America

After 8 September 1943

13.10.1943	Germany/Japan
1991	The Gulf war
1998	Yugoslavia
2001	Afghanistan
2003	Iraq
2011	Libya

'peace' missions of 1982) Italy became involved in 'real' war again, with the first Gulf War (1991), the Kosovo War (1998), the Afghanistan conflict (2001) and the highly divisive participation in the Iraq War (2003), which was imposed by Silvio Berlusconi against the wishes of the Italian president, Carlo Azeglio Ciampi.

Organizationally, Italy's military alliances since 1945 have been much more stable, with membership of NATO (1949) and the presence of numerous US and NATO bases on Italian soil. During the cold war, however, many Italians continued to identify with the Eastern bloc, and not with NATO and the West. The neo-fascist MSI Party (Italian Social Movement) accepted NATO membership, for anti-communist reasons, in 1951. The Socialist Party did so in 1963 and the Communist Party only in the mid-1970s. Peace movements have always taken on a particular strength in Italy, in part because of the non-aligned positions taken up by the Catholic Church. Thus, the 'protective' role of the army has never been uncontroversial in Italy and the army as an institution has usually been challenged by a large number of Italians whether in peacetime or in war. Finally, armed groups were formed, often in secret, supposedly to protect Italy from invasion after 1945. The most important of these organizations was known as *Gladio*, a clandestine 'army' ready to mobilize in the face of foreign aggression from the East and (it appears) against Communist Party structures in Italy.

The second role of the army was an internal one. In a 'normal' state, in peacetime, the army is very rarely involved in the enforcement of 'domestic' law and order. This has not been the case in Italy. The Italian army has frequently been deployed internally to maintain or re-institute public order or to enforce certain state measures. Important Italian military historians have gone as far as to argue that the *central* role of the Italian army was to repress domestic opposition.[23] In part, this function was the natural consequence of the militarized society created out of the Risorgimento, which maintained extremely high levels of military spending and exalted the representative role of the military. In addition, the Italian state has always been able to call on both the regular army and a militarized police force, the *carabinieri*, to carry out these functions. But the constant decision to call on the army internally also reflected the lack of mediation of conflict within Italian society and between that society and the state. The legitimation crises suffered by the Italian state led, all too often, to the use of violence on both sides. For the state, this tactic involved 'sending in' the army to quell labour disputes or street protests. This happened so often as to be seen as 'normal' in Liberal Italy, especially in the south (see Box 2.16). Occasionally, the state lost control to such an extent that a 'state of siege' was declared, which suspended the normal processes of democracy and civil liberties, and imposed martial law. Normal courts were replaced by military tribunals. This happened in Sicily and in Campania in 1862, in Palermo in 1866, in Sicily (again) and in Lunigiana in 1894, across large parts of Italy in 1898, in Reggio Calabria and Messina in 1909.[24] The frequent use of the army, an organization trained in the use of extreme violence, not in mediation or crowd control, led to numerous victims amongst those on the streets, in the fields or outside the factories. The most notorious use of the army in this way was in 1898, when General Bava Beccaris reacted to bread riots in Milan with the use of cannons, killing over 400 demonstrators in the process. The king later awarded Bava Beccaris a medal, praising him for his 'great service ... to our institutions and to civilization'.

Box 2.16   The army and public order: selected list of
'proletarian massacres', 1901–5

27.6.1901   Berra Ferrarese (Ferrara, Emilia) (landworkers' strike) – 3 dead, 23 injured.

5.8.1902   Cassano delle Murge (Bari, Apulia) – 1 dead, 4 injured.

8.9.1902   Candela (Foggia, Apulia) – 5 dead, 12 injured.

13.10.1902   Giarratana (Ragusa, Sicily) – 2 dead, 50 injured, and 1 military policeman killed.

23.2.1903   Petacciato (Campobasso, Molise) – 3 dead, 30 injured.

31.8.1903   Torre Annunziata (Naples, Campania) – 7 dead, 40 injured.

17.5.1904   Cerignola (Apulia) – 3 dead, 14 injured.

4.9.1904   Buggerru (Sardinia) – 3 dead, 20 injured.

14.9.1904   Castelluzzo (Trapani, Sicily) – 2 dead, 20 injured.

18.8.1905   Grammichele (Catania, Sicily) – 14 dead, 68 injured.

Yet the tragedy of this constant recourse to the army was a double one. The army, when called upon to do so, at least in theory, was neither able nor willing to protect many Italian citizens from attack. Fascist squads, armed and in uniform, were able to kill, maim and destroy property with very little intervention from the army or the state. This colossal failure was to delegitimize the state itself for many of its citizens. When called upon to sign a 'state of siege' order to defend Rome from fascist attack in 1922, the king refused to do so, preferring to nominate the leader of the fascists, Mussolini, as prime minister. Mass private violence was legitimized, overlooked by the army whose loyalties were not put to the test. In 1943 the Italian army again failed to defend Italian territory from invasion, and its powers were usurped by foreign armies fighting on Italian soil. The Italian army was delegitimized twice, both through its overuse in internal disputes and through its (lack of) effectiveness as a defending force.

Fascism attempted to militarize Italian society through war, propaganda and intense organization. The rhetoric was of a nation with 'eight million bayonets', and superficial militarization penetrated right through society via the various organizations set up by fascism, such as the *Balilla* (instituted for children aged 8–17 in 1926). Yet, beyond the conquest of Ethiopia and campaigns in Libya, this tactic never created more than a minority of hard-core soldiers. No serious modernization of the army or its equipment was undertaken. The broad majority remained sceptical, as 1940–3 showed. Defeat against Greece was followed by disaster in Russia. The Americans invaded in 1943 without meeting much opposition and German troops also poured into the country. Italy became a theatre of war with Italians playing a secondary role under Hitler, Churchill and Roosevelt. The watershed of 8 September 1943 placed soldiers and generals in a serious dilemma regarding loyalties, obligations and orders. The head of state was the king, and therefore soldiers were, in theory, obliged to follow the monarchy in the overthrow of fascism and the setting up of a 'kingdom of the south'. The Albertine Statute had set up the king as commander of the army, with the right to declare war without the need for parliamentary approval (Article 5). During the period of the parliamentary monarchy the king nominated war and navy ministers. Many supporters of the monarchy joined the Resistance against the Germans, where they allied with anti-fascists, many of whom were communists and republicans. Others, however, left the army and looked to return home. Meanwhile, a significant minority rejected the monarchy and its claims on military loyalty and joined the fascist Republic, and the Nazis, in the centre–north. The events of 8 September 1943 exposed, in dramatic fashion, the divisions long present within the Italian state machine over fascism, the monarchy and the war in a moment of deep crisis and defeat.

The Resistance used military and guerrilla strategies to great effect in combating the German and Italian armies in the centre and north of Italy. This 'new Italian army' was disbanded soon after the end of the war, but the 'military model' remained a strong one for many of those from the Resistance generation. It was only after the failure of the insurrectionary uprisings in July 1948 that this strategy was transformed into a defensive one by parts of the organized Left, and limited stockpiles of arms continued to be maintained by the Communist Party and others. Yet the myth of a future armed struggle (called the 'Hour X' by Christian Democrat propagandists during the cold war) against the state never really died, and was revived, in disastrous fashion, by the 'red' terrorists of the 1970s and 1980s many of whom saw themselves as the heirs of the Resistance tradition – as 'new partisans'.

Other groups have, at times, looked to substitute themselves for the army itself, or to take on the state with military means. The Mafias have always used violence, and private armies, to enforce their extortion and their own idea of order. Some anarchists attempted the road of assassination from the 1870s onwards. In the 1970s and 1980s, terrorists from the Right and the Left used violence to spread their political message, or just to create chaos (as in the 'strategy of tension', see Box 2.1).[25] The Italian state has found it extremely difficult to maintain a monopoly in that most basic area of modern governance, the use of organized violence. While Italy never descended into full-scale civil war (apart from 1943–5, where the civil war was one part of a wider world war fought partly on Italian soil) on the model of Spain or Greece, political and military violence have been a common feature of Italian state–society relations over the last century.

Finally, a central aspect of the state–army relationship has been the issue of military expenditure. In the post-Risorgimento and Liberal states, military spending was extremely high. During the 1850s, 28 per cent of state expenditure was destined for military purposes. This rose to 40 per cent in 1862. The average figure from 1862 to 1896 was around 24 per cent. This sum reached 76 per cent during World War I, before falling back to around 20 per cent right through to the 1940s. Constant debates focused on the need to control this spending, whilst many argued that the high costs were necessary. Domenico Farini, for example, claimed in the 1880s that the army was 'the only cement holding Italy together'. None the less, the financial crises experienced by the Italian state after unification and again in the 1880s and 1890s were in large part due to the dead weight of this expenditure. Other services, especially education, were neglected in favour of the military. In 1871 education and social services expenditure amounted to less than 1 per cent of the total state budget. After World War II, this issue largely slipped off the political agenda, as military spending declined from 3.7 per cent to 1.1 per cent in the fifty years after 1945. It was only in the 1990s and 2000s, with the participation of the Italian army and navy in a number of major international wars and/or peace-keeping operations (in the Gulf, Bosnia, Albania, Afghanistan, Lebanon, Iraq and Libya), that military spending forced its way back onto the political agenda.

Military service and the state

At a more everyday level, the army formed part of the life-experience of millions of Italian men (and, more indirectly, of millions of women), throughout the history of the nation. Military service was instituted soon after unification in 1862, although inefficiencies, cost implications and loopholes allowed many to escape conscription (up to 50 per cent in the south; brigandage was in part a revolt against conscription). Conscription was intended not just to provide the state with a large reserve army in time of war, but also to create a sense of national identity.[26] This function was undermined by the decision to move conscripts and regiments around Italy at regular intervals, a costly process which lessened contacts between the army and society, but facilitated the repressive use of the military domestically (the rationale behind this was to allow the army to be used as a repressive internal force: to construct the institution as detached from the Italian people).[27] Although many resented conscription, and attempted to dodge it (this was especially easy for richer families, and for the clergy), for others the experience was an important one, marking the passage from boy to man, and was often the first long time away from home, as well as offering a rich set of experiences (cultural, social, sexual – the call-up often coincided with ritual visits to brothels), and friendships which often lasted for a lifetime. The rituals of the call-up, with the selection of individual numbers, important for the length and location of military service, and the medical exam, were key parts of this experience. Others tried to avoid conscription by pretending to be mad, or even, in extreme cases, cutting off their own fingers.[28]

Rich networks of military organizations, above all those linked to the alpine forces after 1919 – the *alpini* – but also more generic groupings based around the birth-year of call-ups (many village walls are still decorated with *viva* (year) graffiti), kept the experience alive well after the military service itself, which lasted for up to two years, was just a distant memory. Ex-soldiers kept their uniforms and their 'squad' photos as reminders of that time.[29] After 1945, this experience lost some of its allure, especially without real war to maintain the *camaraderie* under fire of the previous generations. Military service continued, but reforms toned down its military nature. Conscripts were later allowed to declare themselves conscientious objectors, or to opt for civic duties (thanks to a series of reforms in the 1970s).[30] Many thereafter lived at home, not in barracks. The break in the life-cycle represented by the beginning of military service began to lose importance.[31]

In the 1970s, political organizations spread propaganda amongst the conscripts themselves, forming groups such as 'Proletarians in uniform' who marched at demonstrations, in their uniforms, with their faces hidden. The cold war remained the logic behind the continuation of conscription – while the Left supported military service as a supposed democratic bulwark against a reactionary, professional army. Over 11 million Italian men served in the army between 1945 and the 1990s, with a peak figure of 349,000 men in 1989. The time spent on military service was reduced from 18 to 15 months in 1964, and to 12 months in 1975. With the end of the cold war, a series of reforms effectively ended conscription (the last full call-up was of those born in 1985, following the Martino Law, 23.8.2004, n. 226), just as the Italian army was called on again, after 45 years on the home front, to fight wars or to 'keep world order' in Kuwait, Somalia, Albania, Kosovo, Afghanistan and Iraq. Italy moved towards the creation of a largely professional, volunteer army, with the inclusion of women soldiers.

Since 1945, however, the internal role of the army has continued to be a strong one, although troops have been employed more sparingly in internal disputes than during the Liberal period. Often, these functions have been left to the armed police forces or para-militaries (the *carabinieri*) but the army was central in the insurrectionary moments of 1948, 1950, 1960 and 1968. Many Italians lost their lives in these periods of social and political conflict, as the lack of mediation between the state, society and protest movements continued to be a feature of conflict. Italy, unlike Germany and Japan, did not have its army disbanded after 1945, and rearmament took place in the early 1950s. The unique events of 1943 allowed Italy to escape the fate of its former allies, but also led to a certain degree of continuity with the fascist armed forces after the war. Arguably, then, the particular historical events of September 1943 prevented much-needed and wholesale reform of the armed services in Italy.

Military conduct and institutions were always subject to their own, specific legal systems, rules and regulations. Suspected deserters were judged by military law, not the civil or penal codes. Special measures were also inserted into the civil and penal codes relating to the armed forces. In particular, the crime of 'vilification of the armed forces', from the Rocco penal code (1930), was used to prosecute civilians under *military* law, where legal guarantees were much weaker than in the civil or criminal courts. In the post-war period individual judges used this Article to persecute artists, writers and film-makers and to prevent discussion of certain events from Italy's military past. Luchino Visconti was forced to alter his film *Senso* (1954) after threats of prosecution (the film made reference to Italy's defeat at Custoza in 1866). In 1953, two film critics (and ex-soldiers) were successfully prosecuted (with the loss of a rank) under military law for *vilification of the armed forces* after the publication of a screenplay based on events in Greece in the 1940s. The colonies had their own legal systems, based on those in force in Italy.

The use of military law contributed to a general lack of action against those who had committed war crimes during World War II. In 1996 the trial of Erich Priebke, an SS captain who had taken part in the Fosse Ardeatine massacre in Rome in 1944 (when 335 Italians were killed in reprisal for the deaths of 33 German soldiers in a bomb attack in Rome), was held in Rome in a military court. This decision skewed the whole trial towards a discussion within the context of military regulations and the logic of 'following orders'. Much debate during the trial centred on the question of the 'five extra' victims – given that, under military law, reprisal killing (of civilians) was seen as legitimate, even at a ratio of ten-to-one. As a consequence, Priebke was initially found 'not guilty' under military law, but a hastily arranged retrial saw a different result emerge. The trial was dominated by technical, military–legal issues that left those looking for 'justice' confused and angry.

Keeping Order and Judging Illegality: The Legal System[32]

At the top end of the system of legal enforcement stands the judicial system – judges, magistrates, juries, lawyers, courtrooms and trials. The Italian legal system, once again, is modelled on the French system (with some Belgian traits). Following the division into codes, examined above, the legal system is also separated into civil courts and penal courts, as well as into administrative and military courts.

The Legal Process: From Crimes to Trials

The key figure in the Italian legal system is the *Pubblico Ministero* (PM – Public Minister) – an investigating magistrate independent of direct state control. Investigating magistrates look into crimes – they are obliged by law to investigate *all* crimes they are informed of – and indict suspects, in collaboration with the police, the *carabinieri* and other investigating magistrates. This 'requirement' to investigate is in reality dependent upon a number of issues, and is structured by the prevailing political climate, the evidence and time available, the type of crime involved and considerations of public interest. Investigating magistrates have, in reality, a considerable amount of leeway within the Italian system to choose where, and when, to prioritize their activities. They can now form precise groups of magistrates – pools – around specific investigations, as with the anti-Mafia pools in Sicily, or the anti-corruption pools in Milan in the early 1990s. Investigating magistrates also help to decide which investigations should be dropped before trial (or 'archived') a central power particularly with relation to the state itself (see also Box 2.17).

It is widely believed that investigating magistrates have acted politically with regard to these powers. As in all countries, the legal system in Italy is not immune to political pressure. However, Italy's legal system has always been more political than most. The judiciary was remodelled with the 1948 Constitution. Before that, in unified Italy, judges and investigating magistrates were under the direct control of the justice minister and, in many ways, their independence was merely formal. The justice minister could

Box 2.17   Investigating magistrates: the public minister

The 1948 Constitution: Article 107

Members of the judiciary may not be removed from office. They may not be dismissed or suspended from their duties, nor moved to other jurisdictions or functions, save by a decision of the Superior Council of the Judiciary taken for reasons and with guarantees for their defence laid down by the laws on the organization of the judiciary, or with their own consent.

Roles and history

The Public Minister (PM) has always been one of the key components of the Italian legal system, but has very rarely been analysed in historical terms. A PM lay somewhere between what the UK system would think of as a barrister, an investigating magistrate and a judge. Under the 1865 judicial regulations, the PM was defined as 'the representative of executive power within judicial authority under the direction of the Justice Minister'. This dependence remained more or less unchanged until 1941. The state could therefore direct investigations to certain areas, and avoid others. Since 1948 this position of dependence has been reversed. A PM now investigates crimes, either on his/her own initiative or after requests to do so. Under the 1948 Constitution: 'the public prosecutor has a duty to institute criminal proceedings' (Article 112) if informed of crimes. Public Ministers use judicial police for their investigations, and have extensive arrest and search powers. Of course, these activities have always been conditioned by the prevailing political mood. The widespread view that the Italian judiciary is heavily politicized derives from the ways in which investigations have been linked to certain political moments, and *non-investigations* to others.

Furthermore, the PM is part of the decision as to whether or not to go to trial. If a case goes to trial, the PM then appears again, this time as prosecutor. Thus, PMs investigate, invoke arrests and prosecute. These three separate functions have led to confusion, and to abuses of power (and calls for these powers to be 'separated' in some way). At times of political uncertainty, PMs have stepped into the breach to transform Italy through a kind of 'legal revolution', particularly during the struggle against the Mafia (during the 1980s, in Sicily) and against political corruption (during the 1990s), and then again in terms of other criminal organizations in the south and further examples of corruption in the 2000s. Politicians have tried to limit the autonomy of PMs. During the 1990s there were plans to *separate* investigative and prosecuting powers, thus bringing PMs back under political control. Crucially, thanks to the 1948 Constitution, PMs cannot be sacked by politicians, and their promotion depends on the CSM. The 1989 reforms of the criminal procedure codes gave PMs more investigating powers, and other reforms allowed for the formation of groups of investigating magistrates who concentrate on particular areas, such as corruption or organized crime.

sack them or transfer them. Similar powers remained under fascism. The Constitution set up new, intermediate 'buffer' institutions that were designed to guarantee judicial independence. The key body here was the CSM – the *Superior Council of the Magistracy* (see Box 2.9). However, as with the Constitutional Court, the CSM took a long time to get going in the post-war period, not being formally instituted until 1958. There was also considerable continuity of personnel before and after World War II. Many fascist judges, or judges who had worked throughout the fascist period, remained at their posts after 1945, thanks in part to the weak process of purging set up after 1943 (in the south) and 1944–5 (in the centre–north). There is no doubt that the 1948 reforms have guaranteed a large degree of independence from direct political pressure. In addition, the recruitment of the judiciary (via annual public competitions, or *concorsi*) has opened up the system to a non-class-based body of judges, unlike, for example, the extremely elitist nature of the British judiciary.

However, there is no doubt that the Italian judiciary is a politicized institution, despite these important guarantees. For example, there are a number of different political organizations working within the judiciary and these political currents are reflected in the carve-ups that lead to different slates competing for posts on the CSM. The Italian judiciary is thus an openly politicized body, with quasi-political organizations organizing groups of magistrates and judges. Individual members of the judiciary have often made no secret of their passion for political issues and their political opinions and have taken part in quasi-political pressure-group campaigning. This tendency was formalized in the 1960s and 1970s, with the foundation of *Magistratura Democratica* (on the Left) and other politicized organizations for magistrates and PMs. This tendency is aided by the ways in which the judicial governing body, the CSM, was organized – along political lines with a PR voting system since 1975. Complicated reforms passed in 2002 altered this system in an attempt to reduce the corporate power of the CSM. Currently, 16 elected members of the judiciary serve in the CSM as well as 8 elected lay members and 3 institutional figures. It is also true that investigations, or non-investigations, of crimes have always been used as political weapons by judges (and politicians). This instrumental use of justice has, in turn, further delegitimized the legal process. In most cases, magistrates have chosen *not* to take on the rich and powerful, the Mafia and the *camorra*. For years, the Mafia was more or less taboo in Sicilian courts, and only in the 1980s were large numbers of *mafiosi* prosecuted for their crimes, after the efforts of a key group of investigating magistrates in Palermo. In the last twenty years this has also been the case for the Neapolitan Camorra and the 'ndrangheta in Calabria.

Trials, Stage 1: The *Istruttoria* Phase

From unification to the 1989 reforms

Until the 1989 reforms, Italy's penal process was run as a kind of mixed inquisitory process. Two phases led to prosecution for crimes: an inquisitory pre-trial phase and an accusatory trial phase. After unification and under the 1913 codes and the 'Rocco codes' (1930–1) the key phase was that of the *istruttoria*. This phase of the legal process was *written, non-accusatory* and *secret* (although under certain circumstances the 'acts' could be read). A single judge looked at the evidence, interrogated the accused and laid out the various elements of proof against them. Before 1931 a defence lawyer could be present at this phase and the PM had a limited input. Under fascism's legal code the limits on preventative imprisonment were abolished and defence lawyers were excluded from the *istruttoria*. Only when the *istruttoria* was over were defence lawyers informed about the results of the investigations and the evidence against their clients. After this long procedure the process moved on to its second stage, a public trial (see below). The *istruttoria* system was heavily criticized, not least because of the imbalance between the prosecution and the defence, and the lack of guarantees for the accused. Reforms slowly changed this over time – such as that relating to imprisonment in 1913 – but fascism handed more power to the judges and to the PMs. Modernizing reforms after 1945, as in so many other areas, were blocked for years by inertia, political wheeler-dealing and vested interests.

The impact of the 1989 reforms

After an interminable debate a wide-ranging reform of the penal process was introduced in 1989. The idea behind this reform was to abolish the old *istruttoria* phase and bring in a more accusatory system, moving away from the inquisitorial basis of the old system. Under the new reform the decision as to whether a public trial is held or not is left to a preliminary hearing, held under a 'judge for preliminary investigations' – who weighs up the evidence and decides whether to send the case to trial.[33] This whole process is initiated by a PM who, after the investigations, decides either to ask for a trial or to drop the case. If a trial is requested, then a 'preliminary hearing' is held – a pre-instruction phase – in front of a special kind of judge. Here a PM presents the evidence for the prosecution, and the defence presents its case. Defence lawyers are present during this pre-trial phase and are allowed access to evidence. If the case does not carry sufficient weight of evidence in the opinion of the judge, then it is dropped – *archiviato*. If there is enough evidence for a prosecution, the judge orders a trial. This part of the system is thus a further guarantee for the accused and a way, in theory, of preventing overcrowding in the justice system (by filtering out useless trials). Not all cases go through this pre-trial phase, only those of a certain importance. Under the new reforms, PMs are required to inform, by post, those against whom an investigation has reached the point in which a lawyer has the right to make representations. This letter is known as a 'guarantee notice'. Designed to protect the rights of citizens, during the *Tangentopoli* corruption scandals (1992–4) the arrival of a 'guarantee notice' became widely seen as proof of involvement in corruption.

A series of changes to the 1989 reforms have introduced exceptions in the treatment of a number of crimes, especially those relating to the Mafia. In addition, very strong institutional and political factors have combined, at times, to increase or decrease guarantees for various individuals. The political climate during the 1992 corruption investigations led to some cases of summary justice, and it appeared as if the inquisitory system was being reintroduced through the increased powers assigned to the PMs. Institutionally and culturally, pre-trial judges have tended to back the opinion of PMs, even when not supported by enough evidence. The guarantees introduced into the system in 1989 and again in 1999 allowed those with resources and good lawyers to block trial processes almost *ad infinitum*, in part because of the incredibly complicated procedures involved and the different levels of justice. Silvio Berlusconi's own reforms affected the criminal investigations into his own business interests and other alleged crimes. Many trials became a battle against the clock, with procedural issues dominating debate. Often, the whole process ended up in a kind of limbo, as the Statute of Limitations came into play. In short, Italian justice was extremely slow. By the time the whole three-tier process was complete, most people had forgotten what the original accusations were. Finally, the 1989 reforms allowed for various pathways towards sentences avoiding trials, such as an agreement on a guilty verdict in return for shorter sentences.

Trials, Stage 2: The Public Trial

If a trial is deemed necessary, then the *type* of trial depends on the crime involved. Minor civil cases are now held before a 'Justice of the Peace' (literally a 'peace judge') – a kind of low-level magistrate. This institution was set up in 1991 to try and speed up the legal process and clear the massive legal backlog, following frequent condemnations of the Italian state at the European Court of Human Rights. By 1994 the average length of a civil case had reached 1,207 days, and 27 months for a penal case. In 2011, 3.4 million penal cases were awaiting trial. Figures released in 2012 claimed that penal trials were taking an average of 8.3 years to complete. Only a third of all civil cases ever reached a conclusion.[34] In 2001 the Justice of the Peace system was extended to cover minor penal infringements, and encouraged mediation. Peace judges cannot send the accused to prison. Serious crimes are tried in *Corte d'Assise* before three judges and six jury members (chosen from amongst Italian citizens of 'good moral conduct' between the ages of 30 and 65 with at least a basic school qualification). As well as the prosecuting magistrate and the defending lawyer, the victims of the crime, or their families, have the right to legal representation during the trial – this institution is known as the *parte civile*. Trials begin with procedural questions, before proceeding to the *dibattimento* – the debate itself. Witnesses are called by the defence and the prosecution, and questioned by both, as well as by the judges (one of whom directs the trial, deciding on procedural questions) and by the *parte civile* lawyers. At the end of this process, which is often extremely lengthy, both the prosecution and the defence sum up. The judges and jury then retire to consider their verdict, which is read out in open court. The reasons behind the verdict are usually issued some months later, written up by one of the judges in collaboration with the others. Most analysts acknowledge that the 1989 reforms have failed in their intention of speeding up the whole system (in fact, some trials have become longer and more complicated) or to provide more guarantees for the accused and/or victims of crimes.

From here, if the accused is found innocent, the state can appeal against the verdict, asking for it to be changed or the sentence itself to be lengthened. Similarly, a guilty verdict can also be appealed, automatically, by the accused. The verdict is not seen as final until all grades of the justice system have been exhausted (and citizens are often released from prison at this point, pending further trials). In other words, there is a presumption of innocence even after a guilty verdict, until the verdict is confirmed at all levels. In addition, the accused and the prosecution can both appeal to the highest court of all, the *Corte di Cassazione* (CdC – the Cassation court) if they feel that the procedures followed by various court sections have broken the law in some way. The CdC has the power to quash all verdicts and send the case back for reconsideration by other judges, or to confirm earlier decisions.

The accused thus has a number of guarantees within the Italian system. First, there are the various grades of justice, which allow automatic appeal and guarantees against abuse through the possibility to send the case to the CdC. Secondly, the accused can, at any time, call for any judge sitting in a trial to be removed. Reasons must be provided for such an accusation, such as a biased pronouncement of a particular judge, or suspicions about their private role in the case, or their involvement with a previous case involving the same parties. A separate judge then decides on the matter, after which the trial either continues as before, with the same judge, or the judge in question is replaced. Time limits are placed on the possibility of being condemned for various crimes. This Statute of Limitations, in theory, protects citizens from excessively long legal processes. In practice, however, the Statute of Limitations has often allowed wealthy people with top lawyers to effectively block the whole legal process. Silvio Berlusconi made a number of alterations to laws relating to the Statute of Limitations. These reforms had a direct affect on trials involving Berlusconi himself. Finally, a number of recent reforms have added to these guarantees. The constitutional reform known as the 'fair trial' reforms (now Article 111 of the Constitution, 1999) requires all evidence to be repeated in a court by accusers, or else it is not deemed valid. This measure, aimed at reducing the power of supergrasses to make false accusations, and the widespread use of 'written' evidence, but also at guaranteeing the powerful, and politicians, more protection against investigation and prosecution, now makes the trial itself the key moment of the whole justice system Large numbers of trials ended with no outcome either way, as the Statute of Limitations came into play. In 1956 around 56,000 trials or legal processes ended in this way. By 2006 this figure had risen to 206,000.

A further kind of trial, rarely used except in extreme cases, is known as the 'very quick trial' or *direttissimo*. It allows for a near-immediate trial of people 'caught in the act' of committing serious crimes and is mainly used in cases where the state feels the need to make a fast prosecution for reasons of public order or propaganda. Here there is no pre-instruction phase. Retrials are extremely rare in Italy, but can be ordered by the CdC in the case of the emergence of significant new evidence regarding a case. If a retrial (known as a *revisione*) is ordered, then it takes place before three judges and only the new evidence is admissible. Once a retrial is over, there are no other grades of possibility, apart from a possible final appeal to the CdC over questions of procedure, or an amnesty (decided by governments) or a pardon (decided by the President of the Republic).

Superficially, the Italian legal system would seem to present many guarantees for both the state and the accused against unfair accusations or errors in the legal process. In reality, these guarantees are not, and have never been, available to all. The costs of taking forward a case to appeal or of appealing to the CdC are considerable, and many poorer clients are thus forced to accept their fate. More well-to-do clients can keep out of jail and often paralyse the legal processes by drawing out their trials through constant procedural 'tricks' and appeals. This tactic is aided by the extremely lengthy and bureaucratic procedures adopted by Italian courts. Often, cases of this kind, as we have seen, lose the race to beat the Statute of Limitations. Poorer clients cannot afford this type of procedural game, and often end up serving their sentences after the first grade of justice has been completed. In addition, the guarantees within the system have been used to protect the powerful in other ways. In the 1970s and 1980s, numerous verdicts against the Mafia were quashed by Cassation judges for minor administrative blemishes or errors of *form*, not of content. It later transpired that certain leading judges within the CdC were linked to the Mafia and were using their role to help their friends. Such protection was only available for a select few. Other powerful criminals were able to use corrupt networks of doctors and experts to escape prison through loopholes, as with the 'Banda della Magliana' criminal gang in Rome in the 1980s.

Defending Italians: Lawyers

Italy has always 'produced' a high number of law graduates, in part because of the requirement for a law degree for many public service jobs. There are three levels of lawyers: academics, practitioners and magistrates. Practising lawyers can work either as procurators or as attorneys, or both. Procurators are similar to solicitors, representing their clients during the build-up to court proceedings. Attorneys defend clients through legal or written arguments. All must register as lawyers and must have passed bar examinations, as well as completing one year's experience, and their conduct must have been 'unblemished'. Procurators must pass further exams to become attorneys, and there are restrictions on those who can work in higher courts. Senior attorneys can practise in the high court. All lawyers are members of a professional guild that regulates their conduct. Legal aid is available for poorer citizens. All defendants must have legal representation – they cannot defend themselves. Finally, state attorneys are a group of legal experts who defend the state and public administrators. Lawyers' representatives also sit on the CSM and can be appointed to the Court of Cassation. In 1920 there were 25,000 practising lawyers in Italy; by 1987 this figure had reached 50,000 and by 1995, 83,000 (as compared with

32,000 in France, 70,000 in Germany, and 60,000 – plus 8,000 barristers – in the UK); 247,000 Italians were *qualified* as lawyers in 2012. Lawyers have clearly profited from the slow and intricate nature of the legal system. Lack of reform has increased the need for lawyers. The 1970 divorce law, for example, called for two separate legal hearings in order for couples to obtain a divorce. Both required legal representation, and lawyers were thus paid twice.

Histories and Conclusions: Aspects of the Italian Legal System

The Italian legal system has always been slow, extremely complicated and costly. Reform has usually been difficult to achieve and has not produced concrete results. Judges, courts and trials have been a central part of the legitimation crisis suffered by the Italian state. The institutions and personnel of the justice system have tended to be seen by many as distant from the lives of real people and close to the interests of the rich and powerful. From unification to 1948, the judiciary was subject to direct political control, and very rarely were politicians themselves subject to direct investigation. Fascism set up new justice networks and courts that worked against political opponents and denied those accused of political crimes basic legal rights. In other areas, however, the legal system remained largely unchanged under fascism. After 1948, a series of checks and balances were introduced which guaranteed the formal autonomy of magistrates and judges. The CSM, not the government, regulated the judiciary. No investigating magistrate could be sacked, or appointed, by politicians. Continuing recruitment through public competitions also helped to bring the judiciary closer to the people. However, there had been no serious purging of fascist judges after 1945 and many of the basic problems with the system remained. Italian legal processes mixed jury power and judicial power, with the judges having the final say. Strong doubts lingered on concerning the politicization of the judiciary and their 'objectivity'. The failure to take effective action against the 'strategy of tension' in the 1970s was an obvious shortcoming. Little was done against the Mafia.

During the 1980s, things began to change. Certain magistrates began to investigate corruption and organized crime, with some political and social support. Hundreds of *mafiosi* were arrested, tried and imprisoned in Sicily, and magistrates such as Giovanni Falcone and Paolo Borsellino paid a heavy price for this breakthrough – both were murdered by the Mafia in separate bomb attacks in 1992. In Milan, after 1992, a group of judges brought a corrupt political class to its knees, arresting and investigating thousands of politicians, businessmen and even judges. The *Tangentopoli* scandals led to a major rift between the judiciary and certain politicians and parties. A conflict opened up at the heart of the state. The whole basis of the 1948 Constitution was questioned. Later, as the investigations slowed down, successive governments attempted to rein in the independent power of investigating magistrates. Yet, continual accusations against 'politicized' judges and magistrates served to undermine the judiciary and the rule of law in general, threatening another serious legitimation crisis for the Italian state.

A series of trials involving Silvio Berlusconi in the 1990s and 2000s was a dramatic example of the clash between judiciary and politicians (see Boxes

2.10–2.11). Berlusconi used a precise set of strategies to defend himself: claims of conspiracy, the passing of laws in order to shorten or end trials involving himself, constitutional changes bringing in immunity for certain public figures, reforms of the judiciary. All of this led to a further politicization of the entire legal process. It would be difficult to argue that this process was positive for Italy as a whole, and the health of its institutions. Magistrates, as with other institutions, were also branded as an untouchable and privileged 'caste'.

In August 2013 Berlusconi received his first definitive guilty verdict, a four-year sentence for tax fraud. This was a key moment, and had a number of personal and legal consequences for Berlusconi himself. He had to give up his passport, and was banned from standing for office in future elections for at least six years. The Senate would have to decide, moreover, if he was to be kicked out of Parliament immediately under the provisions of the Severino Law (2012), which was applied to all Parliamentarians who had been given a definitive sentence of more than two years. He would also have to choose between house arrest and community service as a way of serving his sentence. A furious debate followed, as Berlusconi and his loyal followers manoeuvred for position. There were calls for a pardon, or an amnesty. Berlusconi threatened repeatedly to bring down the government. Once again, the clear and damaging conflict of interests between Berlusconi the businessman and Berlusconi the politician had come to the fore. In November 2013 the Senate voted to expel Berlusconi from Parliament for six years. An endgame had begun, for Italy herself and for those who had backed Berlusconi's personal-political project.

RAISING MONEY: THE STATE AND TAXATION

> Taxes, taxes, and nothing but taxes.
>
> QUINTINO SELLA, FINANCE MINISTER, 1862

Finance has been a perennial problem for the Italian state. The premises for efficient tax collection are *information* concerning income, property and the activities of a country's citizens, and *consent* on the part of those citizens in the payment of tax. In other words, a state must know who its citizens are, what they do and how much property they own, and those citizens must be willing to finance the state through their taxes. This process has been particularly awkward in Italy given the historical problems encountered by the nascent Italian state (regional differences, disparate administrative systems, lack of adequate central structures, weak financial management). Once we factor in huge military spending and a weak industrial base, this position might appear potentially disastrous. And, in fact, the Italian state found it extremely difficult to raise money, or even to lay the basis for a modern tax-collecting system. Much of the economy was still outside the monetary sector until well into the twentieth century. The great estates, or *latifondi*, functioned largely outside of a modern, cash economy. Sharecropping systems, based in part on cash-exchange but also on the exchange of goods and produce, survived in large parts of Italy until the 1950s (see Chapter 3). Often, state and local authorities had only a very vague idea about patterns of property holdings and commercial trading. This information was essential if tax collection was to be efficient, and fair. A serious survey on a national scale – the *catasto* – was not organized until 1931. Internal customs-type taxes on the movement of goods within Italy, detested by poorer citizens, were not abolished until 1930.

Given the urgent need for money to pay for the army, for frequent wars and for the basic needs of society, the Italian state resorted to the easiest and quickest tax-collecting solution – indirect taxation of the poor. Grain taxes in the past had hit peasants hard – and were extremely unpopular as regressive taxes on food production. None the less, a grain tax was reintroduced by the post-Risorgimento administrations in 1869 (it had been abolished in 1860). This time, however, the tax was aimed at the *grinding* of grain, not the grain itself. It was thought that this would make the tax easier to collect. The immediate reaction to the grist tax was widespread tax revolt, which was put down brutally by the Italian army. Brigandage in the south in the early 1860s had also partly been a tax revolt. However, the state reacted slowly to these protests, and maintained the grist tax right through to 1884, despite its failure to collect significant amounts of revenue. Many grinders simply closed down in protest, or under pressure from below. Only very mild progressive taxation and property taxes were introduced in post-unification Italy. Other indirect taxes included those of the lottery, building taxes and tobacco and petrol taxes.

The Politics of Tax: Giolitti and the Liberal State

The issue of tax had dominated the early unification period and the mildly progressive tax measures imposed by Giolitti in the early twentieth century met with opposition from the better-off members of society. The financial scandals of the 1890s had further undermined the basis of voluntary tax collection and payment, as did the obvious inefficiencies of the state, the lack of public services and the failures of imperialism. The regressive nature of taxation added to the disquiet of the poor. A vicious circle was created, combining tax evasion with poor tax collection. Yet, the state's finances demanded cash, and Giolitti increased taxes on grain (again), sugar and alcohol in 1894, as well as imposing an inheritance tax in 1892. But Giolitti understood that a widened democracy demanded a fairer tax system. In 1900 he argued for tax reforms and claimed that Italy needed to have the 'courage to ask the rich to support the weight of new state spending'. The Left called for more progressive taxation and business taxes. Political demands for high business taxation were particularly strong in the light of the massive profits (known as 'super-profits') made by certain industries during World War I. It was no accident that one of the few areas where there was agreement between the fascists and socialists in 1919–20 was in the demand for the taxation of these industrial 'sharks'.

The bureaucratic logic of the Italian state, reinforced under fascism, also infected the tax system. Citizens were forced to authenticate documents and payments with stamps and different kinds of seals. Often, an expensive visit to a notary was necessary. The state did not trust its citizens to deal with it in an open way, and Italian citizens certainly did not trust the state to use its taxes wisely, or efficiently. Most gritted their teeth, and paid, when they had to. If tax could be avoided, it was.

Fascism and Taxation

Fascism introduced new taxation systems. In 1923, an income tax was brought in, and commercial taxes were set up in 1930 and refined in 1940. Strong limitations were placed on individual spending after 1926 in an attempt to put the state's finances in order. New luxury housing was banned for a year, as was the construction of new bars. Newspapers were limited to six pages and a one-hour-a-day increase in work was imposed. Fascism also used taxes for political and social ends. In 1927 a tax was introduced on the unmarried, in order to promote bigger families. Mussolini called this tax 'a demographic lash to the nation' – tax was being used as a form of social engineering. Fascism also attempted to link taxation, and the financing of the state, with political propaganda and a nationalist mission. Thus, self-taxation programmes were introduced to pay for particular wars and help the state through moments of difficulty. Gold coins and rings were donated 'for the fatherland'. Similar appeals had been made by the liberals during World War I, and in particular after the Caporetto disaster in October 1917. In 1935, 8,000 million lire was raised through a special national loan effort to pay for the Ethiopian campaign. A tax on shares was introduced during the war in 1941.

Taxation since 1945

Since 1945, high taxation combined with high evasion has been a key contributor to, as well as the result of, continuing disaffection with the state. Direct income tax has been collected from salaried workers, whilst those who have declared a 'self-employed' income have often been allowed to evade tax with impunity. Meanwhile, the mismanagement of state funds, visible to *all* citizens, has undermined the consent necessary for efficient tax collection. An extremely complicated tax framework was set up which, when the whole 'tax burden' was considered, made Italians amongst the most taxed citizens in the world. The very complications of the system were an extra burden, adding insult to injury by making the payment of these (high) taxes a frustrating, humiliating and time-consuming experience. Taxes of various kinds had to be paid at various points in the year, to different organizations and institutions. Taxation questions were thus always tied up with problems of legitimacy.

After 1945, the tax system was modernized so as to allow for the annual declaration of income (for the self-employed) in 1951 and new business taxes in 1954. With the signing of the Treaty of Rome in 1957, moves were made towards more European-style taxation systems and levels. Strong consumption taxes were slowly complemented by business and commercial taxation. Direct taxation (from income, at source) was increased in the light of continuing high levels of evasion of indirect tax. Once again, it was the poorest sections of the community who paid for everyone else. Tax systems continued to be extremely complicated and bureaucratic – there was a veritable 'fiscal jungle' of rules, regulations and information.[35] State spending was associated with waste, inefficiency and mismanagement. The *black economy*, outside of the tax system altogether, was the biggest in Europe. Employers used workers without paying contributions (for pensions and health care, for example), leaving them unprotected and outside of state control (and outside the law). This system was so widespread as to be institutionalized, and the black economy was included in official economic statistics.

In the 1970s, tax reform tried to simplify the system, introducing a single form of direct taxation (income tax – *imposta sui redditi delle persone fisiche*, IRPEF 1973, reformed in 1986) and one sales tax (*imposta sul valore aggiunto –* IVA 1972, reformed in 1993 and 1995) paid on every purchase and on many imports. IVA levels currently (in 2013) range from 4 to 22 per cent. A regional tax was also introduced, mainly to pay for health care, which had been brought under the control of regional government. There are also a whole series of business taxes. More serious attempts were made to keep track of dealings and property ownership through the *anagrafe fiscale* (fiscal census), introduced in 1971 and reformed in 1997. In 1980, a solidarity tax was instituted in the wake of economic austerity, which used 0.5 per cent of all incomes.

The rising state debt during the 1980s, 1990s and 2000s provoked the introduction of further local taxes based on property. These taxes were immensely unpopular, and were abolished by Silvio Berlusconi's government in 2008, before being reintroduced with a different name (IMU) by Mario Monti's technical administration in 2011–12. Local government also collected taxes on rubbish collection, on advertising, on the occupation of public land, on water, on property purchases (a tax abolished in 1993), and on businesses. Provincial governments collected taxes for the 'defence of the environment', on local heating and on the occupation of public land. Regional governments imposed taxes on car purchases, on gas and certain forms of petrol use, on rubbish collection and from university students. Thus 'normal' exchanges, such as the purchase of a new car, were taxed heavily. Attempts to collect acceptable sums from tax evaders (such as with the so-called *minimum tax* in the 1990s) met with massive opposition, although some progress was made in this area in the late 1990s. Mixed messages were sent out by Italy's politicians, especially after the arrival of Silvio Berlusconi onto the political scene in 1994.

Not surprisingly, most Italians were never particularly happy to pay these taxes – from employers, to workers, to the middle classes. However, as long as the state gave back as much as it collected in the shape of state benefits, generous pensions and state employment, and continued to turn a blind eye to much evasion, the system managed to survive. For many, the pay-offs were worth the hassle and the costs. By the 1980s, however, this uneasy balance was under threat from the demands of European integration and world recession. Something had to give, and the state was forced to increase taxes still further to meet the Maastricht single currency criteria after 1992. Special taxes were introduced on property and bank accounts, and a one-off *Eurotax* (a kind of obligatory loan, as the state promised to give it back to all citizens who had paid) was brought in to help Italy meet the requirements for the single currency. A tax revolt followed, mixed with a heavy dose of regionalism. The Northern

Leagues demanded an end to the redistribution of their taxes to the south. Corruption scandals further undermined the basis of the system. Many of these scandals involved those who were meant to collect the taxes or chase up tax evaders: the *Guardia di Finanza* (Finance Guards) – a militarized body – were particularly guilty, utilizing their privileged role as *mediators* to demand rake-offs.[36] *Lega* militants burnt their tax books, and called for collective tax evasion as a political act. This type of revolt never took off as a mass tactic, but the demand for lower taxation and more decentralization began to filter through to the political system, which grappled with the still-huge state sector and archaic collection methods. Nobody within Italian politics, however, could deliver on the promises of lower taxation without taking on the powerful public sector unions and state bureaucracy. Even more damaging was the recourse to 'fiscal amnesties' for tax dodgers, which allowed evaders to 're-enter' the legal world through the payment of a fine. These measures, brought in (as in 2002) to recoup much-needed funds, had the effect of legitimizing illegality. Only a fool, it was argued, would pay their taxes on time in Italy. Promises to cut taxes have been frequently made, but rarely if ever carried through.

Finally, Italians have always paid forms of tax to bodies other than the state. Many help to finance the Church through voluntary payments, or finance the flourishing voluntary/charity sector. Other forms of taxation have been far from voluntary. Many Italian businesses and individuals have constantly been forced to pay protection money (usually a percentage of earnings) to organized crime syndicates, especially in the south. This (substantial – up to a half of all profits) payment, known as the *pizzo*, took away a significant proportion of profits from many southern businesses. It was very hard, and dangerous, to resist the *pizzo* – and the *pizzo* itself brought protection and a certain degree of security in situations where trust was singularly lacking.[37] In the south, the *social capital* provided by trust between institutions and between families was often of low quality and in short supply, making any kind of collective action difficult and inhibiting the creation of a modern, civic culture.

ADMINISTERING THE STATE: BUREAUCRACY AND PUBLIC SERVICES

The history of Italy's bureaucracy has been written either as a history of administrators, or as a history of failed reforms, and changing regulations. Some of these histories have reproduced the corporatism of the administration itself, separating changes within the bureaucracy from changes to society. There have also been problems of definition. What do we mean by 'the bureaucracy'? The classic image is of counter clerks, organizers, office workers, typists and tax collectors – but the distinction between these administrators and other state employees (postal workers, school inspectors, librarians) has not always been such a clear one. In general, this section will use the classic, restricted sense of the 'state bureaucracy', meaning administrators of all kinds – from clerks to civil servants to tax inspectors. This definition omits one of the biggest categories of state employees (teachers – nearly a million by the end of the first decade of the 2000s) but will allow us to deal with issues regarding the Italian bureaucracy in a more detailed way.

All modern state institutions require administrators, bureaucrats and bureaucracies. Bureaucracies produce rules, regulations and hierarchies. Some of these rules are written and formal, others are informal and cultural. These systems develop over time in line with regional, geographical, social and political factors. Italy's state administration system evolved out of the Piedmontese state and the Kingdom of Sardinia and slowly spread to the rest of Italy. Yet, many local systems remained in place and informal norms of power varied greatly from city to city and region to region. In this context, how has the Italian bureaucracy developed over time?

Recruitment

In Italy, public officials of all kinds (including the police, university lecturers, *carabinieri* and judges) are recruited by a system of *concorsi*. *Concorsi* are public competitions held at set moments, where an exam is taken and candidates are graded, which then allow for the appointment of the 'winners' of this competition to the jobs required. In theory, this type of recruitment allows for fair competition (within certain rules and standards – such as the requirement for certain types of degrees), removing social, political and clientelistic forms of state recruitment. In practice, these types of practices have often infiltrated the competition process, usually through the back door. The open competition system has, however, opened up a number of professions (such as the judiciary) to wider cross-sections of people than in other countries. Not all public employees, however, are taken on via competitions. In many local contexts, a system of support staff and non-permanent administrators has co-existed with public recruitment systems. These employees have often formed part of clientelistic networks. In Sicily, for example, administrative employees rose from 500 in 1947 to 8,000 in 1971. Many were taken on as 'extra' staff, outside of the competition system. In fact, nobody knew for sure how many employees there were. In Bari University numerous people from the same family were given jobs in certain faculties. In 2010 42 out of 176 lecturers in the Economics Faculty were related in some way. This became a national scandal in the 2000s, and led to a new ethical code being imposed by this institution. This scandal was given a suggestive name in the press: *parentopoli* (or relative-gate).

Rules and Regulations

Italian administration has always been seen as weighed down by particularly elaborate systems of rules, norms and both written and unwritten regulations. In part, this was a legacy of the Piedmontese state (with its centralization and politicized bureaucracy), and in part, fascism increased the documentation and bureaucratic regulations in place at all levels of the administration. In addition, these rules were enforced in legalistic ways by bureaucrats with a technical–legal training. For many branches of the public administration system, a law degree was a requirement. Bureaucrats were seen as interpreters of complicated norms, not servants of Italian citizens. They also *saw themselves* in this way, and the natural, self-perpetuating protection of the powers promoted by secrecy and by knowledge that was not disseminated, created a caste-like approach to public service. Many administrators simply produced, or passed on, documents. Their 'job' consisted in 'a purely formal and literal application of norms'.[38] After unification, 'to administrate meant to move paper between offices; it implied the procedures of formal checking of visas, authorisations … registrations, verbalisations, signatures and stamps' (G. Melis).[39] Bureaucracy had become an end in itself: a nightmarish, useless and endless, Kafkaesque production of paper.

The lack of specific public administration and technical training, beyond the antiquated university system, also played a part in this process. But ordinary Italians also played the bureaucratic game. Clientelism is a two-way process, an *exchange* of resources ('influence', money or power). This exchange has taken place on an everyday basis throughout Italian history – from jumping the queue in a bank because you 'know' the bank clerk right up to rake-offs from public works projects. Mediators were naturally created by such a system, from those who simply obtained the right documents, through to power-brokers for political parties and big business. Administrators thus applied the rules, but not in a uniform fashion. In post-war Naples certain people set themselves up as mediators between the public administration and ordinary citizens. Allum cites the role of *spicciafaccende* – people employed in Naples 'to get documents through the intricate bureaucratic machine'.[40] The resources of time, knowledge and the ability to 'jump the queue' – through the use of this knowledge, or through clientelism, patronage and/or straightforward corruption – were precious commodities given the amount of time taken up by day-to-day administrative practices and petty but necessary document procurement.

The administration also set up its own legal system, with administrative courts and controlling bodies. Certain judges, lawyers and legal experts specialized in administrative law. At the top of this institutional tree lies the Council of State and the Court of Accounts. The former deals with administrative disputes (usually appeals of citizens or institutions against administrative decisions), the latter controls spending. In 1971 the TAR (a series of twenty Regional Administrative Courts) were set up given the inability of the Council of State to deal with an increasing number of administrative disputes and the institution of elected regional councils. The Council of State thus became the final court of appeal for these decisions. By the 1990s and 2000s the administrative law system was becoming increasingly ungovernable, as society in general became more and more litigious. The abundance of rules and the slowness of the system had produced a backlog of 800,000 administrative cases by 1991, despite legal limits on the number of days required for TAR decisions. Many bureaucrats became attached to these rules, and their complexity, using them both to defend themselves from public accountability and as ways of entrenching their own corporative rights and niches of power.

In addition, in the Italian case, these norms were usually *negotiable* and *flexible*; they could be bent by legal and illegal recourse to informal and clientelistic networks of all kinds.

Numbers and 'Southernization'

The Italian bureaucracy has never been especially large in comparison with that of other comparable nations.[41] At the time of unification, there were around 60,000 employees in the state administration sector (with 25,000 in the Kingdom of the Two Sicilies alone). The industrial revolution saw a rise in administrators, from 98,000 (including those working in the military) in 1882 to 286,000 in 1914. Despite the widespread belief that the Italian bureaucracy was enormous – a cliché fed by constant political rhetoric concerning the *elephantisis* of Italy's state machine – the rise in numbers of administrators was neither especially dramatic nor particularly costly. Other factors prevented the development of a modern, 'rational', bureaucracy. The growth in the bureaucracy was also accompanied by a *southernization* of the administration, as state offices were filled with middle-class law students from the *mezzogiorno*. Much has been made of this trend. 'Southernization' was also aided by the drift south of the main ministries with the shift of the capital from Turin (1860–5) to Florence (1865–70) to Rome (after 1870). Special laws to help the south, from those of the 1880s through to the *Cassa per il Mezzogiorno* in the 1950s (see the section on 'The State and the South' in Chapter 3), were administered through southern bureaucrats, who often had strong links to local political elites. Southernization, it is argued, was one factor contributing to the lack of a culture of public service within the Italian bureaucracy. The economic system, it has been argued, 'spoke northern' (with its capital in Milan), whilst the administrative system (and thus the state) increasingly 'spoke southern'. Of course, some of the consequences of this development are clear: such as an increasing conception of public service as a valued job in the south, as perhaps the only realistic vocational choice for many aspirant middle-class graduates. However, we should not slip into stale ethnic explanations for the long-term inefficiencies of the Italian bureaucracy.

Reform and Stasis

Constant attempts have been made to reform the state bureaucracy. Yet the barriers to such reforms have proved far stronger than the will of particular politicians or reformers. Debates over reform were a constant feature of the early Italian state. Yet very little was done or even attempted. Crispi did promote some structural reform in the 1880s, but the general trend was one of immobility, and of reaction to events rather than real long-term planning or organic reform. Fascism established its first unions amongst public and private administrators, and defended the *impiegati* against socialist unions after World War I. Once in power, the regime purged some public services, especially the railways, of 'subversive' elements through the use of forced early retirement. Cuts were made to public spending and the growth of the bureaucracy slowed down. Mussolini also attempted to politicize the bureaucracy and centralize political power. The oaths which all state employees were forced to swear became long political statements: *impiegati* were asked to pledge their 'devotion to the state', and to the king, and to promise that their 'private conduct' would conform to the 'dignity' of their work. *Impiegati* were banned from joining associations or parties whose activities could not 'be reconciled with the tasks of the job' (a hollow claim, since the Fascist Party was the only legal political party in Italy). Rigid hierarchical structures were introduced, zealous fascists were promoted with speed and many *impiegati* felt that they had achieved a sense of real social prestige, perhaps for the first time. However, despite symbolic changes (of language, uniforms, oaths), fascism never succeeded in its aim of creating 'the bureaucrat in the blackshirt' and many went along with the formal aspects of adhesion to the Party for instrumental reasons, not ideological ones. Fascist Party membership was made obligatory for all public bureaucrats in 1938 (when Italian Jews were removed from public service through the anti-Semitic laws) and uniforms were imposed. The culture, however, remained 'that of the liberal era'.[42] Fascism's only real innovatory reforms of the administration came with its decision to create numerous public holding companies, above all IRI (1933), which stood between the public and the private. These organizations were allowed to operate with some autonomy from the state, but were also transmission belts of privileges and political clientelism.

During World War II administrative structures were shattered by civil war and the division of Italy. Part of the state bureaucracy fled north to work for the Italian Social Republic (an estimated 15 per cent of *impiegati*). Others ended up at Brindisi and Salerno with the Kingdom of the South. This chaos took years to sort out after 1945, and was made worse by the half-hearted attempts at purging that both failed to get rid of fascist elements in the bureaucracy and yet frightened many innocent *impiegati*. The republican administration system was not revolutionized – many of the employees were the same, and the laws governing bureaucrats remained more or less unchanged. The state's continuing centralization was also a factor in favour of continuity, not change. Post-war attempts to reform this system tended to produce enormous commission reports, but few actual reforms. Meanwhile, the administrative machine linked to para-state organizations continued to grow: INA-Casa (1949), *La Cassa per il Mezzogiorno* (1950), ENI (Ente Nazionale Idrocarburi – National Oil and Gas Company, 1953), and the setting-up of regional governments (see below) created a whole new set of bureaucrats. One key problem remained the lack of a real administrative elite, in part because of inadequate training. Italy never developed the sophisticated training schools of France, Germany or the UK. Whilst a Superior School for Public Administrators was set up in Caserta in 1957, it never achieved the prestige or importance of, for example, the equivalent school in Paris. A small group of intellectuals attacked the 'cancer' of the bureaucracy, but their voices were marginal ones.[43] Too many Italians were part of the state machine, in one way or another, to be able to distance themselves in any realistic way from its growth, its inefficiencies and its huge resources.

Citizens and Bureaucrats: The Culture of Exchange, Clientelism, Citizens and the Italian State

Italians have always asked a lot of the state, and have blamed the state when things have gone wrong. Everything, it sometimes seems, has been the fault of the government, or the state – from earthquakes to poverty to traffic jams. The failure of the state to respond to these high demands was one of the factors, as we have seen, explaining the semi-permanent legitimation crisis after unification. Nowhere was the lack of legitimation so evident as in the day-to-day workings of public services. Yet, the state–citizen relationship was never simply one of perpetuator and victim, or of patron and client. In the first place, millions of Italians worked for the state, or the *parastate*, or were in some way dependent on the state – no clear separation could be made between the 'state' and its citizens. Moreover, many Italians benefited from the largesse of state-related employment. The state, over time, became a formidable producer of patronage, jobs, benefits and security, especially in the south. Wages were usually low, but there were compensations – short hours, long holidays (three months in the summer for teachers, for example), a virtual immunity from dismissal (*il posto fisso* – the secure job), few controls on activity or productivity, 'baby pensions' (for many years certain categories of state employees could 'retire' after only twenty years' service), generous maternity rights and sickness benefits, discounts on a whole range of services. Public employees were undoubtedly privileged when compared with the private sector, but the state also came to the rescue of private companies in trouble, paying the wages of laid-off workers at Fiat, for example, during the crisis of the early 1980s. Thus, to put it simply, the inefficiencies of the state were also created (and maintained) through the consent of state employees and their families.

Secondly, this deformed relationship, which privileged the informal type of approach to the public administration – ranging from the use of friendships, favours, *raccomandazioni* and specialist knowledge right up to straightforward corruption to bypass, warp or speed up administrative procedures – was one broadly accepted by citizens, as well as the state. There was no moral revolt against this system at any time in Italian history. Italians, broadly, not only accepted this way of doing things, but used the system, when they could, to their own advantage. The system had a mass basis. Loopholes, inefficiencies, petty everyday corruptions and clientelist networks allowed millions of Italians to avoid taxes; build illegal kitchens, houses and even whole neighbourhoods; get elected; or hold up trials long enough for them to be abandoned under the Statute of Limitations. This situation could not, therefore, simply be blamed on the state, or on the lack of reform over the years, or on the governing classes. The state was a convenient scapegoat for the problems of Italy, but the responsibility for the failures of the state went far wider, and deeper. An anthropological revolution would be needed to reform a system based on exchange and mutual benefit. Only when the daily procedures linked to clientelism and patronage were rejected, in practice, by the vast majority of Italians would real reform be possible.

THE STRUCTURE OF THE STATE: NATIONAL AND LOCAL INSTITUTIONS

The State at a Local Level: The Prefects

The Italian state's key representative at a local level has, since 1865, been the *Prefect*, a system based on that in operation in France. Prefects, appointed centrally to each city, with Under-Prefects in provincial towns, controlled public order, oversaw elections and the administration and execution of laws, and until the 1880s, appointed local mayors. They also organized provincial councils. Many of the post-unification Prefects were from the north (31 out of 59 Prefects appointed between 1861 and 1871), who often set up their offices in big city-centre palaces. Luigi Torelli in Palermo held fixed hearings (as had happened under the Bourbon regime) and received visitors in the throne room of a Palermitan palace. Prefects also sent a constant stream of information on political movements and events to Rome. Opponents of the centralization of the new state and the policies towards the south attacked the use and organization of the Prefects. Salvemini coined the term 'Prefectocracy' as part of his critique of the Giolittian system of power. Many Prefects were also part of the nominated Senate, thus highlighting their centralizing and political role. Prefects were able to manipulate the electoral process in favour of the government of the day, and their political patrons. At times of emergency, when martial law was declared, the Prefect's powers were taken over by the military. General Bava Beccaris, for example, became Prefect of Milan from 16 May to 1 September 1898. Giolitti used the Prefects as agents of social and political control and as vital sources of information on local events and trends. Giolitti's Prefects were the key to his territorially based political management of Italy.

During the rise of fascism, many Prefects openly sided with the blackshirts, failing to prevent fascist violence and dissolving a series of democratically elected local councils (one well-known example of this was the Prefect of Milan from August 1920 to May 1923, Alfredo Lusignoli). Fascism further politicized the Prefects, moving them around for instrumental reasons. The Prefects were given new status and more power, especially over public order and security issues (as with the 1934 reforms). Some Prefects used their new powers under fascism to carry out wide-ranging public order operations, as with the 'Iron Prefect' Cesare Mori, and his anti-Mafia round-ups in Sicily in the 1920s. Under fascism the Prefect became 'the complete arbiter of the socio-political–administrative life of each province'.[44]

With the fall of fascism, it appeared as if the end was also nigh for the Prefects. A whole range of critics called for the abolition of the Prefects, from liberals (such as Luigi Einaudi) to the Left parties – the Communists, the Socialists and the Action Party. The Prefects were attacked not just for their role under fascism, but also for their position within an anti-democratic and centralized state, which they represented at a local level. For Einaudi (a future President of Italy), writing in 1944, democracy was incompatible with the Prefecture. 'Away with the Prefects!' he wrote, 'Away with all their offices.'[45] Yet, despite widespread support for their abolition, the Prefects survived, mainly through DC (Christian Democrat) inertia. No governing party wanted to deprive itself of the ability to control internal security and the administration through these strong local institutions, particularly in the chaotic social and economic context of the 1940s. Many bureaucrats also supported retaining the Prefects as important elements of continuity with the past. 'If there hadn't been Prefects, we would have had to invent them,' wrote one such administrator (G. Ortolani, 1949).[46] Thus, the Prefects were left out of the Constitution, and left in place, and their reform was entrusted to normal legal processes. The position of Prefect remained the highest and best-paid in the whole Italian administration system. Slowly, some of the more authoritarian powers given by fascism were taken away, although, paradoxically, the state continued to entrust new areas of control and coordination to the Prefects. After World War II a new generation of Prefects were appointed, many of whom had fought in the Resistance. In the mid-to-late 1940s these Prefects were replaced by more moderate administrators. This shift in power often led to protest, as in 1947 in Milan when the Prefect's Palace was occupied by communist militants and ex-partisans in protest at the removal of the ex-partisan Prefect Ettore Troilo.

A hybrid situation was set in place in the various regions, set up by special statutes after 1945. Prefects remained in the Aosta Valley region for public order reasons, but were abolished in favour of 'government commissioners' in Trentino–Alto Adige (after 1949). A constitutional crisis ensued in Sicily in 1951 when the regional council abolished the Prefects in favour of *Procurators*. After a battle with the central state, the Prefects were re-instated in 1955. Prefects remained in place in Sardinia whilst Friuli-Venezia Giulia replaced Prefects with Government Commissioners, who had, in fact, similar powers. Every so often, the argument for the wholesale abolition of the Prefects would re-emerge, particularly from those unhappy with the lack of change brought about by the Constitution. Calamandrei, in 1955, called the Prefects 'unknowing instruments of the governing party who possess practically unlimited discretional powers'.[47] In 1960 the Communist Party again called for the abolition of the Prefects: 'The Prefects have all the real power in this country – they are a state within the state.'[48]

Modern-day Prefects have had much of their power taken away by decentralization reforms, above all with the setting up of new regional governments (in all the regions) in 1970. A government commissioner was appointed for each region to oversee legislation and administrative organization, powers that were previously held by the Prefect. Prefects remained important in the coordination of public order and for certain other administrative functions, but their public profile was far lower than before. More and more decentralization to the regions weakened their power even further, especially after the regionalist movements of the 1980s and 1990s criticized the role of the Prefects and called, once again, for their abolition. The 1999–2000 reforms were a further blow for the Prefects – and there were calls for regional councils to take control of the police and *carabinieri*, thus making the Prefects all but defunct.

The Local State and Local Government

Like all states, the Italian state is a complicated mix of national and local organizations. In Italy, thanks to the strong local political and cultural histories of many regions, cities and towns, and to 'late' unification, the interplay between the regional, the local and the national has been particularly difficult and has occupied a central role in political debate. Unification centralized downwards, from Piedmont through to the rest of Italy, but once Rome was made the capital, government institutions were concentrated there, as much for symbolic reasons (the desire to contrast Italian state power with that of the Church in its own capital) as for political ones. Federalists were marginalized – from Carlo Cattaneo in 1848 through to the Catholic leader Don Sturzo after World War I. Local power was limited to elected local government, there were no regional governments, there was little decentralization of power, and Prefects, based on the French model, were the real authorities in local areas. For most of the Giolittian period, local government, especially in the south, was simply a transmission belt (up and down) for resources, votes and power, with very little autonomy from centralized decision-making.

The procedures of local government were set out in 1865. Every local authority had an elected council, and a general secretary (the head of the local administration). The number of councillors was proportionate to the population. Voters were tax-paying men over 21, who were also limited by other regulations. The local electorate rose from 3.5 per cent in 1865 to 11.2 per cent in 1889. Turnouts rose from 38 per cent to nearly 60 per cent over the same period. Crucially, the mayor was not elected but nominated centrally after 'advice' from councillors and the Prefect. Councils could be dissolved centrally at any time by the king on the orders of the interior minister, and by the Prefect. There were also a series of areas where councils were obliged to provide services, limiting financial autonomy. In 1888–9 Crispi reformed this system. Most importantly, mayors were thereafter to be directly elected in cities with populations of more than 10,000. Beyond city councils lay the provinces, which covered wider areas of territory and took responsibility, in theory, for matters such as planning, the environment, water supply and energy. Provincial councils were set up by Prefects and consisted of a President and elected members. The provinces were also made more autonomous in 1888–9.

Slowly, city governments were given more clout (reforms introduced in 1903 allowed for the muncipalization of certain services), and more ability to intervene from above. By using these moderate powers to the full, socialist local administrations (from Imola in the 1890s through to many other Padanian towns in the early twentieth century, and on to Milan and Bologna in 1914) terrified local middle-class groups. The radical administration of Rome, led by an anti-clerical mason, Ernesto Nathan (1907–13), which municipalized public services, intervened in education and developed public housing, was an important experiment. The Vatican ban on Catholics voting in national elections had never applied to local government. Even mild attempts at redistribution of wealth were opposed with ferocity (see below for the

Molinella experience). None the less, World War I saw wide powers devolved to local administrations to organize supplies and sell price-controlled goods as well as provide services. The 1920 elections were bitterly fought in many areas and narrow socialist victories in Milan and Bologna were the catalyst for massive opposition which coalesced around the fascists. Fascism made socialist local government one of its main targets. The socialist triumph was the beginning of the end for local democracy, right from the tragic events in Bologna in November 1920, where nine people were killed on the day of the inauguration of the new administration, after clashes with local fascists. Between 1920 and 1922, fascist violence imposed the dissolution of local administrations across Italy, and free local elections were not to be held again until 1945–6; 281 councils were dissolved in 1922, 561 in 1923.

Fascism centralized to an even greater extent than Liberal Italy. In 1926 unelected local administrators – known as *podestà* – were nominated by royal decree for up to five years, and replaced elected mayors. The *podestà* were essentially under the control of Prefects. Local councillors (who only had a consultative role) were also nominated by the Prefect and other organizations. Central decisions rode roughshod over any kind of local autonomy. Development schemes (above all in the Lazio flood plains) were imposed upon whole regions from above, or through quasi-technical development corporations. Whole populations were shifted from place to place. Huge quasi-government bodies (above all IRI) directed industrial growth and planning (and many of these bodies were to remain in operation well into the post-war period). Local politics was thus reduced to the management of power-bases by various fascist leaders, or *ras* (Farinacci in Cremona, Turati in Brescia, Giampaoli in Milan, etc.), and to mediation between industrial powers, local interests and central government (which always, without fail, had the final say). None the less, as during the Liberal period, complicated systems of mediation developed between the local and the national, and local elites and pressure groups influenced central and local policy.

With the fall of fascism, a new model was set up for a far less centralized Italian state, partly as an antidote to the concentration of power that had been the *raison d'être* of the fascist state. Local democracy was immediately reintroduced, first in the *comuni* (the first local elections were held, with PR systems and universal suffrage, in 1945–6) and then in the provinces (with the first elections in the early 1950s). Over time, more and more provincial governments were established but this institution never inspired the same level of debate and political mobilization as city councils. Regional pressure and separatist movements forced the new state to act quickly. Special regional governments with wide powers of administration and tax-collection, as well as their own regional capitals, seats of government and presidents, were set up in Sicily (1946), Sardinia (1948), Trentino–Alto Adige (1948) and Valle d'Aosta (1948) almost immediately after liberation. Later, similar regional powers were given to Friuli-Venezia Giulia (1963). Some provinces, such as Trento, were also given special statutes and powers. However, the 1948 Constitution had provided for regional governments in *all* of Italy's regions (laid out in Articles 114–33). Italy's post-war governments, for various reasons, delayed this measure for 25 years. It was only in 1970 that these regions elected presidents and councillors for the first time, under a PR list system. At first, they had little power, but slowly a series of devolution laws were delegated to the regions, including the management of all health care, tourism, and some education and environmental issues (in 1977).

Each region has its own statute, taking into account the specific historical, social and linguistic nature of different areas. Regions can also pass laws in certain areas ('provided that such legislation does not conflict with the interest of the Nation or of other Regions', Article 117, 1948 Constitution), hold referendums and even challenge the central state. Whilst they have never really became popular institutions, the regions are none the less much less unpopular than central government bodies, although a series of problems have emerged concerning planning coordination with the provinces and the *comuni*, finance, and political alliances with the central state. A government commissioner oversees the functioning of each region and examines all laws, and regions can be dissolved on the orders of the president of the Republic when a council has 'acted against the Constitution' or has 'committed serious violations of the law' or for 'reasons of national security' (Article 126). The central state can also send back regional laws to regions for reassessment or modification (see also Box 2.18).

New regionalist movements in the 1980s, 1990s and 2000s challenged the whole basis of central government power and taxation redistribution. Regionalism in the north demanded that tax collected there should be spent *in the north*, not given to 'Rome the thief' or (even worse) to the south (see the Introduction). Federalism (defined in a number of ways – from the *separation* of Italy into different states, to the granting of wider powers to the existing regions) became a widely accepted demand, across all political parties, even by those who had previously been most in favour of a centralized state. More and more powers were delegated to the regions, and the electoral system was changed, making the president of each region directly electable (the first elections under this system were held in 2000). The increased profile of regional presidents made them, for the first time (during the 1990s), major political players nationally and locally. This was true above all of the super-regions in the north – Lombardy, Veneto and Piedmont – economic power-houses in national, European and world terms. For a time, the regionalist parties controlled these institutions, usually in coalition with other centrist organizations. Major reforms devolved more powers in 2000 (passed by the centre–left) and then again in 2002–3 (the centre–right). Major constitutional reforms, passed in 2005 by the centre-right, that would have devolved further powers to the regions (such as policing and educational systems) were never put into practice thanks to a constitutional referendum in 2006. These measures undermined the very basis of central state power, introducing an uneasy balance with the regions, which began to resemble US or German federal states. Many regional governments had become virtual city-states, forging alliances with local business interests in order to favour particular forms of development and political coalitions. Much power had been taken away from the central state, and the likelihood was that yet more federalist reforms

Box 2.18   The performance of Italian regional government: the Putnam debate

Robert Putnam's influential book *Making Democracy Work* (1993) opened up debates concerning the *performance* of Italian regional government. Putnam's research, based on interviews with government officials, politicians and citizens, looked at a number of regions all over Italy. The key question asked was 'What are the conditions for creating strong, responsive, effective representative institutions?' Through an analysis of these interviews, other measurements of performance, and historical studies, Putnam came to the conclusion that the performance of regions in the centre and north of Italy was far superior to that of similar institutions in the south. This unsurprising conclusion was, however, explained through a series of long-run historical arguments. The 'social capital' of civicness, of trust and of collaboration was far greater in the centre–north than in the south, thanks to hundreds of years of certain kinds of state–citizen relationships and political and social cultural norms. In short, 'in the north, people were citizens, in the south, they were subjects' (Putnam, 1993, p. 130). The south was the un-Tocquevillian part of Italy. Minimal levels of public trust prevented effective government. Southern society was characterized by 'mutual distrust and defection, vertical dependence and exploitation, isolation and disorder, criminality and backwardness [which] have reinforced one another in … interminable vicious circles', whilst northern society was made up of 'a dense network of local associations, by active engagement in community affairs, by egalitarian patterns of politics, by trust and law-abidingness' (Putnam, 1993, p. 182).

There are many problems with this type of conclusion. First, Putnam adheres to an outdated idea of the south that fails to take into account the complicated nature of the *mezzogiorno* and the important new historical work that has deconstructed prevailing ideas of 'the south'. Secondly, Putnam utilizes categories of analysis (such as Banfield's 'amoral familism', see Introduction) which are either obsolete or, in many cases, also applicable to northern society. In particular, the social and cultural development of the north and above all the north-east over the last twenty years would seem to directly contradict Putnam's conclusions. It should also be noted that, just as Putnam's book was being published, a huge corruption scandal, affecting all levels of political society including the regions, was exposed in Milan and other parts of the north. The 'south = corruption' equation simply does not hold in contemporary Italy. Increasingly, in the 2000s, it became clear that criminal organizations had a large presence in the north of Italy. Finally, there is an exaggeration of the role of the rather nebulous concepts of 'social capital' and 'trust' as crucial factors in the effectiveness of government and society.

would strip Rome of more and more management and tax-collecting powers. Corruption scandals in many of these regions, however, undermined the claim that federalism had somehow solved problems supposedly created by a gargantuan and centralized state machine. The suspicion was that federalism had merely increased opportunities for clientelistic and corrupt networks to take root.

Europe and the State[49]

A further key centralization/de-centralization of the Italian state occurred with its involvement with Europe. Italy was one of the main players behind European integration, both through the involvement of key European thinkers (above all Altiero Spinelli) and through political initiative, especially that of the DC. Italy was a signatory to the first European treaty in 1951 (the European Iron and Steel Community) and to the Treaty of Rome in 1957 (one of only six original nations). As such, Italy has enjoyed a central political and economic role in the development of the Common Market and the European Union. 'Europe' has always been extremely popular within Italy and these moves have always had the support of the vast majority of the Italian people. Italy signed up for all subsequent treaties, thereby – as with the other countries in the EU – effectively giving up sovereign power in many areas to European institutions and European law. There was very little debate about these developments in Italy. The low level of popularity and legitimacy of national institutions is one key explanation for this 'lack', as is a low level of attachment to anything we can call the Italian nation, and to the Italian currency, the lira, which disappeared almost without comment at the end of 2001, as Italy joined the euro (but see Box 3.8).

This central role has allowed Italy to obtain some of the most important political posts within the EU, from Franco Maria Malfatti as president of the European Commission in the 1970s (1970–2) to Romano Prodi's appointment to the same post in 1999. In 2011, at the height of the global finance and debt crisis within and outside of the eurozone, ex-European commissioner Mario Monti was appointed as prime minister, as head of a technical government. Many commentators claimed that this new government was formed under pressure from the EU, and from the German and French governments in particular.

European elections, whilst eliciting high turnouts, have always been fought on national political platforms, and not around European issues, and the activities of the European Parliament have never gained more than token coverage in the Italian press and other mass media. Invariably, the major party leaders stand for, and get elected to, the European Parliament (which has maintained its PR system of elections), and then very rarely attend the Parliament itself. This marginalization of the political role of Europe has been a constant ever since the first European elections in the 1970s, although Italy has always been very sensitive towards any criticism of its internal politics from within Europe, and has always milked the system to obtain as much European funding as possible, especially for its poorer regions. European political alliances have been important as forms of legitimation for parties under pressure domestically.

In Italian and European law, Italy has one of the worst records of all EU nations in terms of compliance and ratification. It also maintains a number of laws on its statute books that are palpably out of line with European law, such as the insistence that European residents should still obtain a 'permission of stay' certificate from the local police – a *permesso di soggiorno*. Italy's (lack of) effective tax collection procedures and huge black economy have also created problems with its European partners, as has the widespread (and erroneous) belief that Italy, with its so-called 'porous' borders, is soft on immigrants and has a lax immigration policy.

European agreements have also had a profound influence on domestic Italian politics. This was especially true with the treaty that sanctioned the setting up of a single European currency, ratified at Maastricht in 1992. Italy found it very difficult to meet the entry requirements for the euro and successive governments were forced into 'tax and cut' policies to force down the public debt. These austerity measures not only increased support for anti-taxation parties, especially the *Lega*, but also implied that the old, generous and corrupt welfare state and partitocratic system had to be reformed, or perish. One of the factors that made the *Tangentopoli* scandals possible (1992–4) was precisely the inability of the state and the political system to survive in the old, wasteful way. A political class came crumbling down and the new governors of Italy, who steered the country through the period of entry into the euro, were well-respected financial managers – Amato, Dini, Ciampi, Prodi, Monti (three internationally renowned economists, and two former presidents of the *Banca d'Italia*). The importance of euro-entry was not lost even on the far-left grouping *Rifondazione comunista*, who diligently voted through the all-important 1997 budget, before bringing down Prodi's *Ulivo* coalition over a much weaker austerity package the following year. Public disquiet over tax increases (including a tax on all bank accounts and a special *Eurotax*, which was designed to be paid back) was tempered by widespread support for the euro and European unity. Very few Italians shed a tear for the lira in 2001, a currency that had never become a symbol of national unity or inspired affection in the ways that the dollar or the pound sterling have historically done.

Yet, the euro itself was never popular in Italy, and was widely blamed for a fall in living standards in the 2000s. Anti-euro and anti-European rhetoric became more mainstream in the 1990s and 2000s, starting from the edges of the system (the *Lega*) before being taken up by Silvio Berlusconi, the leader of the centre–right coalition. Anti-political movements, and in particular Beppe Grillo's Five Star MoVement, have called for a referendum on the euro in opposition to the policies of the technocratic Monti government (2011–13), which were seen, with some reason, as being imposed from Brussels and Berlin. For the first time since the war, anti-European ideas were taking root in Italy, partly as a reflection of the collapse of the party system and the increasing hegemony of anti-political tendencies. Europe and its association with the social-democratic post-war consensus (high taxes, redistribution, regulation) came increasingly under attack from populists in the Italian political system. The centre–left were natural allies of the European project, and identified strongly with both the institutions and the outlook of the EU and the eurozone.

3

Economy and Society

CONTENTS

DEBATES AROUND THE ITALIAN ECONOMY AND ITALIAN SOCIETY: FOUR THEMES

Italy and 'Backwardness'

The Italian economy has, at least until the 1980s, traditionally been seen as 'backward', 'late' or 'behind' that of other countries. Italy had a 'late' and 'incomplete' industrial revolution, it never developed a 'proper' industrial society and it never possessed a 'real' industrial working class. Other writers have described the whole of southern Europe, including Italy, as 'semi-peripheral'.[1] In reality, Italy's economic history was not simply late, or simply backward, but *different* from that of other countries. Italy's first industrial revolution did not, for example, create an industrial society like those of Germany, the US or the UK, but it did transform the Italian economy and Italian society. Italy went through a 'slow' or 'soft' industrial revolution where rural labour remained important and the processes linked to mass migration of various kinds were crucial. This form of industrial revolution laid the basis for a rapid transformation to a post-industrial economy in the 1980s and 1990s. Italy has always been compared with other, different models of industrial development. The UK model of a complete industrial revolution was one. But there was also the 'Prussian Model', whereby Germany combined late unification and state intervention with rapid industrial growth. Italy created a new model, but the features of these other 'roads' of development permeate the work of all those who have tried to locate Italy within world economic history. Models are important not just for history, but also for historians. Italy has also been placed, uneasily, within a south European model of 'late' economic development combined with extensive state intervention, weak market presence and a strong tendency towards dictatorship – with Spain, Portugal, Greece and Turkey.

Statistically, Italy was clearly behind the major industrial economies after unification. In 1861 Italy's per capita income was only 60 per cent that of France and half that of Great Britain.[2] This gap was not made up after unification, apart from the period between the end of the nineteenth century and World War I. If we include other indicators of 'backwardness', such as education levels and life expectancy, 'Italy was an unmistakeably backward country' in 1870.[3] But 'backwardness', as many economists and historians have pointed out, can bring advantages. Italy could call on huge and cheap supplies of unskilled labour – a supply described as 'infinite';[4] it was able to develop a mix of big and small industry that allowed for a smoother transition between various industrial 'phases'. Finally, Italy was able to preserve links between industry, rural society and agriculture that were shattered in other nations. Clearly there have been problems, which have prevented the much-vaunted 'catching-up' of Italy – illiteracy, dualism, pre-modern agricultural methods, a lack of skilled labour, suffocating links between the state and industry. It is often claimed that Italy has also been lacking in 'pro-capitalist' ideologies. The two mass cultural organizations working within the civil, political and economic spheres – the Church and socialism – were not capitalist supporters, and many within these organizations were opposed to the structures created by capitalist economics.

Dualism and the 'Southern Question'

Italy's economic history has always been linked to discussions of the 'southern question'. If Italy was 'late' on the industrial scene, the blame lay largely with the underdeveloped south – her ball and chain. Recent historical work has begun to question this dominant interpretation of Italian development. Yet the idea of a backward south dominated political life for much of the nineteenth and twentieth centuries – the concepts of *uneven development* and *dualism* remained at the heart of economic analysis of Italy for 140 years. Many solutions were proposed to the 'southern question' – state-financed development, emigration, tariff reform, colonialism, special legislation and industrial relocation. None of these proposals succeeded in industrializing the south, but they all profoundly affected the development of the *mezzogiorno* from unification onwards.

The State

The relationship between the state and the economy, between the public and private sectors, has always been a crucial aspect of Italian economic history. The complicated interplay between state investment, state banking and private industry has patterned the Italian economy. The state has always been a major economic player and some claim that it has been *the* major economic agent. Giulio Sapelli argues that one of the defining features of southern European countries has, in fact, been 'the overwhelming presence of the state in social and economic life'.[5]

The Pace of Change

A final, general question relates to the speed of economic change in Italy. Over the twentieth century, Italy has experienced mass emigration (of 27 million Italians), extensive internal migrations, the rapid rise and fall of a Fordist industrial economy, the virtual disappearance of whole categories of rural economic enterprises (sharecroppers, *latifondi*, day-labourers) and then of the Fordist industrial workforce. As such, Italy has represented an 'extraordinary laboratory of social and economic change'[6] where industrial and social revolutions were crushed into restricted periods of time.

The very brevity of some of these 'moments' in Italy, and their intensity, contributed to the astonishing power of organized labour and other opposition forces. In turn, these forces also shaped the economic development of Italy. Industry responded to revolt and opposition with its own strategies of change, incorporation and repression. The economy and its development should not be seen as purely the work of landowners, capitalists and politicians. Yet, in other ways and at other times, Italy's development was slow and measured, with the co-habitation of different economic forms and models. Italy was a combination of models, just as it should be seen as a mix of 'northern' and 'southern' characteristics.

ECONOMIC AND SOCIAL ITALIES: COUNTRY, CITY, INDUSTRY

This chapter will draw a picture of the economic history of Italy via a journey through her various sectors. This journey begins in the countryside.

Rural Italy

It can be said that there is by now an industrial and commercial Italy. An agricultural Italy does not yet exist; there are many different agricultural Italies thanks to the great and varied influence of the different climates which are found from the Alps to the Lilibeo and the huge variety of moral, historical, administrative, legislative traditions – which vary greatly from region to region.

STEFANO JACINI ('PROEMIO', INCHIESTA AGRARIA, 1882)

For most of Italy's history, the majority of her citizens have lived and worked in rural areas. The economic forms of this work and habitat were closely linked to cultural, social and territorial structures. The Italian 'peasantry' was never a united force, in any sense. One testimony to this was the wide variety of terms used to describe various types of peasants – 'poor', 'rich', 'middle', 'landless' and so on.[7] Only those ignorant of the reality of rural Italy could possibly see the peasantry as a united bloc. Those who worked on the land were divided in a myriad ways. Territorially, 'peasants' differed from farm to farm, valley to valley and region to region. Peasants on the *latifondi* (great estates) in Sicily were a world away, culturally and in their relation to capitalism, from the day-labourers of the Po Valley, or the fixed-wage rural workers (*salariati fissi*) of the dairy farms around Cremona. Sharecropping contracts varied from area to area. In Apulia and Sicily peasants were grouped in agro-towns, elsewhere they often lived on the land they worked. Female rice-workers migrated vast distances for seasonal work in Piedmont and Emilia. Payment might be in cash, or in kind, or a mixture of both. Some contracts were collective, others individual. Some were written, others verbal. Sometimes middlemen were involved, sometimes not. Women's work varied across regions and farms. The peasant's relationship with the town and the landowner varied greatly across time and space. Landowners were often completely absent, but at other times virtually omnipresent. Rural Italy was thus a complicated mosaic.

In addition to these structural and economic variegations, which were often dictated by the conditions of fertility and markets, other traditions were imposed upon this complex map. There were the diverse political and religious histories, the historical legacies of revolt or passivity, and the strength and weaknesses of the family. In some areas modern capitalist productive relations were introduced into the countryside (most notably across the Po Valley, in Bassa Lombardia and on the Apulian plains) but capitalist farms often existed side by side with more traditional sharecropping systems and small-landholders.

The most controversial structures of rural Italy were the great estates in the south – the *latifondi*.

The Great Estates: *Latifondi*

Large parts of the rural south, since feudal times, had been dominated by great landed estates, known as *latifondi*. *Latifondi* cut across Sicily, Calabria, Lazio and Apulia, but were not necessarily linked to *backward* systems of agriculture. In Apulia, modern techniques were employed by those managing the great estates in the early twentieth century. Often run by absentee landlords, through middlemen and intricate structures of authority and hierarchy, the *latifondi* were complete social systems. Peasants working on the *latifondi* were given job security, and often tiny pockets of land, in return for a semi-feudal relationship with the landlord and a near-complete lack of social rights. For years, the *latifondi* were the political enemy of many southernists, the epitome of backwardness, waste and ancient economic practice. Salvemini declared 'war on the *latifondo*'. For the Sicilian socialist Sebastiano Cammareri Scurti, 'we see the problem of the *latifondo*, for Sicily and for the whole of the South, as the *problem of problems*'. The great estates were not capitalist farms – and in fact could not survive under capitalism.[8] It was only with the peasant struggles of the 1940s and 1950s and the Christian Democrat land reforms that the *latifondi* finally disappeared from the Italian scene. 'Latifondist society and economy disappeared utterly within a few years and left scarcely a trace.'[9]

Various solutions were proposed to this 'problem of problems'. The first, and most simple, was to divide the land up amongst the peasants – creating a massive class of small proprietors. This 'solution' was favoured by Catholic peasant organizations, and many southern democrats, but was opposed by, for example, many socialists (who believed such a class would inevitably become reactionary), and (obviously) by the *latifondi* owners and other southern elites. Division of the land was also the favoured solution to the problems of Spain's great estates at the same time. Crispi proposed radical reforms to the great estate systems in the wake of the Sicilian *Fasci* movement in the 1890s, but his plans were suffocated by the political and social power of big landowners politically and socially. Giolitti ruled in alliance with the political representatives of the *latifondisti* during the early twentieth century.

Millions of *latifondi* peasants simply left Italy altogether as their dreams of change faded: 1.5 million Sicilians departed between 1876 and 1925; 25 per cent of *all* Sicilians emigrated in the twenty years before World War I; 146,000 Sicilians emigrated in 1913 alone. This movement began to change the *latifondi* in unexpected ways. Cash remittances from the USA and elsewhere allowed many peasants at home to buy land on the *latifondi* for the first time. A kind of 'peasant latifundism' began to develop in Sicily and other zones where the great estates had dominated.[10] Cultural changes were also introduced through the more radical attitudes of the 30–50 per cent of Sicilians who returned, either permanently or periodically. These *americani* were unwilling to accept the old ways of life on the *latifondi*. They had seen a new world, and wanted it established in Italy.

After World War I, mass land occupations in the south were an expression of the desire of southern peasants both for land and for the end of the *latifondi* system. Many ex-soldiers joined organizations calling for agrarian reform and for the promises of land, made during the war, to be met. Here was a chance for a revolutionary end to the great estates, but the socialists never contemplated a worker–peasant alliance along the lines of the 1917 Russian–Bolshevik model. Instead of calling for 'land to the peasants', the Italian Left proposed 'socialization', which sounded suspiciously like a socialist version of the great estates.[11]

Latifondo power was finally broken, in the south, by the peasant movements of the post-1944 period, and thanks to the reforms of the early 1950s. In May 1950, the Christian Democrats pushed through the most ambitious programme of land reform in Italian history. Land was to be taken away from big landowners and distributed to peasants. Two types of farms were created: the *podere* (small farm) for landless peasants, and the *quota* (which gave more land to those who had small plots). Land was not simply given in most cases, but had to be paid for in thirty instalments. All peasants on the scheme had to join cooperatives. Special state institutions were set up across the south to administer the reforms, assign the land and provide technical and financial assistance. Over the first ten years in which it was in operation, the law distributed 417,000 hectares of land (not only in the south, but also in large zones of Tuscany). Other measures encouraged the simple purchase of land by small landowners. A further 450,000 hectares were transferred in this way. By the

1960s, the *latifondi* were no more, and the agro-towns were under threat as the reform encouraged peasants to live on their farms. It was no surprise that a group of mainly southern DC deputies ran a vigorous campaign against the reforms, mobilizing some 72 deputies. The centuries-old dream of land had become reality for many peasant families: 113,000 new family farms were created, of which 89,000 were in the south. In Sicily in 1947, 1 per cent of property owners owned half of the arable land; by 1962 this had fallen to one-third.

Yet, the reform's effects were watered down for a number of reasons. Landowners often avoided expropriation through the division of the land amongst their own families. In Sicily, 75 per cent of families who had a right to land received none. Big landowners also used the law's ambiguities to keep their land (making marginal improvements to avoid the designation of their land as 'unimproved'). In addition, the land transferred was usually poor and many quickly abandoned their plots, or used them for subsistence purposes only. Finally, the administrative boards were without peasant representatives and were powerful transmission belts for the Christian Democrats, transferring resources *down* and votes *up*, to and from the central administration. The DC, in this way, became a key decentralized institution across the south.

As Piero Bevilacqua has concluded, the 1950 laws were 'one of the great reforms of the post-war period, thanks to which the Italian republic put down roots of consensus in the countryside [but which] also served to deepen the hegemony of one party and to intensify the private and clientelistic use of public power', and 'the reform had an important social role [but] a limited economic effect'.[12] The effects were, undeniably, conservative – neutralizing the collective aims of the land occupation movement and feeding the familism of southern society. Finally, reforms were also out of time, economically and culturally. Land was distributed just as Italy became an industrial society and just as the old rural Italy was on the verge of disappearance, and the old desire for 'land' was being replaced by new, consumerist aspirations. Millions of southern peasants, disillusioned, left for the northern cities. Mass migration, once again, was the response of the southern people to the failures of political reform, but this time the destinations were Milan, Turin and Genoa, not New York, Buenos Aires or Toronto.

The *latifondi* were also important in the birth and development of the Mafia. Many historians have identified Sicilian *latifondi* managers – known as *gabellotti* – who exercised control over violence within the southern and Sicilian great estates, as the first incarnations of Mafia use of private violence. This type of private violence was also to be found on the *latifondi* of Calabria. The *latifondi* created and reflected a particular kind of southern agrarian landscape and patterns of settlement. Peasants lived in agro-towns (for historical reasons to do mainly with safety and access to water) and were not spread out in farms across the land. Male day-labourers across the south were still being recruited at dawn, with verbal contracts, in the 1950s and 1960s. Once taken on, usually for the day, they faced the long walk to and from work. At harvest time these peasants would often sleep rough on the land or in simple shacks. This was the 'great social disaggregation' described by Antonio Gramsci in his seminal 'Notes on the Southern Question' (1926).

Recent historical work has attempted to reassess the old interpretation of the *latifondi* as entirely wasteful and antiquated economic entities. Marta Petrusewicz's influential research on the biggest *latifondo* in Calabria, that owned by the Barocco family, underlines the advantages of the great estates for the peasants, who were guaranteed employment, credit, services and mediation. The system survived for so long thanks to the provision of collective security and networks of exchange, which formed a 'rational' moral economy, a kind of 'social pact'.[13] The *latifondi* collapsed because the move towards capitalism and the market removed these services, allowing for hiring and firing, and thereby ending the mediation built into the system. 'In its eighty years of existence *latifondismo* had successfully blended the traditional and the modern, in its own autonomous rationality.'[14] Petrusewicz's work, which has provoked much historical debate, has been accused of generalizing from a specific case, and of exaggerating the exchange aspects of the *latifondo* system. Yet, this thesis has the great merit of helping us to break away from a static and politicized version of the history of the *latifondo*, and also from the constant equation, in most of the literature, between Sicily, feudalism, the great estates, absentee landlords and the Mafia (for this kind of account see Box 3.1). The *latifondi* were not merely a Sicilian phenomenon, and cannot be dismissed simply as the most extreme example of southern agricultural backwardness and irrationality.[15]

Beyond the Great Estates: Sharecropping in Central Italy

Sharecropping had deep historical roots in central Italy, being widespread from at least the sixteenth century onwards and represented an alternative form of land ownership and management. Rent was paid in kind, constituting a fixed proportion of the crop – usually half (*mezzo* = half). Sharecroppers worked the land *as families*, and by employing casual labour at key moments throughout the year. The sharecropping family inhabited a house on the land – which was the property of the landowner. This balanced system survived right up until the 1950s and 1960s, when it was finally abandoned in favour of straightforward ownership or rent, and when many sharecroppers, and in particular their children, migrated to the cities. Sharecropping was particularly important in central Italy, above all in Emilia, Tuscany, Umbria and the Marche. Landowners often preferred sharecropping to straight land rental, as it allowed them a considerable degree of control over the form and content of production, and meant that they could off-load the costs of crises (and labour) onto sharecroppers. However, sharecropping did not encourage investment in the land and conflicts emerged continually over who was to pay for land improvement, machinery and technical change. Property-owners often encouraged their sharecroppers to grow lucrative cash crops, whilst sharecroppers were more interested in subsistence produce which would see them through the winter in times of crisis. Landowners relied on sharecropper/ day-labourer divisions to maintain their privileged position in the countryside, as well as on the reluctance of the state to modernize sharecropping contracts, in order to at least remove some of their more 'feudal' elements.[16]

Box 3.1   Emilio Sereni and the *latifondi*

Emilio Sereni's important analysis of the *latifondi* (published for the first time in 1947), and of agrarian Italy in general, played a key part in Marxist accounts of rural Italy, and was taken up by many history textbooks. Sereni, inspired by the work of Gramsci, identified what he called 'the residues of feudalism' in the *latifondi* system – especially in Sicily – including cultural hierarchies, private police forces, wasteful crop rotation and absentee landlords. Peasants were subject to a series of duties and petty taxes throughout the year, and a system of person-alized and oppressive social and economic duties. For Sereni, writing in the 1940s, 'the [*latifondo*] still appears as an economic and administrative unit her-metically closed to the outside world. The cash economy played little part in the internal life of the *latifondo*, where most payments were in kind. Women worked at home, but not on the land. Peasants lived in agro-towns and men were faced with long journeys to work. Water was scarce, investment even more so. This system, and the hereditary laws, forced women into a position of extreme exclu-sion and oppression, a situation made worse when capitalism began to sweep away domestic work and substitute traditional home-based activities, such as bread production. In other *latifondi* areas, beyond Sicily, capitalism had made more inroads into the rural economy, introducing money-based economic rela-tionships. Sereni identified the Mafia as a rural phenomenon, originating in the systems of private violence on the *latifondi* and the armed middlemen, or *gabellotti*, who ran the estates for their absentee owners. For Pino Arlacchi 'labour had to be kept in conditions of constant struggle, insecurity and depend-ence in order to assure the owners that peculiar market set-up which made the *latifondo* profitable'. Elsewhere, rural systems were in desperate need of public investment before they could be properly farmed. On the Agro plains of Lazio, at the end of the nineteenth century, there were

> a few enormous farms, whose names – Casal della Morte, Campomorto, Pantano, Malafede – remind us of the inglorious days of malaria and feudal violence: men dressed in dirty sheep skins, mounted on wild horses, drove buffalo through the ditches, and guided the herds across the desolate plain. For miles around there was not even a house, or a place to stay. Every so often, you came across a Roman tomb or a feudal castle inhabited by a wild people: on the steps you saw naked children, with their bellies swollen, and men, women and old people shivering as the sun went down: they all bore the mark, the unmistakable sign of the fever, the ancient god, the unrelenting queen of the Agro. (Sereni, *Il capitalismo*, p. 167).

For the historian Emilio Sereni sharecroppers represented an outdated form of rural production and an obstacle to progress. He saw sharecropping as a form of transition from pre-capitalist to capitalist agriculture, which none the less encouraged stable links to the land. Sereni criticized the paternalistic features of sharecropping systems, where the whole family worked, and the control mechanisms exercised over the family by the landowner, who decided who could work the land and gave permission for marriage (marriage was a way of extending a family's land, or of increasing the workforce). There was, in sharecropping systems, 'a continuous intervention of the employer in the internal life of the employed'.[17] These clauses were enshrined in the civil codes of the Italian legal system from 1865 onwards. Most historians claim that sharecropping held back the formation of a national market and of a cash economy.

In sharecropping areas, landowner surveillance covered what was grown, farming techniques and the sale of produce. Landowners would sometimes demand a room for themselves in sharecropping homes to use when they pleased and would send their representatives, such as an official 'weigher', to check that their share was fairly calculated. They usually reserved the right to inspect the farmhouse at any time. Sharecropping families were obliged to present landowners with numerous gifts throughout the year, especially on religious festivals or at other occasions of celebration, and had to work for free when asked to do so. Some of these features resembled feudal norms. Sharecroppers were especially vulnerable to bad harvests, when they were often forced to borrow from unscrupulous moneylenders or from the landowner himself just to buy in enough food to survive the winter. During bad times, sharecroppers might try to hide food or falsify the crop produced so as to claw back profits from the landowner. For some, the share-cropper's subordinate situation was akin to that of the working class: 'the sharecropper faced the new century as a "proletarian" more with regard to his social position (isolation, poverty, oppression) than with regard to relationships of production'.[18] Above all, it was relatively easy for sharecroppers to be evicted, and defence against this sanction was one of their key demands. Sharecroppers also resented the short-term contracts they were forced to sign (usually lasting only a year, from 1 November to 31 October) and the 'humiliating'[19] sense of power that the landowner held over them. Yet, this power relationship was not unilateral, and involved exchanges of resources. *Mezzadri* families relied on landowners to intervene on their behalf with the state and in legal matters. This type of patronage was an important resource in nineteenth- and early twentieth-century Italy.

Internally, the sharecropper family was based around rigid hierarchical systems, which were established around gender and age. At the top of the family was the male head, known as a *reggitore* (in Emilia) or a *capoccia* (in Tuscany). This man signed the contract with the landowner, organized work systems and had the final say over all disputes within the family. The *reggitore* was in charge of all relationships with the outside world – he represented the family politically, socially and culturally. Finally, he appointed various members of the family to different tasks, such as the man responsible for the management of the farm animals (known as the *bifolco*). All family members worked in specialized areas, which changed as they became older, both inside and outside of the house, and over the agricultural season. These extended, patriarchal families none the less had strong female figures within their midst. The head of the female part of the family was also given a title (*reggitrice* in Tuscany, *massaia* in Emilia) – she took charge of the women in the family. This individual was not always the wife of the family-leader. Catholics supported sharecropping as a form of mediation between labour and capital, and for its reliance upon the family unit. They saw sharecropping as 'a real society, in which the social quota of one side is the land and its intelligent direction; on the other work and some capital, which circulates: the product is equally divided between the two sides' (Luigi Strati).[20] Sharecropping was therefore a system that fitted well with 'the Christian spirit'.[21] Catholic unions had great success organizing sharecroppers in separate organizations before and after World War I. However, the bitter class struggles of 1919–20, when many sharecroppers allied with rural labourers against the landowners, cut against the grain of this idyllic picture of sharecropping.

Fascism, as with the *latifondi*, helped to prolong the life of the sharecroppers through its 'ruralization' policies, whilst shifting the power which had been lost during the struggles of 1919–20 back to the landowners. After 1945 the sharecroppers won massive concessions from the landowners, including compensation for war damage, a bigger share of the crop and guaranteed investment. Yet this victory was a hollow one. The lure of the towns soon became overwhelming in the 1950s and 1960s, and the prospect of a share-cropping life was not attractive to young people with scooters, cars and access to mass cultural forms. Millions left to work in Bologna, Florence, Perugia and Ancona. Landowners sold up. New sharecropping contracts were outlawed in 1964. All residual *mezzadria* contracts were wiped out by the end of the 1970s. Yet, the sharecropping family business ethic (and individualist spirit) helped to produce quality agricultural production across central Italy, and provided the cultural and economic basis for the vast networks of small, flexible, rural-based family businesses which dominate the Tuscan, Umbrian, Emilian and Marche countryside today. Production moved into the lucrative areas of wine, cheese and ham, products now famous throughout the world.[22] Many sharecropping farms were sold to foreign tourists as holiday homes, or converted into agro-tourist restaurants or hotels. The memory of the sharecropping system, the rules and regulations and cultures linked to the peasant way of life and the struggles of the twentieth century, was kept alive through popular songs, oral history and, in some cases, the development of popular theatre dedicated to the representation of sharecropping traditions. In the two decades after World War II, a way of life that had survived for thousands of years had disappeared from the countryside, but the legacy of sharecropping continued to shape the structures of central Italy in profound and complicated ways.

An Italian Vendée? The Small Landowners

As well as the landless peasants on the great estates, and sharecroppers who rented their farms, there were also those who owned their own land.[23] Small proprietors often struggled to keep their land, and were prey to moneylenders and judicial expropriation, especially in the south. They were in desperate need of credit banks and cooperatives as support. Small property lay at the heart of debates over land reform throughout the history of Italy. Some saw the division of the land, and especially of the *latifondi*, as the only way to reform the conservative, feudal-type aspects of the agrarian systems in Italy. This was the position of the Catholics, who exalted small property and included such proposals in their political and social programmes. Don Sturzo wanted to 'bind man to the land' and the Catholic Popular Party in 1920 vowed to 'conserve, reorder and protect small property', which they thought of as 'sacred'. Catholics dubbed small property 'the backbone of all new social organisation' in 1920.[24] Modest versions of this ideological position were put into practice in 1919 (with a decree which handed small amounts of land to landless peasants), after 1921, when a Catholic was briefly minister for agriculture, and above all with the 1950 agrarian reforms. Fascist policies encouraged small property, especially on its reclamation projects, but did not break up the *latifondi*. Others who supported the divisions of the great estates included some liberals, some southern socialists, and isolated intellectuals and politicians. However, there was vast opposition to the creation of a *new* class of small landed property-owners. Socialists drew a distinction between 'natural' small property, which was already there, and 'artificial' small property, created by dividing the big estates. The socialist Nino Mazzoni argued in 1920 that 'the *latifondo* has, in its tendencies and technical abilities, a tremendous social logic, an adaptation to the conditions of the land, to the climate, to the environment'.[25] Many socialists saw small proprietors as necessarily conservative and counter-revolutionary, an Italian *vendée*, and as uneconomic. On this point they were supported by many liberals and, of course, by the powerful landowning elites in the south.

A huge leap in small landed-property-ownership took place around the time of World War I. In the rural Italy of 1911 the make-up of rural classes was as follows: 41 per cent were day-labourers, 7 per cent were *obbligati* (workers occupied in *cascine*, see below), 21 per cent were sharecroppers, 10 per cent were tenants and 21 per cent small landholders. By 1921 the numbers of day-labourers had decreased to 35 per cent of the active rural population, *obbligati* had fallen to 3 per cent, sharecroppers to 18 per cent and tenants to 8 per cent. The only category to increase in percentage terms between 1911 and 1921 were the small property-owners, who rose by 14 per cent to 35 per cent.[26] Socialist unions were so alarmed by this tendency in Lombardy that they ran a 'don't buy' campaign amongst their peasant members after the war. As Rossi argued in 1931, 'in Italy after 1914, the people of a vast region took possession of land which they had cultivated and hankered after for centuries ... nearly to the surprise of everyone, there took place one of the many silent revolutions which Italy, over many centuries of history, has had occasion to witness'.[27] An important contribution to the rise of fascism came from these new landowners, who were desperate to maintain hold of their recently acquired property.[28]

Occupying the Land: Individuals and Collectives

If the peasants were not to be given land, and could not afford to buy it, they were more than ready to take it. Seizure of land was a traditional form of rural protest and there had been invasions in different parts of the peninsula in 1647, 1789, 1820, 1848, 1860, 1892 and 1904. Two great waves of land occupations swept through the south of Italy in the wake of the two world wars, between 1919 and 1922 and then in the 1940s and early 1950s.

1919–22

Peasant-soldiers were promised land during World War I, and on return from the front they began to take it for themselves. Land occupations began in Lazio in 1915 and exploded across the south and Sicily in 1919–20. In August 1919 in Lazio there were invasions of the land in more than 100 of the small towns and villages in the province of Rome (more than 25,000 hectares were involved). Most of the occupations, at least in the south, were the work of nascent ex-combatant organizations, or were spontaneous. Occupations varied from region to region. Sometimes they were violent. Usually the land taken was not 'unused' but was the best, cultivated land, and ancient disputes about ownership were frequently involved. Buildings, machinery and animals were also seized. Many invasions were ceremonial, mobilizing thousands of people, who marched behind flags to band music. Yet, in other cases, the land was also held for some time and farmed collectively. Thus some occupations were symbolic, involving claims for work, not land (by 'day-labourers'), while others were more 'real', working the land and demanding ownership. This latter type tended to be more revolutionary and involved greater violence. For example, at Civitavecchia (Corneto Tarquinia) in Lazio, 900 peasants invaded communal land in 1919 and utilized it for farming and grazing. Crops grown there were later sold. The intervention of the army brought this particular occupation to a bloody end.

The extent of these occupations should not be exaggerated. Serpieri estimated in 1930 that a total of 50,000 hectares were occupied in 1919–21, with the highest figures in Sicily. Salvemini has calculated that 74,000 hectares were taken without consent and a further 172,000 by 'agreement', out of a total land area of 74,000,000 hectares (much of which was uncultivable).[29] Outside of Lazio and Sicily, invasions were sporadic and small-scale, and never approached the extent of the movement for land in the south after World War II. But there was an ever-present threat to the control of the landowners across much of Italy in 1919 and especially 1920. The psychological shock of the invasions was far greater than their actual impact upon landowner power. Landowners were occasionally taken prisoner by angry peasants. Generally, the socialists and rural unions were suspicious of these movements. Gramsci attacked the futility of land occupation without state support and investment. Occupations could only 'satisfy the primitive thirst for land [of the peasant]'; without help, however, the occupier 'turns into a bandit, not a revolutionary'.[30]

1944–51

Once again, it was war that provoked land occupations in the south in the 1940s. Yet, once again, the desire for land was extremely deep-rooted. Spontaneous occupations began in 1944, in some ways aided by a series of decrees pushed through by the Communist agriculture minister, Fausto Gullo, in July 1944. These measures promoted the occupation of unused land and restricted eviction. The laws insisted that the peasants were organized collectively, into cooperatives or committees. Between 1944 and 1949, 1,187 cooperatives were set up with a membership of more than a quarter of a million southern peasants. Gullo's decrees have been depicted as innovative examples of 'non-reformist reforms', which called for active, collective organization from the peasants of the south. Left-wing parties were deeply involved in the organization and promotion of the occupations, and in debates over the reform of the labour market. The opposition was violent, especially in Sicily, where many union leaders were murdered in the 1940s and the Mafia organized a massacre of peasants (at Portella della Ginestra, in May 1947) to intimidate the movement. Court decisions also invariably went against the peasants. The occupations led to intense debates on the Left about the role of the peasant movement, the 'southern question', collective and individual approaches to occupation, and the role of the land in a socialist society.

The movements continued, with highs and lows, right through the 1940s. In particular, a new wave of occupations followed the Republican Constitution of 1948. In 1946 Gullo had been replaced by Antonio Segni as agriculture minister, and in 1950 Segni was author of the DC agrarian reforms that aimed to diffuse the collective aspects of the movement. These reforms had the opposite effect of the Gullo decrees, encouraging social peace and passivity. The great land occupation movements of 1944–5 and 1949–51 in the south were in favour of *collective* ownership of the land, at least in theory. In practice, however, the desire of most peasants remained that of small property. When this failed to materialize, or when opportunities elsewhere arose, the peasants simply departed, and in huge numbers. It was no accident of history that the greatest migration movements from the south followed the defeat of collective movements for land reform in the south – after 1890 and again after 1950.

Braccianti: Day-labourers and the Rural Proletariat

> Before dawn every square in every town was full of men and boys, each one carrying a hoe: this is the labour market, and these are all workers.
>
> 1875 [SICILY], LEOPOLDO FRANCHETTI AND SIDNEY SONNINO
> (*INCHIESTA IN SICILIA*, FIRENZE: VALLECCHI, 1974)

Braccianti, or day-labourers, were taken on by big farms or by sharecroppers at certain times of high demand, during harvest and threshing. These peasants had a difficult relationship with work. As their 'title' implies, day-labourers worked and were paid by the day – usually from dawn to dusk. Their work was governed by the seasons, and most found it difficult to find employment for more than six months a year. Many relied on credit to make it through the rest of the year. Although day-labourers were to be found across Italy, the precise relationship of this class with the land, the landowners and work varied from zone to zone. Day-labourers had marginal links to the land, and were often nomadic figures, moving from place to place in search of employment. Their job security was nil. Families were necessarily small and pay very low, without any of the benefits of security and housing enjoyed by fixed-wage peasants (see below). *Braccianti* represented a large reserve army of labour for the landowners and sharecroppers, who relied on the flexibility of labour, and the ability to bring in migrant workers to break strikes, to keep wages to a minimum and hours at a maximum.

In Apulia, on the great estates which characterized the bleak Tavolieri plain ('a vista of utter and unbroken desolation in which a traveller could journey for miles without encountering a house, a tree, or a living soul',[31] a huge class of day-labourers, living in large agro-towns, had developed by the start of the twentieth century. As Snowden has written, 'nowhere else in the Mezzogiorno was the workforce so homogeneous or so comprehensively proletarianized'.[32] Apart from backbreaking, poorly paid and insecure work, these peasants had no connection with the land or with property ownership. These *braccianti* were often deeply in debt, and were attracted to the revolutionary ideals of syndicalism and socialism over the first twenty years of the century. By 1920, these organizations were hegemonic. In the Cerignola zone (where the vast majority of the land was in the hands of just three owners) the Prefect reported that the entire class of day-labourers were members of rural unions – 'the organization of the working class is perfect'.[33] Apulia's syndicalists were wiped out by fascist violence between 1920 and 1922 as the landowners battled to save the *latifondi* system, which relied entirely upon the powerlessness of its workforce and their extreme flexibility. The middlemen empowered to manage these estates were the organizers of the fascist squads. They knew full well that the 'only variable' within the production process over which they had control was labour. 'Latifundia could not co-exist with a unionized work force.'[34] Fascism kept the *latifundia* system alive until the great peasant struggles and land reforms of the 1940s and 1950s finally killed it off. Italy was not alone either in possessing *latifondi* or in its large day-labourer classes. In Spain the *braceros* on the great estates of Andalusia formed 'a primitive revolutionary class',[35] and similar debates focused on the division or otherwise of these *latifondi*.

We have already looked at day-labourers on the great estates of Sicily and Apulia, who were part of the specific systems of southern *latifondi*. Yet the largest groups of day-labourers were to be found in central and northern Italy. Here a *rural proletariat* began to emerge around the turn of the nineteenth and twentieth centuries. This class had its stronghold in the Po Valley, the fertile plains which surrounded the massive Po River, running from west to east across Italy into the sea.

The Po Valley

Italy's rural powerhouse has always been in the Po Valley. Here, modern agricultural techniques were introduced from the 1890s onwards. A Fordist-type approach to agriculture was adopted, which used the large, landless, shifting industrial proletariat of day-labourers. The *braccianti* developed as a *dangerous* class, with nothing to lose and no stake in the system.[36] Little mediation was possible between the two worlds of the day-labourer and the landowner. The day-labourers were not identical to factory workers, although there were similarities between the two classes in some of the 'Fordist' aspects of the rural economy in the Po Valley. Day-labourers nurtured a strong sense of social division and resentment towards the landowners, which produced high levels of social solidarity, and a tendency towards riot, revolt and violence. Yet these features should not allow us to overlook the coherence of the day-labourer's world-view, and the 'moral economy' behind *braccianti* protest. Some rural labourers around Ferrara at the turn of the nineteenth and twentieth centuries found work for a mere 130 days a year, and around Ravenna this figure sometimes fell to less than a hundred days a year. The dream of the *braccianti* was to remove the uncertainties of hardship caused by this permanently high level of structural under-employment. They demanded minimum and guaranteed levels of pay, and waged war on the agricultural machines that threatened to make their lives even more desperate.

Towards the end of the nineteenth century these workers began to organize themselves into leagues – demanding contracts, higher pay, shorter hours and guaranteed work. The first important strikes took place around Mantova in the 1890s, and the strikes in the Po Valley in 1900–1 led to the formation of a national landworkers' union – the *Federterra*. Over the next twenty years, socialist and Republican organizers (the latter above all in Romagna) took control – especially in the Po Valley. Ten of the fifteen seats won by the PSI in 1897 were in the Po Valley. The Socialists won 26 per cent of the vote in Emilia in 1900. In 1919 the Socialists gained over two-thirds of the total vote in Ferrara and more than 50 per cent in a number of other areas of the Po Valley.

Networks of socialist and cooperative organizations dominated the economic and social scene. Socialist local government administrations were elected in Imola (1895), and in other Emilian towns. By 1920, 120 out of 130 local councillors in Ferrara, Bologna and Reggio Emilia were Socialists. Huge cooperative networks were established. Local leaders became national figures with impenetrable power bases – Massarenti in Molinella, Prampolini around Reggio Emilia. These organizers often preached a kind of semi-religious socialism that held great sway over the day-labourers and their families. Revolutionary syndicalist unions were also strong in certain areas – Parma, Ferrara and in the south around Apulia – where the call for revolutionary general strikes was often taken up and there were frequent, and violent, clashes with the state and landowners.

The main demands of all these organizations were to do with labour supply and income guarantees. Union leaders looked to control the labour market, and to end the vicious cycles of under-employment, poverty and debt that afflicted most day-labourers. This demand was a revolutionary one, since it threatened to remove the main levers of landowner power over labour and hand them to the unions. To succeed, the unions had to prevent labour being brought in from more moderate zones, such as Piedmont and the Veneto.

Violent battles with emigrant labourers were a constant feature of strikes in the Po Valley in the early twentieth century. Union influence over territory was central to the battle over labour supply and the labour market: hence the use of roadblocks and other forms of control by union leaders during strikes at bargaining times (for strike law see Box 3.2). In some areas, union and political control penetrated the population to such an extent as to be nearly hegemonic. The experience of Molinella was particularly significant. As a young student in the 1890s, Giuseppe Massarenti (1867–1950) began to organize day-labourers in the small Emilian town of Molinella (11,000 population, 7,000 agricultural workers, 32 km from Bologna). In 1897 a 40-day strike led to the first written contract for the agricultural workers in the town, and union recognition. The local union became extremely powerful, winning concessions over labour supply and forging alliances between sharecroppers and day-labourers. Strikes in 1901, 1902 and 1903 all involved sharecroppers. In 1903 Massarenti was forced to flee to Switzerland after a prison sentence was imposed upon him for defamation. He returned in 1905 and became mayor of Molinella in 1906. Massarenti utilized his administrative powers to favour union struggles, including the selective use of taxation, roadblocks and the formation of cooperatives to help strikes to succeed. He also organized mass adhesion to the electoral roll. This 'model' of administration attracted bitter attacks from the landowners, politicians and journalists, who dubbed Molinella the 'Republic of the Shirkers'. Massarenti was accused of being a 'red tsar' who had created a 'state within a state'.

In 1914 the Socialist Party managed to elect *all* members of the council by standing in two lists. Political opposition in the town had been wiped out. But, in the same year, five emigrant labourers, amongst a group brought in to break a day-labourer strike, were killed in clashes with striking peasants at Molinella. Mass persecution of the movement followed.[37] Massarenti, charged with murder and suspended as mayor, fled to San Marino; 3,000 troops were sent to the town. Militant sharecroppers were evicted and 38 workers remained in prison and internment for years, before being freed in 1919 after an amnesty. Massarenti returned to Molinella in the same year, and led even more radical strikes than before. Molinella was at the centre of the bitter struggles of 1919–20. Fines were imposed on landowners for the damage caused by the 1914 repression; evicted sharecroppers were given back their farms, and one contract covered all kinds of rural labourers and rentiers. In 1920 Massarenti was one of the key leaders of a 10-month rural strike in Emilia, which was not without moments of violence, intimidation and sabotage against blacklegs, ordinary workers and landowners. The employers gave in but were preparing their revenge through the violence of the fascist squads. Massarenti became mayor again in November 1920. A series of his followers became key local socialist and union leaders and anti-fascists.

Molinella was the last area in Emilia to fall to the fascists. After the red unions had been crushed, the fascists attempted to force locals to join their unions. Most resisted (passively), despite the unemployment and poverty which resulted. 'If we can't kill them, at least we will make them starve to death' (wrote the local police commissioner). Finally, in October 1926, over

Box 3.2 Unions and the law

The Right to Strike and the Right to Work

Until unified Italy's penal code, strikes without reasonable cause were against the law. In 1889 a new code eliminated this crime. Giolitti allowed unions to grow and claimed that the state would intervene in labour disputes only to maintain law and order (although this policy, as we have seen, was often broken, especially in the south). Fascism abolished the right to strike in 1926.

Documents, Extracts

(i) Fascism and the Trade Unions
Law 3.4.1926, n. 363. On the judicial discipline of labour relations in Italy.

Part III – Lock-outs and Strikes

Lock-outs and strikes are banned.
Organizers of public service strikes face prison sentences of up to two years.
Trade unions are not free associations but part of the state.
Work and production-based controversies are regulated through a state body known as the *Magistratura del lavoro*.
Employment offices control unemployed lists.

(ii) The Fascist Charter of Work (*La Carta del Lavoro*)

This programme did not have the force of a law, or a decree. It was passed by the Fascist Grand Council in April 1927.

Article 1 The Italian nation is an organism whose ends, existence and means of action are superior to those of the individuals or groups who make up its parts. It is a political, economic and moral entity, which is entirely realized within the Fascist state.

Article 2 Work, in all its intellectual, technical and material forms, is a social duty. ... The production process acts together for national ends; its objectives are unitary and can be summarized in the well-being of the producers and the development of national power.

Article 7 The corporate state considers private initiative in the field of production as the efficient and useful instrument for meeting the needs of the nation.

Article 9 The intervention of the state in economic production only takes place when private initiative is insufficient or when the political interests of the state are involved. Such intervention can take the form of control, of encouragement of production or of direct management.

Article 13 The costs of productive and monetary crises must be equally divided between components of the productive process.

200 families were forcibly deported. Massarenti left the town after numerous threats and spent the next five years in prison and internal exile, where he suffered frequent beatings and persecution. Even after his release in 1931 he was not allowed to return to Molinella, and was forced to live as a virtual tramp in Rome. In 1937 he was sent to a mental institution, where he remained until 1944, despite strong evidence of his sanity. An article in June 1944 asked the question: 'Where is Massarenti?' In 1947 a committee was formed to restore all civil rights to Massarenti, who returned to Molinella in triumph in 1948, where he was made a candidate in parliamentary elections. Only sectarian divisions amongst the Socialists prevented his election. He died in 1950 at the age of 83. Historical judgement on Massarenti has ranged from work that beatifies the socialist leader as a martyr and 'the saint of the swamps', to highly critical analyses concentrating on the violence and intimidation (and intense localism) of the Molinella movement. Massarenti remained a local hero, however, with monuments, streets and cooperatives constructed in his name and in his memory.

To return to the history of the Po Valley *braccianti* as a whole, by 1919–20, with the return of day-labourers from the front, where they had been promised 'land', the control over certain parts of Italy by the rural trade unions widened still further. In 1920, the *Federterra* had over a million members. Great victories were won – for the eight-hour day, and above all, with the signing of special contracts. These agreements gave the unions a high degree of influence over the labour market, guaranteeing a certain number of days' work a year to each signed-up member and subverting the workings of the market. During the dramatic strikes of 1920 around Bologna, where children were sent away to allow total concentration on the struggle, the state and the landowners were unable to defeat the unions. At this moment, the 'total hatred' (G. Crainz)[38] reserved for the landowners exploded through the systematic use of sabotage, fires, road-blocks, violence and the apocalyptic threat to ruin the whole Po Valley harvest.

By 1920, however, just as it seemed that the Po Valley labourers had won a historic victory, new forms of landowner resistance were being organized – through methodical violence and the use of armed 'squads'. Fascism made its first inroads into the socialist strongholds of the Po Valley in late 1920. During the 'two black years', 1920–2, Emilia was the scene of hundreds of organized attacks by fascist squads, which destroyed the reformist and union networks of the day-labourers. The gains of 1919–20 were quickly rolled back, and the PSI was thrown out of office in the key cities in the region – Ferrara, Reggio Emilia and especially Bologna (in November 1920) through the use of organized military-style violence.[39] Under fascism, all of the gains of 1919–20 were wiped out, despite the regime's propaganda concerning 'ruralization' and the various 'battles for grain' organized under Mussolini. The corporate state provided basic welfare systems for day-labourers, who were obliged to join fascist unions. During the crises of the 1930s, fascism was even tempted to return to the guaranteed-work policies that the 'red' unions had forced through after World War I. Meanwhile, much of the Po Valley was mechanized. Part of the reclamation programme was aimed at eliminating day-labourers altogether and replacing them with small property owners – a type of *sbracciantizzazione* ('de-day-labourization'). But this policy was not centred on the Po Valley, where day-labourers remained important right up to the 1950s.

The Po Valley since 1945: the end of the world of the braccianti[40]

With the end of the war, Emilia-Romagna was the scene for much blood-letting against the fascists and landowners – so much so that right-wing commentators dubbed one area of Emilia 'the triangle of death'. In part, this was belated revenge for the crimes of the war, and also those of 1920–2, but some of the violence reflected the extremely bitter nature of social conflict on the Po Valley going right back to the 1880s and 1890s, a period evoked in Bernardo Bertolucci's two-part epic film *1900* (1975). In one extreme example of this combination of events, a whole family of landowners, the Manzonis, were murdered in July 1945, near Ravenna. At the subsequent trial, the peasants accused of this crime evoked the long historical period of class struggle, stretching back through fascism to the first clashes of the 1890s.[41]

In 1949 a 36-day strike organized by the *Confederterra* (who had 1.7 million members by that time, most of them day-labourers) saw scenes of social tension and violence, but represented the last struggle of its kind in the Po Valley. The granting of the first national day-labourer contract was a largely symbolic act. Very quickly, almost imperceptibly, *a whole social class disappeared* as mechanization removed the need for large numbers of day-labourers and the lure of the towns proved too much for most families. Motorization, consumerism and the agricultural policies of the European Community all but destroyed the traditional rhythms of rural work. Bologna, Ferrara, Parma, Modena and Ravenna expanded to take in thousands of ex-*braccianti*. At last, there was a realistic alternative, beyond emigration from Italy, to rural unemployment. Yet the radical politics of the region, if anything, were strengthened. Bologna elected Communist mayors from 1945 to 1999, along with most other towns in the region. A more bucolic view of the cold war in the immediate post-war period was that of Giovanni Guareschi, whose hilarious *Don Camillo* stories pitted a Communist mayor against a stubborn priest in a small, Po town. Films based on the *Don Camillo* books, set in Brescello, were immensely popular and depicted a conflict which, deep down, was only skin deep. The reality was rather different, especially in the 1940s and 1950s.

The landscape changed to an empty, monotonous one, only disturbed by an occasional tractor or scarecrow – for a (surreal) picture of rural Emilia in the 1970s, see Bertolucci's film *La strategia del ragno* (*The Spider's Strategem*), 1970. Whole traditions disappeared, whole ways-of-being died out, only preserved through the work of a small group of oral historians, such as Gianni Bosio (see his *Il trattore ad Acquanegra. Piccola e grande storia in una comunità contadini*[42]). No longer did large numbers of people live their lives by the seasons, their lives and incomes intimately linked up with the weather, the time of year and the setting of the sun. The area remained the grain basket of Italy, however, and its export food and wine (most famously Parma ham, Parmesan cheese, pasta, Modenese vinegar and Lambrusco red wine) became staple items across the world. Yet, temporary rural labour did not disappear completely. Some crops still required hand-harvesting (such as tomatoes, although this crop was mainly to be found in the south), a job that was increasingly filled by foreign immigrants, as Italians were reluctant to take on this poorly paid task. Rural day-labouring became a distant memory, but the growth of thousands of small, family-run industries in the region – a model known as *flexible specialization*, in a region which was given the name 'the third Italy' – took root in part thanks to a combination of peasant entrepreneurship and local expertise.[43] Living standards in Emilia-Romagna rose to be amongst the highest in Europe. Once again, Italy's 'soft' model of industrial development provided the possibility of a relatively smooth transition from a Fordist to a post-Fordist economy, allowing the region to become a world leader in a number of specialized sectors.

The Lombard Plains: *Cascine* and *Salariati Fissi*

The most modern of rural proletarians in the rural mosaic of early twentieth-century Italy were the *salariati fissi*, fixed-wage rural workers. Often referred to as *obbligati* (literally, 'forced' workers) because of their permanent location in huge scattered courtyard-type farms, or *cascine*, these workers were employed on fixed wages with (usually) yearly contracts. Large areas of lower Lombardy, the most advanced of all Italy's agricultural zones, as the Jacini inquest had first revealed in the 1880s, used this type of contract. In 1901 in the five zones dominated by *cascine* – Cremona, Crema, Casalmaggiore, Lodi and Pavia – nearly 37 per cent of the rural population worked in this way. Pay, however, was very low and linked to certain and varied rights to housing and product shares, some of which were also 'residues' of feudalism.

Cascine were built on a quadrangular pattern across the Lombard plains, with large inner courtyards and animal stalls. Peasants lived in small houses, usually looking out onto the courtyard itself, which was a place of minutely organized work, community activity, leisure and trade. Many *cascine* produced milk. The number of cows in Lombardy rose from 840,000 in 1881 to 1,160,000 in 1914 (nearly one-fifth of the number for the whole of Italy). *Cascine* were intended as self-sufficient entities, as places of production and of storage. Peasants worked either in the surrounding fields or with livestock inside the farm. Within the *cascine* there was a strongly entrenched hierarchy of tasks, from *mungitori* (milkers) to *capi-bergamini* (milking-stall supervisors). Landowners built the *cascine* so as to be able to oversee even the entry and exit of workers and control their daily lives. This system encouraged a smaller population in the region than in the mixed industry–agriculture zones of upper Lombardy. In lower Lombardy surplus labour was simply not available on such a wide scale and a shifting day-labourer class did not form as it did in Emilia.

Clearly, these *obbligati* were similar to wage workers in terms of their industrial conditions and by the very fact of the collective nature of their work situation, as well as the physical communality produced by the spacious *piazze* or rural courtyards. But the traditional and hierarchical nature of this work and close relationship with the landowners meant that the *obbligati* were a fragmented class inside the *cascine* themselves. *Cascine* were isolated from urban centres, debates and ideas. Any 'class-consciousness' that formed in the *cascine* was not of a classic Marxist kind. *Obbligati* aspirations centred above all on control and regularization of their work, pay and hours. The most radical organizers of this group of peasants were left-wing Catholics in the Cremona area, who organized around the self-management of *cascine* and even the formation of 'farm councils'. The unremitting hostility between the socialist and Catholic peasant movements helped to defeat this organization in the 1920s. As with all other rural systems, the *cascine* struggled through until the 1950s, cutting the number of peasants employed within their buildings and mechanizing production. By the 1960s, few such systems survived, and *cascine* began to be re-used as rural retreats for town dwellers, agro-tourism restaurants and hotels, specialized production centres or even cheap housing for new, foreign immigrants. Some were abandoned completely. Others, especially on the edge of the big cities, were eaten up by the growth of the urban peripheries. Rural-type *cascine* can still be found, for example, in many parts of Milan's urban fabric.

Bonifica: Rural Italy, Water and Malaria – Reclaiming the Land

A key problem facing the Italian state, and the Italian economy, was the large quantity of unusable agricultural land. Much good land was under water, malarial or, alternatively, in dire need of irrigation systems, roads and fertilizer. Large zones of Lombardy had set up modern canal and irrigation systems, and later hydro-electrical power stations, by the end of the nineteenth century, encouraging both modern agricultural production and rural-based industry. This was the work both of the local state and of entrepreneurs, sometimes from abroad. The urgent need for mass *bonifica* – reclamation or public-works projects – was not lost on the Liberal state, and special laws for the south, such as the 1904 Basilicata law, concentrated on public works, the eradication of soil erosion, and irrigation. Huge *bonifica* programmes created vast fertile tracts of land around Ferrara and in other parts of central Italy.[44] Other reclamation schemes began to improve the tragic situation in Lazio and around Rome in the early twentieth century, where malaria was rife: 1.8 million hectares were reclaimed before World War I, a tenth of all farmland in Italy, with the state meeting 75 per cent of the costs.[45] The Giolittian era was particularly important in terms of state spending on these schemes (especially with the measures designed to help the Agro Romano near Rome). These programmes were threatened by natural disasters. For example, the terrible Messina earthquake in 1908 cost the state 107 million lire in six years of reconstruction and aid, as much as was spent in forty years on *bonifica* programmes.

Fascism made its *bonifica* programme the centre of domestic policy, especially in the south. Malaria had been Italy's most important health issue after unification, and Mussolini set out to eradicate the disease. The so-called *bonifica integrale*, begun after 1928, was organized as a campaign of war and run by the veterans' association – against the 'enemies' of water, malaria and 'backwardness'. A massive drainage ditch siphoned off water. Gleaming new cities – Littoria (now Latina), Pomezia, Pontinia, Aprilia and Sabaudia – were constructed entirely in fascist style in the Agro Romano; 60,000 peasants were transferred *en masse* from the Veneto and Romagna and given 5,000 plots of land (with sharecropping contracts), and houses, in the new areas. A total of 0.7 million hectares were reclaimed. The *bonifica* was also a political programme, 'aimed to create a conservative new class of yeoman farmers carefully recruited from the patriotic ranks of the nation's war veterans' (Frank Snowden).[46] At one point, 124,000 labourers were working on the *bonifica integrale* in the Lazio area alone. These infrastructures have largely stood the test of time, despite their totalitarian origins, and helped to eliminate malaria from Lazio, although a new epidemic (which lasted well into 1947) was deliberately created by the retreating German troops in 1943–4. No programmes on this scale were attempted after 1945.

Our journey through the economic history of Italy now shifts to the industrial sector.

INDUSTRIAL ITALY

Italian Industrial Revolutions

Definitions: the first revolution, 1890–1907

An industrial revolution is generally defined as a transformation from a rural to an industrial economy, with high levels of development concentrated in short periods of time. Italy has seen two such industrial revolutions, and one post-industrial revolution, since the 1890s. The first such 'revolution' took place around the 1890s, and was limited in its scope in comparison with what are generally seen as the models of industrial revolution in Germany, or France, or the UK. This was *Italy's version* of such a revolution, with strong dualistic features (above all between north and south), and with the industrialization of large swathes of rural space, especially in the north. No mass emigration to the cities accompanied this first 'revolution', *within* Italy.[47] Population movement did occur on a huge scale, but was directed *outside* of Italy, towards other industrial countries. It was not until the 1950s that the masses of rural workers were to be attracted to the industrial cities of the north from their villages in the Veneto or the south. Italy, hampered by a lack of classic industrial raw materials (coal, iron[48]), developed an alternative strategy that was, in the long run, no less successful than that used elsewhere. It also utilized the advantages it did have – 'white coal' (water power, especially in the north, where modern stations provided the power for Lombard industry and for the city of Milan[49]), other natural resources (sulphur, marble), an extraordinary abundance of cheap labour, market links to both Europe and the Mediterranean basin, the possibility to produce large quantities of a boom product – silk – and, finally, cash flows from its millions of hard-working emigrants, throughout the world.

The seeds of this industrial boom lay with two sectors: textiles and metal-work. Its heart was in the north with private industries: Fiat, Pirelli, Campari, Breda, Falck, Ansaldo, Riva; and in the state-funded central and southern industries – in Terni, Elba, Piombino, Ancona, Florence, Naples and Palermo. Our survey of industrial Italy begins with the crucial textile sector.

The textile industry

Textiles have been the key industrial product for much of Italy's history: 60 per cent of all Italy's industrial workers still worked in that sector in 1911 and textiles made up 20 per cent of Italian industrial production in 1914. This sector remains a central one even today. Textile industries were particularly strong in Lombardy. Here, throughout the last two centuries, this region has been able to develop an integrated economic system marked by strong specialized areas and districts. Lombardy was able to integrate 'agriculture, industry, commerce and finance; big, small and medium-sized industry; family firms and stock companies. All this within a complex whole marked by a pragmatic push towards innovation, by prudent optimism and by the never-ending research for modernity sustained by a tenacious attachment to tradition'.[50] The road to industrial society here was one where links to the land were maintained over long periods. There was a 'soft' industrialization 'based on the gradual interweaving of agricultural and industrial employment among workers'.[51] Whole areas were industrialized without the wholesale expulsion of peasants and rural artisans.

The textile industry in Italy went through a series of phases, too complicated to summarize here.[52] Traditionally, historians have tended to view this type of industry as backward, as merely a stage on the way towards proper, industrial, urban capitalism. Recent work refutes this schematic view, relocating the role of women in the industrial revolution, and mapping out this system as an alternative form of development, with great advantages in the (later) shift to a post-industrial (or post-Fordist) economy. Rural families adopted flexible and varied strategies, as did businessmen, to adapt to changing seasons, work practices, commercial demand and industrial possibilities. Some became *worker-peasants*, maintaining links with the land (as a safety-net, or for certain periods of the year) whilst concentrating their activity in industry. Others opted for a weaker form of this mixed role – as *peasant-workers* – selling their labour to industries for some of the time, perhaps as builders *of* and *in* the cities, whilst prioritizing agricultural activity. Some became pure workers, either in the city or in the countryside. Many moved between these various stages, often without a conscious plan. The flexibility of the Italian rural family allowed this possibility of adaptation to change, but it also *helped to shape* the form and speed of economic and social change. This phenomenon has recently been termed 'pluriactivity'.[53]

For Italy, silk was a crucial product – the largest export good over the first fifty years of Italian history.[54] Silk production required pluriactivity. Numerous difficult and dextrous tasks covered the silk cycle, all tightly linked to the gestation period of the silk worms. Over time, the silk industry moved from the home to the factory, but continued to be dominated by women workers. Silk was concentrated in certain areas of northern Italy for economic and cultural reasons. The numbers of mulberry trees, whose leaves were used to feed the worms, rose from 78,000 to 3 million between 1734 and 1846 in the Como area alone. The Como area had become, according to the Jacini rural inquest of the 1880s, a 'big mulberry orchard'. Slowly, and especially around the turn of the century, this industry became mechanized. Consumer demand widened the need for textile production of all kinds, not just in silk. Later, the Milan fashion industry was to find its business heart in the textile experience and industrial base of Lombardy. The post-industrial boom (see below) also saw textiles play a key role – from the giants of Benetton and Diesel to hundreds of small quality firms across the industrialized countryside of the north-west and north-east. In the 1990s and 2000s this sector came under severe pressure from China and other more competitive economies. The trend towards the decentralization and delocalization of production continued apace. A deep crisis hit the textile industry leading to closures and cut-backs in the areas of specialization.

Ford in Italy

Beyond textiles, Italy began to develop metalwork and consumer goods industries in the last three decades of the nineteenth century. A young entrepreneur called Giovanni Battista Pirelli set up his first factory in Milan in 1872. In 1909, production was moved to the edge of the city to a zone known as the *Bicocca*. Here tyres and cables were produced and exported across Europe and the world. The Milanese company laid cables for energy and telecommunications transmission throughout the world, using a special ship for this purpose. Pirelli also produced goods linked to the motor-car industry. In 1899 Fiat was founded in Turin, and in 1910 Alfa Romeo began production in Milan. The history of Italian industrial capitalism is closely linked to the history of the Fiat motor company, founded by the Agnelli family.[55] Fiat set up Italy's first production lines in 1913 and became a major concern during World War I.

Italy's latecomer status, and the advantages which came with that position (see above) tended to produce a high concentration of production within a few, huge, family-run firms. This oligarchical structure has remained until very recently as a key feature of Italian capitalism. The development of the Fiat company was strongly linked to both US and USSR models of state capitalism. By the 1920s, Fiat was producing 90 per cent of Italy's cars, and the Agnelli family controlled 70 per cent of the company. This was not a US-style managerial capitalist system; there was no real separation between ownership and technical management. In this period, Fiat's production was held back by the lack of internal demand. It was only with the economic miracle of the 1950s and 1960s that the company was able to 'take Italy towards full motorization'.[56] Fiat developed Fordist and Taylorist capitalist techniques in

Italy, building extraordinary temples of capitalist production such as the plants of Lingotto and Mirafiori, which employed up to 50,000 workers. The economy of the virtual company-town of Turin, where the Agnellis owned the national newspaper (*La Stampa*), the football team (*Juventus*), and, it was said, the local government system, was almost entirely devoted to Fiat – either through direct or support production. Fiat also controlled insurance companies, supermarkets, chemical products, newspapers, banks, mineral water, trains: '[It was] more than a kingdom, [it was] an empire.'[57]

The Lingotto plant was completed in 1922, and based on the famous Ford Highland Park factory, with a racing track on the roof, Lingotto took up over 153,000 square metres over four floors and was later widened to over 350,000 square metres, with a factory front which stretched for 2 km. At its peak, the factory produced 40,000 cars a year. Lingotto was always a symbolic place, praised by Le Corbusier as 'a warship ... with bridges, corridors and walkways'. Lingotto organized space in a linear fashion. The city grew around the factory, which in early photos appears like a huge, futuristic construction in the countryside around the city. In 1982, after 60 years of production, the factory closed and became a hotel, offices and an exhibition space. The futuristic roof was used for tourist trips and as a jogging track for executives.

By 1937 Fiat as a whole was producing 55,000 cars a year, and 10,000 lorries and tractors, figures which covered 83 per cent of all Italian production in this sectors. The Mirafiori plant, conceived on an even larger scale, and based on the Ford River Rouge plant in Detroit, as well as on Soviet-type factories, was built in open countryside on the edge of Turin and opened in 1939. Its model was an authoritarian one, with innumerable walls, doors and gates. The factory took up some 376 hectares of space, covering some 6 per cent of the entire area of Turin. The workers' cafe was big enough for 10,000 people. Mirafiori had 37 entry gates, with internal roads and a railway that extended for 22 km and 40 km, respectively. Production lines also ran for 40 km. There were 10,000 telephone sets.

This was 'the Petrograd of Italy', her only real industrial city, where a 'red' workers belt was constructed at the turn of the century with elaborate systems of social solidarity and political mobilization. Even here, however, the industrial revolution in the early twentieth century was a 'soft' one. Migration was common, mobility the norm and the political cohesion of the working-class neighbourhood partly the result of shared forms of cultural discourse.[58] In 1919–20, Turin was the scene of worker mobilization on a scale not seen again until 1943, and then again in 1969. A group of radical intellectual socialists – including Gramsci, Togliatti and Tasca – organized factory councils, democratic organizations and even the occupation of the factories themselves in September 1920. The defeat of this movement paved the way for 20 years of fascism. Mussolini visited Mirafiori in 1939, to be met with the silent protest of the workers. Secret reports told Mussolini what he already knew: 'the great majority of the metalwork workforce who work at Fiat, notwithstanding their formal membership of the fascist party, have remained as they were before, convinced socialists and communists'.[59] These same workers were to give the final push to the fascist regime four years later, in 1943. It was Turin which first rose against Mussolini, with mass strikes under fascist and wartime discipline in March 1943.[60]

In April 1945, the communist secretary of the Committee for National Liberation of the Fiat firm went to the company's director, Vittorio Valletta, and declared that they were now in charge. This revolutionary period was brief, and the company soon regained control. The cold war was a difficult time for militants in the factory. The company kept files on all of its workers, illegally, with information on their political affiliations, and tried to keep out known communists and trade unionists. Later, militant workers were marginalized in isolated parts of the factory. A 1971 investigation found numerous documents regarding workers – 354,077 files had been collected between 1949 and 1971, of which 203,422 were from the 1950s and 1960s, and 150,655 from the period 1967–71.

Fiat attracted thousands of immigrants from within Italy, especially in the period between 1950 and 1973. Many workers had a love–hate relationship with the factory, their work and their bosses. On the one hand, they had an immense pride in their work and the product of the factory. New immigrant workers, on the other hand, were less bound by these traditions, and were at the head of the struggles against production of the late 1960s and 1970s. Southern traditions were a key part of the forms of worker protest in this period. The 'hot autumn' exploded here in 1969, and mass worker struggles continued right through until 1980. In June–July 1969 alone there were 1.1 million hours of strikes, causing the loss of 40,000 cars. Terrorism took hold at Fiat in the 1970s. Between 1976 and 1980, 16 Fiat employees were injured in terrorist attacks, and the first murder took place in 1979.

Italian private capitalism has been described as being under the control of a few, extremely powerful, families.[61] The Agnelli family controlled more than 70 per cent of Fiat for most of the century, and the Falck metal giant was controlled in the same way by the Falck family. Yet these companies, and their fortunes, have always been strongly bound to the state. The state has stepped in to save companies, has ordered their goods, has allowed them to lay off workers and has intervened strongly in collective bargaining. Some commentators have gone so far as to argue that Italy never developed an adequate business class, where control, management and possession of businesses were separated. After becoming an industrial holding in the 1970s, Fiat achieved a virtual monopoly over the Italian car industry, buying Alfa Romeo in 1986. The history of Fiat was closely linked to that of Turin, but in the 1950s and above all during the 1970s, the company expanded to the south of Italy and across the world, including huge plants in Poland, the USSR, and in the south near Naples (1956), and at Melfi (a plant opened in 1994, with over 6,000 employees). Fiat also owned Ferrari, international and national symbol of Italy's motor-industry expertise. Italy's millions of sports fans identified, fanatically, with Ferrari, not with Italian drivers. Italy was also a world leader in the motorbike and scooter sector – producing Vespa and Lambretta scooters and Ducati, Aprilia and MotoGuzzi motorbikes.

By 1950 Fiat was producing 108,700 cars a year; by 1966 this figure had risen to 1.5 million vehicles, with 144,000 employees, with Fiat contributing

5 per cent of total national income. The opening up of the internal market led to a huge increase in demand for cheap utility cars, which was elegantly filled by the 500 and 600 models: 6.4 million of these two models were produced between 1955 and 1975, with a further 1.7 million of the next model, the 850. Italy was transformed by this motorization: 'Italians no longer moved just once in their lives, to emigrate or for military service ... many Italians began to experience the liberty and pleasure to travel and communicate, escaping from the geographical and psychological limits of their daily routine. Many began to discover Italy itself'.[62] Fiat became a world industrial power, producing 6.6 per cent of the world's cars, 16 per cent of those in Europe and 21 per cent of those within the EEC in 1968. This was the peak of the company's position in the world economy, and a slow decline began in the early 1970s that led to a series of crises in the 1980s, 1990s and 2000s (see below). Fiat moved most of its production outside of Italy, although its head offices and decision-making centres remained to some extent in Turin. The managerial expertise of the Italian-Canadian Sergio Marchionne led to a revival of fortunes in the 2000s, but Fiat's interest in Italy itself was increasingly marginal. By the twenty-first century, Fordism in Italy was a distant memory, and its life had been brief.

Debates over Italian Industrial Development

World War I as an economic miracle?

Many historians have also identified a third 'miracle' – which took place during World War I. Here, there was a further 'great leap' in the economy in order to run a massive war machine. The number of munitions factories rose from 221 in 1915 to 1,976 in 1918, involving in all 571,000 workers, of whom 70 per cent were employed in the industrial triangle. Ansaldo alone increased its workforce by 50,000, from 6,000 to 56,000 employees. The state played a key role throughout, and state spending rose by 350 per cent between 1913 and 1919. Industrial employment rose ten times, and the electricity and chemical industries became important national sectors. A 'new class of entrepreneurs and of public and private managers' developed.[63] Production reached record levels: 70 million bullets were produced by munitions factories. Many of those employed were women, who entered the urban industrial workforce for the first time, although the vast majority were sacked after the return of men from the front after 1918.

The issues of protectionism, free trade and tariffs

Much debate amongst historians has been taken up by the question of tariffs and protectionism. During the 1880s, this was an extremely controversial question that occupied the minds of politicians, economists and industrialists. However, it is difficult to understand, either way, what effects tariffs had on the Italian economy and much of this discussion is based around sterile (and pointless) 'what-if' models. What if the tariff had not been imposed when it was? What if it had been higher, or lower? In historical context, the tariffs on imports protected new industries from competition and therefore allowed them to develop, probably contributing to the industrial boom of the 1890s. However, this sheltering from competition also encouraged the growth of capitalism 'without a market', leading to inefficiencies, corruption and dependence on the state. Industrialists, especially in strategic or military sectors, felt safe in the knowledge that the state would almost certainly come to the rescue of companies in trouble. Italy was not alone in imposing tariffs in the 1880s, and the squeeze on exports hit southern agriculture hard, especially those who had invested in wine, oil and fruit production. After 1887, free trade 'aside from a brief interval during and after World War I, was essentially dead'.[64] The free-marketeers were isolated, as they almost always were throughout Italian history. Exports fell by at least a quarter after 1887. Generally, the interpretation of this period is of an unholy alliance (at both a political and an economic level) between northern agrarian and industrial capitalists, and southern latifondists, all mediated through the political nexus of the Liberal and Giolittian system. Generally, again, economists agree that protectionism widened the gap between north and south to a chasm.

THE POST-WAR ECONOMIC MIRACLE

Economic, Cultural and Social Change: Overview, 1950–70

Italy recovered quickly from the post-war 'reconstruction' period to create its own 'economic miracle' in the 1950s and 1960s, with the important contribution of funds from the Marshall Aid programme. Italy's 'miracle' was part of a world boom. This was the 'golden age' of capitalism, which created a new world market for consumer goods and forced Italians into a modern, industrial world. Whilst this period of high economic growth ran right from the early 1950s up to 1973, the 'economic miracle', or 'boom', is commonly placed in the period 1958–63. The 'miracle' was marked by extremely rapid cultural, social and economic change. Italy became an industrialized nation, at least in parts of the north and centre, and centuries-old social categories – the rural day-labourer, the sharecropper – all but disappeared across much of the country. Mass internal migration (10 million Italians moved from one region to another in a ten-year period, more than 17 million moved house) was the most striking effect of and catalyst for change, throwing together different cultures, dialects and customs in the urban environment. With increasing prosperity, many Italians were able to purchase consumer goods for the first time (usually on credit) – televisions (broadcasting began in 1954); cars (the cheap symbols of the boom were the Fiat 500 (1957) and 600 (1955) and the *Topolino*); scooters (the Vespa and the Lambretta); fridges and washing machines. The number of private cars in Italy rose from 364,000 in 1950 to 4.67 million in 1964. Fridges produced by Italian companies shot up from 18,500 in 1951 to 370,000 in 1957 and 3.2 million in 1967. Italy became the biggest European producer of washing machines and fridges, a development that led to something of a revolution within the home and the domestic sphere, as the formerly gloomy kitchens of Italian houses became gleaming and white. Advertising became a permanent feature in Italian homes, especially in the form of *Carosello*, which began transmission in 1957. Mass schooling and urbanization transformed the literacy and cultural outlook of a new generation.

The End of Big Industry and the Rise of Post-industrial Italy: The 1980s and 1990s

The end of Fordism

This boom was a short-lived one. From the end of the 1970s onwards Italy's Fordist industries went through a traumatic and dramatic change – a rapid and complete deindustrialization. In Milan, for example, by the 1980s all the historic factories in the city and its hinterland had closed, or employed tiny fractions of their former workforce. In the 1950s the biggest employer in the city was Pirelli, today it is the local council. Bovisa, the working-class neighbourhood *par excellence*, saw its last big factory close in 1996. Industrial jobs in the Province of Milan fell by 280,000 between 1971 and 1989. Those employed in factories with over 500 employees fell to 163,991 by 1991 (the figure in 1981 had been 272,507). Employees in businesses employing between two and nine employees rose from 496,003 (32 per cent of the total) to 656,805 (41 per cent) between 1981 and 1989. In Italy as a whole, whole industries closed, or changed the way they produced, employing fewer and fewer workers. For example, in the metalwork sector, employees fell from 1,253,600 in 1980 to 758,700 in 1996.

Sesto San Giovanni, a suburb of Milan that was once known as the 'Stalingrad of Italy', represented the extreme end of this trend – with 2 million square metres of ex-industrial space, a third of the whole area of the town.[65] Industrial workers at Sesto fell from 40,000 to 3,000 in just over a decade, wiping out a history of factory work that went back to the early years of the twentieth century. One newspaper reported that young children were heard asking their teachers at an exhibition on the Breda, once an enormous and famous engineering plant at Sesto, 'Were there really factories at Sesto?' By the end of the 1990s, Sesto had taken off as a technological and service centre and much of the legacy of industrial capitalism had disappeared from the landscape and the political make-up of the zone. In the 2000s Sesto was hit by a political scandal linked to speculation over ex-industrial areas. By 1989, the main union federation in Milan – the CGIL (*Confederazione Generale Italiana dei Lavoratori*) – could count on only 90,971 members, a fall of over 40 per cent from 1981.

Many of these factory closures were accompanied by heroic rearguard struggles, in which the formerly militant working class went through the motions of opposition. The end of so much large-scale Fordist production, which had dominated the physical and economic landscape of certain industrial areas for so long, represented a cultural, political and social turning point. No longer would the streets be dominated by thousands of blue-suited

Box 3.3 Migration, economy and society

The static vision of Italian history, so strong in so many of the traditional accounts of unified Italy, bears no relation to the dynamic story of Italians. The famous tendency towards *campanilismo* (attachment to one's home town – literally to its bell-tower) was overcome by the lure of riches and work abroad, and the grinding poverty of rural Italy. Over the first 120 years of Italy's history, many of its inhabitants were almost always on the move. Initially, this movement was above all towards the 'promised lands' – the Americas, northern Europe – but many also migrated within Italy. Fascism cut off this first avenue of movement for twenty years, and outlawed internal migration. Yet millions of Italians still left their homes to find work elsewhere on the peninsula. Many others emigrated for political reasons. After 1945, the scenario changed again. Migration became far more seasonal. In the 1950s, with the economic miracle on the horizon, Italians headed north – specifically to Milan, Turin and Genoa – and to the cities of Rome, Naples and Palermo. This movement was biblical and traumatic, changing forever the face of the rural south and north and transforming urban landscapes and demographies.

Much of these complicated and shifting processes of population movement were packed with contradictions. Emigration brought wealth to 'home' areas (through the *rimesse*) but left villages and land without the most active parts of their population. Families were divided for months if not years at a time – and sometimes forever. Many came home only in their coffins, to be buried in their hometown. Fathers saw their children twice a year. 'White widows' were left in remote southern villages, dependent on weekly or monthly letters. On their return, at Christmas or election time, small towns would fill with men, or with German and French cars. Many Italians learnt a second language for the first time, or to write, or to communicate through photographs and other visual media.

Racism was a common experience. Italians were often humiliated, and banned from public places. In the southern USA they were classified as 'black'. Italians were also exploited, most tragically perhaps in the mines of northern Belgium. Yet, Italians in other countries played the role of the imperialist. In Brazil, Italian settlers, aided by priests, set out on numerous 'civilizing missions' – which involved massacring *indios* and stealing their land. *Indios* children were kidnapped and 'civilized'. Similar events accompanied migrations to Somalia, Libya, Albania and Ethiopia.

workers on a shift change. No longer would Milan be associated with Breda, with Pirelli, with Alfa Romeo – with smoke and chimneys and the factory gate. New identities were in construction.

For the traditional Left, and for the ex-working class, the period 'of the big factory' began to be viewed with nostalgia. In a strange ideological shift, the same critics who had stigmatized the Fordist factory as a dark satanic organization where men were reduced to beasts, now pined for the return of those factories. A kind of 'new apocalypticism' began to take shape on the Left, which started to characterize the '1980s' in the same way as critics had stigmatized the boom thirty years before. This romanticization of the positive effects supposedly produced by big industry – community, production, even legality – was accompanied by a reappraisal of the first economic miracle.

The Milanese ruling class was transformed, as its famous working class disappeared. Media barons (Berlusconi), fashion designers (Armani, Ferré, Versace, Dolce & Gabbana), advertising companies (800,000 television advertisements are produced every year in the city) and financiers (Milan is host to 30 per cent of the national head offices of all banks with a presence in Italy) replaced the old industrial classes. A whole series of new jobs began to dominate the city. By 1987, Milan could call upon 800 DJs, 1,200 make-up artists and 4,700 film dubbers. The landscape of the city changed as factories closed: some were demolished; some were re-used, or had elaborate plans built around them (above all, the Bicocca University/housing Project at the ex-Pirelli area and the Bovisa plans); others were left to crumble, becoming the only available shelter for thousands of immigrants (see also Box 3.4).

Turin saw even more dramatic changes, thanks to the centrality of Fiat in that city. In 1988 journalist Gad Lerner published a study of the working class in Turin. The book, *Workers*, was subtitled 'The life, the houses, the factories of a class which is no more'. The last chapter, entitled 'The Communist Party and the Radiators', tells a story whose implications go far beyond one

---

Box 3.4 The end of Fordism at Fiat

Italy's industrialization and Fordist revolution had come with great speed, and it quickly disappeared. Under pressure from mass militant unionization, and increasing competition, as well as the oil crisis after 1973, the company began to look for different ways of organizing the productive process, and to cut back on its workforce. The number of Fiat's car workers fell from 139,000 to 78,000 between 1979 and 1987, in particular after the 1980 defeat at Turin, which allowed the company to lay off 23,000 workers in one day. Mirafiori's workforce fell from 53,000 (in 1968) to 26,000 (1995). Huge numbers of ex-workers, on unemployment benefit, filled the peripheries of Turin. By the mid-1980s 1,400 robots were at work in Fiat's factories. Half of the robots at work in the whole of Italy were Fiat-controlled. Factories changed from dark and noisy places, full of workers, to clean, quiet and relatively empty spaces. Fordism withdrew from the city, leaving huge empty spaces – 5 million square metres in Turin alone. Production was decentralized – the Fiat Bravo was made partly in Biella, partly in Hungary and partly in Turin. A further crisis in 2001–2 led to the closure of Fiat's Sicilian plant and further lay-offs in Turin. The death of Giovanni Agnelli in January 2003 signalled the end of an era of Italian family-run capitalism. The technocratic and dynamic management of Sergio Marchionne saved Fiat from disaster, bringing the company into the modern age. The cost of this shift was a clear movement away from Italy, whose costs were seen as unsustainable in the short and long run.

neighbourhood in one town. The neighbourhood was Mirafiori Sud, built in 1967 right next to the most important Fiat factory, to house car workers. Here, in the mid-1970s, the Communist Party regularly won around 50 per cent of the vote. By 1987 this vote had fallen to 35 per cent. In the 1994 general elections the constituency was won by a candidate from Berlusconi's right-wing *Forza Italia!*. Lerner tells the 'story of the radiators' to explain what he sees as a radical change in the neighbourhood in the 1980s. What happened was this. In the 1980s, the self-managed collective heating system began to accumulate debts, and could no longer pay for fuel. The response of 96 out of 260 families was to install their own, individual radiator system. 'Friendships were broken, fights nearly broke out ... it was impossible to hold a meeting of the neighbourhood committee; the police were called out on numerous occasions.' Lerner's conclusion was straightforward: 'what is happening at Mirafiori Sud is the final dissolution of any form of workers' identity ... the disappearance of a homogeneous culture and language. The workers' neighbourhood no longer exists ... even if the vast majority of its inhabitants are workers.'[66]

With a series of laws that liberalized the labour market in the 1990s and 2000s, Italy was increasingly divided into 'guaranteed' and 'flexible' employees (in particular the so-called Treu measures in 1997 and the Legge Biagi in 2003). The former still had a series of rights and privileges as public employees or in larger firms, while the latter were usually underpaid, without rights and on short-term contracts. The former were often unsackable (with reference to the 1970 Workers' Statute) while the latter group had no future. In this context, trade unions were seen by many as defenders of the status quo, and as corporate entities who ignored the real situation of many Italians, especially those attempting to enter the labour market for the first time. Many 'flexible' employees were not paid at all. This division was also generational. A whole generation of Italians grew up without having experienced the security of a fixed wage or a long-term contract.

Industrial Districts and Post-industrial Italy

History and roots

Italy's economic development has been marked by the tendency to create *industrial districts*. An industrial district can be defined as 'a community of people and businesses which operate within a limited space, with the presence of economies external to each individual firm, but internal to the district in question. These economies solicit the formation and development of a specialised productive apparatus, in which small firms have a highly relevant role.'[67] Such districts are not a new phenomenon in Italy, despite the fact that much of the current literature ignores the historical roots of this type of industrialization. For example, the area to the immediate north of Milan – Brianza – has long been an industrial district, specializing in furniture, and has been described as 'the historic cradle of Italian design'.[68] This industrial district grew organically from rural society and peasant culture, presenting an alternative model of 'slow industrialization' to the 'rapid industrialization' that characterized most Italian and European regions. Instead of the 'classic' groups of workers and peasants, myriad sectors of peasant-workers and worker-peasants continued to combine agricultural and industrial activity over long periods. From the early days of silkworm farming, where the worms were often nurtured in peasant bedrooms, a tradition of family-based textile manufacture evolved in the area. The furniture industry evolved from the wood-based artisan and peasant traditions of the eighteenth century. A series of small businesses evolved to provide the furniture and fittings for the 700 rooms of Monza's Royal Villa, built between 1780 and 1848. Brianza provided the industrial base for Milan's transition from a Fordist city to a fashion and design capital.

There are hundreds of similar examples across Italy, with products ranging from umbrellas to hats to certain foodstuffs. The town of San Maurizio d'Opaglio on Lake Orta, to the north of Milan and Turin, has a long tradition of tap production, so much so that it has its own Tap Museum. In all, in Italy, there were at least 160 industrial districts operating in the 1990s, taking in 42 per cent of all manufacturing employees. Some were historical districts – such as Vigevano near Milan (for shoes) – and by the 1980s twelve were to be found in the south. These districts combined the advantages of concentrations of services and markets with the flexibility of small industrial production. Over time, big businesses also moved in (such as Nike in the north-east) to take advantage of these specialized territories. Many entrepreneurs employed immigrants, or farmed out parts of their production to countries where labour costs were lower, such as Romania. The protection of small commercial enterprises and artisans by Italian law has helped to shield these districts from moments of crisis. In a period of sharp decline, however, too much specialisation could be a handicap.

Small businesses

The post-industrial boom (which is not post-industrial in any real sense, since here we are generally talking about industries, employing workers) is a *post-Fordist* boom, based (largely) on small business and small factories, and centred on certain historically formed industrial districts. These districts have been at the heart of the 1980s and 1990s export-led boom, based around quality goods – sunglasses, ski boots, chairs, design items, fashion clothing – and centred in the territories of the Veneto and Lombardy, with strong pockets of development right across central Italy and down into parts of the south – above all, Apulia, the Abruzzo and the Molise.

For a long time, many economists, on the Left and the Right, were convinced that small businesses were, by their very nature, inefficient. Yet the Left also exalted small businesses against its chosen enemy in the 1950s and 1960s, 'monopoly capitalism'. The DC, as with small landed property, backed small family businesses for ideological reasons. Today, small businesses are generally glorified as perfect examples of hyper-efficient capitalism, and Fordist production is derided as inefficient. In reality, the extraordinary boom of the 1980s and 1990s in Italy is based around a combination of small and big businesses, and their territorial concentration in industrial districts. Small businesses often had a difficult relationship with public institutions, despite the fact that the state more or less turned a blind eye to tax evasion amongst these enterprises. Internationally, Italy is now a world leader in this sector. In the early 1990s, 70 per cent of Italian employees worked in enterprises with less than 250 workers, compared with 37.5 per cent in Germany, 47 per cent in France, 44.5 per cent in the UK, 67.8 per cent in Spain and 36.6 per cent in the USA. Nearly a quarter of all active Italians worked in businesses with less than 10 employees.

'Padania' and the north-east 'miracle'

The mega-region of Padania was first identified by the Agnelli Research Foundation in 1990. 'Padania' encompassed a series of these industrial districts. In eight central and northern regions, there lay 80 per cent of Italy's businesses and 53 per cent of her investment producing 74 per cent of Italy's exports, with average incomes below only those of the regions around Brussels, Hamburg and Ile de France. Where in the 1960s the factory was the key to understanding social relations, by the 1990s it was *territory* that had become central.

The north-east of Italy was the centre of the economic miracle of the 1980s and 1990s. By the end of the century, there were 10,000 'lire billionaires' in the Province of Treviso alone. Exports from the Province of Vicenza were three times those from the whole of the south. At Rossano-Veneto, where the specialization was bicycle seats, there was a business for every two families. In a 10 km strip between Manzano, San Giovanni al Natisone and Corno di Rosazzo, factories produced four-fifths of all chairs made in Italy, and one-third of those produced in Europe. Some of this production saw the 'double exploitation' of a largely female labour force, both at home and in small factories. In the Province of Treviso 65 per cent of the world's ski boots and 80 per cent of the world's motorbike boots were made. Here there were 55,000 businesses, one for every two inhabitants. Big and small businesses worked on the same territory. The market leader in the key textile sector was Benetton, a multinational that exported 70 per cent of its production, employed 30,000 people and ran 7,000 shops. Tourism was another key sector, especially in Venice with its 800 restaurants, 230 hotels, and 9 million tourists a year. This was the area where the *Lega* was strongest in the 1980s, 1990s and 2000s (see also Chapter 1). Here, people's faith in government was extremely low. In an opinion poll from the 1990s, when asked which institutions they most trusted, respondents put the government below the Church, industrialists' associations, judiciary, local government, the RAI (the State television company – *Radio Televisione Italiana*), banks, the unions and the mass media. A similar poll in 2013 found that nearly 90 per cent of Italians had 'no faith' in Parliament, while only 2% had faith in politicians.

THE STATE AND THE ECONOMY: PUBLIC AND PRIVATE SECTORS

Liberal Italy

The state must direct and not be directed, even in the economic sphere.

GIOVANNI GIOLITTI

State intervention in the Italian economy has always been 'colossal'.[69] Economists have placed Italy with Germany and Japan as amongst nations where the state has intervened to the greatest extent in the economic system.[70] Giolitti nationalized the railways and created a national insurance system. Measures were also introduced in 1903 which allowed local administrations to provide a series of municipal services. Most historians agree on the key role of the state in creating the conditions for Italy's first industrial revolution in the 1890s and early twentieth century, but there are debates over whether this role was as central as, say, that of the private banks or of mass emigration, and over which state activities were important economically (see, for example, Box 3.5). Some economists have called the Italian system 'state capitalism'.[71] This label has been applied by other economists and historians to the whole history of Italian state–economy relations.[72] 'State capitalism' reached a peak with the controlled economic system during World War I. After the war there was some move away from this type of management, but the state still stepped in to save companies in trouble, most notably the giant Ansaldo concern in 1921, a company which constituted 'a veritable military–industrial complex whose survival depended on state purchases'.[73]

Fascism

Fascism began with a period of free-market-inspired policies, under finance minister Alberto De Stefani. The wartime limits on the free market were swept away, the telephone system was privatized and various taxes were abolished (on inheritance and war profits, for example). Salaries fell (as they did throughout the period of fascism) as free trade union bargaining was eroded, through violence and intimidation, and then abolished (by law, along with the abolition of strikes (see Box 3.2). The free market, therefore, was only applied to one player in the capitalist system – the capitalists. Later (from around 1925 onwards), these policies were abandoned in favour of a corporate state, with massive public involvement in the economy.

Some economists and historians have seen the fascist period as one of 'stagnation', others saw it as confirming the economic trends of the Liberal period. Fascism certainly delayed the land reform that Italy so badly needed, cementing her economic dualism. The worst effects of the economic crisis were avoided in comparison with some other industrial nations, but unemployment rose significantly in the early 1930s. Above all, it is difficult to gauge the level of economic support for the regime given the lack of avenues for protest under the fascist state (and problems with official statistics). Fascism laid down some of the infrastructure – railways, land reclamation, motorways – which would later help Italy's boom develop into a 'miracle' after the war.

Labour–capital relations were reshaped within a corporate state where production was promoted as a patriotic duty, and its disruption, by definition, was branded as unpatriotic. The 'interests of the nation' – defined by the fascists as production above all else – took precedence. None the less, fascism had its own unions, who represented, at least officially, the workforce in every sector. It also provided welfare and cultural networks for employees,

Box 3.5   The state and industry: Terni

A key role in Italian industrialization was played by the decision to build a steel factory in Terni, in Umbria. The choice of Terni was a controversial one, given the landlocked nature of the town and the resulting high transport costs. However, the plant was able to use local water supplies for industrial and power supplies, and raw materials from the island of Elba. Terni was chosen as much for military reasons (the ability to defend the plant from attack from the sea) than for industrial ones. Formed in 1884, the Terni company was financed to a large extent by the state. It produced steel for the navy and for the railways: 157,000 tons of steel were produced there in 1885. This was nothing when compared to the 3 million tons a year in the UK and 2 million in Germany, but a massive increase on the mere 4,000 tons produced in Italy in 1881. Terni's development was helped by protectionism but was marked by frequent crises, scandals and accusations of mismanagement. The Terni plant was at the centre of political debate for years. The company was forced to lay off workers in the early 1890s, despite the state's protectionist policies. Other steelworks were opened at Piombino (1897) and Bagnoli (Naples, 1906) and on Elba itself. Terni became a real mega-business during World War I, but was saved from bankruptcy, like many other companies, by a state bail-out in the 1930s.

In the early years, the Terni factory employed peasants from the Umbrian countryside. This small town was dominated by its steelworks, which shaped and built the city. As one Terni resident put it, 'we always talk about the same thing, the steelworks and that's it'. The factory was huge, noisy and smoky. Many described it as 'hell'. Terni was a real company town, one of the very few of its type in Italy, where the company provided a series of social and welfare services – holidays for children, hospitals, sports clubs. Even train times were fixed by the Terni company. This paternalism broke down during the violent class struggles of the 1940s, after which the management moved to Rome 'to avoid contact with the workers'. A deep-rooted culture of resistance developed, expressed also through the names of Terni children – Pensiero (thought), Libero (free), Germinal, Bakunin, Dinamite, Ribelle (rebel) – baptized under a red flag. This history of rebellion also took the form of popular myths and stories, which have been passed down from generation to generation. The Terni firm began to wind down its operations in the 1980s, laying off thousands of workers, as the city attempted to make the difficult adjustment from company town to ex-company town, and to diversify its productive base away from an over-concentration on heavy industry. In the 1990s the company was purchased by a German firm (Thyssen-Krupp) who cut production still further, leading to major protests. A Finnish company took over in 2012, but European anti-trust regulations forced them to put the factory back on the market in 2012. Terni had become part of a global economy.

insurance schemes, and arbitration. The corporate state, for many, was more of a guarantee than the chaotic militancy of pre-fascist Italy. Ideologically, as well, the inclusion of the workers in the Italian nation helped cement a certain type of national identity, although the Fordist working class was never won over to the fascist cause. At an everyday level, each and every individual, however anti-fascist, had to make compromises with the regime, in part to avoid political repression, and in part so as to remain within the economic system.

A key moment in state–economy relations came with the world economic slump of the late 1920s and early 1930s. Italy, under fascism, took specific steps to shield itself from the worst consequences of the recession. The Italian state set up a series of massive state (or 'parastate') holdings, which controlled large sectors of Italian industry and the financial system: in 1931 the regime created IMI (*Istituto Mobiliare Italiano*) to run the building industry, but the most significant of these holdings was IRI (*Istituto per la Ricostruzione Industriale*, established in 1933), the Institute for Italian Reconstruction. IRI took over *one-quarter* of Italy's financial and industrial assets; 90 per cent of those employed in state industries in Campania were under the auspices of IRI. Half of the country's share capital was administered by the holding, including 90 per cent of the nation's shipyards, 40 per cent of her iron production and four-fifths of the shipping companies. IRI was made a permanent organization in 1937. In 1945 IRI controlled 216 share-holding companies with 135,000 employees. In these parastate companies, public managers had relative freedom to act, but were obliged to help out big private concerns. In this way, industry was protected from the worst effects of international crises. IRI, a fascist creation born to save Italy's industry from crisis, soon became a permanent system of state-industrial management. In 1936, the powerful head of IRI, Beneduce, underlined the role of the state in the Italian economy:

> a politics of autarchy in a country poor in capital like Italy must start from the direct role of the state with relation to big industry, just as a politics which aims to create social justice cannot allow that there are super capitalist organizations which are not under the control of the state.   (Report on the IRI budget, 1936)

State holdings continued to be a key part of the Italian economy after 1945. ENI, set up in 1953 to run Italian energy reserves, was particularly important under the management of Enrico Mattei, a Catholic, anti-fascist partisan (1943–5) and dynamic businessman. Mattei challenged US hegemony over oil and energy production, discovered and invested in petrol and gas deposits in the Po Valley and employed an extraordinary network of technicians to modernize the Italian energy system – 1,300 engineers, 300 geologists, 2,000 graduates and 3,000 scientific diploma students. Mattei made his base in Milan, building a whole new zone of the city as his administrative and financial centre – known as *Metanopoli*.

After World War II, the state found itself to be the owner of all national commercial banks, the railways, shipping, all telecommunications, all steel production, shipbuilding, and the vast bulk of the oil and chemical industries.

In addition, electricity was nationalized in 1962 (creating ENEL, the *Ente Nazionale per l'Energia Elettrica*). In the 1950s, state investment (and some elements of central planning) played a key role in laying the bases for the economic miracle. Car companies, in particular Fiat, could benefit from low-cost, locally produced steel and metal (produced largely by the state), a massive road and motorway network (the *autostrada del sole*, which ran for 755 km from Milan to Naples, was completed in record time in 1964, after only eight years of construction work), domestic gas and petrol production and an extensive network of petrol stations. Price controls also encouraged mass motorization. Slowly, the state developed all the trappings of welfare capitalism including a generous pension system and a national health service, but all this came at a cost.

The State Debt

During the 1970s and 1980s, the state debt began to dominate debate around Italy's economic future (although the issue of the debt had always been an object for political discussion, from unification onwards). Public debt quadrupled between 1985 and 1994. By the mid-1990s, the interest on this debt alone amounted to 25 per cent *of all state spending*. The Italian welfare state, and increasing government/administrative costs, were the biggest contributors to the deficit. Political parties raided the state's coffers in order to maintain huge party structures, and a ministry had been set up specifically to control the state sector and share out resources amongst the parties (the Ministry for State Participation, instituted in 1956). The state continued to buy up industries, and run them badly, throughout the post-war period, from the electricity nationalization, to a series of food companies. This 'public neocapitalism'[74] was combined with the 'benign neglect' of the Christian Democrats, who never seriously attempted any planning, despite their near-permanence in power. Mass education brought enormous costs, as well as obvious benefits. An ageing population required more and more pension funds. The black economy and tax evasion meant that the state's coffers were not filled as they should have been. An unholy pact with the middle classes, who depended on the state, and were allowed to avoid taxes, created a vicious circle of dependency and clientelistic networks. Invalidity pensions absorbed 4.5 per cent of national income in 1975, as against 1.3 per cent in France, 1.8 per cent in the UK and 2.3 per cent in Germany; 2.2 per cent of the total population of Italy received this type of pension in 1995, which represented 42 per cent of the total pension budget in 1995. Over a million Italians were in early retirement in 1996, to which were added a quarter of a million 'baby pensioners', of whom 15 per cent were under 45. Politicians were trapped within the system, as their future depended on the existence of these networks. Yet it was clear to everyone by the end of the 1980s that, even in the short term, this type of expenditure could not be maintained. A series of reforms in the 2000s raised the future pension age for all Italians, leaving some people without any protection at all, in a kind of financial limbo. These were the so-called *esodati*, or income-deprived early retirees.

Box 3.6   Unions and the law: The 1948 Constitution

The right to strike was reinstated in 1948. A series of decisions made by the Constitutional Court widened this to include political strikes and boycotts.

Article 1   Italy is a democratic Republic founded on labour.

Article 4 [Work]
(1) The Republic recognizes the right of all citizens to work and promotes such conditions as will make this right effective.
(2) According to capability and choice every citizen has the duty to undertake an activity or a function that will contribute to the material and moral progress of society.

Article 36 [Wages]
(1) Workers shall be entitled to remuneration commensurate with the quantity and quality of their work, and in any case sufficient to ensure to them and their families a free and honourable existence.
(2) The law shall establish limits to the length of the working day.
(3) Workers shall be entitled to a weekly day of rest and to annual paid holidays; they cannot relinquish this right.

Article 37 [Equality of Women at Work]
(1) Working women shall be entitled to equal rights and, for comparable jobs, equal pay with men. The working conditions shall be such as to allow women to fulfil their essential family duties and ensure an adequate protection of mothers and children.

Article 39 [Trade Unions]
(1) The organization of trade unions is free.
(2) No obligation shall be imposed on trade unions except that of registering at local or central offices according to the provisions of the law.
(3) Trade unions shall only be registered on condition that their by-laws shall establish internal organizations based on democratic principles.

Article 40 [Right to Strike]   The right to strike shall be exercised according to the laws which regulate it.

Article 41 [Freedom of Enterprise]
(1) Private economic enterprise shall be free.
(2) It shall not be carried out against the common good or in a way that may harm public security, liberty, and human dignity.
(3) The law shall determine appropriate planning and controls so that public and private economic activities may be directed and coordinated towards social ends.

Article 46 [Workers' Participation]   In order to achieve the economic and social enhancement of labour and in accordance with the requirements of production, the Republic shall recognize the right of workers to take part in the management of companies in the manner and within the limits established by law.

Box 3.7 Unions and the law: the Workers' Statute, May 1970 (extracts) and the 1990s

This statute has the power of a legal document.

Article 14 The right to form trade unions, to join them and to take part in union activity, is guaranteed for all the workers within the workplace.

Article 18 The sacking of a worker without just cause or reason is not permitted, and the worker must be re-employed in the workplace.

Article 20 Meetings: Workers have a right to meet in the workplace outside of working hours, and for up to ten paid hours annually during working hours.

Article 25 Trade union representatives have the right to hang up, in the spaces provided, which the employer is obliged to provide for all workers within the workplace, publications, texts and material of trade union or worker interest.

Article 27 The employer in firms employing more than 200 workers is obliged to provide a permanent room within or close to the working area for the use of the union representatives.

In the 1990s, in the face of constant public service disputes, measures were passed which limited strikes in certain transport sectors. Strikes were to be announced with ten days' notice, and the government could constrain certain numbers of employees to work to keep basic services going.

Something had to give, with Europe pressing for targets to be reached. In 1992, under intense pressure, Prime Minister Giuliano Amato began to dismantle the enormous state machine, and cut back on pensions. A combination of tax increases and cuts in state spending helped Italy meet the demands for European Monetary Union. Some privatization of the huge state sector began, often under the control of large private concerns. The deep-rooted corruption of the political and economic elites was exposed in a series of scandals and bankruptcies throughout the 1990s and 2000s, such as those involving Parmalat, Cirio and other companies (see Box 4.4). Meanwhile, the quality small-business sector exploited a weak lira to create a short-lived post-Fordist boom in the 1990s. Despite everything, the Italian economy moved forward with speed for a time, even as the state itself teetered on the verge of bankruptcy. This short-lived boom came to a shuddering halt towards the end of the first decade of the 2000s, as the euro contributed to the end of Italy's competitive edge. A series of governments presided over by Silvio Berlusconi did little to deal with the spiralling debt after the austerity measures applied in the early part of the decade. The global financial and eurozone crisis threatened to bring the whole edifice crashing down in 2008 (see Box 3.8). In 2011 an emergency, technocratic government led by the economist Mario Monti attempted to implement a harsh austerity programme of cuts and tax rises.

But this strategy proved extremely unpopular. Monti gained only 9 per cent of the vote in the 2013 elections.

The 'Extraordinary Compromise' and the South

Throughout the post-war period, politicians continued to intervene in the economy with special laws, extraordinary measures and specific state funds.

Box 3.8 Italy, the end of the lira and the eurozone

Italy abolished its own, historic currency and adopted the euro on 1 January 2002. On that day, a party in Rome was presided over by Romano Prodi, one of the key architects of the shift to the eurozone, and Italians all over the country visited cashpoint machines to take out the new currency. This moment of euphoria was short-lived. Prices seemed to rise almost immediately on all goods and the advantages traditionally provided by the relatively weak lira were wiped out overnight. The euro also provided a good excuse for many of Italy's structural economic issues, especially for politicians. Giulio Tremonti, finance minister under the Berlusconi governments in the early twenty-first century, was a consistent critic of the single currency, and advocated a one-euro note in order to control spending. Other parties adopted more strident anti-euro propaganda, in particular the *Lega Nord* and, increasingly, Silvio Berlusconi. Later, Beppe Grillo was the first major political figure to float the idea of a referendum on the euro (the Italian people had never been given the chance to decide on this issue).

As the eurozone crisis after 2008 engulfed Greece, Ireland, Spain and Portugal, Italy appeared to be the domino that could not be allowed to fall. European Union leaders were increasingly unhappy with the financial management (or lack of it) imposed by Silvio Berlusconi after 2008. The world's eyes were on Italy, which was often associated with the supposedly generic ills of southern Europe (a large state sector, a corrupt political class, an inefficient political system). Although Italy's banks generally held firm, the Monte Paschi di Siena crisis was a warning sign. Inexorably, it seemed, the cost of servicing Italy's debt rose throughout 2010 and 2011. The word 'spread' now appeared to be on everybody's lips. Angela Merkel and Nicolas Sarkozy openly called for political change in Italy. It was at this point, in the autumn of 2011, that the crisis reached its peak. Berlusconi was forced to resign, and an emergency technical government was put in its place, with the support of both coalitions. The new prime minister was someone who reassured the markets *and* the European institutions, the economist and former European Commissioner Mario Monti. Monti said that Italy had been on the brink of bankruptcy. Economically, at least, Monti managed to steady the ship, and avoid Italy having to ask for a bail-out. Yet, his policies were unpopular and lacking in democratic legitimation. Italians remained pro-European (mainly in comparison with their highly negative view of their own political system) but those heady days at the cashpoints in 2002 seemed light years away.

A model was established which Barca has called the 'extraordinary compromise', which protected the economy from the extremes of the market and used channels of state resources as providers and procurers of political power and consensus.[75] No clear rules were set, or adhered to, to guarantee equality of access within the marketplace. Italy suffered from what was dubbed 'a deficit of competition',[76] especially in the south, which, in addition, failed to prevent mass protest because either the resources were badly distributed or too much of the money fell into the hands of the parties. The Reggio Calabria riots (1969–72) were sparked off by the decision to locate Calabria's regional capital in Catanzaro – a choice that potentially deprived this poor city of access to significant state resources. Important professions – lawyers, journalists, doctors – were sheltered from the market by their inclusion in corporative professional guilds which were kept within the state system after 1948.

THE 'SOUTHERN QUESTION': THE PROBLEM OF PROBLEMS

It is impossible to discuss the development of the Italian economy and Italian society without understanding the key role of the 'southern question'. But it is also important to understand what we mean by the 'southern question'. All countries have poor regions and rich regions. Yet, as Cafagna has argued, in Italy this *dualism* 'had a clear territorial basis'. 'Italian dualism', he concludes, 'was rigorously polarised in geographical terms, with characteristics which were more or less unique in the world.' This unique nature is also supported by Aymard, for whom 'nowhere else has the importance of internal inequalities been as crucial, and in any case nowhere else has it taken so clear a spatial form as in Italy'.[77] (For an example of southern poverty, see Box 3.9.)

The New Southern History and the Critique of the 'Southern Question'

Discussions of the 'southern question' have invariably begun with the assumption that the south, as a whole, was 'backward'. Italy was described as 'a giant with feet of clay'.[78] This 'paradigm of backwardness' is problematic for a number of reasons, pointed out with force by a group of new southern historians in the 1980s, 1990s and 2000s. The paradigm viewed the south as an 'undifferentiated agricultural wasteland', ignoring the differences *within* the south, the 'souths' of the south and pockets of growth, export agriculture and urban change. The paradigm also viewed the south above all as a *problem*, and purely through a comparison with the north, as 'the frustrating tale of what might have been', as 'the negative incarnation of "a question", an obscure problem, almost a social illness'.[79] 'The history of the South was reduced to the history of the Southern Problem while Italian history was made elsewhere.'[80] It is also true that Italy as a whole has often been looked at through the blinkers of a 'paradigm of backwardness' in comparison with other countries, thus reducing Italy to Europe's backward 'south'.[81] New

---

Box 3.9   Matera, the 'Stones' and the 'southern question'

History

The symbol of the 'southern question' after 1945 was Matera in Basilicata. In the early 1950s, 15,000 people were still living in the series of caves and other kinds of dwellings cut into the stones of the hillside of the city – an area known as the *sassi* di Matera. Riccardo Musatti analysed the *sassi* in 1950. He found 1,500 inhabited grottos, almost all without running water, electricity or drains. Animals lived with people. It was decided that a series of new rural villages would be created to put an end to the 'shameful' state of affairs. In July 1950 Prime Minister De Gasperi visited Matera, and announced urgent state aid. A commission was set up to study plans for a new village, and a series of research projects looked at the city in detail. A census was carried out of the *sassi*, and a huge model prepared of the whole area. Meanwhile, a debate was emerging over the form of the new housing. The technicians called for separate farmhouses with their own land, and a collection of services in a central area; the architects defended the original plan of a village arguing that the division of houses would have destroyed the community aspects built up by life in the *sassi*.

A location was finally chosen at La Martella, 7 km from the centre of Matera. Work began in 1952 (following a special state law), and the village was 'opened' by De Gasperi a year later with the arrival of the first residents and a 'symbolic closure of the *sassi*' (M. Talamona, 'Dieci anni di politica dell' Unrra Casas', p. 195). The design of the village looked to re-create the community life of the *sassi* through planning and a minimalist architecture which attempted 'to create a mix of surfaces, sizes and colours which could in some way not constitute a trauma for those who had abandoned … the "Sassi"' (Lodovico Quaroni). Only one other of the three planned villages was ever built. The second village remained empty for years.

In many ways, despite the beauty of the architecture and the good intentions of those involved, the new village was a failure. The timing was wrong, as Italy's economic miracle was imminent. The aim of 're-creating' the rich community of the *sassi*, as those involved fully understood, could not be carried out through architecture alone. Meanwhile, the *sassi* themselves were emptied thanks to a series of special laws in the 1950s. Later, the whole area was designated as a protected archaeological site and is now a popular destination for tourists. Today, there are moves to re-inhabit the *sassi* through the redevelopment of some ex-houses and caves. Mel Gibson's decision to shoot *The Passion* in Matera (2004) also contributed to a revival and rebranding of the *sassi*.

---

historians of the south reject the stale dualisms of the past. They view the south (however defined) as part of a complicated international economic system, with 'souths' within its midst. The state is not seen *a priori* as playing a negative role, but as a collector and dispenser of resources. Thus, these historians also reject some of the rhetorical 'victimism' of previous southern history – which viewed the history of Italy as one long series of crimes against the *mezzogiorno* perpetuated by the Piedmontese state. This 'victimism' was the mirror-image of the dualisms of the past. Finally, the south is pictured as a dynamic, not a static society.

None the less, it is widely accepted, even within the new southern history, that the economic and social divisions between north and south, while not unique to Italy, have 'dogged the heels of national development' of the nation (Cohen and Federico).[82] The divisions were bigger, and more permanent, than in other nations. There was 'an exceptionally pronounced interregional gap'.[83] How have historians tried to explain this 'gap'? The historian Giorgio Candeloro agreed that the industrial revolution of the 1890s increased the distance between north and south, and argued that the backwardness of the south was functional to the development of the north. In other words, in broad agreement with southernists such as Nitti and Salvemini, he claimed that the south was underdeveloped *because* the north was developed, and vice versa. Far from being a ball and chain, the south's backwardness was a crucial part of Italian industrialization. Nitti also saw the south as a kind of colony, which the Italian market exploited for raw materials and labour. Cafagna has argued that economic dualism was not produced by unification, but was already there. Unification 'made dualism clear, but did not provoke it'.[84] Romeo claimed that the early state did what it could in difficult economic circumstances, and that dualism was an inevitable outcome given the differences between north and south, but was exacerbated by the workings of the market.[85]

The State and the South: Subsidy, Reform, Investment

Investment in the south failed to modernize society to the same extent as in the north. In 1905, only 1.8 per cent of land in the south was adequately irrigated, as opposed to 12 per cent in the north. A number of solutions were proposed to deal with these imbalances. One was state investment. In 1902 a Brescian politician, Giuseppe Zanardelli, decided to visit the symbol of southern poverty – Basilicata.[86] For weeks, he crossed the area by mule, at the age of 76. Speeches made at the end of his trip summed up his experiences.

> I have visited nearly the whole region ... and the sad exceptionality of its conditions was worse than I could ever have expected. For days I travelled through bare mountains ... without seeing any signs of production, without even a blade of grass with valleys which were equally unproductive ... we went for hours and hours without even finding a house.[87]

In 1904 (despite Zanardelli's death in 1903) the government passed a series of special laws in favour of Basilicata. Many of the measures depended on a diagnosis of the problems of the region which highlighted the natural backwardness of the area, not its social structure. Hence, the law financed a series of public works programmes and prioritized tree-planting and measures to prevent further soil erosion. This type of reform – which viewed the south as,

above all, *naturally* backward – failed to root out the systems of property ownership that were a key part of the mechanisms producing poverty and
unemployment.[88]

In the 1950s, in addition to the agrarian reforms, the DC poured money
into the south through more straightforward public investment. This was
coordinated through the *Cassa per il Mezzogiorno*, also established in 1950. The
Cassa invested in public works and handed out credit for local businesses.
Modernization slowly took hold of the south. Land was reclaimed, roads and
motorways were constructed, drains dug and fields irrigated. There was no
direct intervention in southern industry, however, until 1957. The history of
the *Cassa* has not been interpreted as a success story. Industries supported by
the fund have been heavily criticized for their inefficiency and lack of strategic planning. Many became known as 'cathedrals in the desert'. Examples
include, or included, the steelworks at Taranto, the Alfa Sud factory near
Naples and the defunct petro-chemical plant at Gela. A new class of political
mediators developed through the administration of the *Cassa* in the south. As
time went on, into the 1970s, more and more money was simply circulating
within the clientelistic networks made up of the parties, voters, clients and
clienteles. State spending was disproportionately geared towards the south,
which received more than a third of state expenditure while 'giving back' less
than a fifth in taxes.

The *Cassa* appeared, on paper, to be a Keynesian organization, inspired by
public works theories of development such as those to be found in the CGIL's
'Plan of work' (1950, see Box 3.10). Yet the intense politicization of the *Cassa*'s
operations, and its use of 'mass clientelism' (G. Sapelli), meant that the virtuous
cycles of Keynesian investment were never able to develop. Resources were
almost always functional to political ends, when they were not simply siphoned
off by organized crime. The south's structural unemployment remained
untouched. Funds were usually distributed as part of a *political exchange*, never
really intended to create autonomous cultures of innovation and change. The
Cassa closed all operations in 1992, just as the DC itself went into terminal decline.

A key area of resource distribution has been the state pension system.
Public employees have enjoyed fabulous advantages over private employees in terms of access to (low) steady pensions. Staff working for the Sicilian
regional government are entitled to early retirement after 25 years (for men)
and 20 years (for women). The pension consists of 80 per cent of the last pay
packet. There are now 10,000 pensioners of this type in Sicily, and the
regional government is forced to use its normal budget to pay the bill. Some
grotesque examples of these 'baby pensions' fed anti-state political movements in the 1980s, 1990s and 2000s. A woman born in 1951 in Messina
worked in a factory from the age of fifteen. In 1977 she began work as a
school keeper, obtaining a permanent contract in 1982. Four months later,
she asked for early retirement. She became a pensioner, at the age of 31,
eleven months after being taken on with a regular contract. Since then (up
to 1998) she has received 260 million lire in pension payments. If she lives to
the age of 79 (the average age for an Italian woman) she will have received
a billion lire.

> **Box 3.10** The trade unions, the Left and planning
>
> In 1949 the biggest and most radical trade union federation, the CGIL, laid out a detailed 'Plan of Work' for Italy, based upon reformist Keynesian principles. A wide-ranging debate took place around the plan.
>
> The CGIL's 'Plan of Work' was explained by Giuseppe Di Vittorio, the union federation's secretary. Di Vittorio underlined the high levels of unemployment in Italy. He argued that 'the greatest national economic problems can be resolved'. He called for the building of power stations, especially in the south.
>
> In addition, he argued for a big state housing programme, the construction of schools and hospitals.
>
> Di Vittorio's analysis was simple, and class-based. 'In Italy', he said, 'to the shame of the ruling classes, those classes which have governed Italy from unification onwards – they have changed their names, but they are still the same – to the great shame of the selfish middle classes, we have thousands of towns without water, without electricity, without sewers, without schools, ambulances, clinics, cemeteries'.
>
> The solution, for Di Vittorio, was straightforward. Progressive taxation, capital investment, centralized economic planning. But Di Vittorio also offered the collaboration of the union movement with these proposed reforms. 'To realize the plan', he argued, 'we are ready to submit ourselves to new sacrifices'. This was a national project that would provide 'an escape from unemployment, poverty, backwardness and which will place Italy on the road of progress and civilization'. Interestingly, the Christian Democratic Party and the Socialists in the centre–left alliances did carry out extensive nationalization and centrally planned investment in houses, health, infrastructure and other public works. They were orthodox Keynesians.

Snapshots from a Changing South: I

Within this broad story of underdevelopment and stagnation, the south has changed greatly over the last century, ever since 'the south' became a 'question'.

Salvemini and Molfetta, 1896–1954

The great southern intellectual Gaetano Salvemini was born in Molfetta, a small town between Barletta and Bari in Apulia, in 1873. He was the second of nine surviving children of the twelve borne by his mother. Salvemini was a teacher and active socialist from the 1880s onwards, and studied at Florence University. He was also among the first historians and sociologists of the south, reporting from the small town of Molfetta on a regular basis, and was elected to Parliament to represent the town after 1919. In 1897 Salvemini wrote a series of three articles on Molfetta for the PSI journal *Critica Sociale*.[89] These articles described the reality of peasant life on the *latifondo*, the poverty and the non-socialism of the local fishermen. For Salvemini (as for Gramsci) the southern peasantry could only be mobilized through the work of 'organic intellectuals', educated middle-class militants who could spread socialist ideas. Throughout the century, Salvemini kept an eye on events in Molfetta, and his personal life was consumed by tragedy. He survived 1908's massive Messina earthquake but lost his wife, five children and a sister.

Finally, after a long exile (under fascism, whose followers called Salvemini 'earthquake brain' and 'the ape of Molfetta') and in one of his last journalistic 'investigations', Salvemini reflected on the changes to Molfetta over half a century of Italian life.[90] By 1954, Molfetta's population had risen to 57,000 from the 14,000 of 1813 and the 30,000 of 1880. The town, however, had always exported people and imported food: 5,000 Molfettians had gone to Venezuela alone, 15,000 lived purely on emigrants' remittances. There were many more small landowners than in 1897, in part thanks to the agrarian reforms of 1950 – the *latifondi* were a distant memory. Salvemini's earlier pessimism about the fishermen had been misplaced – they were by 1954 the best organized and most radical section of the population. Malaria had been eradicated, although water was still scarce. Only 10 per cent were illiterate, although Salvemini noted that many chose to buy what he called 'cretinous' popular magazines. The four cinemas in the town attracted 8,000 people on Sundays. 'The entire population' were football fans. Politically, the Christian Democrats dominated the town, although the Left had a strong presence. Above all, the grinding poverty of the 1890s had gone. 'If I close my eyes and think back 60 years or so, in comparison with today, it seems like I am living in a different world.' 'Then, most day-labourers went barefoot: today, men, women and children all have shoes.' 'The material progress – that is the passage from an animal-like way of life to a human one – has been immense for the mass of the population,' Salvemini concluded. And the 'economic miracle' had only just begun in 1954. Molfettians would soon leave in great numbers for the industrial triangle of the north, bringing further wealth to the north, and to the south, through their work in the factories of Milan, Genoa and Turin.

The Changing South: II

Sicily: from hovels to palaces

The south had changed, it had transformed itself over the twentieth century, but this progress had not been straightforward or linear. In an influential analysis from the 1970s, Jane and Peter Schneider also took a small town, which they called Villamura, as an object of their study. The Schneiders concluded that this Sicilian town had *modernized*, but not *developed*: 'Societies that modernize in the absence of economic development', they wrote, 'are vulnerable to the ideologies and life-styles of industrial metropolitan centres … a modernizing society may experience rapid and marked social change, but does not control it or direct it.'[91] Sicily had experienced great changes in standards of living, in access to education and to mass cultural forms, in consumption levels, but this had not been matched by *development* within the economic system or, in fact, the political system. Everyday business, administrative and political activity was marked by a dependence on clientelism, patronage, corruption and violence. None the less, the structural changes were dramatic. Fewer and fewer people worked in the agricultural sector. Women were allowed access to the education system on par with men. Families had declined in size, if not in importance.

Housing had improved beyond all measure. Before 1945, 75 per cent of houses in Villamura had no indoor plumbing; by 1960 nearly all were so equipped. The home 'became an icon, signalling membership in society as well as being cherished for its comfort and appearance'.[92] Often, the construction of houses, by their owners, had taken years or even decades. Half-built, unfinished houses became a common feature of the southern urban/rural landscape. New houses were built with separate bedrooms for the children, with clean, bright tiles and gleaming bathrooms. Separation within the home was so important, as a symbol of the leap in status implied by the ability not to sleep all in one room (a feature noted by almost all commentators on the 'old' south), that long corridors were built to accommodate the various rooms. This tendency had begun through remittances from emigrants in the early twentieth century – when the houses built were known as 'American houses', with white-washed walls. When the Jacini inquiry reported on housing in the south in the 1880s it found dwellings of rough stone, with leaky cane ceilings and dirt floors, frequently with no windows and hence no light. Often animals were kept inside the house. The toilet was a hole in the floor. The family slept together, on the floor or sometimes in hammocks. By comparison with this past, the sparkling new houses of the 1980s, 1990s and 2000s in Sicily were like the palaces of the rich noble families in the 1890s.

Eboli: mediation and the state

Christ Stopped at Eboli, the book by Carlo Levi set in Basilicata, is not about Eboli at all. Eboli, none the less, partly thanks to this title, became a symbol of the 'immobile south, far from the state and at the margins of history'.[93] Eboli is a medium-sized coastal town in Campania, studied in detail by the anthropologist Gabriella Gribaudi. Looking closely at Eboli, Gribaudi draws out the ways in which complicated systems of struggles have been internalized, changed and demobilized through mediation and the distribution of resources. Traditions of political and social conflict impact upon contemporary debates through the importance of networks, territory and family histories. This centrality of mediation has remained, and reinforced itself over time. In the south the state is often 'not seen as an impartial arbiter, but as a resource to which one gained access through connections'.[94] Models of clientelism and patronage, far from dying out, have been reinforced through successive waves of state intervention and special laws. 'It is precisely the pervasive and centralising presence of public institutions, and their near total economic monopoly, which provokes the perversion of accumulative mechanisms, hijacks intelligence and entrepreneurship, and consolidates networks of parasitic mediation which lead to inefficiency and corruption.'[95] This is 'a vicious circle with deep roots' in Eboli, despite trends of economic, cultural and social progress similar to those in Sicily and Molfetta.

The South Today

New developments in the south, in particular in the Abruzzo, Molise and Apulia, 'have shattered the old mould'[96] built around rigid concepts of dualism and uneven development. The whole south has become richer, so much so in some regions that commentators have claimed that the Abruzzo is no longer part of the *mezzogiorno*. However, the concept of *modernization without development* remains an important one, and the presence of organized crime continues to be a crucial component of southern society. It is claimed that 90 per cent of shops in Catania in Sicily are forced to pay money to protection rackets. A further estimate claimed that 12.5 per cent of the GDP in the south originated from criminal activity. In 1988, anti-Mafia commissioner Domenico Sica declared that three Italian regions were no longer under the full control of the state – Calabria, Sicily and Campania. An alternative economic 'system' flourished thanks to the drug trade and other illegal activities, and invested its profits in the north and other parts of the world. Structural unemployment is still very high, especially amongst the young – in 1992 unemployment stood at 4.3 per cent in Lombardy, and 22 per cent in Campania and Sicily – and is largely a southern phenomenon. In addition, state services are of a lower standard but the dependence on the state is far greater. The 'southern question', however defined, remained a crucial one for the Italian state and Italian society in the twenty-first century.

chapter
4
Politics

CONTENTS

ANALYSING ITALIAN POLITICS

The Rules of the Game and Political Cultures[1]

> For your friends you interpret the law, for your enemies you apply it.
>
> GIOVANNI GIOLITTI

> How, gentlemen, can you expect to stop theft and fraud in our country when we have seen these crimes committed with impunity in the highest spheres?
>
> FRANCESCO CRISPI[2]

> Laws are applied to enemies, but only interpreted as regards friends.
>
> GIOVANNI GIOLITTI

Crucial to any understanding of Italian politics (and of the Italian state, the economy and the nation) have been the overarching rules by which the system has governed itself, *and* the extent to which these rules have been adhered to. As we saw in Chapter 2, two basic sets of rules have structured Italian politics since unification, the 1848 Albertine Statute and the 1948 Constitution. Most other rules have operated *within* these frameworks.

Two broad tendencies have characterized diagnoses of the failures of Italian political systems since unification. One tendency emphasizes the inadequacies and effects of the *rules of the game*. That is, certain kinds of institutional frameworks – electoral systems, parliamentary systems, administrative organization – produced specific types of politics and political cultures. Hence, institutional reform was needed to create change. With different rules, politics might have worked more efficiently. Other commentators have always stressed the anthropological and cultural factors shaping Italian politics – familism, the tendency towards clientelism and *parentela*, the role of the south, Italy's Mediterranean history, the character of Italians.[3] Institutional reform, if we accept this scenario, would make little difference. The problems were and are much more deep-rooted. A cultural revolution was required, which would include the tendency to adhere to the rules of the game. And not all the rules of the game were written down; in fact, some of the most important rules were and are cultural norms, rules about what could and could not be done, or illegal rules, written down in some cases but not part of the legal or constitutional political framework.

This chapter will utilize both of these ways of understanding Italian politics. The rules of the game were and are crucial, but so are the anthropological and cultural frameworks within which those rules were formed, re-formed, and function. Thus, the tools adopted by political scientists can help us understand the successes and failures of Italian politics, but we also need to draw on the work of historians, anthropologists and ethnographers to be able to draw out how Italian politics has worked, or not worked.

Generally, again, historians have tended to depict Italian politics as a series of failures and semi-catastrophes, saved only by the praiseworthy efforts of certain 'illuminated' elites – the leaders of the Risorgimento (above all Cavour), Giolitti, the Action Party (1943–6) and, depending on which version you accept, the Communists or Christian Democracy. This type of 'catastrophic' analysis ignores the progress made by Italy and the Italian state since 1860. It is also an intensely politicized and top–down analysis – pulling out a kind of virtuous thread (usually linked to specific personalities) from Italian history. Which thread you choose depends on your political persuasion. Much of this is also based on counterfactual history, an exercise in historical wishful thinking. What most of these studies fail to do is to understand the contradictions of Italian political history. We are not dealing merely with a horror story, where the 'good guys' always lose, or where to win it was necessary to resort to immoral methods. Italian politics produced extraordinary results, in difficult situations, but it also contributed to its own legitimation crises. The politicization of history has been particularly strong in Italy as a result of the deep political and social divisions over time, and this in turn produced divided and largely irreconcilable historical narratives. This type of analysis has come under serious challenge in recent years from what has been called the 'new Risorgimento history' (see Box 1.1).

DEFINITIONS AND KEYWORDS

Certain concepts, 'keywords' and dualisms need to be laid out before any discussion of the political history of Italy can be attempted. Some of these concepts are 'ways of being', anthropological states, some delineate political sensibilities or trends, others specific historical moments, and others political ideologies and cultures. The list is necessarily incomplete, and the rest of this chapter will integrate these concepts and definitions with the history of Italian politics. One key area of discussion has always concerned the extent to which Italian politics and political systems have been marked by continuities, or breaks, and if so, how have these continuities, or breaks, translated themselves into politics. Some concepts have already been dealt with in previous chapters, and will be referred to here in passing, others will be introduced further ahead.

Transformism: Changing Sides

Italian politicians, and sometimes whole parties, have regularly changed sides. This process, whereby new alliances arose from short-term ends, and not from political principle and ideology, and could therefore be broken at any time, was first noted with Depretis in 1876 and became part of political discourse during the 1880s. The Giolittian period is usually seen as the peak of transformism, yet many fascists came from the world of socialism and syndicalism, not least Mussolini himself, and became ferocious anti-socialists. This process, however, is not so much one of transformism but one of renegadism – the *permanent* changing of political sides, not temporary shifts (more common in the Liberal period). Transformism did not disappear after 1945, despite the rigid barriers of the cold war. The Socialist Party formed an alliance with the Christian Democrats in 1962, fourteen years after having fought the acrimonious election campaign of 1948. The Communist Party supported DC governments from 1976 to 1979 (the 'historic compromise'). Within the huge DC party, politicians regularly moved from faction to faction. After 1989, transformism once again became the norm in a fluid post-cold war world. The regionalist *Lega* stood with Berlusconi in 1994, then supported a centre–left government in 1995, before standing alone in 1996, and then again with Berlusconi in 2001. Lamberto Dini was finance minister in the 1994 Berlusconi government, and then prime minister of a centre–left backed government (plus the *Lega*) in 1995. Numerous deputies changed sides in the 2000s, leading to the fall of a number of governments over this period. A 'transfer market' in deputies and senators also emerged, with offers of ministerial posts or even simply cash in return for political support. This type of movement was most common amongst centrist groups and individual deputies, who rapidly moved from alliance to alliance and formed new groups to take advantage of short-term political crises.

The key political feature of transformism is therefore the lack of a clear distinction between government and opposition. In this sense, the most 'transformist' periods of Italian political history have been 1860–1914, 1962–79, 1992–2001 and 2006–2013 although transformism was not absent from other moments, and even under fascism did not disappear altogether. In Spain after 1875 a similar system developed, in conjunction with *caciquismo*, which became known as '*il turno – el turno*', 'whereby two political parties automatically rotated in power through the mechanism of contrived elections'.[4] Giulio Bollati also underlined the behavioural aspects of transformism, the

> gap between declared intentions and actual behaviour; the ability to make the themes and words of one's adversary one's own, to empty them of significance; the willingness to let oneself be won over; disagreement in public – and agreement behind closed doors … its [transformism's] aim is power for its own sake.[5]

Why has this type of political activity always been so strong in Italy, and what effects has it had? How can we explain the birth and survival of transformism? Some answers to these questions are historical – the lack of mass parties in Liberal Italy (see below), the impossibility of a coherent national policy in a country with such strong economic and social dualisms and the strong bureaucratic centralism of the new state. For Fontana, a common national project was impossible in Italy, and thus 'political and parliamentary aggregation took place on the basis of particularistic and personal interests which were often contradictory'.[6] Huge state intervention in the economy encouraged politicians not to cut themselves off from the resources that could be used to maintain power. Institutional arrangements allowed transformism within the political system. Politicians could change sides with very little consequence for themselves or their parties, but with enough effect to make these changes worthwhile. Gramsci argued that it was Italy's 'passive revolution' (the Risorgimento) which created the basis for transformism as a means of exercising power. The decline of mass parties in the 1990s and 2000s also meant that loyalties were less binding.

One key *effect* of transformism, over time, has been to create, or exacerbate, a cynicism towards politics amongst ordinary citizens. Politics, although characterized by strong ideologies, became seen as essentially the 'art of the possible', the means by which resources could be accessed and used by the powerful, and the renegotiation of the link between the powerful and the powerless. Numerous political commentators have attacked the transformism of Italy's politicians, from Labriola to Salvemini to Mussolini to Berlusconi. Croce, however, defended the 'realism' and unity of transformism and attacked those who compared abstract liberal models with the Italian system. Elite theorists such as Mosca and Pareto analysed the transformism of Italian politics in their seminal works of the 1880s. For Mosca the 'members [of Parliament] only represent a quantity of private interests, the sum of which are a long way from becoming a public interest'.[7] Transformism in the post-1945 period has often been confused with *consociationism*.

Consociationism

During the 1970s, sociologists worked out a theory to describe the sharing out of power between political parties. This system became known as *consociationism*. The public 'cake' was divided in various ways between all parties, including the opposition. Similar systems had also developed in Belgium, Holland and Austria. Consociationism reached its peak during the period of the 'historic compromise' (1976–9) but can also be applied to the phase when the Socialist Party supported various Giolitti-led governments in the late nineteenth and early twentieth centuries, and to the Resistance coalitions between 1943 and 1947. Consociationism saw the division of the spoils and state positions amongst all the parties, and not just *within* governing parties. This system was also known as *lottizzazione* (the most obvious example of this being the ways in which the public television channels have been shared out politically). Within governments, positions were shared out through a complicated system that connected party factions to certain numbers of posts. Sharing of power and positions in this way became known as 'following the Cencelli Manual' after a minor Christian Democrat politician who devised a method for this division of the spoils (see Box 4.1). Moments of consociationism were usually justified by an emergency-type situation – the end-of-century crisis for Giolitti, the collapse of fascism, the economic crisis and terrorism in the 1970s. Similar types of governments emerged after the 1992 crises. Consociationism sat neatly with clientelism and corruption, and tended to play down the practical role of ideologies (which remained strong in public, if not in private). This was thus largely an unwritten pact. Politicians usually justified consociationism through an appeal to the values of what they dubbed 'pluralism'. With political fragmentation and the decline of mass parties, broader if fragile coalitions began to emerge at the end of the first decade of the twenty-first century. The technocratic Monti government was supported by centre–left and centre–right coalitions, and a similar 'grand coalition' was put together after the inconclusive 2013 elections under the premiership of Enrico Letta. It appeared as if a new consociationist consensus was in place, in part because of the challenge from anti-political movements outside of the system. President Giorgio Napolitano was the architect of these 'emergency' coalitions, which he compared to the 'historic compromise' alliances of the 1970s. It remains to be seen whether these coalitions were part of a long-term trend, or were an uneasy response to a deep-rooted economic and political crisis. In any case, these 'catch-all' emergency or technocratic governments seemed to confirm a shift towards post-democracy or post-politics, and this was a trend which was being seen across Europe – for example with the coalitions in Germany, Greece and the UK.

Caesarism and the Cult of Leadership

Italian politics, for long periods, was structured around the power of certain leaders. Charismatic figures stood at the centre of the Liberal system (Depretis, Crispi, Giolitti), fascism (Mussolini), the DC state (De Gasperi, Fanfani, Moro, Andreotti) and the centre–left (Nenni, Craxi) and then the 'second republic' (Berlusconi and Bossi). Parties themselves were also structured around charismatic and, in some cases, almost unchallengeable leaders. This was especially true of the PCI under Togliatti (leader from 1927 to 1964) and, of course, the

---

Box 4.1   The scientific spoils system: the 'Cencelli Manual'

In the late 1960s, after PR had been introduced to govern the internal democracy of the DC with its numerous factions, a method was required to calculate
the distribution of positions of power within the party and with the DC's various
allies. In 1968 Massimiliano Cencelli was under-secretary to the minister of
tourism, Adolfo Sarti. Cencelli became famous for devising a mathematical formula to organize this sharing of the spoils. This method became known as the
'Cencelli Manual'. Of course, people cannot be divided into fractions so one of
the key features of this system was to decide how to deal with percentages, and
how to round up (or down) power distribution. Occasionally, individuals would
break with this rigid system, and create new ministries (as with Andreotti's
inspired invention of a 'minister for youth' during one crisis) to accommodate
friends. The Cencelli Manual became a way of doing politics 'which infected the
state' (R. Venditti, *Il manuale Cencelli*). Some analysts even went as far as to
claim that the real constitution of Italy was the Cencelli Manual. The spoils system continued well after the decline of the DC; it became part of Italy's political
culture, a methodology adopted by all parties under the guise of 'pluralism'.

The system worked like this. If we take the example of Leone's second government (1968), there were 22 ministers and 47 under-secretaries to share out.
By multiplying the percentages of each DC faction by the number of ministers,
and then by the number of under-secretaries, and then dividing by 100, a figure
was arrived at for each faction. Thus the 12 per cent of Taviani's faction became
2.64 ministers (rounded up to 3), 5.64 (rounded up to 6) under-secretaries, and
so on. Another faction only reached 0.34 per cent in the party, and thus had no
right to a ministry, but did have the 'right' to one under-secretary.

The effects of this system were many. First, any idea of merit was absent.
Secondly, any imbalance in the complex calculations could lead to a government
crisis. Thirdly, the sharing of the spoils undermined legitimacy, but also legiti-
mated this kind of management of power. The logic of the Cencelli Manual
reached right down into Italian society, to institutions such as universities, opera
houses and cultural foundations.

Fascist Party (*Partito Nazionale Fascista* – PNF) under Mussolini. The Socialists
were always more divided, and more pluralist, and more liable to split (as they
did in 1921, 1922, 1947, 1964 and 1992). The PCI only split once, at its death, in
1990. Christian Democracy had too many rival factions to ever allow one
leader to take control, at least after the De Gasperi period in the 1950s, and
Fanfani, Moro, Rumor, Andreotti and De Mita switched roles within the party
over long periods of time. Craxi exercised rigid control over the PSI from 1976
to 1992, with disastrous results for his party, which collapsed electorally after
Tangentopoli (the massive corruption scandals exposed after 1992) and then
crumbled into a myriad of tiny groupings.

Berlusconi's *Forza Italia!* organization was a new kind of 'personal' party,
formed in 1994, under the total control of its leader and shaped around that

leader's media empire. It was difficult if not impossible to imagine *Forza Italia!* without Berlusconi, something that did not apply to any of the other major organizations. The end of the Cold War led to a much more fluid political system, with broad alliances replacing the party-based blocs which had ruled the roost for more than forty years. (On the Left, umbrella groups formed and re-formed with alarming regularity (the *Ulivo*, the Democrats, the *Margherita*, all between 1996 and 2002), L'Unione (which embraced even more groups) and the Democratic Party, which was formed in 2007. Many of these organizations were more labels than actual organizations, and were riven by personalized factions named after party grandees (Bersaniani, Renziani and so on). The only real, old-style parties which had survived the end of the cold war and *Tangentopoli* were the DS (*Democratici di sinistra* – a centre–left party, which later merged into the Democratic Party), *Rifondazione Comunista* (which seemed to go into terminal decline in the first decade of the twenty-first century) and, on the Right, *Alleanza Nazionale* (ex-MSI), which merged with Berlusconi and then split. All the other organizations were either of a different type (*Forza Italia!*, the *Ulivo*, the *Margherita*) or born from social movements in the 1980s (the Greens, the *Lega*). The introduction of primaries for the selection of candidates (usually for the centre-left) also underlined the increasing importance of personalities and leadership. Similar tendencies could be seen on the far left, with the rise of Nicola Vendola in the 2000s.

An Internet-based protest movement, formed by the comedian Beppe Grillo in 2010, began to enjoy electoral success soon afterwards, and won an extraordinary 25 per cent of the vote in the 2013 general elections. Grillo's Five Star MoVement (the capital V stood for 'F*** Off' in Italian) was an entirely new form of loose organization, but which contained strong elements of personalization linked to those seen with Berlusconi throughout the 1990s and 2000s. Grillo's followers were often called *Grillini*, and Grillo himself attempted to exercise complete control over the movement, despite its frequent recourse to Internet-based democratic processes. Previous populist movements, such as *L'uomo qualunque* in the 1940s, had also been centred on strong, charismatic leaders.

In the 1990s and 2000s a series of Internet or loosely based movements rose and fell, sometimes over single issues. These movements could often mobilize large numbers of people – as with the extraordinary women's demonstrations (which went under the name of *Se non ora quando? If not now when?*) of early 2011 – but rarely had a long-term political impact. Many faded quickly from public life. Only the post-political, 'neither right nor left', Five Star MoVement was able to elect significant numbers of candidates at a local and national level. Most of the movements were not interested in traditional political struggles (including elections) and preferred to work outside of the parliamentary or electoral spheres.

How can we explain the tendency of individuals to dominate parties and the political system? First, unstable governments did not signify instability in terms of personnel, as we have already seen (and see the list of governments in Appendix 1). Secondly, weak parties in the Liberal period, and then again after 1992, encouraged the grouping of political movements around strong personalities, as did the general withdrawal from politics in the 1980s and 1990s and the rise of militant anti-political politics in the 1990s and 2000s. Mass interest in politics was often lacking – by design in the Liberal period; through social and cultural change in the 1980s, 1990s and 2000s. By the end of the first decade of the twenty-first century, many 'political' activists rejected politics and the political system entirely. Thirdly, fascism, born from the chaos and violence of the post-World War I period, actively encouraged the cult of the leader and was structured in such a way (politically, and through propaganda) as to centralize power around one man. Mussolini took on a number of state roles beyond that of prime minister – he was also interior minister from 1926 to 1943, and foreign minister between 1922 and 1929 and from 1932 to 1936. Emilio Gentile has called this system 'totalitarian caesarism'.[8] Fourthly, the Left parties (especially the PCI) adopted 'democratic centralism', which essentially left internal power in the hands of the central committee, and placed great value on party discipline, following the Stalinist model. Communists also had their own 'cults of personality', especially around Stalin and Togliatti. This was much less true of the non-Communist parties on the Left, the Socialists and the Action Party, for example, who placed more faith in real internal party democracy and thus saw changes of leadership and frequent splits. Discipline paid off, politically, in the short and long run. The DC ran itself by using complicated systems of internal democracy, which allowed the party to maintain power, and not to split, given the existence of a very broad coalition within its ranks.

Finally, after 1992, the break-up of the old party-based system, and the virtual disappearance of mass parties, led to the emergence of myriad groupings with extremely strong leaders, who were virtually unchallengeable despite the formal existence of internal party democracy (Berlusconi, Bossi, Fini, Grillo). All of these parties, however, did have internal factions. It has been argued that 'Caesarism [i.e. identification with a strong leader] is the predominant form of mass identification in periods of social fragmentation and mass psychological regression'.[9] Sociologists and anthropologists have claimed that Italy's individualist and post-industrial society, and the withdrawal from active politics, has led increasingly to identification with strong leader figures, of whom the ultimate example has been Berlusconi, and the latest and most innovative figure that of Beppe Grillo.

Historically, the leadership role of the monarchy has often been neglected. Recent research has shown how important the monarchy was to early attempts at nation-building, and the king built up his public image through the use of the mass media and as the representative of Italy at home and abroad, above all at times of crisis. Monarchs provided a reference point outside and above the dirty world of politics. Kings were also seen as the main negative symbol of the nation, and the state, for subversives and for many democrats. Hence the constant attempts to assassinate the king at various moments in Italian history, right up to an unsuccessful bomb attack in Milan in 1928. King Umberto I was assassinated by an anarchist at Monza in 1900.

Moreover, the king played a key role at various turning points in Italian history – in particular in 1915, 1922 and 1943. By leaving Rome in 1943, after twenty years of co-habitation with fascism, the king lost legitimacy at all levels (and the monarchy had been systematically stripped of its powers under the regime). Even the fascists turned to Republicanism.[10] None the less, the monarchy was still able to attract a surprising amount of votes in the 1946 referendum (see Box 4.2) and a small minority of Italians continued to vote for monarchist parties right up to the 1960s.

Mediation, Clientelism, *Raccomandazioni*,[11] Patronage

Italy has sometimes been defined as *cleptocracy*. That is, a country where the government exists merely to increase the personal and economic power of those within it and of the ruling elites. In a cleptocracy corruption often involves the misuse or misappropriation of public resources. Clientelism is a key aspect of a cleptocracy, in terms of the consensus such systems sometimes achieve.

At a basic, anthropological level, clientelism involves an exchange of resources between a patron and a client. These exchanges are voluntary and reciprocal. *Political* clientelism is the most important concept in the context of this chapter.[12] The resources exchanged between political clients are votes, on the one hand, and state-based resources on the other. However, these resources should be understood in a wider sense – they are not always simply jobs, or even cash, but can be much more ephemeral 'goods' such as trust, the promise of a future 'recommendation', or even the banking of such resources for future use.

In Italy, the use of clientelism has always been widespread, although its form and content have changed over time and place. Pre-modern forms of clientelism dominated the post-unification and Liberal periods, based around personal links and 'notables'. This system survived until changes to the suffrage extended politics into a mass system. Later, mass parties set up new kinds of clientelist networks. Percy Allum (writing about post-war Naples) argued that 'the politician conceives of his task as that of scattering among the needy masses some crumbs of the state's resources'.[13]

Historical and political studies have shown in detail how political bosses have constructed clienteles.[14] In the nineteenth century the key mediators in the clientelist political systems were lawyers, notaries and councillors. Parliamentary deputies organized their political support through *grandi elettori*, local bigwigs who were able to mobilize voters. As Musella has argued, 'electoral choices were conditioned by individual, personal and familial interests and relations and local problems and values'.[15] In Naples in the early twentieth century political leaders were surrounded by:

> small groups of personal friends or activists, united via favours conceded through the public purse and grouped together in hierarchies, [who] made up the initial force of the *clientela*, and against whom isolated individuals could not resist, if not from within other clienteles.[16]

Box 4.2   The Referendum on the Republic, June 1946

The results of the referendum, 2 June 1946

Yes (Republic): 12,700,000 (54%)
No (Monarchy): 10,700,000 (46%)

The king left Italy on 13 June for Portugal.

The regional break-down of the vote (figures given as a percentage)

Regions	Republic	Monarchy	Cities and towns	Republic	Monarchy
Venice Tridentina	85.0	15.0	Turin	60.0	40.0
Emilia	77.0	23.0	Rome	46.0	54.0
Umbria	71.9	28.1	Ravenna	91.2	8.8
Tuscany	71.6	28.4	Cesena	91.3	8.7
Marche	70.1	29.9	Carrara	88.1	11.9
Liguria	69.0	31.0	Livorno	80.5	19.5
Lombardy	64.1	35.9	Messina	14.6	85.4
Valle d'Aosta	63.5	36.5	Palermo	15.8	84.2
Veneto	59.3	40.7	Catania	18.2	81.4
Piedmont	57.1	42.9	Naples	20.1	79.9
Lazio	48.6	51.4	Bari	25.2	74.8
Abruzzi	43.1	56.9	Province of	43.8	56.2
Lucania	40.6	59.4	Cuneo		
Calabria	39.7	60.3			
Sardinia	39.1	60.3			
Sicily	35.3	64.7			
Apulia	32.7	67.3			
Campania	23.5	76.5			
Total	**54.3**	**45.7**			

The Constitution and the monarchy

Article XIII [House of Savoy]

(1) The members and descendants of the House of Savoy shall not be entitled to vote and may not hold any public or elective office.
(2) Former kings of the House of Savoy, their wives and male descendants may not enter the national territory or remain in it.
(3) Property within the national territory belonging to the former kings of the House of Savoy, their wives and male descendants, shall revert to the State. The transfer and the establishment of property rights or the said estate that have taken place after June 2 1946, shall be null and void.

In 2002 votes were held in both Houses of Parliament to overturn these constitutional provisions.

Often, political clientelism has been associated exclusively with southern political systems, although there are numerous examples of clientelist systems in the north of Italy, both in the Liberal period and in Republican Italy. The history of the DC in the Veneto, and the rise of local boss Antonio Bisaglia to the upper echelons of the party in the late 1950s through to the 1970s, is perhaps the most well-documented example of boss-type politics in the north.[17] In 1992, the *Tangentopoli* scandals revealed a deep-rooted system of political corruption that stretched across all the major parties.[18] Scandals continued throughout the 1990s and 2000s. It was clear that it was not enough simply to change the personnel in charge, but that the *system* itself and cultural aspects of corruption needed to be transformed in some way. The assumption has been, however, that political clientelism works best where resources are scarce – in situations of high unemployment and poverty.

Looking beyond Italy, it is clear that clientelism has not been confined to her shores. In Spain, at the turn of the century, a debate began over what became known as *caciquismo* – where a *cacique* was, as Carr writes, 'a person who in a pueblo or district exercises excessive influence in political or administrative matters'. This type of clientelism went to the very heart of Spanish politics – 'it was not a parliamentary regime with abuses: the abuses were the system itself'.[19] As in Italy, this clientelism involved exchanges of power, resources, protection and votes. A *cacique* would protect his clientele from taxation or perhaps from military service, in return for electoral support. More recently, Sapelli has argued that what he calls 'neo-caciquism' – where 'party organizations continue to depend on the personal relationship which the person elected has with a society that is intrinsically based on the amoral family' – is the key element to an understanding of the way politics works in southern Europe: 'a land of clientelism and patronage … characterized by the presence of status systems not by contractural ones'.[20]

It is beyond question that clientelism has had a negative influence on Italian politics, in a number of different ways: widespread use of clientelism delegitimizes the system and the actors within that system. Nor does clientelism produce authority. Once politicians can no longer deliver the goods, they can be substituted; their power rests on the ability to distribute resources. Clientelism undermines people's faith in the official rules of the game, and in the institutions themselves. Politics in a clientelist system colonizes civil society, and private interests are able to penetrate politics with ease. In Luigi Graziano's detailed study of the use of clientelism in a small southern town, one politician spoke frankly about his idea of his role and his power base:

> there are many needs amongst the people and I help them to be met: I give out commercial permits, building permissions, you make friends. … I have had many people taken on by the *Comune*, all friends: what should I do … give work to my enemies? … by now I have built up my *clientela*. But I have done so as a professional and as an administrator. (Interview, 1974)[21]

It is worth considering the argument that the Italian state was 'infiltrated' partly as a means of consolidating democracy and maintaining social peace (M. Ferrara).[22] Clearly, part of the rationale behind the clientelistic use of the state was to create consensus around the political system and the state. Yet such a system can only create short-term, instrumental forms of consensus. As soon as the resources are no longer available to be distributed in the old way, or the costs of the whole system become too high (for example, in terms of inefficiencies and high taxes), any 'support' will inevitably slip away.

Clientelism is also very expensive – an irrational and extremely wasteful way of distributing resources and running a state. Invalidity pensions rose from 1.2 to 3.4 million during the 1960s alone. For a long time, the system survived thanks to massive use of public funds. All the parties had access to their own clientelist power-bases, such as the *Cassa per il Mezzogiorno* (the DC) and the pensions system (INPS – *Istituto Nazionale di Previdenza Sociale* – the state pension system, was run by the tiny Social Democratic Party between 1949 and 1965). It was only with the deep crisis of the 1990s and the looming appointment with European Monetary Union that the vicious clientelist circles began to break down. This was inevitable: 'the clientelist process, by its very nature, was destined to undermine itself' (P. McCarthy).[23] Clientelism produced bad government, which led to a decline in support, which forced politicians to use even more clientelism to survive. Antonio Gava reached the peak of the clientelist tree in 1983, when he was appointed Post Office minister.[24] During his four years in charge he managed to get 3,808 people from the province of Naples (20 per cent of all such jobs in Italy) taken on as Post Office staff, including forty disabled people from his home-town. This was a system of 'mass clientelism' and of 'mass bribery'. In the early 1990s parts of the clientelist–party system were dismantled by a legal revolution. However, the old practices were soon reconstructed across Italy, often under the guise of managerial capitalism and private–public partnerships that flourished around the increasingly powerful regional governments (see Box 4.4).

It would be naive to claim that this break-up of many of the more generous features of political clientelism in the 1990s ended clientelism altogether. As Dorothy Zinn has shown in her pioneering research on a small town in Basilicata, the culture of clientelism is deeply ingrained in people's worldview.[25] Whole lives are shaped by clientelism and *raccomandazioni* – from the hospital where you are born, to school exams and university degrees, through to job opportunities and pensions. On a daily basis, everyone accepts the constant ways in which personal relationships, favours and contacts are used to get 'normal' tasks completed. Those without such contacts are helpless, unable to get onto even the first rung of the social ladder. Yet, there is also widespread criticism of the ways in which the system works – creating frustration and anger. The so-called Baronial system within universities was a classic and depressing example of the exercise of power for its own sake. Merit was ignored in favour of the creation of networks of clients and patrons. Once you were outside the system, you had no chance of having a career.

Italian politics has also been marked by high levels of straightforward political corruption. Bribes were paid to win contracts (locally and nationally), money was raked off to fund political parties, and funds were used to cover up other scandals. Corruption has taken the form both of individual profit (politicians using the system to enrich themselves) and of party-funding via illegal means. In part, this corruption was a natural outcome of the various forms assumed by the system over time (the lack of alternation in power, the intervention of the state, consociationism, the high cost of politics). Some accounts of Italian political history concentrate on the series of scandals that arose. Scandal itself was part of the political power-game, as in the Giolitti–Crispi duel over the Banca Romana scandal in the 1890s. The description of a party, or a politician, as 'honest' was often part of electoral propaganda. At certain times, the 'moral question' dominated debate – from Cavallotti to Berlinguer. Corruption was also at the heart of the collapse of the first republic in the early 1990s. It was left to the courts to investigate individual corruption, justified by many politicians as necessary to pay the extremely high costs of political campaigning and political organization. Only once, with the Lockheed scandal in the 1970s (see Box 4.3), did the Constitutional Court intervene to investigate political corruption, but soon afterwards its powers to do so ever again were removed. Various solutions were tried to prevent corruption – including the public financing of political parties (after 1974). The total failure of this reform emerged in the *Tangentopoli* scandals after 1992, when 25,000 separate investigations into corruption were opened, many of which involved politicians. After 1992, the mass party structures of the first republic (daily papers, full-time staff, radio stations, party schools, congresses, youth organizations) were streamlined, and the 'light' party, on the model of *Forza Italia!*, became more popular. Yet corruption continued at a local and national level. A cultural revolution would be needed to dismantle the clientelist practices which marked Italian politics. The illusion that an anti-political class could be elected to replace the political caste which had governed Italy was a strong one, especially amongst those who supported Beppe Grillo's Five Star MoVement. Yet without deep-rooted reform of structures, simply changing the people in charge was a short-term solution that was destined to fail.

The so-called *Tangentopoli* corruption scandals (1992–3) were seen as a watershed in Italy in terms of the use of public funds and the financing of political parties, as well as the management of the economic system. Yet, despite thousands of arrests and hundreds of trials, corruption continued to infect the political and business sectors. A new wave of scandals struck various areas of Italian public life in the twenty-first century, in areas ranging from football to regional government. Politicians from both the centre–right and the centre–left were involved. Numerous councils were dissolved by central government or placed under the control of commissioners after mayors had been forced to resign, including those of Bologna (2010), Parma (1994, 2011), Reggio Calabria (dissolved due to Mafia infiltration 2012). This

---

Box 4.3   The Lockheed scandal: bribery and exchange

In 1976, the Lockheed company decided to pay a series of bribes in order to promote the sale of its anti-submarine aircrafts and the Hercules 130 in Italy. They employed a consultant, university professor Antonio Lefèbvre, who in turn used his brother Ovidio to conclude the formal part of the agreement and work out how much money was to be paid. An engineer, Camillo Crociani, played the part of mediator with the minister, Tanassi, and with the army. A key role was played by the secretary to the defence minister (Palmiotti), who also decided to take a little amount for himself. Note the secretive nature of the operation, its ritualized features, the various places utilized and the levels of mediation involved.

The cast (this was the second part of the bribe to be paid)

Antonio Lefèbvre, Professor and consultant to Lockheed
Ovidio Lefèbvre, Antonio's brother
Camillo Crociani, Engineer
Bruno Palmiotti, secretary to defence minister Mario Tanassi

Ovidio Lefèbvre got the cash together (360 million lire) divided into L.100,000 banknotes. He put them into envelopes and then in a brown bag with soft sides.

Palmiotti and Lefèbvre met in an office near the Ministry. The bag was handed over. Nobody had a look inside to count the money. Everything was done on trust. A company representative was also there.

Palmiotti had told the bribers that 'he would not have been indifferent to a gesture of personal homage'. An extra payment of 10 million lire was given to him in another envelope.

After this exchange the Company representative and Lefèbvre visited the ministry were they saw a copy of the decree-law which they had 'bought' with the bribe they had paid. The empty bag was returned a few days later, under the pretence that it had been 'forgotten'.

For further details see the 'Final Sentence, Constitutional Court Investigation into the Lockheed Scandal, 2 August 1979', in V. M. Caferra, *Il sistema della corruzione. Le ragioni, i soggetti, i luoghi* (Bari: Laterza, 1992), pp. 31–3.

---

pattern of scandals seemed to confirm that Italy had the characteristics of a cleptocracy, where the system itself was marked by a culture of clientelism and corruption, and where the simple arrest of protagonists of these deeds did nothing to alter the tendency towards the misuse of public and private funds (see Box 4.4). Corruption was not just an Italian problem, of course. It was also almost certainly the case that Italy's active and relatively independent judiciary exposed more scandals than in many other countries. Yet, the slow and inefficient nature of the legal system meant that, in the end, the chances of being found guilty were slim, especially if you had a good lawyer.

Box 4.4   Cleptocracy? A selection of corruption, financial and other scandals in Italy, 2006–2013

Calciopoli (2006)

This sporting scandal uncovered a network of power and control centred on numerous football clubs. The focus of the scandal was Juventus, Italy's biggest and most successful club, and the one with the most fans. The scandal became known as *Calciopoli*, a play on the term used for the 1992–3 corruption scandals in Milan, (*Tangentopoli*) which could roughly be translated as Footballgate. General Manager Luciano Moggi was accused of manipulating referees and the transfer market in order to buy influence and guarantee success. The evidence was provided in the main by thousands of phone tap transcriptions. The outcome of the scandal was traumatic for the football authorities, clubs and fans, with numerous resignations, arrests and the forced relegation of Juventus to Serie B. Juventus were also stripped of two Serie A titles. Other clubs were also relegated, or received points deductions, or both. The criminal cases linked to the scandal were drawn out and controversial, and some were still ongoing in 2013. Many Juventus fans claim that the scandal was a conspiracy organized by rivals Inter, and they dubbed the whole affair *Farsopoli* (a farce, farce-gate).

Parmalat (2003) (*Lattopoli*)

Parmalat is one of Italy's biggest multinational food companies, producing milk and numerous other food-based products. It was run by the Tanzi family after Calisto Tanzi set it up in the early 1960s. The company grew rapidly and expanded into numerous sectors including television, Formula 1 and football. In 2003 a huge financial hole (of some €14 million) was revealed at the heart of the company, which eventually led to its bankruptcy. Massive financial irregularities were uncovered at a whole series of levels. Tanzi was arrested and eventually given an eight-year prison sentence in 2011 for stock manipulation. He remained in prison in 2013. A further trial for fraudulent accounting is ongoing, as are other trials.

Monte dei Paschi di Siena (2012–2013)

One of the oldest banks in the world, the Monte dei Paschi di Siena became embroiled in a major scandal in 2013. In 2007 the bank had purchased the Banca Antonveneta, but then the financial crisis hit, leaving the bank heavily exposed. In an attempt to dig themselves out of the crisis, the bank only made things worse and it was forced to ask for state aid in 2009. 'Creative accounting' meant that many debts were hidden from balance sheets. In 2012, the extent of this was revealed. Job losses were announced alongside the closure of numerous branches. The bank asked for a second bailout and the scandal became a major issue in the election campaign of 2012–13. Arrests followed and the bank's head of communications killed himself in 2013.

Regione Lombardia (2010–2013)

More than one single scandal, Lombardy's regional government was beset by a series of connected scandals which eventually led to early elections in 2013. Roberto Formigoni, a Catholic who had been one of the founders of the *Comunione e Liberazione* movement in the late 1960s and had joined Berlusconi's *Forza Italia!* movement in 1998, was President of the Region from April 1995 to February 2013, winning four elections. After Formigoni's victory in 2010, a number of arrests and investigations hit the regional government, many of which were linked to accusations of corruption (especially in the health service) and some for connections to organized crime. A further investigation was linked to the alleged collection of false signatures used to ratify candidates for the 2010 elections. This combination of circumstances led to the collapse of the administration and new elections in 2013, which saw the victory of the centre–right coalition led by the *Lega Nord* and Roberto Maroni.

Regione Lazio (2012–2013)

Renata Polverini was elected president of the Lazio region in 2010 as head of a centre–right coalition. She had been an activist in the neo-fascist trade union movement. In 2012 a system of corruption was uncovered which involved large sums being spent by councillors for private ends, including inflated expenses for individuals and political parties. Lurid details emerged in the press about parties and holidays paid for with public funds. Franco Fiorito from the centre-right coalition became the key figure in terms of public opinion. Known as Er Batman thanks to a failed attempt to ride a Harley Davidson motorbike while standing up, he was arrested and later charged with offences involving corruption and the misuse of public funds. Ironically, Fiorito had taken part, as a young neo-fascist militant, in the famous demonstration against Bettino Craxi in Rome in 1993 which became one of the symbolic moments of the *Tangentopoli* scandals. Polverini resigned in September 2012 and new elections were held in February 2013 on the same day as the General Elections, with victory going to the centre–left coalition.

Parties and *Partitocrazia* (Rule by Parties)

During the Liberal period both governments *and* parties were weak, at least until after World War I, and political power was held by oligarchic elites, based around personalities (Cavour, Giolitti, Sonnino, Turati) with links to important economic interests. Stronger parties began to emerge within the parliamentary system with the end of World War I and the entry into Parliament of large numbers of Socialist and Catholic deputies. Fascism stripped Parliament of most of its powers, removed elections and set up a party–state machine which ruled for twenty years. Although most accounts of Italian fascism concentrate on Mussolini, the role of the Fascist Party (the PNF) was crucial (see below) and party structures replaced, to a large extent, the structures of Italian liberal parliamentary democracy. After 1945, mass democracy returned and with it Italy entered into an age of mass parties.

These political parties then held political power. This may seem a truism. But in many other democracies, it is the government, not the parties, who hold power. In Italy, since 1945 (and before 1922), governments have usually been extremely weak. From 1945 to 1992, this power vacuum was filled by strong parties. Parties also permeated every level of society and the economy. As Bufacchi and Burgess put it, 'Italy is a republic of parties, a sort of hegemonic party-state based upon the complete co-penetration between party and state.'[26]

This system became known as 'rule-by-parties', or *partitocracy* – a term first coined in the 1960s,[27] but whose use became commonplace in the 1970s and 1980s. Various definitions of 'partitocracy' exist. Some claim that this was a system of *one-party rule* (the Fascist Party, and then the DC) – linked to the widespread use of clientelism, a huge state sector and the forms of government set up under fascism or in 1948.[28] Parties and their representatives penetrated into all levels of civil and cultural society. Others stress the multi-party nature of partitocracy, still linked to clientelism and the spoils system but stretching across all parties in consociational structures.[29] In general, partitocracy has been blamed for many ills present in Italian society – above all, the inefficient and illogical ways in which parties divided up the state and its resources amongst themselves (*lottizzazione*), the clientelistic use of public resources and the lack of reform. Since 1992, with the collapse or decline of all the major and minor parties, partitocracy has faded from the scene. New parties have emerged with much weaker structures and smaller memberships (*Forza Italia!*, the *Margherita* coalition, the PD, the Five Star MoVement). Yet, the practices of spoils-sharing have remained. Both the centre–left and the centre–right governments of 1996–2001 and since 2001 proceeded to divide up state organizations amongst themselves. Cultures of partitocracy and spoils-system practices, therefore, were much more deeply ingrained than the parties themselves (and could be said to go right back to the Liberal period). This was less like partitocracy, and more like a *cleptocracy* (or a 'republic of thieves').[30] Since 1992, a kind of *partitocracy without parties* can be said to have developed, although all the major groupings have formed themselves into structures resembling parties and have become more and more similar to the old-style party forms (without the mass member-ships of the past).

Crises and the Legitimacy of the Opposition

It is difficult to reconcile the idea of Italian politics as transformist and con-sociationist with another key feature of the system – its tendency to fall into crisis and the huge gulf, at times, between government and opposition. It could be argued that Italy's political system has experienced three deep historical crises. These moments were, broadly, 1919–22, 1943–5, and (the longest of all) 1992–2013. This last crisis is ongoing. Each crisis has led to an institutional revolution (apart from, as I write, the last one). All of these crises have been marked by a chasm (usually expressed through ideological differences – nation/anti-nation; communism/anti-communism; fascism/anti-fascism) whereby the government has claimed that the opposition has had no right to govern, and the opposition has contested the government's legitimacy. In the first period, there was no middle ground between fascism, liberalism and anti-fascism. The failure to build democratic alliances led to the collapse of democracy itself. Fascism's collapse in 1943 coincided with that of the Italian state, and forced democrats to ally briefly in the construc-tion of a new institutional framework. However, the Cold War created a new, insurmountable gulf with both sides contesting the other's legitimacy.

This was a 'democracy without democratic alternatives' (M. Salvadori).[31] No Communist ministers held office between 1947 and 1994. This gulf was only (partially) breached in the face of the deep crisis (terrorism, inflation) during the 1970s. After 1992, the right to govern of various governments con-tinued to come under challenge on numerous occasions. Berlusconi argued that the Dini government (1995–6), for example, was *illegitimate* because it was supported by deputies (from the *Lega Nord*) who had changed sides *en masse* less than a year after a general election. After 2001, despite his massive victory, many Italians both in the political system and in civil society argued that Berlusconi had no right to govern thanks to his massive control of private interests, above all within the media. At times, this illegitimacy label was applied to smaller parties (such as the neo-fascists, kept out of governments until 1994). Here it is clear that the Italian political system, culturally and institutionally, was not 'normal' in a European, liberal democratic sense, despite the alternance between Left and Right after 1992.[32] Reciprocal accusa-tions of non-democracy or illegitimacy continued to dog Italian politics after 2001. The neck and neck result in 2006 led to claims on both sides of vote rigging and arguments from the centre–right that they were the real victors from the election. The Monti government of 2011–13 was made up entirely of non-elected technocrats, and replaced an elected Berlusconi government. An increasing democratic deficit seemed to be infecting the heart of the Italian political system.

These various concepts and ways of understanding Italian politics should be kept in mind as the account now moves on to the history of the organiza-tions that have run the political system since unification – the parties.

ORGANIZING POLITICS

The 'Liberal Party'

> In Italy there are no real parties similar to those in the great constitutional countries.
>
> LUIGI LUZZATTI (1874)

> You should see the pandemonium at Montecitorio [the Italian parliament] when the moment approaches for an important division. The agents of the government run through the rooms and corridors, to gather votes, subsidies, decorations, canals, bridges, roads, everything is promised; and sometimes an act of justice, long denied, is the price of a parliamentary vote.
>
> FRANCESCO CRISPI (ELECTORAL ADDRESS, 1886)

A key 'lack' for Italy in the post-Risorgimento phase has always been identified in the absence of a strong liberal party. This 'lack' of a 'normal' centre–right political organization is sometimes also applied to the post-war period. Gramsci claimed that the only real political organizations in Italy were the freemasons. Italy never produced a coherent conservative party, not linked to the Church, and the growth of an 'abnormal' Right after 1992 (Berlusconi, the neo-fascists, the regionalists) only reinforced claims of this absence at the heart of Italian politics. In the post-unification and Liberal periods, the liberals were always divided (although never clearly on principle) and never constructed a mass party with deep local roots. This, as with so many other features of Italian politics, such as transformism, was both a symptom *and* a cause of Italy's political problems. Italy 'lacked' a mass liberal party for a whole series of reasons – the ways in which elections were managed by the state (the liberals did not *need* a party; no sitting government lost an election apart from Pelloux in 1900), the historical formation of Italian civil society and the bourgeoisie, the political culture of Italy's politicians and their conception of politics (as essentially the work of elites), and the overwhelming weight of the idea of 'the nation' in Italian politics after unification. This was also true of Spain around the same period, where 'no Cabinet ever lost an election'.[33] The lofty concept of the 'free deputy', working in the interests of the nation, developed, in reality, into the triumph of particular, local and clientelist interests. Yet Italy was not alone, particularly in southern Europe, in possessing a liberal party of this kind. In Spain there was, as Carr noted, 'a conglomeration of factions without a programme' and 'a loose federation of groups each of which owed primary allegiance to a chief'.[34]

The liberals concentrated, in the absence of party structures, on 'the management of power' (P. Pombeni).[35] 'Liberal' organizations only really came to life at election time. Newspapers were largely maintained and controlled by individuals (such as Crispi's La Riforma). In the absence of strong parties, the temptation was always to resort to the rule of strong leaders. In times of crisis, in particular, the liberals collapsed into fragments. In the 1919 elections, for example, there were 26 separate 'liberal' lists. Thus the 'liberal party' was 'the great absentee from Italian political life' (A. W. Salomone).[36] This fact should not be analysed in isolation from the other historical and cultural trends (such as the formation of an Italian bourgeoisie, its regional bases and its links to politics). It is also wise to avoid, as in other spheres, the creation of an 'ideal-model' of politics in comparison with which Italy, inevitably, has failed at every level.

Other parties, modern mass parties, began to develop from the 1890s onwards – the most important of these was the Italian Socialist Party.[37]

MASS PARTIES: THE LEFT[38]

The Socialist Party (*Partito Socialista Italiano*)

Formation: 1892; Dissolution: 1993.

Splits/divisions: 1912 (reformists expelled); 1921 (Communist Party formed); 1922 (reformists expelled, and form new party); 1947 (Social Democrats leave to form new party, which later becomes the PSDI); 1964 (Left Socialists leave to form PSIUP – *Partito socialista d'unità proletaria*); 1992– (since 1992 the remains of the PSI have fragmented into numerous smaller groupings).

Participation in national governments (coalitions): 1945–7; 1962–92.[39]

History

Formed in 1892 as a workers' party in Genoa, specifically in opposition to anarchism, the early Socialist Party was a combination of a strong industrial base (Milan, Turin, Naples) and extremely well-organized rural proletarian leagues, mainly in the Po Valley. Many early Socialist leaders, such as Prampolini, Costa and Massarenti, worked in rural areas, and exercised a form of semi-religious power over their membership. This form of socialism, based on reformist municipal control and cooperatives, linked up with similar urban-based ideas proposed by Milan-based leaders – above all by Filippo Turati and Anna Kuliscioff and the urban trade union movement. Socialists began to win local elections in the 1890s and to construct important networks of economic and organic reformist institutions that threatened the market power of smaller commercial interests. By 1914 the PSI was in government in Milan and Bologna and controlled more than a quarter of all municipal governments in Emilia–Romagna. In Parliament, the PSI was a much more moderate organization, and frequently worked with the liberals, especially in the Giolittian system, to promote moderate reforms. Socialists made little impact in the south, apart from their input into the Sicilian *Fasci* in the 1890s and amongst the day-labourers on the Apulian plain. Anti-clericalism, sometimes of a violent kind, was a constant feature of socialist ideology, although at times this was combined with radical Catholic ideas and even the concept of Christ-as-socialist.

With the radicalization imposed by the imperialist Libyan campaigns, a combative-left revolutionary wing began to emerge under the leadership of a young and charismatic orator – Benito Mussolini. At the 1912 congress, these revolutionaries managed to expel a number of important reformist leaders from the party. This marginalization of the moderate wing of the party continued throughout the period running up to the success of fascism in the 1920s. These bitter divisions within the party – which appeared to be simply over the 'choice' between reform and revolution but in reality were far more complicated and contradictory – were crystallized formally in the so-called *minimalist* and *maximalist* programmes adopted by the party in 1900. In fact, the left-wing grouping which formed around Giacinto Menotti Serrati during World War I called themselves the 'maximalists' both in homage to the Bolshevik Revolution and in opposition to the reformists. But the maximalists were neither united nor similar to the Bolsheviks in other ways – they had strong links to the union movement, and, despite their rhetoric, did not really believe in or prepare for violent revolution.

Socialist reaction to World War I was mixed. Many left the party, tempted by forms of populist nationalism. The most important of these dissidents was Mussolini himself, expelled from the PSI for his support of the war effort in 1914. Officially, the PSI adopted an ambiguous policy of 'neither adhere, nor sabotage' towards the war, somewhere between the wholesale patriotism of the German SPD (Social Democratic Party – *Sozialdemokratische Partei Deutschland*) and the radical anti-nationalism of the Russian Bolsheviks. This line allowed for party unity, and for the support of civil disobedience or even outright rebellion against the war (as in Turin and Milan in spring 1917). The peasant and working-class masses were far ahead of the Socialists here, often refusing to fight or sabotaging the war effort on the home front. Another division opened up within the party after military catastrophe at Caporetto in October 1917. Important reformist leaders, such as Turati, underlined the need to defend Italy from invasion, whilst others moved towards a more radical 'defeatist' policy. After the 'mutilated victory' in November 1918, the Socialists campaigned openly on an anti-war platform. With the revolutionary movements of 1919–20, the Socialists began to pick up thousands of new members, and became the biggest party in Parliament (156 seats in 1919) as well as controlling winning majorities on more than 2,000 local councils in 1920 (2,115 out of 8,346 in the whole of Italy). The maximalists managed to take over the party in November 1919 and the reformists were marginalized and ostracized. None the less, the vast majority of the base of the party and the unions remained reformist and the unions (apart from the important syndicalist groupings) were still largely controlled by cautious moderates.[40] New 'communist' groupings began to emerge within the party, above all that linked to Antonio Gramsci and the newspaper *L'Ordine Nuovo* in Turin. New ideas began to circulate concerning workers' democracy and alternatives to the trade unions. As before, the party's weakness was in the south. In 1920, when membership reached 208,952, only 0.43 per cent of these members were in Basilicata, and 2.5 per cent in Lazio, whilst nearly 19 per cent were to be found in Piedmont, 18 per cent in Emilia and 17 per cent in Lombardy.

In the face of fascist violence, the Socialists were unable to organize serious armed resistance (apart from in a few isolated cases) and thousands of militants were killed, beaten up, humiliated or forced to flee. Socialist

Box 4.5   Violence and the rise of fascism

The squads and violence

Fascism came to power through the use of organized and systematic violence. Fascist 'squads' used beatings, murders and humiliation to crush socialist and trade union organizations, terrify militants and re-impose the power of the landowners in the Po Valley and Tuscan sharecropping regions. Squads had local roots and were led by local leaders, who became known as *ras* ('leader' in Ethiopian) – Italo Balbo in Ferrara, Roberto Farinacci in Cremona, Dino Grandi in Bologna. They were often funded by landowners and had modern equipment – trucks, guns, uniforms – to back up their activities. The *biennio nero* (1921–2) left thousands dead and ended with the virtual disappearance of free trade unions and the Socialists. Many left-wing leaders were forced into exile. The state generally stood back and watched, or even aided the fascists. Only rarely (as in Sarzana in 1921) did the army or the police take on the fascists. Socialists and unions were generally powerless to resist, weakened by internal division and the lack of preparation even for the defence of their property and their own supporters. Yet, in some cases, the fascists were unable to conquer certain areas, most famously in Bari in 1921 and in Parma in 1922.

The squads in action: Roccastrada, Grossetto, July 1921

In July 1921, 50 fascists descended on the small town of Roccastrada near Grossetto in order to impose the flying of the Italian flag. This 'expedition' was accompanied by the usual rites of beatings, the enforced drinking of castor oil and the destruction of Socialist and union property. As they were leaving, a blackshirt was killed by a gunshot. This sparked off an orgy of violence: crops were burnt, and ten people were shot dead by the fascists, more or less at random, including two 68-year-old peasants, a young married couple and a 24-year-old woman who tried to protect her father. The police report wrote that 'people were killed with wild fury, with no regard for the age or the condition of the victims'. As in so many other cases no action was taken against the perpetrators of these crimes. The fascists in this particular case were identified but never arrested.

organizations were systematically destroyed and the party was forced out of local government by fascist violence (see Box 4.5). In Parliament, the party was unsure over tactics, withdrawing from the institutions altogether in 1924 after the murder of the socialist reformist Giacomo Matteotti. The party suffered two major splits (to the left in 1921, to the right in 1922) that weakened it even further. Most PSI leaders were arrested or forced into exile by 1926. For nearly twenty years, the official PSI ceased to exist on Italian soil.

Under fascism, the party survived through strong exile networks (above all in France, but also in Switzerland and amongst emigrant communities across the globe) and groups of militants in prison and internal exile. Many came together in Spain to fight for the Republicans in the Civil War. Clandestine networks also worked within Italy. After 1943, Socialist leaders returned and took active part in the resistance, forming the Matteotti brigades and taking part in the experience of the committees for national liberation. This period saw the party move towards Stalinist positions. The depth and survival of Socialist support was shown by the results of the 1946 elections. Yet the party split again (to the right) over support for the PCI and the USSR in 1947 (with the formation of the PSDI, a small party which managed to win a constant 4–5 per cent of the vote). In 1948, the PSI stood together with the PCI in the 'popular front' coalition, a decision that proved electorally disastrous for the Socialists, who lost their hegemony on the left to the Communists, a hegem-ony they were never to regain. Although a mass party, the PSI never managed to build up the same sub-cultures as the Communists, nor to forge the same links with the industrial working class and the trade unions after 1945. The PSI was always a more liberal party than the PCI, and attracted wide groups of intellectuals to its ranks in the post-war period.

A real break with Moscow only took place after the invasion of Hungary in 1956, although the PSI had stood alone in the elections of 1953. Nenni handed back his 'Stalin prize' and many of those who left the PCI gravitated towards the Socialists. Nenni began to argue for a centre–left alliance with DC, in order to reform Italy. This decision cost the party yet another split, this time to the left with the departure of an important group of intellectuals and militants under the banner of the PSIUP (in 1964). Socialists entered govern-ment for the first time since 1947 in 1962, and were to stay there, with some short gaps, until 1992. Historians generally agree that this first centre–left government was the most successful in terms of reform (education, the nationalization of electricity) although many of the more radical aspects of the programme were not carried out (such as urban planning reforms). Centre–left administrations were also set up across Italy at local government level. On the downside, the Socialists became a key part of the clientelistic and partito-cratic spoils system, a development that created vicious circles of corruption and shifted the party further to the right. Ideas of 'revolutionary' or 'non-reformist' reforms (proposed by important figures within the PSI, such as Lombardi) were never put into practice. In addition, the reformist basics (as the social democrat Saragat put it, 'here we need houses, schools, hospitals') were only implemented at great expense and with much inefficiency.

In the 1970s, a new approach to Socialist party politics took control under the leadership of Bettino Craxi. Craxi reinvented the party as a post-labourist body, breaking not just with the symbols of socialism (the hammer and sickle), but also with its traditional base (the industrial working class). The party adopted a modernist and strongman rhetoric that proved extremely popular with the new middle classes of an increasingly wealthy Italy. Craxi was prime minister for four years, the longest term of any post-war prime minister (and, excepting Mussolini, of any prime minister in Italian history). Yet few reforms were pushed through and the Socialists appeared increasingly as a clientelistic and 'business politics' party. Craxi presided over a huge increase in the public debt, despite the ephemeral 1980s boom. Craxi's model was Mitterrand, but his party never achieved more than 14 per cent of the vote and never threatened to replace the PCI as the central party on the Left, as the Socialists had done in France. This house of cards collapsed in 1992, when an extraordinary system of political corruption was exposed in Milan, the Socialist Party's (and Craxi's) political capital. The PSI imploded, with its leader exiled (where he died claiming bitterly that his party had been victim of a judicial, communist-inspired conspiracy). Most Socialist Party voters abandoned the party for Berlusconi's *Forza Italia!* while the party itself split into a number of small groupings, who claimed to represent either the traditions of Craxism or of traditional, more left-leaning Italian socialism. By the second decade of the twenty-first century, despite pockets of Socialists here and there, and tiny groupings at a local level, it would be fair to say that the Socialist Party had ceased to exist.

The Italian Communist Party (Partito Comunista Italiano, PCI)

Formation: 1921; Dissolution: 1990–1.

Splits/divisions: 1969 (*Il Manifesto* group); 1990–1 (*Rifondazione comunista*) *Partito democratico della Sinistra*, from 1998, *Democratici di sinistra*, from 2007 *Partito Democratico*).

National governments (coalitions); 1944–7; 1990–4; 1996–2001; 2006–8; 2013– The PCI/PDS/PD also supported governments externally in 1976–9, 1995–6, 2011–13.

History

Italian communism had its roots in the various subversive and revolutionary factions that arose within the Socialist Party in the first quarter of the twentieth century. These groups were all made up of revolutionaries, opposed to the reformist line of the old guard within the PSI. They were also generally opposed to parliamentarianism and strongly advocated links with Moscow and the Bolsheviks. When Lenin called for the expulsion of reformists from left-wing parties across the world, and the PSI leadership refused to comply, these groups left the Socialists to form the Italian Communist Party, after a dramatic conference in Livorno in 1921. This traumatic split took place just as fascism was beginning to destroy left-wing institutions across Italy, and was a key factor in the lack of anti-fascist unity at a crucial moment. Of the 216,377 members of the PSI in 1921, 172,487 were represented at Livorno. The maximalist 'unity' motion obtained nearly 100,000 votes, the Communists nearly 60,000 and the reformists 14,700. Unable to accept this defeat, the communist delegates walked out of the meeting and reconvened in another theatre nearby, setting up the Italian Communist Party.[41]

Thus, the new party was a strong minority within the PSI, with important bases of support in Florence, Milan and Turin, and amongst rural workers in places such as Ravenna, Forli and Grosseto, but without the support of the majority of PSI members or even of the working class, which remained over-whelmingly reformist and moderate. The PCI programme was largely theo-retical and inspired by the Third International. By the end of 1921 the party had recruited nearly 43,000 members. Yet, as with the rest of the Left, the PCI disintegrated in the face of fascist violence and its membership slumped to less than 10,000 by September 1923. In a climate of intimidation, the party still managed to elect 19 deputies to Parliament in 1924. By 1926, however, many PCI leaders were under arrest or in internal exile, and other militants had fled abroad. The party became an underground organization in Italy, whilst oper-ating openly in other countries from the USSR to France and Switzerland. PCI tactics began to slavishly follow the Stalinist line, and dissidents were expelled, or marginalized. Leading members of the party were expelled in the late 1920s and early 1930s. Many Italians were sent to Soviet concentration camps, including some of those who had gone to the USSR to escape repres-sion in Italy.[42] Communists participated along with other anti-fascists in the Spanish Civil War, where Togliatti was a key figure in 'United Front' organization.

The PCI's clandestine status and its ideological and financial links to Moscow helped the party to survive the fascist period. In 1943, Communist militants were among the organizers of the strikes which helped to bring down Mussolini, and as the resistance began, the Communist brigades (known as the Garibaldi brigades) were the best organized and most numerous of all the resistance groupings (some two-thirds of all partisans were part of these brigades). Meanwhile, in the 1930s, Communist leaders had begun to rethink the disastrous period of the *biennio rosso*. Togliatti produced an analysis of fascism that concentrated on the role of the middle classes and acknowledged the popularity of the regime.[43] Gramsci elaborated a theory of hegemony and the 'war of movement' that was to form the backbone of the PCI's strategy.[44] A frontal attack on the state was replaced with long-term alliances, above all with the 'productive middle classes' and the idea of 'structural' or 'non-re-formist' reforms, which were to transform society from within, and not over-night. All this was given the grand title 'the Italian road to socialism' and grouped under the broad heading of 'progressive democracy'. Never again would communists help to create the conditions for the collapse of democracy. None the less, this position was never made crystal clear to the PCI base. Togliatti and others maintained, for some time, a strategy of *doppiezza*, or 'duplicity'. They preached reform and moderation, but also allowed the base to think, or made it plain at a local level, that revolution was still on the agenda. This policy masked a real conflict over long-term aims within the party, and was only really to be eliminated (in favour of secret preparations for defensive struggle, in the case of a threat to democracy) after 1948.

Togliatti sealed this institutional pact with the other anti-fascist parties with the 'about-turn' (*svolta*) at Salerno in March 1944, on his return to Italy after eighteen years of exile. The 'revolutionary' PCI accepted the leadership of the king (in the short run) and co-habitation in government with Catholics and even monarchists. 'There is room for everyone', Togliatti stated, 'who desires to fight for the liberty of Italy.' In April, Togliatti became vice-president of a new government led by Marshal Badoglio. After the liberation, Communists joined the post-war governments, with Togliatti becoming minister of justice, pushing through an amnesty that allowed many fascists to escape punishment. The party played a full and important part in the drawing up of the 1948 Constitution. Yet, even as that document was signed, the Cold War was beginning to shape Italian politics. In 1947, in fact, the Communists were thrown out of the Italian government by De Gasperi (a move linked to US foreign policy and aid).

Communists thus played a key role in the resistance, and the role of Stalin's Russia in defeating Hitler gave the USSR enormous credibility and popularity in Western Europe. Millions of Italians flocked to join the PCI, making the party the biggest Communist Party (and perhaps the biggest party, full stop) in the Western world. The PCI was not just a political organization, but a state within a state, with party schools, newspapers, radio stations, sports and leisure organizations, women's groups, holiday homes, magazines, festivals and much, much more.[45] Many cities were run by the Communists from 1945 onwards, in particular Bologna, capital of what Togliatti called 'red Emilia'. By the end of the war the PCI had over 300,000 members, and this figure rose to an incredible 1.7 million by September 1945. In five months, 1.4 million Italians had joined the Communist Party. Electorally, however, the strength of the Socialist tradition was still equal to that of the Communists. In the 1946 elections the PCI won 4.3 million votes, and the PSI 4.7 million. By January 1948 party membership had reached 2.3 million. Yet this boom came to an abrupt end in the April 1948 election (see Box 4.6). The popular front won only 8.1 million votes, less than the two parties combined in 1946 and a result well behind that of the DC, who were able to govern alone. The defeat was traumatic, and never again were Socialists and Communists to stand together electorally against the DC. The PCI became the permanent and 'untouchable' political opposition – a position it was to maintain right up to 1976. This system, in which the opposition was not 'permitted' to govern, in a world dominated by the Cold War, was described by political scientists as 'imperfect bipolarism' or a 'blocked' system.[46]

The bankruptcy of *doppiezza* was soon to follow. On 4 July 1948, a young right-wing student shot Togliatti on the steps of Parliament. Mass reaction was swift, and dramatic. Tram tracks were soldered together at Genoa, strikes spread across the whole of the country (despite Togliatti's own attempts to calm the situation down), arms kept well oiled for three years reappeared on the streets. Road blocks were set up. Party leaders hesitated between revolutionary rhetoric (the front page of *L'Unità* screamed 'Down with the government of murderers!') and caution. In Rome, PCI leader D'Onofrio was greeted with cries of 'Give us the order to go'. But the order for the insurrection was never given, and the PCI soon began to demobilize the masses, avoiding the consequences of a frontal assault on the state. Duplicity, from that moment, was dead and the only arms that were kept from then on were clearly intended as defensive weapons, not revolutionary arsenals.

Kept out of government by the cold war, the PCI was unable to test its ideas of progressive democracy and structural reforms. At a local level (in cities such as Bologna and Modena), the party limited itself largely to innovative planning,

---

Box 4.6 Political sub-cultures

The 1948 election: concentrations of votes for the Left Coalition (a selection)

Cities	Vote for FDP (Popular Democratic Front), 18.4.1948 (%)
Provincial capitals	
La Spezia	51.3
Imperia	50.4
Ferrara	56.2
Forlì	52.2
Livorno	56.1
Perugia	56.7
Ravenna	58.3
Other cities (more than 30,000 inhabitants)	
Piombino	75.5
Sesto San Giovanni	54.4
Gubbio	61.6
Vigevano	50.7
Ostoni	59.2
Imola	61.3
Carpi	67.6
Cortona	56.7
Lugo	54.3
Prato	52.5
Spoleto	53.0

Source: Istituto Centrale di Statistica, Ministero dell'Interno, Elezioni politiche del 1948, *Elezioni della Camera dei Deputati*, Roma, 1949, 2 vols.

The Catholics, 1948

In the 1948 elections in the Province of Bergamo the Christian Democrats won 73.6 per cent of the votes. In Brescia itself their vote was 61.4 per cent and in Como 60.4 per cent. The results for the Popular Front in these three areas were 14.3, 28.4 and 23.9 per cent, respectively.

Other parties also concentrated their support in certain sub-cultural areas. The Socialists always did well in Milan, Mantova, Cremona, Varese (until the 1980s), Terni, Perugia and Novara. The Monarchists had strong support in Naples and Salerno. The neo-fascists found strong support in Bolzano, Trieste, Chieti, Latina and L'Aquila, as well as parts of Rome and Lazio. Republican Party strength was concentrated in areas of Romagna, such as Ravenna and Forli.

Red sub-cultures: the PCI after 1945

In the Tuscan comune of Certaldo in 1949 (a town of 12,000 people) there were more than 2,000 members of the Italian Communist Party, with 41 party cells (8 of which were factory-based, 10 street-based, 15 village-based, and 8 for women). The local chamber of labour could count on 4,000 members.

'good government' and political symbolism. Communist sub-cultures were reinforced throughout the 1950s.[47] Organic links were constructed with the CGIL, the 'red' union federation. The party was still dominated by Moscow, and right through to the shock of 1956, the cult of Stalin was extremely strong. Stalin's death was a traumatic moment for many Italian Communists. *L'Unità*, the official party daily, wrote that 'the man who has done the most for the liberation of the human race is dead'. After the invasion of Hungary in 1956, however, many communist intellectuals rebelled, and hundreds of thousands left the party (never to return). Togliatti made tentative attempts to break with the USSR, but the party was too tied up with the Soviet world, and the Soviet myth. A whole generation of young people rebelled against the system, of which the PCI was a key part, after 1968. Although the Communists managed to 'ride the tiger' of the worker and student rebellion, especially in the factories, the ability of the party to control the situation was in decline.

PCI votes continued to increase, however, as the party presented itself as a moderate and honest alternative to the DC. In the 1970s the party managed to form centre–left governments with the PSI in Turin, Rome, Naples and Milan, but not at a national level. In the wake of the Chilean coup of 1973, the new leader Enrico Berlinguer began to draw up plans for what he called a 'historic compromise'. This consisted of an alliance between communism and the DC, in defence of democracy and in favour of reform. Berlinguer argued, in the wake of Chile, that 51 per cent of the votes were not enough to govern Italy. Between 1976 (the peak of the PCI's electoral support) and 1979 the Communists supported DC governments at a time of deep economic and social crisis, and of terrorism. This policy, however, never convinced PCI militants, who saw themselves allied with the enemies of old. Reforms were moderate and hampered by inflation that reached 22 per cent. Party membership and electoral support began to decline. The sub-cultures began to fragment under the pressure of consumerism, individualism and mass cultural trends.

The final 'break' with Moscow took place in the 1980s. Berlinguer opposed the invasion of Afghanistan, and the PCI finally accepted Italian membership of NATO. A last crisis in this relationship came in 1990, with the end of the official cold war (a phoney cold war was to rage on in Italy for at least the next ten years). Achille Occhetto, the last leader of the PCI, attempted to modernize the party through a radical rethink of its strategy, its past and its name (as well as the 'communist' experience'). This strategy was also inspired by the ideas of Gorbachev in attempting to democratize and reform the Soviet system. In 1991, the PCI died (and split), becoming the *Democratic Party of the Left* (PDS) and later the *Democratic Left* (DS). Occhetto's *svolta* filled reams of newspaper articles, but took the party towards its worst electoral result ever, in 1992. Occhetto had drastically underestimated the importance to many Communists of the symbolism of the party name, its history, and its pride as a specific entity.[48]

A small split became a major one when *Rifondazione Comunista* obtained 5.6 per cent of the vote and, in some places, such as Milan, even overtook the PDS, albeit briefly. Before the *svolta*, the PCI was still a mass party, with 1,422,000 members, 10,310 sections and 128 federations. Over the next decade, much of this membership was to disappear, and the huge party bureaucracy was dismantled (the party still employed 1,750 full-time staff in 1992). Even the famous party daily, *L'Unità*, went bankrupt for a time and disappeared from the news-stands.

After 1992, the Left blundered towards a centre–left electoral alliance, achieving local success (victories in Naples, Rome, Palermo) and national defeat. Only with the Ulivo coalition in 1996, inspired by the Catholic economist Roman Prodi, did the umbrella model bear fruit. Yet political in-fighting and Machiavellism undermined the Prodi project and the five years of DS-backed governments were only the prelude to a disastrous defeat, born from disunity, in 2001. Many of the more traditional aspects of communist culture were kept alive by *Rifondazione*, which also encapsulated the 'culture of opposition' enshrined in part of the Italian Left after 1945. Yet, *Rifondazione* and other connected groupings failed to reach the 4 per cent threshold needed to enter Parliament in 2008 and 2013 while standing outside the major coalitions. New umbrella formations collected the remnants of what had once been a powerful culture on the far left. The PCI had twice seen its social base eliminated by social change – from the day-labourers in the 1950s to the industrial working class in the 1980s. Some commentators claimed that, by the 1990s, what remained of the PCI represented merely the most moral and 'honest' part of Italy's conservative majority. The party had no real strategy for transforming the conservatism of Italian society, only a technical plan to reform the state, making it more efficient and appealing to the remains of the working class and those working in the state sector.[49]

MASS PARTIES: THE CHURCH AND THE CENTRE GROUND OF POLITICS – CATHOLIC POLITICAL PARTIES

The Italian Popular Party (*Partito Popolare Italiano*, PPI)

Formation: 1919; Dissolution: 1926.

Leaders: Don Luigi Sturzo, 1919–23; Alcide De Gasperi, 1924–6.

The Russian Revolution and the potential for political Catholicism in Italy finally convinced the Vatican in 1919 to sanction the formation of a Catholic political party. Before 1919, Catholics had been elected *as* Catholics in small numbers in 1904 and in larger numbers in 1913 following the Gentiloni pact between the Liberals and political Catholics. The Italian Popular Party (PPI) was formed in Rome in January 1919, under the leadership of a Sicilian priest, Don Luigi Sturzo. The first PPI programme was an organic and radical plan for political and economic reform, aimed at the maintenance of the status quo through major change. Politically, the PPI called for PR and votes for women, whilst in the economic sphere, the party glorified the small landowner, arguing for the redistribution of the land of the big estates and the protection and extension of small property. The PPI was an anti-socialist and inter-class party, arguing for reform not revolution, and social peace not social conflict. A modern aspect of the programme was its emphasis on decentralization. Yet the PPI was also deeply divided – between a moderate reformist centre (led by Sturzo), a deeply clerical right and a revolutionary far left linked to union movements in the Po Valley and the Veneto.[50]

One hundred PPI deputies were elected in the 1919 elections, an extraordinary result for a party formed just nine months earlier. The party did well in the north and north-east, moderately in the centre and badly in the south, where the Liberals still held sway (see Box 4.7). In Parliament, PPI deputies remained in opposition until 1921, when three Catholic ministers were appointed. Mussolini included Catholics in his first cabinet in 1922 and Catholic votes were crucial to the passage of the new electoral law in 1923. Many Catholics were attracted to the law-and-order policies of fascism. However, the fascists made life increasingly difficult for the PPI in the 1920s, and began to destroy party offices and institutions as well as to intimidate PPI members and leaders. A priest, Don Minzoni, was killed by fascists near Ferrara in 1923. Sturzo remained strongly anti-fascist, but many in his party and in the official Church hierarchy disagreed – he was forced to resign as PPI leader in 1923 (and was then forced out of Italy). Catholic pacifists had long been a target of fascist attack, especially since World War I. By 1926 all the Catholic political leaders had been forced out of office or into exile. The PPI was dissolved in 1926, along with all other non-fascist parties. Allum argues that the PPI represented the second attempt at a political Catholic organization in Italy, after the *Opera dei Congressi* (1874). Both failed after being abandoned by the Vatican.

Catholic political anti-fascism was much weaker than that of either the Communists or the Socialists. It was only in the early 1940s that the first seeds of Christian Democracy began to form. Alcide De Gasperi, the last secretary of the PPI, who had been working in the Vatican under fascism, helped to set up a Christian Democrat Party (DC) in 1942 and Catholic-inspired partisan groups fought the German and Italian fascists, especially in the Veneto, in Friuli and in Piedmont. After the war, the Catholic political centre quickly became the heart of all political alliances, taking up moderate anti-fascist positions and occupying the state machine. The DC also took up a clear anti-communist and pro-US political stance. Italian Christian Democracy became so omnipresent and gargantuan that it was known as 'the white whale'. This beast was to govern Italy for nearly fifty years.

The 'White Whale': the Christian Democrats (DC), 1942–94

Formed: 1942; Dissolution: 1992.

Splits/divisions: 1994 (*Partito Popolare Italiano, CdU, CCd, UdeuR, La Margherita*, and various other groupings).

National governments as DC (coalitions): 1944–94.

History

The cold war international system meant that it was virtually impossible for the DC to lose elections. After the dismissal of the Left in 1947 (on orders from the US) the Christian Democratic Party (the DC) governed either alone, or

---

Box 4.7 The Catholic vote over time

The Catholic vote before and after fascism: from the Popular Party to the DC and beyond (percentage votes, selected general elections)

Region	1921 (PPI)	1946 (DC)	1948 (DC)	1992 (DC)
Piedmont	22.0	35.0	48.0	21.04
Liguria	22.0	33.0	46.0	21.85
Lombardy	26.0	39.0	53.0	24.11
Veneto	36.0	49.0	61.0	31.50
Trentino	32.0	57.0	71.0	21.52
Venezia-Giulia	3.2	46.6	57.0	28.13
Emilia-Romagna	19.3	23.0	33.0	19.53
Tuscany	19.0	28.0	39.0	22.05
Marche	30.0	31.0	47.0	31.49
Umbria	16.0	36.0	37.0	24.83
Lazio	22.0	33.0	52.0	31.04
Abruzzo/Molise	7.0	42.0	54.0	40.40
Campania	14.0	34.0	50.0	41.09
Apulia	10.0	33.0	49.0	35.79
Basilicata	4.0	31.0	48.0	44.45
Calabria	19.0	34.0	49.0	36.65
Sicily	13.2	34.0	48.0	41.18
Sardinia	11.0	41.0	51.0	33.65
Italy	**20.4**	**35.2**	**49.0**	29.70

with smaller centrist parties, until the early 1960s.[51] There then followed a period of centre–left governments (at first with the Socialists, or with the support of the Communists, and then with the Socialists again). The only party with whom the DC never governed were the neo-fascists, after the failed attempt to use their votes in 1960 (for the governments and various coalitions, see Box 4.8 and Appendix 1). Right up to the end of the 1970s, the DC kept control of all the key positions within the state machine – apart from the Italian presidency that was also occupied by a Social Democrat from 1964 to 1971, and a Socialist from 1978 to 1985.

But what kind of party was the DC? It was a *mass* party, which used the support of Church and Catholic organizations at a series of levels. The party claimed to have well over a million members. The Church was important ideologically (the Pope excommunicated communists in 1948, and reforms within the Church after 1960 tended to influence the DC), organizationally and financially. The DC became symbiotic with the state, building up stable relationships (and clienteles) within public institutions. Over time, the DC used various methods to construct consensus. Public resources were distributed widely and generously (as Chubb wrote, this was 'a party that has transformed the Italian state into a huge patronage machine'[52]); political alliances were built up with centre parties; mass Catholic associations played a central role.[53] Given its near

---

Box 4.8   Political alliances: coalitions, parties, formations (up to 1992)

1945–7   Tripartism: DC/PCI/PSI (stable period – one prime minister: De
            Gasperi)

1947–53   Centrism: PLI (Liberal Party)/DC/PRI (Republican Party)/PSDI
            (stable period – one prime minister: De Gasperi)
1953–60   Centrism: DC/PLI/PSDI/PRI (instability – five different prime ministers)
1960–2   Transition: PLI/DC/PRI/PSDI/PSI (instability – search for different
            coalition pattern to the Right failed in 1960)
1962–4   Centre–left: DC/PRI/PSDI/PSI
1964–8   Centre–left: DC/PRI/PSDI/PSI (stable – one prime minister: Moro)
1968–71   Centre–left: DC/PRI/PSDI/PSI (instability – three prime ministers)
1972–3   Centrism: DC/PLI/PSDI/PRI
1973–5   Centre–left: DC/PSDI/PRI/PSI
1976–9   National Solidarity: DC/PCI/PSI
1979–92   *Pentapartito*: DC/PSI/PLI/PSDI/PRI

---

semi-permanence in government, the DC could afford to be generous in this way. Power was important in its own right. As Giulio Andreotti famously said, 'power consumes those who do not have it'. An *internal* spoils system also developed, with elaborate factions, PR voting (the DC was an extremely democratic party internally, much more so than the PCI) and scientific distribution of the spoils – through the so-called 'Cencelli Manual' (see Box 4.1). DC policy was to never carry out too much reform, and in fact the actuation of the Constitution was systematically blocked until the 1950s and 1960s. Calamandrei called this 'majority obstructionism'. The administration was left unreformed; purging of fascists stopped and the economy was 'managed' by 'benign neglect'. After the agrarian reforms of 1950 (a perfect example of the construction of consensus through the use of the state) the DC was only pushed into long-awaited reform (for example of the education system) by the Socialists in the 1960s. Stable electoral support was constructed across Italy, from south to north (see Box 4.17). In addition, strong conservative forces in the DC deferred or watered down any radical reform. Yet, the DC always contained innovative and reforming factions – the group around Dossetti in the 1950s, La Pira in Florence in the 1950s and 1960s, Donat Cattin in the 1970s, Fanfani's first governments, Moro's work with the Socialists, the anti-Mafia movements around the 'Palermo spring' and *La Rete* in the 1980s and 1990s, Mario Segni's referendum movements in the 1990s, the 'honest' Catholicism of Martinazzoli or Zaccagnini. Time and again, figures emerged who talked of renewal and change. Time and again, nothing actually changed, centrally.

The priority for the DC hierarchies was always the maintenance of power (and of the Western bloc). To this end, everything was justified, from cohabitation with the Mafia, to the construction of an anti-communist (and secret) reserve army, to the organization of the 'strategy of tension' (see Box 2.1, Chapter 2). The party's *raison d'être* was as a cold warrior, but it was also flexible enough to govern with the Socialists and to pull the Communists into the fold in the 1970s, as well as presiding over the economic miracle and the secularization of civil society. The DC effectively created a *material constitution* (L. Elia),[54] which operated alongside the real, written Constitution during its fifty years in power. The DC itself, and the way it behaved, developed into the constitution which ran Italy. Strong links were also constructed with the Catholic Union Federation (CISL – *Confederazione Italiana Sindacati Lavoratori*) and the powerful small farmers' organization (the *Coldiretti*). Enrico Mattei also constructed wide-ranging power networks around ENI, the state oil and gas corporation.

By the 1970s, the DC was a vast organizational machine. The 1973 National Congress, for example, held in Rome, saw the party claim 1.7 million members, represented by 734 delegates. A massive stage was constructed in front of a reproduction of the party symbol, and in huge letters, the phrase 'A united and democratic commitment to push forward, in peace and liberty, Italy and Europe'. Across Italy and amongst emigrant communities, 13,000 preparatory meetings were held. Committees which sat included the Committee for the Verification of Powers, the Committee for the Acceptance of Candidate Lists, and the Motion Committee. Political representatives of the DC attended the congress, as well as observers from Latin America, Asia and Africa, the President of the Chilean Senate and the Norwegian prime minister. The mayor of Rome was there, as were major figures from all the other parties and trade unions except for the neo-fascist party. A long and interminable 'debate' dominated the public part of the congress, with lengthy interventions from the various DC leaders over four days (Moro's speech alone runs to some 25 pages of the congress proceedings). The really important business, of course, took place behind the scenes, with the elections of representatives from the various party factions. This vote would decide the distribution of jobs in any successive government. Six factions stood candidates for the DC central secretariat, and the votes of all the delegates and those elected were minutely recorded. The simple costs of keeping this organization going were, clearly, enormous. Fanfani, when in charge of the party, had increased the number of party functionaries from 37,000 to 200,000. The party was forced to look for illegal sources of funds to survive, given its inability to reform itself, or the state.

The DC was thus a mixture of mass party, sub-cultural organization and huge clientelistic machine, managed through the control of the state and the filtering down of resources through ministers, junior ministers and local representatives. Specific areas were controlled by specific bosses. In the south, there was Gava in Naples; Bosco in Caserta; Vetrone in Benevento; De Mita in Avellino. The southern system functioned through patronage, organized crime and the straightforward distribution of state funding (pensions, jobs, contracts). In the north, Catholic ideology was more important, as were credit associations. Later, with the mass welfare state, health care became a key source of patronage. As we have seen in the sections on clientelism, partitocracy and consociationism, by the end of the 1980s this system was close to breaking point.

In 1992 the DC was still able to win nearly 30 per cent of the vote, although this was seen as an enormous defeat at the time. By 1994, the 'white whale' had ceased to exist. The end of the cold war had not led the voters 'to vote for who we really are' (as Antonio Gava had claimed, optimistically). On the contrary, there was no longer any need to 'hold your nose and vote DC', as the right-wing journalist Indro Montanelli famously wrote. The unity of the voters, and of the Catholics themselves, was no longer necessary for the survival of an anti-communist Italy. Communism had died on its own. The DC had been destroyed by its massive involvement in political corruption, exposed dramatically by the *Tangentopoli* scandals in 1992–3. The DC had been at the heart of all the partitocratic networks which infected the Italian state, and had constructed the clientelist system around which the first republic revolved. It was therefore natural that the highest number of corrupt politicians were from the DC (although many of those caught up in the scandals were later to claim that the whole investigation had been politically motivated, as did the Socialists). Two symbols of this corruption were particularly powerful. One was the ageing treasurer of the DC, Salvatore Citaristi, who was caught up in hundreds of investigations. Another was DC secretary and former prime minister Forlani, literally foaming at the mouth on live TV as he responded weakly to a series of aggressive questions from the investigating magistrate Antonio Di Pietro. Of the old leadership only 'Beelzebub', Giulio Andreotti, was able to survive politically, despite the much more serious charge of Mafia collusion, although a large number of minor leaders 'recycled' themselves into positions of prestige in the new political structures of the second republic. The continuing key role of the centre ground meant that a DC kind of 'catch-all' party was still needed in Italy, even if the DC itself could no longer perform that function.

After 1992, the DC split into a number of Catholic-inspired groupings. Some attempted to stand alone, in the centre, whilst others gravitated towards the Left or the Right. All claimed to be the heirs of the best parts of the DC tradition. Among the main organizations were the centre–left-inspired PPI, which took the name of Don Sturzo's party from 1919. This party later dissolved itself into the *Ulivo* umbrella organization and later into *La Margherita*. The innovative reformist ideas of Mario Segni (who inspired the referendums of the 1990s) and Leoluca Orlando (with the anti-Mafia social movements in the south, and the anti-corruption parties in the north) were all marginalized within the political power games centred on Parliament. On the centre–right, other groups took up the DC mantle, using a similar symbol to that of the old DC and allying themselves with Berlusconi and Fini. Slowly, these groups came together to form a single centre–right Catholic party, representing a moderate wing of the centre–right, with an ideological concentration on 'Catholic' (schools, abortion) and family-inspired issues. Nonetheless, the epoch of one, vast, Catholic-inspired party was over, forever. The 'white whale' was extinct.

Although the DC ceased to exist as a monolithic party in the mid-1990s, its legacy was a powerful one. Many of the key politicians of the 1990s and 2000s came from the Christian Democrat diaspora, and the DC style of politics was certainly present within the parliamentary system well into the twenty-first century. The idea of a gigantic, catch-all party linked to the Church was no longer practical, but the Church remained a key player in Italian political life, working effectively across ideological and party lines. A galaxy of small and medium-sized 'Catholic' parties and groups emerged who formed alliances to the left or to the right. Many ex-DC politicians simply joined 'new' left- or right-wing organizations. The party itself was gone, but its influence remained high. For example, Enrico Letta, Prime Minister in 2013, had been a young member of the DC and Roberto Formigoni, who was President of the Lombard Region from 1995 to 2013, also came from the DC. Pressure groups and economic forces linked to the Church exerted a powerful cultural and political role, such as *Comunione e Liberazione*, Milan's Catholic University, the Catholic press, banks, radio and TV networks and the huge *Compagnia delle Opere* business association.

THE FAR RIGHT: FASCIST AND NEO-FASCIST PARTIES

The Fascist Party, 1921–45 (*Partito Nazionale Fascista*, PNF)

The PNF, the national fascist party, was formed in November 1921 in Rome. This body drew together the disparate elements of fascism – from the violent *squadristi*, with their local bases and leadership, to the military-style *arditi* and *fasci di combattimento*, to the more 'political' elements of fascism centred on Mussolini. Slowly, fascism moved from movement to regime, as fascist violence became less central (although the party was always a military-type organization, as Gentile has persuasively argued). The role of the party under the regime has been largely neglected by historians and social scientists – the PNF has largely been seen as a bureaucratic colossus, or merely as an adjunct of Mussolini's power. Recently, however, a number of studies have begun to appear which underline the centrality of the Fascist Party, and its constitutional importance, especially following the 1926 and 1928 reforms (after which the head of the government was automatically also head of the party). Through authoritarian reform and violence, the PNF played a key role in the governance of Italy after the installation of the regime. Within this new constitutional system, the Fascist Grand Council (set up in December 1922) became fundamental.[55] The PNF was also significant as a means of dominating society – as an instrument of cultural propaganda and education. Many intellectuals and politicians from the post-war period had experience within the PNF, and not always had they been constrained to join or participate.

In addition, the PNF represented the ideological and organizational link to the 'revolutionary' moments of 1919–22 which provided the historical legitimation for the regime. History was rewritten via these organizations. For example, in 1923, the families of fascists who had died during the march on Rome (1922) were awarded state *war* pensions. Mussolini's downfall also underlined the crucial constitutional powers held by the PNF by the 1940s.[56] Finally, the PNF was important for state bureaucrats (all of whom were obliged to join the party in the 1930s). PNF members found it easier to get jobs in general, as a kind of second, party-led bureaucracy was set up. As with liberalism before, and the DC afterwards, however, membership of the PNF was not necessarily an ideological decision. As De Luna has written, 'fascism had a bureaucratic conception of politics – joining the PNF was like getting a birth certificate: there was no ethical component'.[57] Debates around the PNF concern the importance of its military features, and the extent to which the party represented a new form of organization with respect to the parties which had existed in Liberal Italy.[58]

The PNF was a mass party, with a membership far superior to that of any of the parties from Liberal Italy in the early 1920s. By 1923 the PNF could already count on nearly 800,000 members. During the 1930s, youth organizations, women's organizations and cultural bodies were formed, and the party recruited more than a million members.[59] As Salvati has written, 'culturally and politically, more than organisationally, the structure of the party filled the empty space between the citizen and the state, that gap between the petty bourgeoisie and the law which had marked the first twenty years of the century'.[60] Party organization provided the regime with a way of educating and preparing leaders, and with the means to control and integrate local organizations, and to suppress or soften rebellions (the party was purged of militants on various occasions). This was a double-edged sword, however: 'the greatest arena of potential contestation of the Duce's overwhelming authority remained the Fascist party' (Bosworth).[61] The party became a key part of the state machine, so much so that it was difficult to distinguish the one from the other. By the end of the 1930s the PNF had 2.6 million members.

The Grand Council controlled the electoral systems set up by fascism (and thus the construction of a new political class). Grand Council members decided the lists of those to be 'elected' by plebiscite. All Grand Council members were given parliamentary immunity and some analysts have argued that this organization became, or acted like, a *collective* head of state. Here, the role of Mussolini is, of course, crucial. Who had final say? How much power did Mussolini really wield? Once again, as we have argued, the removal of Mussolini by the Grand Council in 1943 would seem to point in one direction, although it is clear that this moment followed twenty years of dictatorship, was initiated by the king and some leading fascists, and came at a time when Mussolini was extremely unpopular in Italy as a whole. None the less, institutionally, the Grand Council vote does appear something like a vote of no confidence. Parliament, or at least the role played by a 'parliament' in a totalitarian regime, became the Grand Council, at least in theory. In practice, little actual power was exercised until 1943. The Grand Council always contained the 'great names of the fascist movement',[62] who were not in the early Mussolini cabinets. After July 1943, these traditions continued only within the Republic of Salò, whose importance has only recently begun to attract the serious attention of historians.[63] In the rest of Italy, the PNF was dissolved, fascist symbols were torn down, and the fascist militia disbanded. The legacy of the PNF, however, remained strong within the political cultures and structures of Italian civil society and the state machine, especially given the continuities which marked the transition back to democracy and the minimal purging of fascist officials.

After Mussolini: The Italian Social Movement (*Movimento Sociale Italiano*), 1946–94, National Alliance (*Alleanza Nazionale*), 1994–2009

Founded: 26.12.1946; Party dissolved in 1994: *Alleanza Nazionale* (AN) formed in 1994.

Splits: 1956 (*Ordine Nuovo*); 1995 (*Fiamma-tricolore*); 2003 (*Libertà di Azione/ Azione Sociale*); 2007 (*La Destra*).

Alleanza Nazionale fused into *The People of Freedom*, 2009. *Futuro e Libertà* group leave, 2010, *Fratelli d'Italia*, 2012.

Fascism and right-wing politics did not disappear in 1945. Many Italians remained committed fascists, often in silence, whilst others were still attracted by the policies and the ideologies of the regime which had ruled the country for twenty years. The strong monarchist legacy was revealed by the 10 million Italians who voted against the Republic in 1946, especially in the south. In fact, the resistance had little effect in the south (militarily, and above all ideologically). There were a number of strands to right-wing politics after the war. The first and most important was a fairly straightforward re-edition of the Fascist Party, formed by neo-fascists in 1946 and given the title of the Italian Social Movement (MSI).[64]

The MSI had its strongholds in the south, but managed to pick up support everywhere in Italy (especially in Rome), and was also important in the German, Austrian and Yugoslavian border regions. MSI policies were anti-communist, and exalted the record of the fascist regime, whilst picking up on the shift to more social policies under the Republic of Salò. Neo-fascists developed their own version of history and their own ceremonies to combat those of the new Republic. Until the 1990s, apart from brief periods in the 1960s, the MSI was a political untouchable, marginalized by all the major political parties within the democratic system. In national elections, the party won between 5 and 10 per cent of the vote, with a peak on the back of the protests of 1968, which also radicalized extreme right-wing elements in Italian society. In fact, right-wing leaders even managed to take control of violent social protests in Reggio Calabria (1969–72). Many young people were attracted to fascist ideologies in this period. The MSI's best electoral performances were in the 1972 general election, with 8.7 per cent, and in 1983 with 8.8 per cent. Neo-fascists were also recruited by the secret services to carry out terrorist attacks, often as part of the 'strategy of tension', and neo-fascists formed their own trade union federation.

Politically, the DC was tempted to use MSI support on a number of occasions, but the only attempt to set up formal alliances in Parliament failed after violent anti-fascist demonstrations in Genoa in 1960. Outside of the system, the MSI was able to survive the political earthquake of 1992–4. The end of the cold war, and the receding memory of fascism, allowed the MSI back into the political fold, under a new 'moderate' leadership (that of Gianfranco Fini) and after a renewal which led to (at least officially) the dropping of the more 'fascist' aspects of MSI ideology, a new name (*Alleanza Nazionale*) and even a critique of some aspects of Mussolini's regime, such as the alliance with

Germany and the anti-Semitic laws. None the less, at the base, many of the old attitudes remained and significant groups of members were 'nostalgic' for a return to old-style fascism. In numerous AN offices there were portraits of Mussolini, and some of those in the party were openly 'fascist'. Yet, AN also moved away from corporatist and statist positions and much closer to the mainstream of Italian democracy. In fact, well before the 1990s, the MSI had shown itself to be 'open to modernity' and 'hoping to establish relations with other parties, with a particular interest in the Socialist Party'. The MSI was thus ready, unlike other European far-right parties (such as the National Front in France), to 'escape from its neo-fascist ghetto'.[65] The dramatic events of the 1990s gave the party this opportunity, and AN became a governing party at a local and national level in 1994 and after 2001. A series of splits to the right dogged the party's progress towards the centre, splits which were sometimes sparked by specific events, such as Fini's visit to Israel in 2003.

The broad centre–right umbrella alliance presided over by Berlusconi was called the *Pole of Freedoms* and later the *House of Liberties* (*La Casa delle Libertà* or *CdL*). In 2007 Berlusconi announced that Forza Italia and AN would fuse into *The People of Freedom* organization (*Il Popolo della Libertà* or PdL). The PdL also included ex-Catholics, ex-Communists, ex-Liberals and ex-Socialists. This merger finally took place in 2009. In 2010, former AN leader Gianfranco Fini left to set up yet another grouping called *Futuro e Libertà*. This organization then supported a centrist coalition in 2012–13, where it gained 0.4 per cent of the vote.

Further to the right, far-right groupings and parties continued to emerge and re-form, and claim a link to the now defunct MSI. Nostalgia for the fascism of Mussolini was fairly widespread, and new far-right organizations created spaces in many Italian cities. Young people were often attracted to these spaces and their ideas. This was a movement that included the so-called 'Casa Pound' activists in Rome and elsewhere.

THE SECOND AND THIRD REPUBLIC: NEW PARTIES AND MOVEMENTS AFTER 1992[66]

The events of 1992–4 have been dealt with elsewhere in this volume. After 1992, all the major parties from the 'First Republic' disappeared from the political scene, to be replaced either with new editions of old parties (*Alleanza Nazionale*, the PDS) or with completely new groupings – above all, Silvio Berlusconi's *Forza Italia!*

Berlusconi's Personal and 'Business Party': *Forza Italia!* 1994–2009; The *People of Freedom* (*Il Popolo della Libertà*) 2009–2013; *Forza Italia!* 2013–

Forza Italia! (FI) represented a completely new type of party when set up by media magnate Silvio Berlusconi in January 1994. Without a mass membership or any of the trappings of traditional parties (local sections were known as 'clubs'), FI grew from the entrepreneurial and media experience of

Berlusconi's Fininvest media empire. Using modern sales and consumer-oriented techniques, and the undoubted charisma of its leader and boss, FI was perfectly suited to the post-political society which the Italy of the 1990s had become. Incredibly, Berlusconi managed to win the elections of April 1994 in alliance with the right-wing *Alleanza Nazionale* (ex-MSI, see above) in the south and the regionalist Leagues in the north of Italy. *Forza Italia!* placed itself in the old-fashioned anti-communist camp – as a bulwark against the rule of the Left in Italy – in combination with its 'postmodern' elements. In addition, there were no internal elections, no delegates and no party democracy. Berlusconi was the undisputed leader and the first congress of FI was not held until 1998. In terms of policy, Berlusconi adopted an anti-tax programme, linking elements of Thatcherism and free market ideology with forms of populism (as in the famous slogan from the 1994 elections which promised to 'create a million jobs'). These elements led Bossi to call Berlusconi 'the Peron of the provinces'. Berlusconi was also able to use his vast media empire to promote his own political ambitions.

In reality, these free market ambitions were tempered not only by Berlusconi's own conflict of interests, which was often discussed but never resolved – a position unique in a Western democracy, of a confusion of media control and political power – but also by the need to ally with various moderate 'statist' parties: AN, the Catholic centre. In power in 1994, FI was paralysed by Berlusconi's personal battles with the judiciary and by the impossibility of uniting a nationalist party with a regionalist movement. Berlusconi's government fell after only nine months in power, as the *Lega* withdrew its support. None the less, against all the odds and in the face of the lack of a 'proper' or a 'normal Right' in Italy, FI survived the debacle of 1994 and the continuing judicial problems of Berlusconi himself to remain the biggest non-Left party and control a series of important local councils, such as Milan. In 2000–1, Berlusconi managed to construct a much more solid alliance with the *Lega* and AN, as well as the Catholic centre–right, within an umbrella grouping known as the House of Liberties. *Forza Italia!* reinforced its position as the natural home for former DC and PSI voters, becoming the biggest political party in Italy and showing signs of the creation of a political and organizational life which was in some way autonomous from Berlusconi and his business interests (see Box 4.10).

Yet, time and again, the organization was identified almost entirely with Berlusconi's personality and his business empire. Rebels were marginalized and forced out. Internal democracy was non-existent. Loyalty was everything. The party was closely, almost intimately, connected to the vast media and sporting galaxy of companies which Berlusconi had set up and continued to run. His TV stations promoted his own political vision. He was the centre of the party. Nobody seriously challenged his leadership. What this meant, however, was a dangerous identification of the needs of the collectivity with the needs, foibles and trials of one man. Another clear danger was that the movement could not survive a future without Berlusconi. Italy did not have a 'normal', moderate, right-wing or centre-right party. Debate was often reduced to a simplistic, and damaging, for-or-against Berlusconi equation.

Box 4.9   Silvio Berlusconi 'takes the field', January 1994

The entire speech was just 1,000 words long. It took 9 minutes and 24 seconds. Berlusconi was sitting in a 'room', in a trademark blue suit. The 'programme' was then sent as a video-tape to the news channels. The 'room' was in fact fake. It was a TV studio, set up in Berlusconi's house in Macherio, outside Milan, with pretend books and two family photos behind him. In front of him, there were blank sheets of paper, which he held in order to provide gravitas. It is said that a stocking was put over the camera to soften the atmosphere. Berlusconi flashed his famous smile. A political star was born. The first channel to show the message was, appropriately, Berlusconi's own Rete 4, presented by his most faithful anchor-man of all, Emilio Fede. The speech emphasized Berlusconi's personal success story, the Communist roots of the left in Italy (who were painted as *the* enemy) and his belief in the free market. The language was direct, non-political and clear.

'Italy is the country I love', 26 January 1994 (extracts)

> I have chosen to take the field and to take an interest in public affairs because I do not want to live in an illiberal country, governed by people who have links to a past which has failed. In order to carry out this new life choice, I have today resigned from every institutional position in the business group of which I was the founder ... If the political system is to work, it is essential that there emerges a 'pole of Liberty' ... we believe in individuals, in families, in business, in competition, in economic growth, in efficiency. (Silvio Berlusconi)*

* The text of the speech is included in Silvio Berlusconi, *L'Italia che ho in mente. I discorsi 'a braccio' di Silvio Berlusconi*, Mondadori, Milan, 2000, pp. 289–92. Crainz, *Il paese reale*, pp. 308–9 and Paul Ginsborg, *Berlusconi*, pp. 65–6. For a series of speeches made by Berlusconi between 1994 and 2000 see the volume cited above.

The toxic effects of this conflict of interests infected Italian politics at all levels. Institutions suffered as a result, as did public debate.

After the defeat in 2006, in late 2007 Berlusconi announced a supposedly new grouping which was to be called *The People of Freedom*, and would reinforce discipline in the coalition. The *Lega* remained outside of this organization (although it remained as part of the centre–right electoral alliance) which easily won the elections in 2008. Although AN and FI merged into the PdL in 2009, there were tensions over Berlusconi's total control of the organization. In 2010 Gianfranco Fini left to form a new grouping, in a move which greatly weakened the government. Berlusconi's party remained largely loyal, disciplined and 'personal'. Despite this, it was constructed in his image. In November 2013, Berlusconi relaunched *Forza Italia!* but a significant group of his Deputies left to set up a new, more moderate, centre–right grouping. The key issues at stake were, once again, personal issues, linked to Berlusconi's

Box 4.10   Silvio Berlusconi's business empire, 2013

1. Construction of an empire, 1962–90 (the core of Berlusconi's business empire was built between the 1960s and the 1990s)

   1962: Cantieri Riuniti Milanesi
   1963: Edilnord
   1969: Milano2 built (officially opened in 1971)
   1973: Milano3 built
   1974: Cable TV Telemilano
   1979: Publitalia formed (advertising concessions company)
   1980: Canale 5 founded
   1983: Purchase of Italia 1 TV station
   1984: Purchase of Rete 4 TV station
   1986: Purchase of AC Milan football club
   1988: Purchase of Standa supermarkets (sold in 1998)
   1990: Purchase of Arnoldo Mondadori SpA

2. The Empire (figures and information below relate to the situation in 2012–13 with some reference to earlier periods).

Fininvest (set up 1975–8): Silvio Berlusconi owns over 61% of the shares in this financial holding company. The rest are held by his five children. Its president in 2013 was his eldest daughter Marina Berlusconi.*
   The Fininvest group controls all or part of the following companies. It employed some 22,000 people directly in 2012. It also had a 2% share in the Mediobanca investment bank in 2013.

- **TV, Radio and Internet**: Mediaset SpA (41.1%)/Kirch Media (2.6%), *Mediaset* (the president since 1994 has been Fedele Confalonieri) 100%, Rti (Reti televisive italiane: Canale 5, Italia 1, Rete 4), Mediatrade (production company), Videotime (production company), Elettronica Industriale (technical services), Publitalia 80 (advertising) Mediadigit (digital TV and internet), Euroset; 60% Gestevision Telecinco; 40% Publiespaña; 40% Albacom.
- **Publishing**: Mondadori SpA 50.1%. Mondadori controls 31% of the books market and 45% of the magazine sector, including *Panorama, Donna Moderna, Chi, TV Sorrisi e Canzoni*; publishing houses in the group include Mondolibri, Elemond, Einaudi, Mondadori Pubblicità, Mondadori Informatica, Mondadori.com, Sperling & Kupfer, Le Monnier. Marina Berlusconi is president of Mondadori.
- **Housing and Construction**: Edilnord2000 63% (sold to Silvio Berlusconi's brother Paolo Berlusconi in 1992).
- **Financial Services**: Mediolanum SpA 35.5% (Insurance and savings). Banca Assicurazione Prodotti Finanziari, Banca Mediolanum, Mediolanum Inter. Funds Limited, Mediolanum Gestione Fondi Mediolanum Vita SpA, Partner Time SpA, Finbanc Inversiones, Mediolanum State Street.
- **Cinema**: Medusa Film SpA 100% (film production company; in 2000 this company had a 23% market share; the President in 2013 was Marina Berlusconi), Medusa Video, Cinema5.
- **Sport**: AC Milan SpA 100% (Serie A football team, honorary president Silvio Berlusconi-*amministratore delegato* Adriano Galliani).

* The presence of numerous companies that hold shares in the company has led to a series of judicial investigations into Finivest's business affairs.

Box 4.11   Silvio Berlusconi's language: political and marketing strategy

Berlusconi's language was made up of finely tuned political slogans which, taken together, created a kind of outlook on life and a political philosophy. Some of these were linked to his business acumen and ideas, such as the well-known 'I sell sales' remark from the 1980s. Others showed how he understood television, which, he said, 'allows people to hang out with their families. You need to know how to use it.' In 1986, Berlusconi underlined his political connections when he said that 'I am a businessman. I believe in the West, in the free market, in social progress. I obviously have sympathy with those who have the same ideas as me. I have been friends with [Bettino] Craxi for a long time. I respect him.' Berlusconi's language was direct and full of jokes and asides, and lacking in traditional 'politichese'. It looked outwards, not inwards, and it made frequent reference to himself (often in the third person). In his public statements, he usually tried to create or reinforce a community, either in a positive sense – Berlusconi-fans, or Milan supporters – or negatively – as with anti-communism.

A key political moment came in 1993 when Berlusconi backed the neo-fascist candidate Gianfranco Fini in the mayoral elections in Rome. This was important not only in the way it legitimized a party which had been outside of the political mainstream since the war, but also in the way that it showed how Berlusconi was ready to take a direct interest in the political system. At the same time, Berlusconi said that Fini 'is someone who brings together the moderate forces in this country which, if they are united, can guarantee the development of Italy'. Berlusconi often compared himself to God and underlined his sense of 'sacrifice'. He was at the same time ordinary and special, glamorous and down-to-earth, and he was a winner, in sport and in life.

He was also a political innovator, inventing ways of selling his product to the voters. In 2001 he signed a so-called 'Contract with the Italians' live on television. He said: 'If at the end of this five years of our government we have not carried out at least four or five of these objectives, Silvio Berlusconi gives a formal pledge that he will not stand in the following elections'. In the end, nobody really remembered if the pledges had been met, or not (most of them hadn't). What mattered were the promises and above all the spectacle of the contract live on television. Form was much more important than content.

In his long battle with the judiciary over twenty years or so, Berlusconi frequently made populist appeals which attempted to mobilize 'the people' in his favour. In court in 2003 he said: 'If it is true that the law is the same for everyone it is more equal for me than for the others because the majority of Italians have voted for me'.

Often, Berlusconi would say things which caused controversy. Usually, he would later argue that he had been misquoted. In reality, these so-called gaffes were carefully constructed to appeal to a specific audience, and to keep Berlusconi himself at the centre of media attention. For example, in 2008, Berlusconi made this remark about President Obama: 'I told President Medvedev that Obama has got everything going for him: he is young, good-looking and sun-tanned and I think we can work with him'. The reference to Obama as 'sun-tanned' was reported around the world, and was widely perceived as a gaffe, but Berlusconi later repeated the remark. In this way, he was showing that he had no respect for the powerful, and was able to use the 'humour' of the masses. The same could be said of his frequent use of sexist stereotypes and homophobic language. Berlusconi's words and phrases entered dictionaries, becoming part of the language. His catch-phrase '*Mi consenta...*' (if you would allow me) was associated with a whole epoch, and the term Bunga Bunga also seemed to encapsulate the decadence of the late Berlusconian period. He was loved and hated in equal measure, but he also was able to dominate debate and attract attention in a way that no other leader could aspire to.

legal problems and the possibility of his exclusion from Parliament. The centre–right was paralysed by the conflict of interest, which had been at the heart of the movement since 1994, and no clear outcome was in sight.

The Democratic Party (*Partito Democratico*, PD), 2007–

In 2007 the two main currents which had survived the death of the two major and mass parties that had dominated Italian political life since 1945 came together to form the Democratic Party. The Party was born amidst great fanfare. It brought together the remnants of the moderate wing of the Italian Communist Party and various centre and centre-left Catholic groups who had previously been linked to the Christian Democrats, along with a few scattered intellectuals and others. This was a relatively large and multi-faceted organization, albeit with nothing like the cultural and social weight, or the membership, of the mass parties in their post-war heyday. The first leader of the PD was the ex-communist journalist and writer Walter Veltroni, who was mayor of Rome at the time and had served as Minister of Culture in the first Prodi government in 1996–8. Veltroni had edited the PCI's daily newspaper, *L'Unità*.

In many ways, the formation of the PD seemed to be the long-term outcome of the 'historic compromise' from the 1970s, as the galaxy of centre-left groupings and coalitions which stood against Berlusconi and his allies in the 1990s and 2000s came together in one party. The PD was a gargantuan organization, top heavy and weighed down by an association with the past and with politics and professional politicians in general, despite an attempt at razzmatazz and modernity in terms of some of the campaigning and ideas introduced by Veltroni in particular. It struggled to present a new face to the electorate, and its base was ageing and tired. Primaries brought in fresh blood, often from outside of the party itself, but there were divisions over alliances (to the left, or to the centre? Veltroni cut the ties with the left, later leaders rebuilt them) and over policy (free market Blairism was advocated by many, but corporate conservatism usually prevailed, as did the links with the union movement). Moreover, the party was divided into a myriad of factions, many of which were grouped around individual 'leaders'. It often seemed less than the sum of its parts. The young mayor of Florence, Matteo Renzi (born in 1975) called for the old leadership to be 'discarded' or scrapped. This term gave him his nickname 'the scrapper', and he emerged as a key figure in the reconfiguration of Italian politics within the so-called 'Third Republic'. In December 2013 Renzi was elected as Secretary of the PD, winning over 70% of the vote in the primaries.

Beppe Grillo and The Five Star MoVement (*MoVimento Cinque Stelle*, M5S), 2009–

Beppe Grillo was born in Genoa in 1948. He became a successful comedian and was a frequent presence on television in the 1970s and 1980s. In 1981 he met the French comedian Coluch on a film set. Coluch used similar language in the political context to that later utilized by Grillo. In 1987 Grillo made a

Box 4.12   Primaries, Italian-style, 2005–13

The first primaries in Italy were held to decide on some candidates for the *Lega Nord* in the 1990s, but they became a fixed part of the political scene, at least for the centre–left, in 2005. In that year 4.3 million people turned out to select Romano Prodi as the candidate for the General Elections, which he duly won. This was an undoubted success and, it could be argued, gave a boost to Prodi's subsequent campaign, which he narrowly won. Further primaries were held for a series of regional and mayoral candidates over the ensuing years, although the rules for voters and voting were changed with bewildering regularity. The primaries often saw outsiders win in local contests, while the national Democratic Party primaries were usually more conservative, confirming the moderate wing of the party (such as in 2012 when Pier Luigi Bersani beat the young pretender Matteo Renzi, mayor of Florence, to become the centre–left candidate in the 2013 elections). Primaries were divided into closed contests (only for those in a certain party) and open campaigns (where anybody could vote, under certain conditions). In most cases a small financial contribution was asked for by the organizers. Occasionally, there were claims that the system was being abused, or that opponents were taking part in order to distort the results.

Selection of the centre–left candidate for the 2006 general elections, 16 October 2005 (4,311,149 votes)[a]

Romano Prodi	3,182,000	74.1%
Fausto Bertinotti	631,592	14.7%
Clemente Mastella	196,014	4.6%
Antonio Di Pietro	142,143	3.3%
Pecoraro Scanio	95,388	2.2%

Selection of the (first) leader of the *Partito Democratico*, 14 October 2007 (3,554,169 votes)[b]

Walter Veltroni	2,694,721	75.82%
Rosy Bindi	459,398	12.93%
Enrico Letta	391,775	11.02%

Selection of the (second) leader of the *Partito Democratico*, 25 October 2009 (3,102,709 votes)

Pier Luigi Bersani	1,623,239	52.30%
Dario Franceschini	1,045,123	33.68%
Ignazio Marino	380,904	12.28%

Selection of the centre–left candidate for the 2013 elections[c]

1st Round, 25 November 2012 (total votes 3,110,210)

Bersani	1,395,096	44.9%
Matteo Renzi	1,104,958	35.5%
Nichi Vendola	485,689	15.6%
Others	24,108	4.0%

2nd round, 2 December 2012 (total votes 2,802,382)

Bersani	1,706,457	60.9%
Renzi	1,095,925	39.1%

Selection of the Secretary of the PD (8.12.2013)

Renzi	1,895,332	67.55%
Gianni Cuperlo	510,970	18.21%
Giuseppe Civati	399,473	14.24%

Open primaries were also held for mayoral and other candidates over the same period. PD candidates often lost in these primaries to candidates from outside the party.

[a] Voting was open to all those over 18, who had to show an identity document and pay one euro.

[b] Primaries were also used to elect the candidates to the so-called Constituent Assembly of the party and for the selection of regional secretaries.

[c] Voters had to register for these primaries before the vote and sign up to the programme of the coalition.

joke linking the Socialist Party to corruption, and was apparently forced out of the television sector for a number of years. Outside of TV, Grillo built a huge fan base through his powerful and funny stand-up one-man shows, which became increasingly political, or anti-political, as the 1990s wore on. He developed an act based on rage against the current political class, combined with strong doses of environmentalism, calls for client and share-holder power, a critique of the banking and financial sectors and an increasing interest in the possibilities of the Internet. This last development was a remarkable turnaround in many ways. Grillo would end earlier versions of his show by smashing a computer to pieces on stage.

Grillo came into contact with an Internet entrepreneur and strategist and market researcher called Gianroberto Casaleggio in 2004. They set up a highly successful blog in 2005 (www.beppegrillo.it), which quickly became the focal point for a new movement. At first, this movement was also organized around a series of stunts and public events, including two successful so-called V-days (*F*** off* days) in 2007 and 2008. Casaleggio and Grillo formed a loose political-anti-political 'movement' called the Five Star MoVement in 2009, with its own symbol, programme and a 'non-statute' (to distinguish it from the other parties). The five stars refer to the various threads in the movement – associationism (through so-called *Meet-up* groups of militants), the environment, connectivity, and water, transport and development. Five Star followers and militants appear to be relatively young and well educated, and spread across Italy, although the beginnings of the movement were concentrated in the north. They were not particularly anti-European, but they

---

4.13 Populist movements in Italy: *Fronte dell'Uomo Qualunque* (1944–9)

Qualunquismo – an apathy towards politics, also often seen as a kind of superficiality or an opportunistic attitude towards problems. This 'ideology' is often linked to the idea that all politicians are corrupt, the same etc.

Leader and founder: Guglielmo Giannini.

This political movement set itself up as the voice of the 'common man' and the middle classes, and in opposition to political parties and ideologies. It appeared to be anti-communist but in some senses also anti-capitalist and spread its word through a newspaper that used crude satire and blunt language, such as the phrase '*non ci rompete più le scatole*' ('don't break our balls'). The movement won 5.3 per cent of the vote in 1946 for the Constituent Assembly, electing 30 representatives. In the local elections that followed the movement did extremely well, beating the Christian Democrats, for example, in Rome. Both the Christian Democrats and the Communists attacked the FUQ as a pro-fascist movement. In 1947, the movement split around the attitude towards the DC. By 1949 it had disappeared, many voters preferring to back the neo-fascist and/or monarchist parties. The movement gave birth to the negative term *qualunquismo*, a phrase used to attack similar movements and attitudes in the ensuing decades.

did tend to be strongly anti-trade union. Many also had what can only be described as a catastrophic view about Italy's future. Grillo himself was a charismatic leader whose language was violent and direct.

The movement's programme was largely negative, consisting in a series of laws to be abrogated and cuts to be made to the 'costs of politics'. There was a heavy concentration on the clean nature of candidates and on the differences in behaviour of Five Star elected representatives. Election expenses were handed back to the state. Much of this took its cue from a series of seemingly endless political corruption scandals in Italy (see Boxes 4.3 and 4.4), and from investigations into the costs of politics and the abuses of power of the political 'caste'. The success of the book *La Casta* (*The Caste*) was highly significant (see Box 4.14).

In addition, Grillo called for a referendum on Italy's membership of the euro and for a guaranteed income for those who had been hit by austerity cuts, which he rejected. The movement also had a strong ecological slant and was opposed to certain major public works programmes, such as the high-speed train link through the Val di Susa in Piedmont. These policies were not linked to any traditional idea of 'left' or 'right' and thus were clearly part of a post-political and post-ideological political outlook. However, some commentators placed the movement clearly on the left of the political spectrum. The preferred (and in fact only) form of communication used by the movement was the Internet, and the web was used to choose candidates and decide on expulsions and policies. TV was rejected entirely, as were other forms of campaigning such as posters.

Soon after the success of the V-days, Five Star candidates began to stand in local elections. Success was swift. In 2012 a 39-year-old Five Star militant and bank assistant called Federico Pizzarotti (whom nobody had heard of previously and who had never held office) was elected as mayor of Parma (following a series of corruption scandals in that city), winning 60.2 per cent in the second round run-off against the PD candidate. Grillo swam from Reggio Calabria to Sicily to launch the movement's candidates for the regional elections there in October 2012, the results of which saw the Five Star MoVement become the biggest 'party' on the island and hold the balance of power, with 15 regional deputies elected. During the 2013 national election campaign Grillo embarked on what he called a 'Tsunami Tour', filling squares and piazzas across Italy. The final results were extraordinary. Grillo's party won over 25 per cent of the votes cast and became the biggest single 'party' inside Italy (although when the emigrant vote was counted the biggest party was the PD). Once in Parliament, Grillo's deputies refused to do a deal with the PD, and went into opposition once a new coalition government was formed in April 2013. Almost all of those elected had no previous political experience.

A number of questions remained about the movement and were the subject of debate. What was the real basis of Internet-based democracy? Some have criticized the movement as having a festishistic attitude towards the web, which was seen as emancipatory in itself. Others have underlined the televisual roots of Grillo's appeal. As Giuliano Santoro has written, 'the Genovese

---

Box. 4.14   *The Caste*: Italy and the cost of politics

Italy's politicians managed to build a system of privileges for themselves over the years that attracted increasing attention and criticism towards the end of the twentieth and the beginning of the twenty-first century. This system included extremely generous pension-type payments known as *vitalizi* (a kind of life contract), high wages, and expenses for all kinds of items. In 2011, this meant that a deputy needed to serve for just five years to pick up this pension at the age of 65. The fact that many deputies and local representatives were elected for long periods of time entrenched many of these privileges. In the 2000s journalists began to expose this system in detail. In 2007 Gian Antonio Stella and Sergio Rizzo from *Il Corriere della Sera* published a book called *La Casta* (*The Caste*), which had the subtitle 'How Italian politicians have become untouchable'. The book became a runaway bestseller, shifting some 1.2 million copies in 2007 alone. It detailed a series of institutional abuses of power, of politicians with criminal records, and of waste, inefficiency and cronyism. As Santoro has written, '[The book] *The Caste* was the spark that lit the fire. It created a powerful frame for debate, which played on the anger of the Italians towards a political system which, for decades, had appeared to be entirely static' (Giuliano Santoro, *Un Grillo qualunque. Il Movimento 5 Stelle e il populismo digitale nella crisi dei partiti italiani* (Rome: Castelvecchi, 2013)).

Further studies and investigations exposed the clientelistic networks that controlled appointments and promotion in many institutions. These stories of privilege and institutionalized corruption were important weapons in the hands of anti-political forces, which railed against the entire system. For example, the Five Star MoVement cut the pay of its elected representatives, handed back the electoral expenses given to them by the state, and selected its candidates via the Internet. The pressure from the success of this book (and others), added to the increasing power of the anti-political movement in Italy, led to a number of reforms of these systems in the second decade of the twenty-first century. But the overwhelming impression was that Italy's 'political class', the 'caste', was extremely loath to reform itself.

---

comedian represents the colonisation by television of new forms of communication'. Was Grillo a populist leader in the same mould as Berlusconi himself? Or was this something truly new, a post-political, post-televisual (Grillo and his candidates rarely appeared on TV political chat shows or on television at all), post-ideological movement? Would Grillo's movement stay the course, and become a permanent feature of the Italian political landscape, or would it fade like so many other populist movements in Italy and elsewhere, from the *Poujadists* in France to *L'Uomo Qualunque* in Italy in the 1940s and the *Lega Nord* in the 1990s and 2000s (see Box 4.13)? Whatever the outcome, the anti-political forces which had given rise to Grillo's success were not likely to disappear in the short run. Italian political life had entered a new phase, without mass parties, and with mass disenchantment with the entire system. No

Box 4.15 Populist movements in Italy: the programme of the Five Star MoVement (2013) (selection)

State and Citizens

'The current organization of the State is bureaucratic, over-large, costly, inefficient. Parliament no longer represents the citizens'
[we call for the]
Abolition of Provinces
Abolition of election expenses
A maximum of two terms for all Parliamentarians and all other public officers
Abrogative and propositive referendums without a quorum

Energy

A series of measures aimed at reducing CO_2 emissions and at more efficient energy use

Information

Free Internet for all
Elimination of public funding for newspapers
No national television station can be owned by any private individual. Shares must be spread with a maximum concentration of 10 per cent (similar measures for the press)
Abolition of the Journalist Corporation/Guild
One public TV station, without advertising
Nationalization of the landline phone network

Economy

Class action
Abolition of stock options
Abolition of monopolies
Reduction of the public debt through cuts to public spending and the elimination of waste, as well as giving citizens direct access to information through the Internet without the need for intermediaries
Unemployment benefit

Transport

Cycle lanes in cities and the countryside
A tax on cars in city centres with only one driver
A halt to the high-speed rail link in Val di Susa
Broadband in the entire country

Health

Free care and equal access

Education

Free Internet in schools
Elimination of printed schoolbooks
English taught from nursery schools onwards
State financing only to state schools
University lectures online

viable alternative had yet appeared by 2013, however, leaving the old political class still clinging onto power.

Debates over the Political 'Rules of the Game'

All of these parties have always operated within particular sets of rules and frameworks, and political debate has been marked by discussion over these rules themselves, and their effect on the functioning, efficiency and shape of the political system. Debates over these political *rules of the game* dragged on throughout the post-unification and Liberal period, and have dogged political debate in Republican Italy. One theme has dominated these debates: that of the electoral system and (until 1946) the linked question of the suffrage.

The electoral system

Those who believed in the crucial importance of the rules of the game in shaping Italian politics have concentrated to a large extent on the failings or otherwise of its electoral systems. Two areas have been at the heart of discussions over the electoral system. First (until 1919 at least), the enlargement of the suffrage and the question of the vote for women – over who could vote, and who could not. A second crucial area has been that of the *form* of the system – proportional representation, first-past-the-post, or a mixture of these two systems. Whilst it would be foolish to still claim, as many commentators did in the early 1990s, for example, that it would be enough to change the electoral system to transform Italian politics, it is none the less equally obvious that electoral systems, the ways in which votes are collected and seats distributed, have an important role in patterning political systems and voting patterns. It should be added, however, that these frequent debates over the electoral system have often proved to be a substitute for real reform of the institutions governing the political framework of Italy.

Italy's long road to universal suffrage

From 1861 until 1909, Italy was a country where very few people could vote, and few of those who could vote, did so (see the figures on turnout in Box 4.16). Half the population were excluded on the basis of their sex, and most men because of restrictions involving literacy, property and age. To be able to vote in 1870 you had to be 25 years old, a man, literate and pay a minimum of 40 lire per year in direct taxes. Only 2 per cent of the population (about half a million adult males) fulfilled all these criteria at that time. Thanks to abstentionism of up to 50 per cent, only around 1 per cent of Italians were involved in the electoral process in a direct way. At the same time one-third of Germans and nearly half of all French people had the vote. These figures alone are not enough to demonstrate that there was an abyss between the political system and the mass of the Italian people after unification.

In fact, recent historical work has underlined the difficulties the political class faced in enlarging the suffrage.[67] None the less, the absence of the masses from the structures of democracy certainly contributed to the general lack of identification with the state and the low legitimacy enjoyed by Italian politicians.

This tiny electorate was not only a problem for the designation of Italy as a *democracy*, it also encouraged corruption. A deputy needed only to 'shift' a few hundred votes to gain election. Changes to the electoral lists were easy to manipulate. In many cases, no opposition candidate bothered to stand, especially in the south. There were 50 uncontested seats in the 1874 election, and 36 in 1876, 75 per cent of which were to be found in the *mezzogiorno* (out of a total of 443 constituencies). In many other constituencies, the opposition had no hope of winning. If we put together these uncontested seats with those where the opposition won less than fifty votes, we arrive at a figure of nearly a quarter of all seats in the 1860s and 1870s. A quarter of Italy's deputies over the first twenty years of the country's existence were elected without opposition.

Slowly, and amidst much debate, the suffrage was enlarged. Garibaldi and his League of Democracy had called for universal suffrage, as did Crispi for a time, yet a motion for complete universal suffrage was defeated by 300 votes in 1882. In Italy, unlike in other European countries, there was no mass movement in favour of universal suffrage, and many of those in the main social-democratic party – the PSI – remained opposed to the suffrage right up until the eve of World War I. This opposition was not a formal one. Universal suffrage was part of the 'minimum' programme of the PSI from 1900 onwards. But the party never really campaigned on this issue and many leaders were profoundly suspicious of giving the vote to the southern peasantry, and to women. The reformist Bonomi argued in 1904 that 'the suffrage is in itself only an instrument, and without a force who could use it in a valid way, it could cause damage to those who invoke it'. For Salvemini, a voice in the wilderness within the PSI on this question, universal suffrage was the only way to break the clientelism which lay at the basis of Giolitti's political system, especially in the south. Catholics were also excluded from the system through the Papal ban on voting (which many ignored), which was not completely removed until 1919 (although the low turnout in that election perhaps shows that it was not only the *non expedit* which was keeping people away from the polls). Slowly, the Catholics also began to use the system. Three openly Catholic deputies were elected in 1904, 16 in 1909 and 29 in 1913 (thanks largely to a secret agreement with Giolitti, known as the Gentiloni pact).

The only convincing explanation for this anomaly (the lack of a mass movement for the suffrage) lies with the particular effects of the 'southern question' on Italian politics. Italian socialism was born in the north, and was deeply suspicious of the southern peasantry. A battle for the completion of Italian democracy could have brought together the northern and southern masses, but most Italian socialists preferred the strategy of evolution through social change. As a result, Italy's political elites were able to decide electoral changes in the virtual absence of mass pressure for change. When universal suffrage was 'conceded', it was not in response to protest (1882 and 1913 were not periods of strong mass support for democratic change). The first election

Box 4.16 General election turnouts, 1948–2013[a]

Year	Electorate	Voters (valid votes)	Turnout (%)
1948	29,117,270	26,264,458	90.2
1953	30,272,236	27,087,701	89.5
1958	32,434,835	29,560,269	91.1
1963	34,199,184	30,752,871	89.9
1968	35,566,493	31,790,428	89.4
1972	37,049,351	33,403,528	90.2
1976	40,426,658	36,709,578	90.8
1979	42,203,354	36,671,309	86.9
1983	44,526,357	36,906,005	82.9
1987	45,692,417	38,571,508	84.4
1992	47,435,689	39,243,506	82.7
1994 PR	48,135,041	38,717,043	80.4
First-Past-the-Post (FPTP)	48,235,213	38,504,158	79.8
1996 PR	48,744,846	37,484,398	76.9
FPTP	48,846,238	37,295,109	76.4
2001 PR	49,256,295	37,122,776	75.4
FPTP	49,358,947	37,259,705	75.5
2006	49,805,563[b]	39,203,156	78.7
2008	50,066,615	37,575,711	75.1
2013	50,399,841	34,984,851	69.4

[a] These turnout percentages and figures are calculated on the basis of valid votes with relation to the total electorate. I have deducted invalid votes such as blank, spoiled and incorrectly compiled ballot papers. Invalid votes have sometimes reached a relatively high figure, such as 7.9 per cent of votes cast in the first-past-the-post section of the election in 1996. All figures from Luca Ricolfi et al. (eds), *L'Italia al voto: Le elezioni politiche dal 1948 al 2008* (Turin: UTET, 2013).
[b] Includes Italians voting in overseas constituencies.

with a system close to universal suffrage was marked by the entry of the Catholics into Italian politics in a systematic fashion with the Gentiloni pact. Thus, Italy's political class only felt safe in allowing the masses to vote when they had the mass Catholic vote under control, which, it was assumed, would vote in a moderate fashion. This strategy collapsed in 1919, when the Catholics formed their own democratic party.

Debates over the Form of Voting
Lists, constituencies, voters, 1882–1913

For more than five years in the late 1870s and early 1880s (but the debate had been ongoing since the early 1870s) Parliament thrashed out a new electoral law. The debate was conditioned by general agreement that the peasantry as a whole could *not* be given the vote, either because the peasants were seen as too revolutionary (by the Right), or as too reactionary and 'backward' (by the Left, and most of the socialists). Much of the debate concentrated on the 'capacity' of the people to vote. Thus, the franchise was to be expanded, but still limited by literacy tests and by a milder property qualification (or a primary education certificate). In this way, and above all by lowering the voting age from 25 to 21, the potential electorate was raised by 1.4 million, to 2 million (from 2 per cent to 7 per cent of the population). Crucially, public administrators and councillors were also admitted to the voting lists, whether or not they met the other criteria. A new structure was introduced for constituencies, with larger, multi-member constituencies replacing the older, smaller areas (electing between two and five deputies each). Before 1882, a run-off took place if turnout was less than a third or if no one candidate reached more than 50 per cent of the vote. The new system was extremely complicated, and introduced a kind of proportionalism, with the minority grouping having a right to seats in bigger constituencies.

The elections in 1882, held immediately after the reform, led to a renewal of Italy's political class, with 44 per cent of the deputies from the old Parliament failing to be elected. A further long debate followed around the multi-member constituency system. In 1891 Parliament voted by a large majority to return to the old single-member, two-round constituency system. Part of this discussion also concerned the position of the political parties in the electoral process. Exclusionary rules kept the numbers of voters down, especially in the south. In 1900, only 3.8 per cent of the Sicilian population had the right to vote, which, when added to abstentionism which reached levels of 66 per cent in parts of the south (as in Basilicata in 1900), left the system more or less as it had been in 1861. It was this system which was criticized with such force in the famous series of articles published by Salvemini in 1909 under the title 'The Ministry of the Underworld'. Meanwhile, in the north, the situation was very different: 10 per cent of the Piedmontese population could vote in 1900, and more than half did so. Central governments also intervened heavily in the electoral process. Crispi, in the wake of the repression of the Sicilian Fasci in 1894, pruned the electoral roll by 847,000, a massive restriction of the suffrage. Prefects, notables, 'Grand Electors' and local elites 'constructed the electorate' at the behest of national leaders and political organizations. Prefects also played a central role in the clientelist electoral systems which developed in Spain with *caciquismo* at the turn of the century (see Box 4.17).[68]

This was one way of 'bending the rules', but it was also clear that the electoral rules of the game were frequently, and blatantly, broken in Liberal Italy. The role of mediators and 'vote-catchers' was well documented in many constituencies and cases of electoral fraud were frequent. Accusations of fraud, in addition, were the common currency of political debate, and could be used to discredit opponents. Rules were bent over the formation and revision of electoral lists, the design of constituencies (gerrymandering) and through 'simple' corruption and ballot-stuffing. Public employees were moved round to pack

Box 4.17   Election results, 1860–1913

Year	Electorate	Voters	Turnout (%)	Right (%)	Left (%)	Extreme Left (%)	Not noted (%)
1861	419,846	239,746	57.10	47.63	25.96	2.48	23.93
1865	498,952	271,552	54.42	41.99	36.31	4.87	16.84
1867	498,427	258,119	51.80	44.22	38.34	3.65	13.79
1870	530,911	240,731	45.34	47.24	38.78	2.56	11.42
1874	571,628	319,493	66.32	44.69	43.11	2.56	9.65
1876	419,846	239,746	57.10	23.43	62.60	5.51	8.46
1880	620,491	369,953	59.60	30.12	53.91	8.86	8.07
1882	2,018,394	1,222,555	60.57	24.61	58.27	9.06	8.07
1886	2,416,174	1,406,658	58.22	32.48	52.17	9.06	6.30
1890	2,752,364	1,479,475	53.75	31.69	51.77	8.86	7.68
1892	2,926,667	1,643,417	56.15	28.54	53.25	11.22	6.89
1895	2,122,612	1,257,888	59.26	30.51	48.23	12.20	9.06
1897	2,121,338	1,242,657	58.58	37.80	40.55	15.94	5.71
1900	2,248,509	1,310,480	58.28	30.91	43.70	19.88	5.51
1904	2,541,327	1,593,886	62.72	26.77	45.67	19.09	8.46
1909	2,930,473	1,903,687	64.96	29.13	43.11	23.03	4.72
1913	8,644,699	5,100,615	59.00	28.15	33.27	28.94	9.65

Figures elaborated from M. S. Piretti, *Le elezioni politiche in Italia dal 1848 a oggi* (Bari: Laterza, 1995).

constituencies. In 1880 in Genoa the Prefect signed up 549 new voters just before the election. The winning candidate had a majority of 349 votes. Signs and codes were used to control the voter, as much as the candidate. In Caserta (14th Legislature) a number of ballot papers contained strange added information – 'To Jacobo Comin A', 'Honest Jacobo Comin' and so on. These codes were part of the 'exchange vote', a practice which survives to this day. All this undermined the legitimacy of elections as democratic, free processes. As Salvemini wrote, 'An election is a game which has its rules. If some or all of the players break these rules on purpose and if – which is even worse – the referee falsifies the game, the whole system will no longer function, and in the end nobody will take it seriously any more.'[69]

Giolitti adopted an instrumental stance towards the suffrage. In 1913 he extended voting rights again, this time to all male literates over the age of 21 and to illiterates over the age of 30, or as soon as they had completed their military service. All tax restrictions were abolished. The electorate rose by 5.3 million to 8.6 million, which represented 24 per cent of the population. Politics was also opened up by the institution of pay for deputies. The actual voting process was always a matter for extraordinary and interminable debates. The compromise reached in 1913 was a voting slip brought into the voting booth by the voter, and deposited in a special envelope, called the 'Bertolini envelope' after its inventor. The special feature of the envelope was that the name of the voter could be read without opening the envelope itself.

After World War I a number of political factors led to an agreement on a move to a PR voting system. The Liberals were afraid of disappearing altogether, the new Catholic party had PR at the top of its political programme and the Socialists stressed the democratic nature of the new system. In July 1919 a majority of 240 deputies voted the reform through. It was decided that constituencies would elect five deputies each. The Liberals, however, managed to keep the system of the Bertolini envelope. Catholic deputy Meda joked that the government did not want to throw away the millions of envelopes it had kept in government stores. The alternative was a government-produced ballot paper, which guaranteed more openness and spared the parties the high costs of producing millions of voting slips. In reality, the system was not a real proportional one, given the small numbers of deputies in each constituency and the tendency of the parties to concentrate on personalities, not party lists. Liberal lists contained hybrid collections of politicians, known as blocs, which went against the spirit if not the letter of the law.

Proportional representation: 1919–21

In 1919 Italy was divided into 54 constituencies with between 5 and 20 members each. Voters chose between party lists and the suffrage was further extended to all males over 21, and to those under 21 if they had served in the army (which of course many had done by 1919). Preference votes were also allowed. Thus the electorate rose again, from 8.6 to 11.2 million. The 1919 elections brought a new Italy to power: 84 new Catholic deputies and 131 new Socialist deputies took their seats. The only sign of continuity was in the Liberal bloc, where 112 deputies were re-elected. However, the change to PR had moderated the renewal in the air after the war. For the 1921 elections, the government promised to enlarge the small constituencies used in 1919. Now, each constituency had to elect at least 10 deputies. Giolitti again tried to tinker with the system, and contemplated a return, by decree, to the first-past-the-post system.

Fascist electoral reform, 1923

From 1919 onwards PR had come under attack from all sides (as in the 1980s and 1990s, it was blamed for creating instability and the possibility of corruption). Fascism, once in power, set about reforming the system so as to maintain control of the reins of government. Mussolini presented a plan which gave an absolute majority to the list which gained the most votes, in the name of stability and in opposition to the political chaos of the post-war years. Italy, in addition, was to be drawn up as one, giant, constituency. This law (the 'Acerbo law') was put to various parliamentary commissions in 1922 and was passed on 14 November 1923 with the support of many Liberals and Catholics. Fascism's coup of 1922 had been translated into law. The Fascists

Box 4.18a   General elections, 1919–24

Political group/party	1919 %	1919 Seats	1921 %	1921 Seats	1924 %	1924 Seats
PPI (Catholics)	20.5	**100**	20.4	**108**	9	**39**
					5.9[a]	**24**
Socialist Party	32.3	**156**	24.7	**123**		
					5[b]	**22**
Ex-combatants Party	4.1	**20**	1.7	**10**	–	–
National Blocs	–	–	19.1	**105**	–	–
Fascist Party	–	–	0.5	**2**	64.9	**374**
Communist Party	–	–	4.6	**15**	3.7	**19**
Liberal Party	8.6	**41**	7.1	**43**	3.3	**15**
Democratic Party	10.9	**60**	4.7	**29**	1.6	**10**
Democratic Liberals	15.9	**96**	10.4	**68**	–	–
Others	7.7	**36**	8.5	**32**	6.6	**32**

[a] Reformist Socialists.
[b] Maximalist Socialists.

duly drew up a list with Liberals and dissident Catholics. Amidst violence and intimidation, the 1924 elections were held using the new law (see below). But there was no need for the law's extra seats for the majority list. The opposition was wiped out at the polls (the Left only elected 65 deputies via three parties and the Catholics could only send 39 representatives to Rome). Mussolini was not content with his huge majority, and proceeded to phase out liberal democracy altogether. A plan to reintroduce a first-past-the-post system was put forward by the Fascists in 1925. This new reform, however, passed in January 1925, was never to be used. By 1928, once the opposition had been removed from the scene, the regime was ready to abolish voting altogether, at least in terms of a *choice* between various parties. Elections were replaced with plebiscites, which were more to do with propaganda than democracy. Normal elections did not return until 1946.

Rules, Debates, Voting, Elections: 1943–93
PR

Universal suffrage was the central demand of all the anti-fascist groupings, and was promised as early as June 1944 in a decree-law issued by the new Italian government. Immediately, a discussion began concerning the new electoral system. For a time, it seemed as if the old positions had not changed. Leading Liberals from pre-fascist Italy, such as Orlando, Croce and Nitti, still opposed PR. Orlando even argued that PR had been 'the cause of all Italian problems, at least in the political field'. The Catholics, as before, backed PR, and were much stronger than in Liberal Italy. On the Left, there was general agreement in favour of PR, with some arguing for extra seats for the bigger parties to ensure stability. The first actual (local) elections, however, did not take place until March 1946. A series of battles took place over technical issues – preference votes, constituencies and seat distribution. In the end, constituencies were based around provinces, with from 7 to 36 seats in each. Obligatory voting was rejected (only after much discussion). The electoral law, a very 'pure' form of PR with preference votes, was passed in March 1946. Parties were given great freedom to draw up lists, and candidates could stand in more than one constituency. PR guaranteed representation in Parliament for even the tiniest parties. Voters chose between party lists in large constituencies and parties drew up the lists of candidates. If a deputy died, or retired, the next person in the electoral list took their place; there were no by-elections. Ballot papers were made up of various party symbols with names underneath. Similar systems were adopted for local elections and (after 1979) for European elections.

The first national elections elected the Constituent Assembly, which itself was to decide upon the rest of the electoral system, including the question of an elected Senate. Slightly different systems were introduced for the Lower House and the Senate. Voters were faced with a ballot paper with various party lists, on which they indicated from one to four names and a vote for the party of their choice. The Senate was also assigned a PR system, after much wheeler-dealing, and given a higher voting age. Without PR, the Left would have been completely wiped out in the 'cold war' general election of 1948.

Elections and the 1948 Constitution[70]

Under the 1948 Constitution, electoral *systems* were to be shaped by ordinary laws, and not by the Constitution. This left the way open, much later on, for a referendum campaign which was to transform Italy.

The attempt to change the system: the 'swindle law', 1953

After their triumph in the elections of April 1948 (48.5 per cent of the vote, with absolute majorities in both Houses of Parliament) the DC and its allies attempted to change the rules again, in order to guarantee their position in power for the foreseeable future. In October 1952 a proposal was presented to the House for a new electoral law, following set-backs in local elections. The law aimed at giving extra seats to the biggest set of party lists, but only if they reached a certain level of vote. The parallels with the fascist law of 1923 were obvious. Immediately, the opposition began to organize a massive campaign, inside and outside of Parliament, against what they called the 'swindle law'. In Parliament, the opposition set up complicated obstructionist systems, including 2,000 amendments and even the overturning of the ballot box (invoking memories of 1899). De Gasperi, in the end, had to use confidence motions to get the law through in time. Yet, after all this effort, the law never entered into operation. In 1953 the DC lost 2 million votes, and failed to reach

---

Box 4.18b Elections for the Constituent Assembly, 2 June 1946

Party	Votes for list	%	Seats
Democrazia Cristiana (DC)	8,101,004	35.2	207
Partito comunista italiano (PCI)	4,356,686	18.9	104
Partito socialista d'unità proletaria (PSIUP)	4,758,129	20.7	115
Unione democratica nazionale	1,560,638	6.8	41
Uomo qualunque	1,211,956	5.3	30
Partito repubblicano italiano	1,003,007	4.4	23
Others	2,019,059	8.7	36

Box 4.18c General election, 18 April 1948

Party	Votes for list	%	Seats
Democrazia Cristiana (DC)	12,741,299	48.5	305
Fronte democratico popolare	8,137,047	31.0	183
Unità socialista (PCI and PSI)	1,858,346	7.1	33
Blocco nazionale	1,004,889	3.8	19
Partito nazionale monarchico	1,211,956	2.8	30
Partito repubblicano italiano	1,003,007	2.5	23
Movimento sociale italiano	526,670	2.0	6
Others	619,010	2.4	5

the 50 per cent they needed (calculated in 'groups of lists') to gain the 'prize' of more seats. After this defeat, the DC left the system alone until it was forced to change it in the 1990s.

The Shift to Bi-polarism: 1993–2006[71]

From 1953 right up to the 1990s, many commentators criticized the ways in which the particular form of PR used in Italy had contributed to the degeneration of the political system. PR, it was argued, gave disproportionate power to the minor parties in the governing coalition, leading to horse-trading and the scientific sharing of the spoils. It also led to government instability, party fragmentation and insecurity, and favoured systems of clientelism and corruption. Preference voting was used in such a way as to identify sources of support and reward clientelist politics. In 1991, a referendum on the abolition of these preferences was passed against the wishes of the major parties. This was the first

Box 4.18d General elections, 1953–92: votes, percentage of votes, seats

Parties	1953	1958	1963	1968	1972	1976	1979	1983	1987	1992
DC(Christian Democrats)	10.864.282 40.1%/263	12.522.279 42.3%/273	11.775.970 38.3%/260	12.441.553 39.1%/266	12.919.270 38.7%/266	14.218.298 38.7%/263	14.046.290 38.3%/262	12.153.081 32.9%/225	13.241.188 34.3%/234	11.637.569 29.7%/206
PCI (Communist Party)	6.121.922 22.6% 143	6.704.706 22.7% 140	7.768.228 25.3% 166	8.557.404 26.9% 177	9.072.454 27.1% 179	12.622.728 34.4% 227	11.139.231 30.4 201	11.032.318 29.9% 198	10.254.591 26.6% 177	PDS[a]:6.317.962 16.1% 107
PSI (Socialist Party)	3.441.305 12.7% 75	4.208.111 14.2% 84	4.257.300 13.8% 87	4.605.832[b] 14.5% 91	3.210.427 9.6% 61	3.542.998 9.6% 57	3.596.802 9.8 62	4.223.362 11.4% 73	5.505.690 14.3% 94	5.343.808 13.6% 92
Monarchist Parties	1.855.842 6.9% 40	1.436.807[c] 4.8% 25	....	PSIUP 1.414.544 4.4; 23	648.763 1.9 0 seats	DP[d] 556,022 1.5%; 6	Radicals 1.264.870 3.5%; 18	809.810 2.2 11	988.180 2.6% 13	486.344 1.2% 7
MSI (Neo-fascists)	1.582.567 5.8%/29	1.407.913 4.8%/24	1.571.187 5.1%/27	1.414.794 4.5%/24	2.896.762 8.7%/56	2.245.376 6.1%/35	1.930.639 5.3%/30	2.511.487 8.8%/42	2.282.256 5.9%/35	2.107.272 5.4%/34
PSDI (Social Democrats)	1.223.251 4.5%/19	1.345.750 4.6%/22	1.876.409 6.1%/33	--------	1.717.539 5.1%/29	1.237.270 3.4%/15	1.407.535 3.8%/20	1.508.234 4.1%/23	1.140.910 2.9%/17	1.066.672 2.7%/16
PLI(Liberal Party)	816.267 3.3%/13	1.046.939 3.5%/17	2.143.954 7%/39	1.851.060 5.8%/31	1.297.105 3.9%/20	478.335 1.3%/5	712.646 1.9%/9	1.066.980 2.9%/16	810.216 2.1%/11	1.121.854 2.9%/17
Others	1,187,307 4.4%/8	891,128 3.1%/11	1,364,983 4.4%/18	1518066 4.8%/16	1652387 5%/19	1826246 5%/22	2573295 7%/28	3475422 9.5%/41	2915216 7.5%/35	4958550 11.4%/52
							Lega	125.311 0.3%/1	1454091 3.8%/14	3.395.384 8.6%/55
								Greens	969.330 2.5%/13	1.093.037 2.8%/16
									PRC (Left Communists)	2.201.428 5.6% 35

[a] The PCI became the PDS in 1991. Rifondazione Comunista split from the new grouping.

[b] In 1968 the PSI and the PSDI stood together as the PSU. Meanwhile, a split in 1964 had led to the formation of the PSIUP.

[c] Two separate monarchist parties stood in 1958.

[d] Democrazia Proletaria, a far-left grouping, stood in general elections from 1976 until 1987.

jolt to the system which had become known as the 'First Republic'. In 1993, thanks to a campaign by the centre–left, and against the far right and the smaller parties, a massive majority of Italians voted to wipe out the PR system which had been used for all general elections since 1948 (PR was kept for European elections).[72]

The parties were forced to act, and they did so in the most complicated and moderate way possible. A horrible compromise was produced – which became known as the *Mattarellum* after its signatory Sergio Mattarella (the law was passed in August 1993). Three-quarters of seats would be elected through a UK-style first-past-the-post system, with the remaining 25 per cent assigned by PR. Each voter had *two* votes for the Lower House, and they could split their vote. In the Upper House a similar system was introduced, but with only one vote being cast. Incredibly complicated methods were used to distribute votes and seats. A 4 per cent cut-off point was introduced in the PR section of the vote. The year 1994 saw the first election with this system. What the *Mattarellum* did was keep the medium-sized parties in Parliament, but it encouraged alliances, especially in the first-past-the-post section. Generally, the part of the political spectrum that has built more successful alliances, or has been less divided, has won in elections since 1993 under two different electoral systems – the centre–right (1994, 2001, 2008) or the centre–left (1996, 2006). See Box 4.18e for details.

Twice, campaigners pushed through referendums to abolish the PR part of the ballot altogether. Twice, these proposals were defeated, but only because the referendums failed to reach the 50 per cent quorum, the second time by a mere whisker. Centre–left parties, especially the ex-PCI (now the DS), called time and again for a French two-round system, but failed to reach the necessary consensus in Parliament. Yet, a change of system could not transform the ingrained habits of Italian political life. Politicians continued to change sides with great regularity within Parliament, and from election to election. There were 116 deputies in the 'mixed group' in Parliament by 1999 (elected in 1996). The fall of governments did not lead to immediate new elections (in 1994 and 1998, for example). Little serious campaigning took place at a local level – the idea of a constituency deputy simply did not exist in Italy. Candidates were moved around from election to election, and sometimes were not seen between one election and the next; they did not open offices in their constituencies nor did they hold 'surgeries'. In fact, the link between deputies and local areas was less than it had been under PR and in the Liberal period. There were some exceptions to this rule (such as with Massimo D'Alema's constituency in Gallipoli in the south). Party leaders were virtually certain of election (they always had the insurance of the PR section of the vote). Horse-trading was immense.

What the new system created was a hybrid first-past-the-post system, which demanded pre-electoral alliances (not *post*-electoral alliances, as had been the case with PR) and programmatic agreements. If one were to be extremely cynical, it could be argued that now the 'Cencelli Manual' is also applied before the election, not just afterwards. Small parties did not disappear, but became part of broad umbrella coalitions. Leaders became more important. Agreements were also reached over stand-downs and individual seats. By-elections became part of the Italian system (although they were all but ignored by the voters). The alliances which have been successful since 1994 have tended to coalesce around single leaders, and have built the widest alliances possible. The rhetoric of bi-polarism, however, has been as important as the reality.[73]

Box 4.18e General elections: mixed first-past-the-post/PR system, 1994–2001 Votes (%) and seats (Lower House). Percentages refer to the PR part of the ballot, seats to both sections of the ballot. Results of main parties and coalitions represented in Parliament only.

	1994	1996	2001
Forza Italia!	8,119,287 21% 366[a] (with Lega and AN)	7,712,149 20.6% 246 (with AN)	10,863,545 29.5% 352 (with AN and Lega and others)
PDS (DS)	7,855,610 20.4% 202 (Progressives – with PRC)	7,894,118 21.1% 284 (Ulivo)	6,115,902 16.6% 248 (Ulivo with La Margherita and others)
Rifondazione	2,334,029 6.1% 11 (with PDS)	3,213,748 8.6% 35[b]	1,859,492 5% 11
AN	5,202,698 13.5% (with FI)	5,870,491 15.7% (with FI)	4,439,552 12% (with FI coalition)
Lega Nord	3,237,026 8.4% (with FI)	3,776,354 10.1% 59	1,456,490 3.9% (with FI coalition)
PPI	4,268,940 11.1% 46 (with Patto Segni)	2,554,072 6.8%	– –
Patto Segni	1,795,270 4.7% (with PPI)	–	–
La Margherita	–	–	5,356,838 14.5% (with DS)
CCD/CDU	–	2,189,563 5.8% (with FI)	1,189,765 3.2% (with FI coalition)
Others (seats)	5 seats	6 seats	6 seats
Total	630	630	630[c] (617)

[a] Total seats from two coalitions, with AN in the centre–south (an alliance known as the Pole of Good Government) and with the Lega in the centre–north (the Pole of Freedoms).
[b] In 1996 Rifondazione did a stand-down deal with the Ulivo coalition.
[c] Due to a complicated series of circumstances, 13 seats were not assigned to any party after the 2001 elections.

The 'Porcellum', Instability, Crisis and Anti-politics: 2006–13

In September 2005 a proposal for a new electoral law was presented to Parliament. In theory, this marked a return to proportional representation, but in reality it took away huge amounts of power from the voters and handed it back to party leaders. The law was passed in December 2005. Blocked lists and the removal of all preferences meant that most of those who were to be elected were effectively chosen by party leaders *before* the election. Small parties were discriminated against by this new system, and advantages were gained by becoming part of an electoral coalition. Despite drafting the law, and expressing his satisfaction that it had been passed, Roberto Calderoli of the *Lega Nord* later dubbed the reform *'una porcata'* ('a pig's ear' or a total mess). This term led to the law becoming known as *'Il Porcellum'*, a combination of the phrase used for the previous law (*Il Mattarellum*) and the word *porcata*. Calderoli explained that the electoral law was designed to prevent a clear majority emerging in Parliament.

For the first time in the history of the Italian republic, an electoral law was passed by one side of the political spectrum (the centre–right) without the consent of the other side. The law also made it obligatory for each party to provide a programme and the name of its leader when registering their symbol. Coalitions can assign a coalition leader to their alliance, and this can be included on the ballot paper itself.

The reform set down a 2 per cent threshold before a party within a coalition gained any seats (as long as the coalition itself got 10 per cent overall) and a majority bonus of (at least) 340 seats for the winning coalition in the lower house.[74] In the Senate, however, majority bonuses were assigned to the winning list in each region, as opposed to nationally.[75] Parties standing outside of a coalition needed to win at least 4 per cent of the national vote in order to gain any seats. Different systems applied in the regions of the Molise, Trentino-Alto Adige and the Valle d'Aosta.

The law was extremely unpopular for a number of reasons, above all the fact that voters could not choose individual candidates, or reject them. But, as it favoured the two major parties, this was a reform that proved resistant to change. The 'Porcellum' was widely seen as a way of reinforcing the power of the political 'caste' in Italy, and of guaranteeing the election of candidates who should have been excluded on the grounds of their criminal records or their involvement in corruption. There were lengthy debates between the parties over changes to the law in the years that followed, but Italy went to the polls in 2008 and 2013 with exactly the same system. A referendum in June 2009 to abrogate parts of the law failed to attract the necessary numbers of voters to affect the law. A further attempt to change the law by referendum was thrown out by the Constitutional Court in 2012. The law remained unaltered because it suited the major parties (the only forces with the power to change it) and left power almost entirely in the hands of the party leaders. Despite numerous promises to reform the law, and protests from all sides (including those from President Napolitano and the Constitutional Court) the law was still in place in 2013.

In 2000 Italy's electoral and parliamentary system had been further complicated by a constitutional law that allocated seats to Italian emigrants voting abroad in special, newly created super-constituencies. Previously, some of these emigrants had returned home to vote. This law has made calculations of voting and turnout more difficult since its first use in 2001. Twelve deputies and six senators are now elected from lists voted for by Italians living abroad. Turnout has been much lower in these constituencies than in Italy itself.

The first election using the 'Porcellum', in 2006, was Italy's 'Florida moment'. The result was decided by a mere 26,000 votes and by votes that came in from Italians abroad. There were numerous accusations of electoral fraud (from both sides) and Berlusconi refused to concede defeat. The system left the broad centre–left coalition with a tiny majority in the Senate, making it almost impossible for them to govern. Prodi's government finally fell in February 2008, after a small number of senators changed sides and voted against the government. New elections were called. Later, one of the senators who had switched coalitions claimed that he had been paid to do so.

The 2008 campaign on the left was led by Walter Veltroni, the first leader of the newly formed *Partito Democratico*, who resigned as mayor of Rome in order to head up a coalition which excluded the far left but included Antonio Di Pietro's anti-corruption party. Berlusconi won easily despite the fact that his coalition lost nearly two million votes between 2006 and 2008. He even had a solid majority in the Senate (the only time this has happened in the history of the Porcellum up to 2013).

Berlusconi's solid majority suffered a major blow in the summer of 2010 when former ally Gianfranco Fini formed a new parliamentary group called *Futuro e Libertà*, which could initially count on 33 deputies. In November 2010 the ministers and vice-ministers from this group left the government. Fini and his group criticized what they saw as the authoritarian aspects of Berlusconi's government as well as highlighting the ongoing issue of conflicts of interest. Fini's group came very close to bringing down the Berlusconi government in December 2010, when a confidence vote was won by just three votes. This split left Berlusconi with a tiny majority, although his government struggled on until November 2011 as the financial crisis deepened.

Back to Consociationism? Mario Monti's 'technical' government, 2011–13

In November 2011, Italy's increasing bond yields precipitated a political crisis. Silvio Berlusconi resigned under pressure from international leaders, the stock markets, the EU and Italy's president, Giorgio Napolitano. A technical government was formed, led by former European Commissioner Mario Monti, who was made a life senator by Napolitano. None of the members of this government had been elected, and most were university professors. It was often referred to as the 'Government of the Professors'. Monti tried to implement swingeing austerity measures and he did raise taxes. Not surprisingly, these policies proved to be unpopular with the electorate, yet they were backed by a broad coalition in Parliament.

Box 4.18f General elections, 2006–13, blocked list PR system: votes, percentages, seats

Elections, 2006–13

	2006 (Lower House)	2006 (Senate)	2008 (Lower House)	2008 (Senate)	2013[a] (Lower House)	2013 (Senate)
Casa della Libertà	18,995,697 49.69 281	17,359,754 49.87 156				
L'Unione	19,036,986 49.8 348[b]	17,118,364 49.18 158				
PdL (with Lega)			17,064,314 46.81 344	15,678,144 46.94 174	9,123,109 29.18 125	9,405,679 30,71 117
Pd			13,686,501[c] 37.54 246	12,620,660 37.79 134	10,047,642 29,54 345	9,686,683 31,63 123
UdC			2,050,309 5.62 36	1,898,842 5.69 3		
Monti (includes UdC)					3,591,629 10.56 47	2,797,486 9.13 19
MoVimento 5 Stelle					8,689,168 25.5 109	7,285,850 23,79 54

[a] Seat totals include votes from Italians abroad, and, for the Senate, seats from Trentino-Alto Adige.
[b] Including the majority bonus plus seats from Italians voting abroad.
[c] With IdV.

A New 'Grand Coalition': 2013–

After the difficult experience of Monti's technical emergency government, new elections were called in February 2013. Once again, the Porcellum failed to produce a working majority in both houses. The Senate was left without a clear majority for any coalition, leading to months of uncertainly as attempts were made to form a government. Beppe Grillo's anti-political movement held the balance of power, but refused to do a deal with either left or right. Finally, at the end of April 2013, a new broad coalition administration was formed with ministers from both the centre–right and the centre–left, but without the support of the far left or the Five Star MoVement. For the second time in succession, a grand coalition was in charge. Bi-polarism was not working. The government's future appeared incredibly uncertain, and was closely connected to the fate of Silvio Berlusconi in a series of ongoing criminal trials. Italy's political system was stuck in a deep, 'organic' crisis, and the country was in economic decline. The way out of this crisis was unclear, and the fate of Europe was at stake. In November 2013, Berlusconi's expulsion from Parliament led to a split in the centre-right and weakened the grand coalition.

Women and the Vote

On various occasions, the issue of real universal suffrage was raised in Parliament and in the country as a whole. Most Italian politicians in the

Liberal period, however, 'took it for granted that women should not be given the vote'.[76] All attempts to give the vote to women, even if only in local elections, were given short shrift until World War I, and Italy never produced a radical movement on the lines of the suffragettes. During the debates on the 1912–13 reforms women were again excluded (by 209 votes to 48). In 1914 the Socialist Party had proposed a law on universal suffrage including women and in 1917 the trade unions had joined this struggle. The vote for women was also part of the Catholic political programme, and all sides assumed that women would largely vote in a moderate way. In 1918–19 (with Catholics and Socialists a major presence in the House) a law finally reached Parliament. Turati made a famous speech in defence of the vote for prostitutes (who were none the less excluded in the law).

Universal suffrage was passed by the Lower House in September 1919 (by 174 votes to 55) but did not have time to reach the Senate before the elections. Reform was then repeatedly delayed. In 1923, Mussolini conceded the vote to certain categories of women (to those who had been decorated for wartime services, to mothers of those killed in the war, to female 'heads of families' and to those who paid certain levels of taxation) for local elections only. Yet fascism then intervened to abolish local elections altogether, making the law obsolete, and women did not get to actually vote (or stand for Parliament) until 1946, after a reform passed in February 1945. Even in the first version of this 'universal suffrage' prostitutes were again excluded, but they were finally given their democratic rights in 1947. The effects of the women's vote have been little studied and undervalued by historians. Women were (and are) heavily under-represented in Parliament (there were only 21 in the Constituent Assembly) and continued to be so within the First Republic. The first woman under-secretary was appointed in 1951, and the first minister not until 1976 (Tina Anselmi). Some progress was made in the 1970s, with the appointment of women to some of the most important positions within the parliamentary machine (such as Nilde Iotti as president of the Lower House). However, the gender gap continued to be a strong cultural block to women within politics. Berlusconi's second government in 2001 had only one woman minister although Enrico Letta's grand coalition administration made something of a break with tradition, with seven women in the cabinet.[77]

CONCLUSION: ITALY, DEMOCRACY AND POLITICS

At various times the question of what kind of democracy Italy has been, and if it has been a democracy at all, has exercised the minds of commentators, historians and political scientists. In 1945 Ferruccio Parri and Benedetto Croce disagreed over the democratic nature of pre-fascist Italy. Parri argued that the restricted suffrage and the frequent use of repressive measures by Liberal governments precluded the characterization of pre-fascist Italy as a democratic state. Croce replied that 'Italy from 1860 to 1922 was one of the most democratic states in Europe'. In 1952 Salvemini returned to this debate in a series of articles for the Florentine journal *Il Ponte*. Salvemini, quite correctly, claimed that the response to this key question depended on one's definition of democracy – on which *model* of democracy was being used to compare with Italy. For Salvemini pre-fascist Italy had not been a democracy, but an oligarchy (the rule of the few over the many). The very lack of a mass movement in favour of democratic rights, and the instrumental way in which the suffrage was 'conceded' to the people, underlined the rotten, undemocratic core at the heart of Italian society. Today Italy is a democracy in the formal sense, but there are conflicts of interest between public and private power that infect the state at all levels. The 'Berlusconi era' has done irreparable damage to Italy's economy and the legitimacy of its institutions. Italy's rich history demands deep analysis, both of her leaders, and of her peoples, but her story has not been a happy one. As Salvemini wrote in 1952, 'When the reality is barbaric, a mirror will reflect a barbaric image.'

1911, 1961, 2011: Celebrating the Nation, Contesting the Nation

The way that a nation celebrates itself tells us much about that nation's history and identity, and its relationship with its own past. In 1911 Italy had celebrated its fiftieth anniversary amidst pomp and circumstance. Italy's ruling elites saw the country's fiftieth anniversary as an opportunity to present their understanding of how the Italian state operated to unite the nation and to orientate their presence on the world stage. In Rome the Altar of the Fatherland, a massive marble memorial structure in the heart of the capital, was inaugurated in June 1911. The monument was a tribute to Victor Emmanuel II and a direct attempt to stress the importance of a new kind of religion, that of the nation, with the king as its figurehead. This huge structure was also a direct challenge to the Catholic Church, right in the centre of the new nation's capital. Not surprisingly, the Church refused to participate in the jubilee and the Vatican argued that 'A single Fatherland does not exist'. Later, in his review of the jubilee, the liberal philosopher Benedetto Croce claimed that 'social unity' was being superseded by new forms of individualism that undermined a sense of public interest and had led to a situation in which the words 'king', 'nation', and 'Fatherland' did not hold a unifying meaning.

Despite the efforts of the celebration organizers to disguise it, the Italy of 1911 remained a young country with deep-rooted political, regional and social problems. The structure of the state and the nation had been contested by many of those who had taken part in the Risorgimento, numerous democrats and republicans challenged the powerful role of the monarchy and cast a shadow over the unitary aspirations of the new Italy, and anti-Italian strands existed in Italian society both on the left and in the south. The 1911 jubilee, therefore, was not so much about declaring the achievement of Italian unity as it was about outlining what the present government believed would be the path to national unification.

Fifty years later, the Italy of 1961 was a very different place. It was a Republic, and a country that was going places, and at the centre of Europe. The 'economic miracle' was in full flow and it appeared to many as if the nation was really on the move, perhaps for the first time. In order to celebrate this anniversary a plethora of exhibitions and events were organized in Turin, the first capital of Italy and the site of much of her manufacturing industry. Millions of visitors marvelled at the sites of the exhibition and new structures that had been built for the celebrations. Yet, behind the scenes there were intense debates over the form and content of the exhibitions. The nation itself was not brought into question, but the direction it was taking was the subject of debate. Difficult historical questions from the more distant and recent past (the monarchy, fascism) were largely avoided. The future appeared bright, for all social classes. Money was being made. Unemployment was virtually non-existent in large parts of the north. Deep tensions in society were not yet evident, although they would explode in the 1960s in Turin itself.

On 17 March 2011, Italy celebrated its 150th birthday. On that day, in 1861, Victor Emmanuel II had become the first king of Italy. It was not a day of revolution, but of a bureaucratic (albeit highly symbolic) political unification. The day was designated as a national holiday on a one-off basis in 2011. Flags were raised across Italy to celebrate the nation's 150th birthday. The central event took place in Parliament and the two houses were united to hear a speech from Giorgio Napolitano, the president of the Republic. Official celebrations were also planned for many key places of memory linked to the history of the unification process and Italy in general. In Rome the sites for these included the Gianicolo hill (where fighting had taken place in 1848), the Altar of the Fatherland (constructed for the 1911 celebrations) and the Pantheon (where some of Italy's monarchs are buried). Mimicking the long process of unification, the sesquicentennial commemorations, which began in 2010, continued throughout 2011, with further set pieces on 25 April and 2 June, and will be followed by a series of different and ongoing events until 2020.

In 2011 the symbols of Italy itself were challenged from within the very heart of government by a powerful and well-organized political minority. Yet, to the surprise of many (including the organizers), the 2011 celebrations saw widespread and sustained participation by Italians across the peninsula and so proved to be a powerful moment of national unity at a time of considerable division. In some ways, this enthusiasm for the celebrations was a reaction to the activities of the *Lega Nord* as well as to the deepening political crisis in Italy. Amidst all this upheaval, the role of President Napolitano became increasingly central as the year went on. It was Napolitano who led the celebrations at various key moments and who became identified with Italy itself. It could be argued that if 2011 was a battle between the nation and the anti-nation, it was Italy that came out as the winner.

Attitudes to national symbols and celebrations have shifted in recent years. With the increasing symbolic and political power of the regionalist *Lega Nord*, the left as a whole has moved closer towards an acceptance and use of national symbols. At times, this has created something of an unholy alliance between the nationalist right (whose position on the nation state has remained constant) and the left. One example of this was the widely praised 'show' by Roberto Benigni at the San Remo music festival on 17 February 2011, which saw 19 million Italians tune in. Benigni's fairly acritical approach to the role, for example, of King Victor Emmanuel II during the unification period, was applauded across the political spectrum, with the exception of the *Lega*.

These are not new issues. For years, and especially since the rise of the Leagues in the North in the late 1980s, a long-running debate had taken place over the future of Italy as a nation-state (as well as its past). This ranged from the academic level through to journalism and popular narratives and can be summarized through the title of one of the most important contributions, Gian Enrico Rusconi's *Se cessiamo di essere una nazione* (*If we stop being a nation*, 1993).[78] This debate took place just as mass immigration began to influence the cultural identity of populations within Italy for the first time. By the beginning of the twenty-first century, there were over five million foreign immigrants resident in Italy. Italy was now a multi-ethnic country, and this had not only called into question the meaning of *italianità*, but had also created new forms of national identity (as *Italians*) in opposition to immigration and immigrants. Interestingly, the Northern League (which has rarely identified itself with a country called 'Italy') was at the forefront of anti-immigrant political campaigns, which tended to base themselves around narratives of Italy for the Italians and defence of the nation's borders. Debates over national identity, therefore, were never straightforward or linear, and neither were the political debates that ensued from or were linked to national commemorations. In the academic sphere, many pointed towards new forms of national identity linked to the symbols and institutions of the Republic, above all the Constitution and the president of Italy. A new form of 'constitutional patriotism' has been identified, with support for the 1948 Constitution being seen as the glue keeping Italy together.[79] Again it was Roberto Benigni who seemed to capture this mood, with another popular one-man TV show, this time dedicated to the Constitution itself (*La più bella al mondo*, 20.12.2012).

The Italy of 2011 was a nation unsure of its future. A deep financial crisis due largely to Italy's long-running debt problems ran alongside almost daily reports of corruption involving politicians (from both left and right) and the business community. The role of Berlusconi in government had been deeply divisive, and clashes between public institutions (above all the battle between the judiciary and the political class) saw politics itself become ever more delegitimized in the minds of many Italians. Berlusconi and the LN leader, Umberto Bossi, were themselves, in part, products of an anti-political culture around the time of the '*Tangentopoli*' scandals which swept away the political parties that had governed Italy since 1945. The success of the journalistic investigation into the privileges enjoyed by politicians in Italy (published as *La Casta*, see Box 4.14) and the high profile of anti-political movements – in particular ex-comedian Grillo's Five Star MoVement (see Box 4.15) – provided further evidence of a system in deep crisis. In this context, the 2011commemorations came at a difficult time for Italy, in stark contrast with the economic and political situation in 1961, which was a time of boom and political stability, with most people favouring the big parties which had stretched their tentacles right across the country and into all spheres of life.

Yet, while the publicity and accounts of the events of March and June 2011 which are discussed in detail below were often centred on the activities of the *Lega*, there is no doubt that they also saw what appeared to be wide-ranging and often surprisingly high levels of participation on the part of the general population, from all walks of life and social classes. This was a rare moment of unity and national celebration, in a country increasingly divided not just at the level of politics, but also around the facts and truth of each individual account. During 2011 itself, the dominant narrative changed from one of an account of the celebrations as a series of events which would underline how divided Italy was, to a narrative which saw the commemorations as doing the exact opposite of this, as a sign of unity and connection with the symbols of the nation-state. This narrative took on particular power as the year went on, particularly after the June celebrations, and it was pushed by the national press in addition to, most crucially, key national and local institutions, from the president of Italy right down to many local mayors and other administrators, as well as in schools all over Italy.

Constitutional patriotism is a concept that has also been applied to other countries or transnational entities with significant regional or linguistic heterogeneity within their borders, such as Switzerland, Spain or the European Union.[80] This constitutional patriotism has been seen in various ways in recent years, including the successful referendum campaign against changes to the Constitution in 2006 and the use of the Constitution text in political demonstrations and public events. The Constitution itself has been read aloud or simply carried as part of political protests on numerous occasions in recent years, or certain articles have been recited again and again (for example during anti-war demonstrations). Increasingly, it seems that the defence of the Constitution itself has become a strong element of national identity for many Italians.

Unlike in 1961, many of the events linked to the 2011 commemorations were interested in discussing and highlighting the problematic aspects of Italy's past, and not simply celebrating a particular past. This was evident in the vast exhibition staged in Turin, under the stewardship of historians Walter Barberis and Giovanni De Luna and with the collective title '*Fare gli italiani*' (Making Italians). This interactive exhibition, designed by the highly successful artistic group Studio Azzurro, promised to 'tell the story of the last century and a half in a critical way, showing what has held Italians together and the factors which, on the other hand, have maintained or increased divisions. This will be done by using a wide range of stories and language.' Space was given over to difficult themes that had been avoided in 1911 and 1961 such as migration and immigration, mafias, all of which were organized in thematic 'islands' where there were installations, film shows, music and photographic material on show. The migrations island, for example, was overhung by a vast fishing net containing bags and boxes tied up with string, a reference both to the internal migration of the past (a crucial theme for Turin itself, and a movement which had been at its peak in 1961) as well as to the migrants today attempting to reach Italy across the Mediterranean sea. The exhibition also included reflections on the use of memory itself, and on the past commemorations of national unification, including that of 1961.

Thus, 2011 also saw a number of 'commemorative' events which were not merely commemorative, and were very much part of an interrogation of what made up 'Italy', a country unsure of its own past and its own future,[81] riven by divisions over that past and that future. Moreover, newer historical methodologies were also employed in the make-up of these events linked to the 2011 commemorations. There was an acceptance of the way that Italy has been marked by a tendency towards what has been dubbed divided memory, where, as Luisa Passerini has put it, 'Memory is a battlefield, where nothing is neutral and where everything is continually contested.'[82] Throughout Italy's 150-year lifespan, in fact 'events have been interpreted in contrasting ways, and the facts themselves often contested ... Individual events as well as history itself have been understood in a bewildering variety of ways. The state and other public bodies have rarely been able to build durable and commonly agreed practices of commemoration. There has been no closure, no "truth", little reconciliation.'[83]

The evidence since 2011, however, is that the high levels of participation in the celebrations of that year were not necessarily part of a long-term trend. Italy remained a deeply divided and troubled nation, unable to agree about how to understand its past or about what should be done in the present. It was also a nation where leadership and politics itself had lost much of its legitimacy. The 2011 celebrations had seen moments of unity, but the future remained bleak, economically, politically and socially. The re-election of Napolitano as president in 2013 was a reflection of the relative success of the 2011 commemorations. But the difficulties Italy experienced in forming a new government and the increasing strength of anti-political forces pointed towards a future marked by uncertainty, crisis and decline. This book is an attempt to understand where Italy is at the moment, but above all it tries to provide material for a debate about where Italy has come from. What exactly was being celebrated, or contested in 2011? And where was Italy going in 2013? It is to be hoped that some of the possible answers to these crucial questions can be found in this volume.

Appendix 1 Italian Governments from 1860

GOVERNMENTS, CRISES, APPOINTMENTS

After 1860, the president of the Council of Ministers was appointed by the king. Governments 'fell' after a no-confidence vote in Parliament or when, more generically, the 'conditions were no longer right' for a particular government to carry on, or after particular moments of tension (such as with the resignation of Crispi after the defeat at Adowa in 1896). In 'normal' government crises the king would appoint someone else to try and form another government. Once ministers were selected, they would be sworn in and the government would officially take office. Elections were held regularly, except after changes to electoral systems (1882, 1891, 1912), which tended to be followed immediately by new elections. In the post-unification and Liberal periods, governments were generally brief – 58 in 62 years (with an average life of just over 12 months). The longest-lasting governments were that presided over by Minghetti (1873–6) and Giolitti's first and second governments. As with the post-1945 period, presidents of the Council of Ministers were far more stable than governments. Depretis presided over eight governments, Di Rudini over five, Giolitti over four.

After 1922, Mussolini was president of the Council for more than 20 years without, after 1926, the need to subject himself to elections. None the less, fascist governments did not remain unchanged. Mussolini frequently shuffled his pack of ministers and went through the constitutional motions of putting laws through Parliament. Gradually, however, the party and the dictator removed even these symbolic features of the normal processes of government.

Under the 1948 Constitution, the president of the Council was appointed by the president of the Republic to form a government in the first instance after an election. Government crises occurred following the fall of a particular government after a vote of no confidence in Parliament or, as in the Liberal period, when there was a general feeling that a government's time had come. In such cases, the ex-president of the Council would offer his resignation to the president, who then had three choices – to call an early election (which happened in 1972, 1994 and 1996), to choose a new person to try and form a government, or to ask the *same* person to attempt to form a new government. In most cases, presidents (after consulting all the party leaders and others) chose the second or the third options. The time period and modalities of these 'crises' were fixed by the Constitution.

STABILITY AND INSTABILITY: FACTS AND FIGURES, POST-1945

From 1945 to 1994 Italy was run by 52 governments, which lasted for an average of eleven months. The most durable government was the first Bettino Craxi administration which governed from August 1983 up to June 1986 (1,058 days). The shortest were Andreotti's first government (9 days) and Fanfani's first (12 days). Yet, these 52 governments were led by only 22 different prime ministers. De Gasperi ran eight governments (for a total of 2,688 consecutive days), Andreotti seven, Fanfani six and Moro five. Some ministries have also seen considerable degrees of stability. Andreotti was minister of defence from 1959 to 1966 and Emilio Colombo presided over the treasury from 1963 to 1968. Under-secretaries changed much more frequently, as they were the key component of resource exchange amongst various Christian Democrat factions via the 'Cencelli Manual' (see Box 4.1). Increasingly, the 'material constitution' set up by the DC and its allies dictated when governments fell and were born, marginalizing the role of Parliament and the president of the Republic. After 1994, with the new electoral system in place, government stability generally tended to increase, especially after 1996. The period 1994–2002 saw eight governments, but Berlusconi's second government ran through from 2001 to 2005, and after a mini-crisis, Berlusconi continued in power until 2006. Fragmentation and uncertainty followed with the new electoral system after 2006. Prodi's second government was on borrowed time, and Berlusconi's 2008 administration (although elected with a solid majority) slowly fell apart. After 2011, the main coalitions were unable to form governments on their own and this, allied to the effects of the 2006 electoral system, led to two successive administrations with cross-coalition backing.

LISTING GOVERNMENTS

Given our analysis above, the list below is open to different interpretations. During a crisis, a 'caretaker' government (usually the outgoing one) ran things until the new government was formed. Thus, there are different ways in which the length of governments can be calculated – either leaving gaps between the official 'fall' of an old government and the formation of a new one, or connecting up the dates to include the crisis period. Following convention, I have used the former method for governments up to 1946, and the latter after 1948. In addition, semi-caretaker governments – known as electoral governments – were often set up to take the country through until the date of the next general election. The governments linked to the euro crisis in 2011 and 2013 were also referred to as 'presidential governments' because of the key role played by the president of the Republic in their formation.

Governments and Prime Ministers of Italy, 1860–

January 1860–June 1861	Cavour
June 1861–March 1862	Ricasoli
March 1862–December 1862	Rattazzi
December 1862–March 1863	Farini
March 1863–September 1864	Minghetti
September 1864–December 1865	La Marmora
December 1865–June 1866	La Marmora
June 1866–April 1867	Ricasoli
April 1867–October 1867	Rattazzi
October 1867–January 1868	Menabrea
January 1868–May 1869	Menabrea
May 1869–December 1869	Menabrea
December 1869–June 1873	Lanza
July 1873–March 1876	Minghetti
March 1876–December 1877	Depretis
December 1877–March 1878	Depretis
March 1878–December 1878	Cairoli
December 1878–July 1879	Depretis
July 1879–November 1879	Cairoli
November 1879–May 1881	Cairoli
May 1881–May 1883	Depretis
May 1883–March 1884	Depretis
March 1884–June 1885	Depretis
June 1885–April 1887	Depretis
April 1887–July 1887	Depretis
August 1887–March 1889	Crispi
March 1889–February 1891	Crispi
February 1891–May 1892	Rudini
May 1892–November 1893	Giolitti
December 1893–June 1894	Crispi
June 1894–March 1896	Crispi
March 1896–July 1896	Di Rudini
July 1896–December 1897	Di Rudini
December 1897–June 1898	Di Rudini
June 1898	Di Rudini
June 1898–May 1899	Pelloux
May 1899–June 1900	Pelloux
June 1900–February 1901	Saracco
February 1901–October 1903	Zanardelli
November 1903–March 1905	Giolitti
March 1905–December 1905	Fortis
December 1905–February 1906	Fortis
February 1906–May 1906	Sonnino
May 1906–December 1909	Giolitti
December 1909–March 1910	Sonnino
March 1910–March 1911	Luzzatti
March 1911–March 1914	Giolitti

March 1914–October 1914   Salandra
November 1914–June 1916   Salandra
June 1916–October 1917   Boselli
October 1917–June 1919   Orlando
June 1919–May 1920   Nitti
May 1920–June 1920   Nitti
June 1920–June 1921   Giolitti
July 1921–February 1922   Bonomi
February 1922–July 1922   Facta
July 1922–October 1922   Facta
October 1922–July 1943   Mussolini

Fall of Mussolini and dissolution of Fascist Party
July 1943–April 1944   Badoglio
April 1944–June 1944   Badoglio
June 1944–November 1944   Bonomi
December 1944–June 1945   Bonomi
June 1945–December 1945   Parri
December 1945–July 1946   De Gasperi I

Elections to Constituent Assembly and Referendum on the Republic, June 1946
July 1946–February 1947   De Gasperi II
February 1947–May 1947   De Gasperi III
May 1947–May 1948   De Gasperi IV
1948 Constitution passed

I Legislature: 8 May 1948–24 June 1953
May 1948–January 1950   De Gasperi V
January 1950–July 1951   De Gasperi VI
July 1951–June 1953   De Gasperi VII

II Legislature: 25 June 1953–11 June 1958
July 1953–August 1953   De Gasperi VIII
August 1953–January 1954   Pella I
January 1954–February 1954   Fanfani I
February 1954–July 1955   Scelba
July 1955–May 1957   Segni I
May 1957–June 1958   Zoli

III Legislature: 12 June 1958–15 May 1963
June 1958–February 1959   Fanfani II
February 1959–March 1960   Segni II
March 1960–July 1960   Tambroni I
July 1960–February 1962   Fanfani III
February 1962–May 1963   Fanfani IV

IV Legislature: 16 May 1963–4 June 1968
June 1963–December 1963   Leone I
December 1963–July 1964   Moro I
July 1964–February 1966   Moro II
February 1966–June 1968   Moro III

V Legislature: 5 June 1968–24 May 1972

June 1968–December 1968	Leone II
December 1968–July 1969	Rumor I
August 1969–February 1970	Rumor II
March 1970–July 1970	Rumor III
August 1970–May 1972	Colombo I

VI Legislature: 25 May 1972–4 July 1976

May 1972–June 1972	Andreotti I
June 1972–June 1973	Andreotti II
July 1973–March 1974	Rumor IV
March 1974–October 1974	Rumor V
November 1974–January 1976	Moro IV
February 1976–July 1976	Moro V

VII Legislature: 5 July 1976–19 June 1979

July 1976–January 1978	Andreotti III
March 1978–January 1979	Andreotti IV
March 1979	Andreotti V

VIII Legislature: 20 June 1979–11 July 1983

June 1979–March 1980	Cossiga I
April 1980–September 1980	Cossiga II
October 1980–May 1981	Forlani I
June 1981–August 1982	Spadolini I
August 1982–November 1982	Spadolini II
December 1982–July 1983	Fanfani V

IX Legislature: 12 July 1983–7 July 1987

July 1983–June 1986	Craxi I
August 1986–March 1987	Craxi II
April 1987	Fanfani VI

X Legislature: 2 July 1987–22 April 1992

July 1987–March 1988	Goria
April 1988–May 1989	De Mita
July 1989–March 1991	Andreotti VI
April 1991–April 1992	Andreotti VII

XI Legislature: 23 April 1992–8 May 1994

| April 1992–April 1993 | Amato I |
| April 1993–April 1994 | Ciampi I |

XII Legislature: 15 April 1994–8 May 1996

| May 1994–December 1994 | Berlusconi I |
| January 1995–May 1996 | Dini |

XIII Legislature: 9 May 1996–13 May 2001

| May 1996–October 1998 | Prodi I |

October 1998–December 1999   D'Alema I
December 1999–April 2000   D'Alema II
April 2000–May 2001   Amato II

XIV Legislature: 14 May 2001–27 April 2006
June 2001–April 2005   Berlusconi II
April 2005–May 2006   Berlusconi III

XV Legislature: 28 April 2006–6 February 2008
May 2006–May 2008   Prodi II

XVI Legislature: 29 April 2008–22 December 2012
May 2008–November 2011   Berlusconi IV
November 2011–December 2012   Monti

XVII Legislature:
April 2013–February 2014   (Enrico) Letta
February 2014–   Renzi

Appendix 2   Italian Heads of State from 1860

Vittorio Emanuele II, 1861–78
Umberto I 1878–1900
Vittorio Emanuele III 1900–46
Umberto II 1946

Date of election	Name	Number of voting rounds	Voters	Quorum	Votes
28 June 1946	Enrico De Nicola	1	537	323	396
11 May 1948	Luigi Einaudi	4	900	451	518
29 April 1955	Giovanni Gronchi	4	843	422	658
11 May 1962	Antonio Segni	9	854	428	443
28 December 1964	Giuseppe Saragat	21	963	482	648
24 December 1971	Giovanni Leone	23	1,008	505	518
8 July 1978	Sandro Pertini	16	1,010	506	832
3 July 1985	Francesco Cossiga	1	1,011	674	752
28 May 1992	Oscar Luigi Scalfaro	16	1,014	508	672
13 May 1999	Carlo Azeglio Ciampi	1	1,011	674	707
15 May 2006	Giorgio Napolitano	4	1009	505	543
20 April 2013	Giorgio Napolitano	6	1007	504	738

Notes

The bibliography that follows these notes has been fully updated to take account of works published since 2003. Not all of these new works are cited in the notes below to avoid repetition.

Since the first edition of this book was published, two important volumes have appeared which have broadened our understanding of Italian history and of how that history should be studied, Nick Carter's *Modern Italy in Historical Perspective* and Claudia Baldoli's *A History of Italy*. The approach to Italian history in these books underlines how new methodologies have increasingly been employed in order to understand modern Italy.

INTRODUCTION: STUDYING ITALY

1. D. Mack Smith, *Modern Italy: a Political History* (New Haven, CT: Yale University Press, 1997); M. Clark, *Modern Italy, 1871–1995*, 2nd edn (London: Longman, 1996); C. Duggan, *A Concise History of Italy* (Cambridge: Cambridge University Press, 1994); C. Seton-Watson, *Italy from Liberalism to Fascism, 1870–1925* (London: Methuen, 1967); J. A. Davis (ed.), *Italy in the Nineteenth Century, 1796–1900* (Oxford: Oxford University Press, 2000); P. Ginsborg, *A History of Contemporary Italy: Society and Politics, 1943–1988* (London: Penguin, 1990); P. Ginsborg, *Italy and its Discontents: Family, Civil Society, State, 1980–2001* (London: Penguin, 2002); P. McCarthy (ed.), *Italy since 1945* (Oxford: Oxford University Press, 2000); D. Sassoon, *Contemporary Italy: Politics, Economy, and Society*, 2nd edn (London: Longman, 1996); A. Lyttelton (ed.), *Liberal and Fascist Italy, 1900–1945* (Oxford: Oxford University Press, 2002). An excellent synthesis of Italian social history is J. Dunnage, *Twentieth Century Italy: a Social History* (London: Longman, 2002). For collections of documents and extracts in English (in the traditional form of selected pieces and commentaries, not in the box form used here) see D. Mack Smith, *The Making of Italy, 1796–1866* (London: Macmillan, 1988) and S. Clough and S. Saladino, *A History of Modern Italy: Documents, Readings and Commentary* (New York and London: Columbia University Press, 1968).
2. F. Spotts and T. Weiser, *Italy: A Difficult Democracy* (Cambridge: Cambridge University Press, 1986); S. Gundle and S. Parker, *The New Italian Republic: from the Fall of the Berlin Wall to Berlusconi* (London: Routledge, 1996); D. Hine, *Governing*

Italy (Oxford: Oxford University Press, 1993). In addition, there are a number of excellent comparative European politics textbooks which cover Italy, such as P. Allum, *State and Society in Western Europe* (Cambridge: Polity, 1995) and Y. Meny, *Government and Politics in Western Europe* (Oxford: Oxford University Press, 1998). See also D. Forgacs and R. Lumley (eds), *Italian Cultural Studies* (Cambridge: Cambridge University Press, 1997).

3. A thorough and thoughtful discussion of the question of periodization, concentrating on the three post-war eras of 1918, 1945 and 1989 in a comparative perspective, can be found in C. Levy, '1918–1945–1989: The Making and Unmaking of Stable Societies in Western Europe', in C. Levy and M. Roseman (eds), *Three Postwar Eras in Comparison: Western Europe, 1918–1945–1989* (Basingstoke: Palgrave Macmillan, 2002), pp. 1–39.

   For a provocative analysis of the use of school textbooks in historical teaching and the debates over history, see D. Bidussa, 'Dalla storia alla prosodia? Il dibattito sui libri di testo', *I viaggi di Erodoto*, 41/42 (2000), pp. 68–73. Of course, a thematic approach carries its own dangers, most obviously the artificial separation of material into various areas, when, clearly, all of this material cuts across at least two or three themes. No area is exclusively social, political, economic or national. The reader is actively encouraged not to read this book from cover to cover, but to move around the volume in a more flexible way.

4. For this particular massacre and the debates surrounding it, see A. Portelli, 'The Massacre at Civitella Val di Chiana (Tuscany, June 29, 1944). Myth and Politics, Mourning and Common Sense', in his *The Battle of Valle Giulia: Oral History and the Art of Dialogue* (Wisconsin: Wisconsin University Press, 1997), pp. 140–60; G. Contini, *La memoria divisa* (Milan: Rizzoli, 1997) and. J. Foot, *Italy's Divided Memory* (New York: Palgrave, 2009). The quote is from G. Contini, 'Introduzione' to G. Contini (ed.), *Un'isola in terra ferma. Storia orale di una comunità mineraria dell'Amiata* (Siena: Il Leccio, 1995), p. 10,

5. L. Barzini, *The Italians* (London: Penguin, 1968).

6. For a discussion of the various periodizations used by historians, sociologists and economists, see S. Guarracino, 'Le periodizzazioni del Novecento', *I viaggi di Erodoto*, 41/42 (2000), pp. 151–8. In general see, above all, E. Hobsbawm, *Age of Extremes: the Short Twentieth Century, 1914–1991* (London: M. Joseph, 1994) and M. Mazower, *Dark Continent: Europe's Twentieth Century* (London: Allen Lane, 1998). See also C. Levy and M. Roseman (eds), *Three Postwar Eras in Comparison: Western Europe, 1918–1945–1989* (London: Palgrave Macmillan, 2002).

7. For example, S. Colarizi, *Il novecento italiano* (Milan: Rizzoli, 2000) and G. Bocca, *Il secolo sbagliato* (Milan: Mondadori, 2000).

8. P. Craveri, *La Repubblica dal 1958 al 1992* (Milan: TEA, 1992).

9. L. Pes, 'Descrivere il territorio: il punto di vista storico', *I viaggi di Erodoto*, 12, 34 (1998), pp. 50–1.

10. For example, A. Portelli, *The Death of Luigi Trastulli and other Stories: Form and Meaning in Oral History* (New York: State University of New York Press, 1991), C. Ginzburg, *Miti emblemi spie* (Turin: Einaudi, 1974) and C. Ginzburg, *The Cheese and the Worms: The Cosmos of a Sixteenth-Century Miller* (London: Routledge, 1980).

11. Many of these comparative points were discussed at a round table on *Civil Wars in the Twentieth Century (Greece, Ireland, Israel, Italy, Spain)* held at the International Past and Present history conference in London in July 2002 and chaired by Roy

Foster. The question of Italy's civil wars in the twentieth century needs to be put in the context of the debates concerning a European civil war. See, for an overview, P. Preston, 'The Great Civil War: European Politics, 1914–1945', in T. Blanning (ed.), *The Oxford History of Contemporary Europe* (Oxford: Oxford University Press, 1995), pp. 148–81; and G. Ranzato (ed.), *Guerre fratricide. Le guerre civili in età contemporanea* (Turin: Bollati Boringhieri, 1994).

12. See, for example, Foot, *Italy's Divided Memory*; F. Focardi, *Il cattivo tedesco e il bravo italiano: La rimozione delle colpe della seconda guerra mondiale* (Bari: Laterza, 2013); E. Gobetti, *Alleati del nemico: L'occupazione italiana in Jugoslavia (1941–1943)* (Bari: Laterza, 2013).

13. Giulio Sapelli has made a very convincing case for including Italy in southern Europe (with Spain, Greece, Turkey and Portugal) using (in the main) economic and political indicators. However, even here Italy appears to emerge with a number of exceptions which distance her from Sapelli's own south European 'model' (postwar democracy, a different economic history), *Southern Europe since 1945: Tradition and Modernity in Portugal, Spain, Italy, Greece and Turkey* (London: Longman, 1995). Other work on 'southern Europe' either varies the countries included (Turkey is often left out) or makes rather sweeping generalizations to justify the term used, such as late industrialization or clientelistic state structures, whilst playing down, for example, the influence of France on Piedmont and the unification of Italy, or of Austrian occupation on Lombardy and the Veneto; see for example, J. Kurth and J. Petras (eds), *Mediterranean Paradoxes* (Oxford: Berg, 1993). Yet, this work is in contrast to many studies of southern Europe which make no attempt whatsoever to argue for the comparative framework they employ, such as A. Williams (ed.), *Southern Europe Transformed: Political and Economic Change in Greece, Italy, Portugal and Spain* (London: Harper and Row, 1984) or R. Hudson and J. Lewis (eds), *Uneven Development in Southern Europe: Studies of Accumulation, Class, Migration and the State* (London: Methuen, 1985), which none the less includes an excellent comparative historical analysis by S. Giner, 'Political Economy, Legitimation and the State in Southern Europe', pp. 309–51. For Italy and the Mediterranean see the classic work of Fernand Braudel, *The Mediterranean* (London and New York, 1973), 2 vols, and the extraordinary research and synthesis by P. Holden and N. Purcell, *The Corrupting Sea: A Study of Mediterranean History* (Oxford: Blackwell, 2000). For a critical survey of anthropological work on the Mediterranean region up to the mid-1970s see J. Davis, *People of the Mediterranean: An Essay in Comparative Social Anthropology* (London: Routledge & Kegan Paul, 1977). See also the essays collected in P. Katzenstein et al. (eds), *Comparative Theory and Political Experience: Mario Einaudi and the Liberal Tradition* (London and Ithaca: Cornell University Press, 1990), and E. Dal Lago and R. Halpern (eds), *The American South and the Italian Mezzogiorno: Essays in Comparative History* (Basingstoke: Palgrave, 2002).

14. See R. Bosworth, *Italy: The Least of the Great Powers* (1979) and *Italy and the Wider World: 1860–1960* (London: Routledge, 1996).

15. G. Levi, 'Italy: Catholicism, Power, Democracy and the Failure of the Past', in P. Furtado (ed.), *Histories of Nations: How their Identities Were Forged* (London: Thames and Hudson, 2012), pp. 266–7.

16. For a taste of the comparative work (of differing quality) on democracy and dictatorship in southern Europe, see L. Morlino, *Democracy between Consolidation and Crisis* (Oxford: Oxford University Press, 1998); G. Pridham (ed.), *Encouraging Democracy: The International Context of Regime Transition in Southern Europe*

(New York: St Martin's Press, 1991); G. Pridham (ed.), *Transitions to Democracy: Comparative Perspectives from Southern Europe, Latin America and Eastern Europe* (Aldershot: Dartmouth, 1995); and U. Liebert and M. Cotta (eds), *Parliament and Democratic Consolidation in Southern Europe* (London and New York: Pinter, 1990).

17. C. Crouch, *Post-Democracy* (Cambridge: Polity, 2004).
18. The literature on Italian fascism is vast, see R. De Felice, *Mussolini*, 7 volumes (Turin: Einaudi, 1965–97), *Interpretations of Fascism* (Cambridge, MA: Harvard University Press, 1977) and *Fascism, an Informal Introduction to its Theory and Practice* (New Brunswick: Transaction, 1976) (for the beginning of the debate); L. Passerini, *Fascism in Popular Memory: the Cultural Experience of the Turin Working Class* (Cambridge: Cambridge University Press, 1987); R. Bosworth, *The Italian Dictatorship: Problems and Perspectives in the Interpretation of Mussolini and Fascism* (London: Arnold, 1998), and other references in the bibliography.
19. Levi, 'Italy', pp. 266, 270.
20. See J. Agnew, *Place and Politics: The Geographical Mediation of Space and Society* (London: Allen and Unwin, 1987) and J. Agnew, *Place and Politics in Modern Italy* (Chicago: Chicago University Press, 2002).
21. S. Gundle and N. O'Sullivan, 'The Mass Media and the Political Crisis', in Gundle and Parker, *The New Italian Republic*, p. 216.
22. See P. Aprile, *Terroni. Tutto quello che è stato fatto perché gli italiani del Sud diventassero Meridionali* (Rome: Piemme, 2010), which has sold more than a quarter of a million copies. An English translation appeared in 2011, *Terroni. All That Has Been Done to Ensure That the Italians of the South Became 'Southerners'* (New York: Bordighera, 2011).
23. For the debates around Pansa and the Resistance in general see P. Cooke, *The Legacy of the Italian Resistance* (London: Palgrave, 2011) and Foot, *Italy's Divided Memory*.
24. P. Ginsborg, '"Prologue" to *Salviamo l'Italia* (Turin: Einaudi, 2010)', *California Italian Studies*, 2, 1, http://escholarship.org/uc/item/1dz8v1nn

1 THE NATION

1. P. Bevilacqua, 'New and Old in the Southern Question', *Modern Italy*, 1, 2 (1996), pp. 81–92; *Breve storia dell'Italia meridionale dall'Ottocento a oggi* (Rome: Donzelli, 1993); J. Dickie, *Darkest Italy: The Nation and Stereotypes of the Mezzogiorno, 1860–1900* (New York: St Martin's Press, 1999); R. Lumley and J. Morris (eds), *The New History of the Italian South: The Mezzogiorno Revisited* (Exeter: Exeter University Press, 1997); N. Moe, *The View from Vesuvius: Italian Culture and the Southern Question* (Berkeley, CA: University of California Press, 2002); E. Dal Lago and R. Halpern (eds), *The American South and the Italian Mezzogiorno: Essays in Comparative History* (Basingstoke: Palgrave, 2002).
2. A. Smith, *National Identity* (London: Penguin, 1991).
3. L. Gallino, *Dizionario di Sociologia* (Turin: UTET, 1993), p. 443.
4. G. E. Rusconi (ed.), *Nazione, etnia, cittadinanza in Italia e in Europa. Per un discorso storico-culturale* (Brescia: Editrice La Scuola, 1993), p. 7.
5. Rusconi, *Nazione*, p. 26.
6. J. Dickie, 'Imagined Italies', in D. Forgacs and R. Lumley (eds), *Italian Cultural Studies* (Cambridge: Cambridge University Press, 1997), p. 20.

7. B. Anderson, *Imagined Communities: Reflections on the Origin and Spread of Nationalism*, new edn (London: Verso, 1991), p. 6.

8. Dickie, 'Imagined Italies', p. 22.

9. Dickie, *Darkest Italy*, p. 19.

10. See D. Pick, *Faces of Degeneration: a European Disorder, 1848–1918* (Cambridge: Cambridge University Press, 1989), and D. Horn, *Social Bodies: Science, Reproduction and Italian Modernity* (Princeton, NJ: Princeton University Press, 1994).

11. See also the crucial research published by S. Patriarca, *Italian Vices: Nation and Character from the Risorgimento to the Republic* (Cambridge: Cambridge University Press, 2010), and the monumental seven-volume collective work (which is due to reach nearly 4,600 pages) overseen by M. Isnenghi, *Gli Italiani in guerra. Conflitti, identità, memorie dal Risorgimento ai nostri giorni* (Turin: UTET, 2008), and in particular volume 1 for the Risorgimento, Mario Isnenghi and Eva Cecchinato (eds), *Fare l'Italia: unità e disunità nel Risorgimento* (Turin: UTET, 2008).

12. This idea of a 'mass movement' has come in for some trenchant criticism; see for example the fascinating debates around Banti's work in *Nations and Nationalism*, 15, 3 (2009).

13. L. Riall, *Risorgimento: The History of Italy from Napoleon to Nation State* (London: Palgrave, 2009), p. 123.

14. Riall, *Risorgimento*, p. 124.

15. A. M. Banti and P. Ginsborg (eds), *Il Risorgimento* (Turin: Einaudi, 2007), p. xxiii.

16. T. De Mauro, *Storia linguistica dell'Italia Unita* (Bari: Laterza, 1963).

17. D. Gabaccia, *Italy's Many Diasporas* (London: UCL Press, 2000).

18. 'L'italiano? No grazie, io parlo dialetto', *Corriere della Sera*, 21 April 2007, www.treccani.it/magazine/lingua_italiana/speciali/italiano_dialetti/Cerruti.html

19. www.ef-italia.it/epi/europe/italy/

20. L. Rastello, *La frontiera addosso. Cosi si deportano i diritti umani* (Rome: Laterza, 2010).

21. R. King (ed.), *The Mediterranean Passage: Migration and New Cultural Encounters in Southern Europe* (Liverpool: Liverpool University Press, 2001); R. King and N. Mai, *Out of Albania: From Crisis Migration to Social Inclusion in Italy* (London: Berghahn Books, 2008); Fabrizio Gatti, *Bilal. Viaggiare, lavorare, morire da clandestini* (Milan: Rizzoli, 2008). See also the documentary at http://static.repubblica.it/repubblica/lampedusa/

22. See for this reform I. Sales, 'Federalismo italiano', *Meridiana*, 43 (2002), pp. 238–52.

23. See, for example, E. Franzina, *Merica! Merica! Emigrazione e colonizzazione nelle lettere dei contadini veneti e friulani in America latina (1876–1902)* (Milan: Feltrinelli, 1979).

24. Gabaccia, *Italy's Many Diasporas*.

25. Eleven Italians were lynched in 1891 in New Orleans; P. Salvietti, *Corda e sapone: Storie di linciaggi degli italiani negli Stati Uniti* (Rome: Donzelli, 2003). For more general questions, see M. Frye Jacobson, *Whiteness of a Different Colour: European Immigrants and the Alchemy of Race* (Cambridge and London: Harvard University Press, 1998).

26. P. Brunello, *Pionieri. Gli italiani in Brasile e il mito della frontiera* (Rome: Donzelli, 1994).

27. For a comparative analysis of migration from (and to) Southern Europe, see Sapelli, *Southern Europe since 1945*, ch. 3.

28. M. Gallerano, *La nuova legge sulla cittadinanza italiana* (Rimini: Maggioli, 1994).

29. T. Perlmutter, 'All Roads Lead to Rome: the Domestic and Geopolitics of "Enfranchising" Italians Abroad' (paper given to the Council for European Studies Conference, Chicago, April 2000).

30. See also the reflections of G. Salvemini in 1952, 'Fu L'Italia prefascista una democrazia?', *Il Ponte*, VIII, I (January 1952), pp. 11–23.

31. An absurd concept in itself – we cannot measure national identity just as we cannot measure ideology. To do so would be to assume that national identity was a single entity, which merely varied in strength.

32. See E. Forcella and A. Monticone, *Plotone di esecuzione. I processi della prima guerra mondiale* (Bari: Laterza, 1998). Of the 5–6 million men mobilized by Italy, some 870,000 had been denounced to the military judges by the end of the war, around 15 per cent. A large part of this figure refers to emigrants who failed to turn up after conscription (some 470,000 men). By September 1919, 350,000 trials had taken place with 210,000 guilty verdicts: 100,000 were for desertion, 25,000 for acts of indiscipline and 10,000 for acts of self-injury; 15,000 life sentences were handed out, with 4,000 death sentences of which 3,000 ended in amnestics and 750 were carried out. In addition, there were at least 150 summary executions at the front, see M. Isenghi, 'La Grande Guerra', in M. Isenghi (ed.), *I luoghi dell'identità* (Bari: Laterza, 1997), pp. 273–329.

33. E. Galli della Loggia, *La morte della patria* (Bari: Laterza, 1999), pp. 7–10. For Caporetto see G. Procacci, 'The Disaster of Caporetto', in J. Dickie, J. Foot and F. Snowden (eds), *Disastro! Disasters in Italy since 1860: Culture, Politics, Society* (New York: Palgrave, 2002), pp. 141–61.

34. Speech in Milan, 25 October 1932, www.mussolinibenito.it/discorsodel25_10_1932.htm

35. E. Leed, *No Man's Land: Combat and Identity in World War One* (Cambridge: Cambridge University Press, 1979).

36. See G. Sabbatucci, 'La vittoria mutilata', in G. Belardelli et al. (eds), *Miti e storia dell'Italia unita* (Bologna: Il Mulino, 1999), pp. 101–6.

37. Cited in E. Gentile, *La Grande Italia. Ascesa e declino del mito della nazione nel ventesimo secolo* (Milan: Mondadori, 1997), p. 142.

38. Cited in Gentile, *La Grande Italia*, p. 144.

39. L. Passerini, *Fascism in Popular Memory: The Cultural Experience of the Turin Working Class* (Cambridge: Cambridge University Press, 1987).

40. See Mussolini's declaration of war, in M. Isenghi, *Le guerre degli italiani. Parole, immagini, ricordi, 1848–1945* (Milan: Mondadori, 1989), pp. 41–5.

41. N. Revelli, 'La ritirata di Russia', in M. Isenghi (ed.), *I luoghi della memoria* (Bari: Laterza, 1997), p. 374.

42. C. Pavone, *Una guerra civile. Saggio storico sulla moralità della Resistenza* (Turin: Bollati Boringhieri, 1991). An English translation finally appeared in 2013. *A Civil War. A History of the Italian Resistance*, S. Pugliese ed. (London: Verso, 2013).

43. R. Absalom, *A Strange Alliance: Aspects of Escape and Survival in Italy, 1943–1945* (Florence: Olschki, 1991).

44. E. Aga Rossi, *Una Nazione allo sbando. L'armistizio italiano del settembre 1943* (Bologna: Il Mulino, 1993), p. 132.

45. R. De Felice, *Il rosso e il nero* (Milan: Baldini & Castoldi, 1995), p. 35.

46. M. Franzinelli, 'L'8 settembre', in Isenghi (ed), *I luoghi della memoria*, p. 244.

47. Pavone, *Una guerra civile*, p. 36.

48. C. Brice, '"The King was Pale". Italy's National–Popular Monarchy and the Construction of Disasters, 1882–1885', in Dickie et al. (eds), *Disastro!*, pp. 61–79; J. Dickie, 'A Patriotic Disaster: the Messina–Reggio Calabria earthquake of 1908', in G. Bedani and B. Haddock (eds), *The Politics of Italian National Identity* (Cardiff: University of Wales Press, 2000); J. Dickie, *Una catastrofe patriottica. 1908: il terremoto di Messina* (Bari: Laterza, 2008).
49. See for a survey, W. Lamont (ed.), *Historical Controversies and Historians* (London: UCL Press, 1998), and for France in particular, H. Rousso, *The Vichy Syndrome: History and Memory in France since 1944* (Boston: Harvard University Press, 1991).
50. R. d'Amico, *Burocrazia e ente Regione. L'appunto amministrativo della Regione sicilian* (Bologna: Il Mulino, 1978); M. Tocco, *Libro nero di Sicilia. Dietro le quinte della politica, degli affari e della cronaca della Regione Siciliana* (Milan: Sugarco editore, 1972).
51. E. Banfield, *The Moral Basis of a Backward Society* (Glencoe, IL: Free Press, 1958), p. 10.
52. I have not repeated the usual historical arguments put forward for Italy's 'weak' sense of national identity – late unification, regional history, dialects, illiteracy, etc. – as these are readily available in any of the current traditional Italian history textbooks.
53. J. Foot, 'The Family and the "Economic Miracle": Social Transformation, Work, Leisure and Development at Bovisa and Comasina (Milan), 1950–1970', *Contemporary European History*, 4, 3 (1995), pp. 315–38.
54. R. Putnam et al., *Making Democracy Work: Civic Traditions in Modern Italy* (Princeton NJ: Princeton University Press, 1993), p. 130.
55. J. Schneider (ed.), *Italy's Southern Question: Orientalism in One Country?* (Oxford: Berg, 1998), p. 8.

2 THE STATE

1. Two points should be noted here regarding the organization of this chapter. The political side of state organization will be dealt with (mainly) in Chapter 4, while the fate of public industry will be examined in Chapter 3. An obvious area, which has been neglected here, is the relationship between the Italian state and international organizations, above all the European Union. Some discussion will be included in this chapter and Chapters 3–4, but for further information see Ginsborg, *Italy and its Discontents*; F. Francioni (ed.), *Italy and EC Membership Evaluated* (London: Pinter, 1992); and S. Pistone (ed.), *L'Italia e l'unità europea* (Turin: Einaudi, 1982). Other areas omitted due to lack of space are those involving the police and *carabinieri*, and the education system.
2. J. Habermas, *Legitimation Crisis* (Cambridge: Polity, 1988), p. 46.
3. For hegemony, see J. Femia, *Gramsci's Political Thought: Hegemony, Consciousness and the Revolutionary Process* (Oxford: Clarendon Press, 1987), and M. Mann, *Consciousness and Action amongst the Western Working Class* (London: Macmillan, 1973). If we follow Mann's early analysis of the three levels through which power is exercised, the Italian state has very rarely come close to the third level of 'power-management' – it has never exercised significant degrees of *hegemony* over its people.
4. Ginsborg, *A History of Contemporary Italy*, p. 51.
5. There is no adequate history of Italian reformism. For Giolitti, see A. De Grand, *The Hunchback's Tailor: Giovanni Giolitti and Liberal Italy from the Challenge of Mass*

Politics to the Rise of Fascism, 1882–1922 (Westport CT: Praeger, 2001), and R. Romanelli, *Il comando impossibile: Stato e società nell'Italia liberale* (Bologna: Il Mulino, 1995). For the post-war period, see Vittorio Foa's seminal *Il cavallo e la torre. Riflessioni su una vita* (Turin: Einaudi, 1991).

6. G. Salvemini, *Opere*, V, *Scritti sulla scuola* (Milan: Feltrinelli, 1966), p. xiii.

7. See F. Turati, *Rifare l'Italia* (Milan: Lega nazionale delle cooperative, 1920), or the work of E. Rossi, *Abolire la miseria* (Bari: Laterza, 1977).

8. For the debates over the Risorgimento, see L. Riall, *The Italian Risorgimento: State, Society and National Unification* (London: Routledge, 1994), and R. Romeo, *Risorgimento e capitalismo* (Bari: Laterza, 1959).

9. For familism see Chapter 1 and Chapter 3.

10. D. Gambetta, 'Mafia: the Price of Distrust', in D. Gambetta (ed.), *Trust: Making and Breaking Cooperative Relations* (electronic edition, Dept. of Sociology, University of Oxford), pp. 158–75.

11. Of course, criminal organizations have not been confined to Sicily, or to the Mafia. For the *camorra* (Campania/Naples) see T. Behan, *The Camorra* (London: Routledge, 1995), reprinted as *See Naples and Die: The Camorra and Organized Crime* (London: I. B. Tauris, 2002).

12. For an international history of 1968, including Italy, see R. Fraser, *1968: A Student Generation in Revolt* (London: Chatto and Windus, 1987) and R. Gildea et al eds., *Europe's 1968. Voices of Revolt* (Oxford: OUP, 2013).

13. P. Pombeni, 'The Roots of the Italian Political Crisis: A View from History, 1918, 1945, 1989…and After', in C. Levy and M. Roseman (eds), *Three Postwar Eras in Comparison: Western Europe, 1918–1945–1989* (Basingstoke: Palgrave, 2002), p. 277.

14. The classic international comparison is with the French Fourth Republic, a similar document with similar intentions. The transition to a very different, presidential system (with the Fifth Republic, set up in 1958) never happened in Italy, despite almost constant debate after 1948. For the text of these constitutions see S. Finer (ed.), *Five Constitutions* (London: Penguin, 1979).

15. Pombeni, 'Roots of the Italian Political Crisis'.

16. Finally, at a local level, councils, provinces and regions have always had legal powers, within limits. Laws have also been produced locally. These powers have changed over time in line with changes to the federalist structure of the state over the century. Regional governments can legislate in a number of areas, specified by Article 117 of the Constitution (for the 'ordinary' regions) and the statutes (for the special regions). This right has only been in place since the institution of various regions since 1945. A series of restrictions apply to these laws: they must conform to the Constitution and regional statutes and to European law, and, more vaguely, they must be 'in line with' the reforms of the central state and 'the interests of the state and other regions'. Regional laws have to work within the broad principles set out by central legislation in each area. These controls are exercised by the government commissioners in each region and by the Constitutional Court. Decentralization reforms introduced in 2000 and ratified by referendum in 2001 allowed regions to free themselves from many of these restrictions for the first time, and regional presidents could sign their own laws without reference to state or government officers or institutions. Regional laws are drawn up by regional governments, and need to be passed by the appropriate committees and the regional chamber before becoming law, after being signed by the regional president.

17. Royal decree 1398, 18 October 1930. See *The Italian Penal Code* (Littleton, CO: Fred Rothman, 1978) for an English translation. For the 1913 code of penal procedure, see *Codice di procedura penale per il Regno d'Italia* (Rome: Camera dei deputati, 1914); for the 1865 code, see *Codice di procedura penale per il Regno d'Italia* (Naples: Giovanni Jovene, 1882).

18. When passing sentence, judges were obliged to take into account the motives of the offender, their criminal record, their behaviour since the offence and their personal, domestic and social conditions.

19. The infamous Article 587, which was only reformed in 1981, read as follows: 'Whoever causes death of a spouse, daughter or sister upon discovering them to be having illicit carnal relations, and in a state of rage caused by the affront to his own honour or that of his family, shall be punished by imprisonment for from three to seven years', see T. Padovani, 'I delitti nelle relazioni private', in L. Violante (ed.), *La criminalità, Storia d'Italia, Annali*, 12 (Turin: Einaudi, 1997), pp. 219–46; and E. Cantarella, 'Homicides of Honor: the Development of Italian Adultery Law over Two Millennia', in D. Kertzer and R. Saller (eds), *The Family in Italy from Antiquity to the Present* (New Haven, CT: Yale University Press, 1991), pp. 229–46.

20. At the time, some argued for the abolition of the 1931 codes, and a return to the Liberal codes. Others, such as the leading constitutionalist Piero Calamandrei, called for the 'disinfection' of the 1931 codes of their fascist elements. Calamandrei claimed that a return to the Liberal codes would have been a regressive and damaging move and that the Rocco codes were not entirely fascist. However, even this 'disinfection' was very slow to occur and is still not entirely completed. See 'Sulla riforma dei codici' (1945), in N. Bobbio (ed.), *Piero Calamandrei, Scritti e discorsi politici*, vol. 1 (Florence: La nuova Italia, 1966), pp. 86–99.

21. M. Ainis, 'La chiarezza delle leggi', in L. Violante (ed.), *Legge Diritto Giustizia, Storia d'Italia, Annali*, 14 (Turin: Einaudi, 1998), p. 916.

22. See also, for the Italian African Police, R. Girlando, *PAI. Polizia dell'Africa italiana* (Campobasso: Italia editrice, 1996).

23. G. Rochat and G. Massobrio, *Breve storia dell'esercito italiano dal 1861 al 1943* (Turin: Einaudi, 1978).

24. L. Violante, 'La repressione del dissenso politico nell'Italia liberale: stati d'assedio e giustizia militare', *Rivista di storia contemporanea*, v (1976), pp. 481–524.

25. For example, the extraordinary violence which took place in Reggio Calabria between 1969 and 1972, sparked by a debate over the location of the capital of Calabria's new regional government, see Ginsborg, *A History of Contemporary Italy*, pp. 338–40; and F. D'Agostino, *Reggio Calabria. I moti del luglio 1970–febbraio 1971* (Milan, 1972).

26. Other kinds of military service operated in the colonies, for example local Ethiopians were recruited into the Italian army during the 1890s and 1930s. The so-called *askari* fought alongside the Italians in both these periods. This is an under-studied area; for an analysis, see C. Pipitone, 'The Black Army: Survey on the Culture of the Italian Officer in East Africa' (unpublished paper delivered at the Italian Colonialism and Post-Colonial Legacies Conference, ASMI, London, 30 November–1 December 2001).

27. G. Rochat, 'L'esercito italiano negli ultimi cento anni', *Storia d'Italia*, vol. V, *I documenti*, 2 (Turin: Einaudi, 1973), pp. 1867–902.

28. P. Del Negro, *Esercito, Stato, Società: saggi di storia militare* (Bologna: Cappelli editore, 1979).

29. G. Oliva, 'La Naja', in M. Isnenghi (ed.), *I luoghi della memoria* (Bari: Laterza, 1997), pp. 95–109.

30. These reforms were opposed by the Right, and the structures set in place were particularly bureaucratic, allowing for various 'tests' of the 'sincerity' of individuals before they could be rewarded with the status of 'conscientious objector' and allowed to work, more or less for nothing, in other state sectors for up to two years. For the texts of these laws, see C. Santoro, *Obiezioni di coscienza al servizio militare, all'aborto, al lavoro* (Salerno: Edizioni il sapere, 1995).

31. There were always a number of volunteer soldiers in the army, in addition to conscripts, and career officers. Conscription was not the only way to serve in the Italian army. Volunteer service has a strong tradition in Italian history, from Garibaldi's armies onwards, and took on particular importance at times of war.

32. It would not be useful here to go deeply into the intricacies of the whole legal system. However, it is worth noting that administrative decisions and administrative law have a whole, separate, set of institutes governed, at the top, by regional administrative courts (the TAR), whose decisions can be appealed to the Council of State in Rome.

33. These judges also decide on a number of other matters: namely cautionary arrests and requests for bail; phone tapping and bugging authorizations; house arrests.

34. Ginsborg, *Italy and its Discontents*, p. 844.

35. E. Gorrieri, *La giungla retributiva* (Bologna: Il Mulino, 1972).

36. For the importance of mediators, see G. Gribaudi, *Mediatori. Antropologia del potere democristiano nel Mezzogiorno* (Turin: Rosenberg and Sellier, 1980).

37. For an analysis of this kind, see D. Gambetta, *The Sicilian Mafia: the Business of Private Protection* (Cambridge, MA: Harvard University Press, 1993).

38. P. Kivel Mazuy, 'L'orario di lavoro', in M. Rusciano and L. Zoppoli (eds), *Il lavoro pubblico* (Bologna: Il Mulino, 1993), p. 545.

39. G. Melis, *Storia dell'amministrazione italiana (1861–1993)* (Bologna: Il Mulino, 1996), p. 72.

40. P. Allum, *Politics and Society in Post-war Naples* (Cambridge: Cambridge University Press, 1973), p. 48. See also D. L. Zinn, *La raccomandazione. Clientelismo vecchio e nuovo* (Rome: Donzelli, 2001).

41. Here is a rough guide to the numbers of state employees in Italy: 1923 – 540,847; 1938 – 787,862; 1943 – 1,380,904; 1948 – 1,075,042; 1963 – 1,417,529; 1983 – 2,274,602; 1991 – 2,325,304. If we include all state companies, such as the railways, this last figure reaches 4.2 million. This figure had fallen to 3.42 million by 2010.

42. Melis, *Storia*, p. 318.

43. See E. Rossi, *Il Malgoverno* (Bari: Laterza, 1954).

44. M. C. Mascambruno, *Il Prefetto*, I, *Dalle origini all'avvento delle Regioni* (Milan: Giuffrè, 1988), p. 95.

45. L. Einaudi, 'Via il prefetto!', in *Italia e il secondo Risorgimento* (17 July 1944), now in L. Einaudi, *Il Buongoverno* (Bari: Laterza, 1955), pp. 52–9.

46. Cited in Mascambruno, *Il Prefetto*, p. 117.

47. Calamandrei (1955), cited in Mascambruno, *Il Prefetto*, p. 153.

48. 'Via i prefetti!' *L'Unità*, 11 November 1960.

49. There is no space here to discuss Italy's international political role in more detail. For the relationship between Italy and the G7/G8 see Ginsborg, *Italy and its Discontents*, pp. 1–2. Italy was only admitted to the UN in 1955.

3 ECONOMY AND SOCIETY

1. See, for example, I. Wallerstein, who said 'one can interpret the whole political development of Italy, Spain, Portugal, Greece and Turkey in the interwar period as one grand response to the sense and reality of "having been left behind"', from 'The Relevance of the Concept of Semiperiphery to Southern Europe', in G. Arrighi (ed.), *Semiperipheral Development: The Politics of Southern Europe in the Twentieth Century* (Beverly Hills, CA: Sage, 1985), p. 37. The question as to whether Italy was part of the 'semiperiphery' now seems a rather odd one, and Peter Lange had already contested this description in his reply to Wallerstein in the same volume, 'Semiperiphery and Core in the European Context: Reflections on the Postwar Italian Experience', pp. 179–214. For Lange, Italy was clearly part of the 'core', even by the mid-1970s.
2. J. Cohen and G. Federico, *The Growth of the Italian Economy, 1820–1960* (Cambridge: Cambridge University Press, 2001), p. 1.
3. G. Federico and G. Toniolo, 'Italy', pp. 197–214 in R. Sylla and G. Toniolo (eds), *Patterns of European Industrialization: The Nineteenth Century* (London: Routledge, 1991), p. 201.
4. Cohen and Federico, *The Growth*, p. 61.
5. Sapelli, *Southern Europe since 1945*, p. 10. See also N. Carter, 'Rethinking the Italian Liberal State', *Bulletin of Italian Politics*, 3, 2 (2011), pp. 225–45 and 'The Economy of Liberal Italy: a Roundtable Discussion with Brian A'Hearn, Nick Carter, Giovanni Federico and Vera Zamagni on Stefano Fenoaltea's *The Reinterpretation of Italian Economic History: From Unification to the Great War*. Cambridge, CUP, 2011', *Modern Italy*, 18, 1 (2013), pp. 81–94.
6. G. Sapelli, 'Dalla periferia all'integrazione europea', in R. Romano (ed.), *Storia dell'economia italiana*, III, *L'età contemporanea: un paese nuovo* (Turin: Einaudi, 1991), pp. 59–141.
7. A. Serpieri, *La guerra e le classi rurali italiane* (Bari: Laterza, 1930); P. Bevilacqua (ed.), *Storia dell'agricoltura italiana in età contemporanea* (Venice: Marsilio, 1989–91), vols 1–3.
8. G. C. Marino, *Socialismo nel latifondo. Sebastiano Cammareri Scurti nel movimento contadino della Sicilia occidentale (1896–1912)* (Palermo: ESA, 1972), p. 262.
9. P. Arlacchi, *Mafia, Peasants and Great Estates: Society in Traditional Calabria* (Cambridge: Cambridge University Press, 1983), p. 203.
10. G. Lorenzoni, *Inchiesta Parlamentare sulle Condizioni dei Contadini nelle Provincie Meridionali e nella Sicilia*, vol. 6 (Rome: Tipografia Nazionale di Giovanni Bertero, 1910).
11. This had long been the programme of the Left and the peasant unions. As Pasquale Villari noted in 1896, 'the socialists argued for one thing and the peasants wanted another. The former called for the common use of land, and the latter drew up maps which divided the land', *La Sicilia e il socialismo* (Milan: Treves, 1896), p. 97.
12. Cited in J. Schneider and P. Schneider, *Festival of the Poor: Fertility Decline and the Ideology of Class in Sicily, 1860–1980* (Tucson: University of Arizona Press, 1996), p. 252.

13. M. Petrusewicz, 'The Demise of Latifondismo', in R. Lumley and J. Morris (eds), *A New History of the Italian South: the Mezzogiorno Revisited* (Exeter: Exeter University Press, 1997), p. 21.

14. Ibid., p. 39.

15. For the latest debates over the *latifondi*, see the notes to Petrusewicz in Lumley and Morris, *A New History*, and Cohen and Federico, *The Growth*, pp. 26–38.

16. For an account which emphasizes the exploitative features of the sharecropping system in Tuscany, see F. Snowden, *The Fascist Revolution in Tuscany, 1919–1922* (Cambridge: Cambridge University Press, 1989), pp. 7–14. See also S. Oglethorpe, 'Change and Memory: The Central Italy Countryside, 1945–1970' (unpublished PhD thesis, UCL, 2009).

17. E. Sereni, *Il capitalismo nelle campagne (1860–1900)* (Turin: Einaudi, 1975 [1947]), p. 180.

18. P. Clemente et al., *Mezzadri, letterati e padroni nella Toscana dell'Ottocento* (Palermo: Sellerio, 1980), p. 88.

19. D. Kertzer, *Family Life in Central Italy, 1880–1910: Sharecropping, Wage Labor and Coresidence* (New Brunswick: Rutgers University Press, 1984), p. 28.

20. L. Strati, *La mezzadria e la nuova agricoltura* (1908), cited in F. Bogliari (ed.), *Il movimento contadino in Italia. Dall'unità al fascismo* (Turin: Loescher, 1980), p. 239.

21. Ibid.

22. G. Becattini, 'Dal "settore" industriale al "distretto" industriale. Alcune considerazioni sull'unità di indagine dell'economia industriale', *Rivista di Economia e Politica Industriale*, v (1979), pp. 7–21; A. Bonomi, *Il capitalismo molecolare* (Turin: Einaudi, 1997).

23. On the history of small property note the comments of S. Jacini, *La proprietà fondiaria e le popolazioni agricole in Lombardia* (Milan, 1857), cited in J. Davis, *Conflict and Control: Law and Order in Nineteenth-Century Italy* (London: Macmillan, 1988), p. 114; V. Castronovo, 'La storia economica', in *Storia d'Italia*, vol. 4 (Turin: Einaudi, 1973), pp. 235–6.

24. I. Cappelloto, 'La mozione agraria', *L'Italia*, 11 December 1920.

25. N. Mazzoni, *Il problema della terra e il socialismo* (Milan: PSI, 1920).

26. Bogliari, *Il movimento contadino*, pp. 265–6.

27. R. Rossi, *Inchiesta sulla piccola proprietà coltivatrice formateasi nel dopoguerra*, III, *Lombardia* (Rome, 1931), p. 67.

28. See A. D'Orsi, *La rivoluzione bolscevica. Fascismo, classi, ideologie* (1917–1922) (Milan: Franco Angeli, 1985).

29. G. Salvemini, *The Fascist Dictatorship in Italy*, vol. 1 (New York: H. Holt, 1928), p. 39.

30. Antonio Gramsci, *L'ordine nuovo*, 3:1 (1920), now in *Selections from Political Writings, 1910–1920* (London: Lawrence and Wishart, 1977), pp. 146–9.

31. F. Snowden, *Violence and the Great Estates in the South of Italy: Apulia, 1900–1922* (Cambridge: Cambridge University Press, 1986), p. 23.

32. Ibid., p. 20. Of course Italy was not the only country to possess great estates or landscapes of this type. Journeying in Estremadura in Spain William Beckford wrote that in five hours he did not see 'any animals, bipeds or quadrupeds'. The big estates of Andalusia are compared to those of the mezzogiorno by R. Carr, *Spain, 1808–1975* (Oxford: Clarendon, 1982), p. 16.

33. Cited in Snowden, *Violence and the Great Estates*, p. 167.

34. Snowden, *Violence and the Great Estates*, p. 202.

35. Carr, *Spain*, p. 16.

36. G. Crainz, *Padania. Il mondo dei braccianti dall'Ottocento alla fuga dalle campagne* (Rome: Donzelli, 1994); F. Cazzola, *Storia delle campagne padane dall'Ottocento a oggi* (Milan: Bruno Mondadori, 1996).

37. G. Mazzoni, *Un uomo, una città: Giuseppe Massarenti a Molinella* (Bologna: Coop Il Nove, 1990), p. 76.

38. Crainz, *Padania*.

39. P. Corner, *Fascism in Ferrara, 1915–1925* (Oxford: Oxford University Press, 1975); A. Cardoza, *Agrarian Elites and Italian Fascism: the Province of Bologna, 1901–1926* (Princeton, NJ: Princeton University Press, 1983). There is no space in this volume to touch on the vast debates and literature concerning comparative accounts of fascism and the Right; see, for a taster, C. Levy, 'Fascism, National Socialism and Conservatives in Europe, 1914–1945: Issues for Comparativists', *Contemporary European History*, 8, 1 (1999), pp. 97–126; C. Delzell (ed.), *Mediterranean Fascism, 1919–1945* (New York: Harper and Row, 1970); H. Rogger and E. Weber (eds), *The European Right: A Historical Profile* (Berkeley: University of California Press, 1965); A. De Grand, *Fascist Italy and Nazi Germany: The 'Fascist' Style of Rule* (London: Routledge, 1995); R. J. B. Bosworth and P. Dogliani (eds), *Italian Fascism: History, Memory and Representation* (London: Macmillan, 1999); R. Bessel (ed.), *Fascist Italy and Nazi Germany: Comparisons and Contrasts* (Cambridge: Cambridge University Press, 1996); R. Griffin (ed.), *International Fascism, Theories, Causes and the New Consensus* (London: Arnold, 1998). Very little work compares Mussolini's regime with those in Spain, Greece or Portugal (or Japan). Most comparisons are still made with Hitler and the Nazis. See, for some reflections on the Italian, German and Spanish cases, P. Preston, *The Politics of Revenge: Fascism and the Military in Twentieth-century Spain* (London: Routledge, 1995).

40. Crainz, *Padania*.

41. G. Crainz, 'La violenza postbellica in Emilia fra "guerra civile" e conflitti antichi', in P. Pezzino and G. Ranzato (eds), *Laboratorio di storia. Studi in onore di Claudio Pavone* (Milan: Franco Angeli, 1994), pp. 191–205.

42. G. Bosio, *Il trattore ad Acquanegra* (Bari: De Donato, 1981).

43. See Ginsborg, *Italy and its Discontents*, pp. 117–19; A. Amin, 'Small Firms in Italy: Myths and Realities', in N. R. Gilbert, R. Burrows and A. Pollert (eds), *Fordism and Flexibility: Divisions and Change* (New York: St. Martin's Press, 1992), and M. J. Piore and C. F. Sabel, *The Second Industrial Divide* (New York: Basic Books, 1984). Much of the work on Italy initially concentrated on the so-called area of the Third Italy (Emilia–Romagna) and the flexible specialization identified by Piore and Sabel. Recently, there has been far more focus on other areas, above all the north-east. Some comparison can be made here with Spain where the family-run farms of the Basque region (*el caserío*) have often been credited with forming the basis for later small industrial development. As Carr writes, 'without any alteration of techniques, the *caserío* could become, in the twentieth century, a commercialized concern with off-the-farm sales to the towns', *Spain*, p. 6.

44. For a description of the Ferrarese swamps before this reclamation, see Sereni, *Il capitalismo nelle campagne*, p. 188.

45. P. Bevilacqua and M. Rossi-Doria, *Le bonifiche in Italia dal '700 a oggi* (Bari: Laterza, 1984), pp. 64–5.

46. F. Snowden, 'From Triumph to Disaster: Fascism and Malaria in the Pontine Marshes, 1928–1946', in Dickie et al. (eds), *Disastro!*, p. 124.

47. There are numerous (ongoing) debates about the extent and causes of this 'revolution'. For an overview see Cohen and Federico, *The Growth*. Some have argued that there was no real revolution, but a series of economic cycles. Others underlined the key role of German credit and savings banks in the 1890s. Other debates have concentrated on the role of the agrarian economy. It may be that historians simply expected there to be an industrial revolution at some point – another case of Italy being seen only in relation to the models imposed by other countries.

48. In 1861 the UK produced 85 million tons of coal, Germany 18.7 million, Belgium 10 million, France 9.5 million and Italy a mere 34,000 tons.

49. Here great progress was made, through hydro-electric projects and Pirelli-built cables. Between 1900 and 1914 electricity production rose by 16 times, reaching the level of France and 75 per cent that of the UK.

50. D. Bigazzi, 'Un inventario del progetto del saper fare', in A. Pansera (ed.), *L'anima dell'industria: un secolo di disegno industriale nel Milanese* (Milan: Skira, 1996), p. 11.

51. A. Bull and P. Corner, *From Peasant to Entrepreneur: The Survival of the Family Economy in Italy* (Oxford: Berg, 1993), p. 4. See also P. Corner, *Contadini e industrializzazione: società rurale e impresa in Italia dal 1840 al 1940* (Bari: Laterza, 1993).

52. For silk, see A. Bull, 'The Lombard Silk Workers in the Nineteenth Century: an Industrial Workforce in a Rural Setting', *The Italianist*, 7 (1987), pp. 104–9; P. Corner, 'Il contadino-operaio dell'Italia Padana', in Bevilacqua (ed.), *Storia*, II (1990), pp. 751–83.

53. Corner, 'Il contadino-operaio dell'Italia Padana', p. 782.

54. Silk represented one-third of all exports from Italy in 1887, M. Meriggi, *Storia dell'Italia settentrionale dall'Ottocento a oggi* (Rome: Donzelli, 1996), p. 67. Crucial here was the market role of Milan, with its stock exchange and sophisticated banking and market services.

55. And with Italy in general, see E. Galli della Loggia, 'La Fiat e l'Italia', in C. Annibaldi and G. Berta (eds), *Grande impresa e sviluppo italiano* (Bologna: Il Mulino, 1999), pp. 7–36.

56. F. Barca (ed.), *Storia del capitalismo italiano dal dopoguerra a oggi* (Rome: Donzelli editore, 1997).

57. M. Revelli, *Lavorare in Fiat* (Milan: Garzanti, 1989), p. 5.

58. See, above all, M. Gribaudi's work on Turin, *Mondo operaio e mito operaio. Spazi e percorsi sociali a Torino nel primo Novecento* (Turin: Einaudi, 1987).

59. L. Gianotti, *Gli operai della Fiat hanno cento anni* (Rome: Riuniti, 1999), p. 21.

60. T. Mason, 'The Turin Strikes of March 1943', in T. Mason, *Nazism, Fascism and the Working Class: Essays by Tim Mason* (Cambridge: Cambridge University Press, 1995), pp. 274–95.

61. F. Amatori and F. Brioschi, 'Le grandi imprese private: famiglie e coalizioni', in Barca, *Storia*, pp. 117–53.

62. P. Bairati, *Valletta* (Turin: UTET, 1983).

63. M. De Cecco and A. Pedone, 'Le istituzioni dell'economia', in R. Romanelli (ed.), *Storia dello Stato Italiano dall'Unità a oggi* (Rome: Donzelli, 1995), p. 261.

64. Cohen and Federico, *The Growth*, p. 39.

65. *La Repubblica*, 27 November 1997.

66. G. Lerner, *Operai. Viaggio all'interno della Fiat. La vita, le case, le fabbriche di una classe che non c'è più* (Milan: Feltrinelli, 1988), pp. 177, 178, 180.

67. S. Brusco and S. Paba, 'Per una storia dei distretti industriali italiani dal secondo dopoguerra agli anni Novanta', in Barca, *Storia*, pp. 277–8.

68. A. Branzi, 'Italian Design and the Complexity of Modernity', in G. Celant (ed.), *The Italian Metamorphosis, 1943–1968* (New York: Guggenheim Museum, 1994), p. 602.

69. V. Zamagni, *Lo stato italiano e l'economia. Storia dell'intervento pubblico dall'unificazione ai giorni nostri* (Florence: Le Monnier, 1981).

70. V. Zamagni, *The Economic History of Italy, 1860–1990* (Oxford: Oxford University Press, 1993) p. 154.

71. F. Bonelli, 'Il capitalismo italiano. Linee generali d'interpretazione', in *Storia d'Italia, Annali 1, Dal feudalismo al capitalismo* (Turin: Einaudi, 1979), pp. 1193–256.

72. See for example, V. Zamagni, 'Alcune tesi sull'intervento dello stato in una prospettiva di lungo periodo', in P. L. Ciocca (ed.), *Il progresso economico in Italia* (Bologna: Il Mulino, 1994), pp. 151–60; G. Federico and R. Giannetti, 'Italy: Stalling and Surpassing', in J. Foreman-Peck and G. Federico (eds), *The Mediterranean Response to Globalisation before 1950* (London), pp. 269–96.

73. Cohen and Federico, *The Growth*, p. 66.

74. Barca, *Storia*, p. 101.

75. Ibid., p. 12.

76. Ibid., p. 42.

77. L. Cafagna, 'La industrializzazione ritardata tra Ottocento e Novecento', *La Storia*, vol. 6, *L'Età Contemporanea*, 1, 'I quadri generali' (Turin: UTET, 1988), pp. 54 and 66; M. Aymard, 'Nation-states and Interregional Disparities of Development', in G. Arrighi (ed.), *Semiperipheral Development: The Politics of Southern Europe in the Twentieth Century* (Beverly Hills, CA: Sage, 1985), p. 53.

78. G. Toniolo, *An Economic History of Liberal Italy, 1850–1918* (London and New York: Routledge, 1990), p. 49.

79. P. Bevilacqua, *Breve storia dell'Italia meridionale dall'Ottocento a oggi* (Rome: Donzelli, 1993), pp. iix, ix.

80. J. Morris, in Morris and Lumley, *A New History*, p. 3.

81. A. Gerschenkon, *Economic Backwardness in Historical Perspective* (Cambridge MA: Belknap Press, 1962). On backwardness and Italy, see also J. Agnew, 'The Myth of Backward Italy in Modern Europe', in B. Allen and M. Russo (eds), *Revisioning Italy: National Identity and Global Culture* (Minneapolis: University of Minnesota Press, 1997), pp. 23–42, who writes that '*true* modernity…is always around the corner or elsewhere, not in Italy'.

82. Cohen and Federico, *The Growth*, p. 26.

83. Ibid., p. 51.

84. L. Cafagna, cited in M. Meriggi, 'L'unificazione nazionale in Italia e in Germania', in *Storia Contemporanea* (Rome: Donzelli, 1997), p. 148.

85. Romeo, *Risorgimento e capitalismo*.

86. Nitti wrote in 1902 that 'to confront the problem of Basilicata signifies taking on the problems of the whole rural south'. In 1907, 75 per cent of Basilicata residents were classified as illiterate. Labour organizations were almost non-existent. Between 1898 and 1907 there was one strike in Basilicata.

87. Giuseppe Zanardelli, 'Discorso pronunciato a Potenza il 29 Settembre 1902', now in P. Corti (ed.), *Inchiesta Zanardelli sulla Basilicata* (Turin: Einaudi, 1976).
88. Corti (ed.), *Inchiesta*; see also Cohen and Federico, *The Growth*, who call the special laws 'little more than token measures', p. 28.
89. G. Salvemini, 'Un Comune dell'Italia meridionale: Molfetta', pp. 3–23, *Critica Sociale*, 1 and 16 March and 1 April 1897.
90. G. Salvemini, 'Molfetta 1954', in G. Salvemini, *Scritti sulla questione meridicnale, 1896–1955* (Turin: Einaudi, 1955), pp. 645–59.
91. J. Schneider and P. Schneider, *Culture and Political Economy in Western Sicily* (New York: Academic Press, 1976), p. 3.
92. Schneider and Schneider, *Festival of the Poor*, p. 280.
93. G. Gribaudi, *A Eboli. Il mondo meridionale in cent'anni di trasformazioni* (Venice: Marsilio, 1990).
94. Morris, in Humley and Morris, *The New History*, p. 12.
95. Gribaudi, *A Eboli*, p. 292.
96. Cohen and Federico, *The Growth*, p. 4.

4 POLITICS

1. Space does not permit separate discussion of a number of key issues with relation to Italian politics – political violence and the role of the extra-parliamentary Left (anarchists, revolutionaries) and Right, as well as the key area of referendums.
2. Francesco Crispi, 1865, cited in C. Duggan, *Francesco Crispi, 1818–1901: From Nation to Nationalism* (Oxford: Oxford University Press, 2002), p. 239.
3. For a sophisticated combination of these approaches, see P. Ginsborg, 'Italian Political Culture in Historical Perspective', *Modern Italy*, 1, 1 (1995), pp. 3–17.
4. J. Kurth, 'A Tale of Four Countries: Parallel Politics in Southern Europe, 1815–1990,' in J. Kurth and J. Petras (eds), *Mediterranean Paradoxes* (Oxford: Berg, 1993), p. 35.
5. Quoted in S. Fontana, 'Towards a History of Transformism (1883–1983)', in M. Donovan (ed.), *Italy*, Volume II (Dartmouth: Ashgate, 1998), pp. 305–21.
6. Ibid., p. 309.
7. G. Mosca, *Sulla teorica dei governi e sul governo parlamentare* (Palermo, 1884).
8. E. Gentile, 'Mussolini's Charisma', *Modern Italy*, 3, 2 (1998), pp. 219–35. For Mussolini, see also L. Passerini, *Mussolini immaginario. Storia di una biografia, 1915–1939* (Bari: Laterza, 1991), and S. Luzzatto, *Il corpo del duce. Un cadavere tra immaginazione, storia e memoria* (Turin: Einaudi, 1998).
9. G. Sapelli, 'The Italian Crisis and Capitalism', *Modern Italy*, 1, 1 (1995), p. 93.
10. For a history of the Republican ideal in Italy, see A. G. Ricci, *La Repubblica* (Bologna: Il Mulino, 2001).
11. On the difficulties of translating this term, which signifies something similar to 'putting a word in for' (recommending), but has a much wider cultural set of meanings, see D. L. Zinn, *La Raccomandazione. Clientelismo vecchio e nuovo* (Rome: Donzelli, 2001).
12. Political scientists have often downplayed the exchange aspects of clientelism. Graziano, for example, has defined clientelism as 'the ways in which party leaders seek to use the institutions and public resources for their own ends', cited in

G. Van Loenen, 'Weimar or Byzantium: Two Opposing Approaches to the Italian Party System', *European Journal of Political Research*, 18 (1990), p. 246. The anthropologist Signorelli takes a much wider, and yet more personal, view of clientelism, which she defines as 'the use of public resources for private ends, and private resources (family, friendship, others) for public ends' (*Chi può e chi aspetti. Giovani e clientelismo in un'area interna del Mezzogiorno*) (Naples: Liguori editore, 1983).

13. P. A. Allum, *Potere e società a Napoli nel dopoguerra* (Turin: Einaudi, 1975), p. 408.

14. P. Allum, *Politics and Society in Post-war Naples* (Cambridge: Cambridge University Press, 1973); Chubb, *Patronage, Power and Poverty*.

15. L. Musella, *Individui, amici, clienti. Relazioni personali e circuiti politici in Italia meridionale tra Otto e Novecento* (Bologna: Il Mulino, 1994), p. 213.

16. G. Saredo, 'Inquest on Politics in Naples', cited in Musella, *Individui*, p. 205.

17. P. McCarthy, *La crisi dello Stato italiano. Costume e vita politica nell'Italia* (Rome: Riuniti, 1996); G. Pansa, *Bisaglia. Una carriera democristiana* (Milan: Sugarco, 1975).

18. See J. Foot, *Milan since the Miracle: City, Culture and Identity* (Oxford: Berg, 2001).

19. R. Carr, *Spain 1808–1975* (Oxford: Clarendon, 1982), p. 460.

20. Carr, *Spain*, pp. 366–79; G. Sapelli, *Southern Europe since 1945: Tradition and Modernity in Portugal, Spain, Italy, Greece and Turkey* (London: Longman, 1995), pp. 120 and 10 and in general Chapter 7.

21. Cited in L. Graziano, *Clientelismo e sistema politico. Il caso dell'Italia* (Milan: Franco Angeli, 1980), pp. 197–8.

22. M. Ferrara, 'The Rise and Fall of Democratic Universalism: Health Care Reform in Italy, 1978–1994', *Journal of Health Politics, Policy and Law*, 20, 2 (1995), p. 18.

23. McCarthy, *La crisi dello Stato*, p. 99.

24. Although in some cases peripheral politicians had far more patronage power than those in the centre.

25. *La raccomadazione*.

26. V. Bufacchi and S. Burgess, *L'Italia contesa. Dieci anni di lotta politica da Mani Pulite a Berlusconi* (Rome: Carocci, 2002), p. 18.

27. By Giuseppe Maranini, see *Storia del potere in Italia, 1848–1967* (Milan: Corbaccio, 1995).

28. M. Calise, 'The Italian Particracy: Beyond President and Parliament', *Political Science Quarterly*, 109, 3 (1994), p. 18.

29. A. Pizzorno, 'Le difficoltà del consociativismo', in A. Pizzorno, *Le radici della politica assoluta* (Milan: Feltrinelli, 1993), pp. 285–313.

30. G. Sapelli, *Cleptocrazia. Il meccanismi unico della corruzione tra economia e politica* (Milan: Feltrinelli, 1994).

31. M. Salvadori, *Storia d'Italia e crisi di regime. Alle radici della politica italiana* (Bologna: Il Mulino, 1994), p. 63. For the cold war in general, see M. Walker, *The Cold War and the Making of the Modern World* (London: Fourth Estate, 1993), and in Italy, C. Duggan and C. Wagstaff (eds), *Italy in the Cold War, Politics, Culture and Society* (Oxford: Berg, 1995). For a comparative discussion of the removal or resignation of communist parties in Belgium, France and Italy in March–June 1947, see A. Boxhoorn, *The Cold War and the Rift in the Governments of National Unity: Belgium, France and Italy in the Spring of 1947, a Comparison* (Amsterdam: Historisch Seminarium, van de Universiteit Van Amsterdam, 1993); see also B. Bongiovanni, *Storia della guerra fredda* (Bari: Laterza, 2001) and M. Del Pero, *La guerra fredda* (Rome: Carocci, 2001).

32. See S. Parker, 'The End of Italian Exceptionalism? Assessing the Transition to the Second Republic', *The Italianist*, 19 (1999), pp. 251–83.

33. J. Romero-Maura, 'Caciquismo as a Political System', in E. Gellner and J. Waterbury, *Patrons and Clients in Mediterranean Societies* (London: Duckworth, 1977), p. 54.

34. Carr, *Spain*, p. 365.

35. P. Pombeni, *Partiti e sistemi politici nella storia contemporanea (1830–1968)* (Bologna: Il Mulino, 1985), p. 456. For an excellent discussion of the debates surrounding the Liberals in post-unification Italy, see H. Ullrich, 'L'organizzazione politica dei liberali italiani nel Parlamento e nel Paese (1870–1914)', in R. Lill and N. Matteucci, *Il liberalismo in Italia e in Germania dalla rivoluzione del '48 alla prima guerra mondiale* (Bologna: Il Mulino, 1980), pp. 403–51.

36. A. W. Salomone, *Italian Democracy in the Making* (Philadelphia: University of Pennsylvania Press, 1945), p. 51.

37. The Republican Party were also important, if very regionally limited – their main strength was in the Romagna region, see M. Ridolfi, *Il partito della repubblica. I repubblicani in Romagna e le origini del Pri nell'Italia liberale (1972–1895)* (Milan: Franco Angeli, 1990); M. Ridolfi, *Il circolo virtuoso. Sociabilità democratica, associazionismo e rappresentanza politicale nell'Ottocento* (Florence: Centro editoriale Toscano, 1990); M. Ridolfi, *Il PSI e la nascita del partito di massa, 1892–1922* (Bari: Laterza, 1992).

38. Important parties which are not discussed in detail here include the Action Party (1943–6). For information on this organization, see G. De Luna, *Storia del Partito d'Azione (1942–1947)* (Rome: Riuniti, 1997). For the extra-parliamentary Left, see L. Bobbio, *Lotta Continua. Storia di un' organizzazione rivoluzionaria* (Rome: Savelli, 1979). For Rifondazione comunista and La Rete see J. Foot, 'The Left Opposition and the Crisis. Rifondazione Comunista and La Rete: 1989–1994', in S. Gundle and S. Parker (eds), *The New Italian Republic: From the Fall of the Berlin Wall to Berlusconi* (London: Routledge, 1996), pp. 173–88.

39. The PSI supported a number of liberal governments in the 1890s and early twentieth century, without ever becoming part of formal coalitions. The party was out of government between 1972 and 1973.

40. For the history of the revolutionary syndicalists, see C. Levy, 'Currents of Italian Syndicalism before 1926', *International Review of Social History*, 45 (2000), pp. 209–50.

41. In October 1922 a further split in the PSI saw the expulsion of the reformists, but there was no reunification with the Communist Party.

42. For a fascinating study of these victims see www.gulag-italia.it.

43. P. Togliatti, *Lectures on Fascism* (London: Lawrence and Wishart, 1976).

44. J. Femia, *Gramsci's Political Thought: Hegemony, Consciousness and the Revolutionary Process* (Oxford: Clarendon Press, 1987).

45. D. Kertzer, *Comrades and Christians: Religion and Political Struggle in Communist Italy* (Cambridge: Cambridge University Press, 1980); S. Gundle, *Between Hollywood and Moscow: The Italian Communists and the Challenge of Mass Culture, 1943–1991* (Durham, NC: Duke University Press, 2000).

46. G. Galli, *Il bipartitismo imperfetto* (Bologna: Il Mulino, 1966). For the debates amongst political scientists concerning the Italian political system, see P. Farneti, *The Italian Party System (1945–1980)* (London: Pinter, 1985); G. Pasquino, 'Sources of Stability and Instability in the Italian Party System', *West European Politics*, 6

(1983), pp. 93–110; G. Sartori, *Parties and Party Systems: A Framework for Analysis* (Cambridge: Cambridge University Press, 1976).

47. Gundle, *Between Hollywood and Moscow*; D. Kertzer, *Politics and Symbols: The Italian Communist Party and the Fall of Communism* (New Haven, CT: Yale University Press, 1996), see also Box 4.4.

48. D. Kertzer, 'The 19th Congress of the PCI: the Role of Symbolism in the Communist Crisis', in R. Leonardi and F. Anderlini (eds), *Italian Politics: A Review*, vol. 6 (London: Pinter, 1992), pp. 69–82.

49. M. Flores, 'Il Pds', *Linea d'ombra*, 72 (1992), pp. 6–7; see also M. Flores and N. Gallerano, *Sul PCI. Un'interpretazione storica* (Bologna: Il Mulino, 1992). For a comparative analysis (the material available here, on both communism and socialism, is vast) see D. Sassoon, *One Hundred Years of Socialism: the West European Left in the Twentieth Century* (London: Tauris, 1996); G. Di Palma, 'Eurocommunism?' *Comparative Politics*, IX (April 1977), pp. 357–75; D. Blackmer and S. Tarrow (eds), *Communism in Italy and France* (Princeton, NJ: Princeton University Press, 1977); R. Blackburn (ed.), *After the Fall: The Failure of Communism and the Future of Socialism* (London: Verso, 1991); M. J. Bull and P. Heywood, *West European Communist Parties After the Revolutions of 1989* (Basingstoke: Macmillan, 1994); R. Dunphy, *From Eurocommunism to Eurosocialism: The Search for a Post-Communist European Left* (Dundee: Department of Political Science, 1993); P. Anderson and P. Camiller (eds), *Mapping the West European Left* (London: Verso, 1994).

50. See J. Foot, 'White Bolsheviks'? The Catholic Left and the Socialists in Italy – 1919–1920', *Historical Journal*, 40, 2 (1997), pp. 415–33.

51. For the DC and coalitions, see the wide-ranging study by G. Pridham, *Political Parties and Coalitional Behaviour in Italy* (London: Routledge, 1988).

52. Chubb, *Patronage, Power and Poverty*, p. 10.

53. Allum calculated that in the 1970s there were 1,800 Catholic publications in Italy, with a total of 16,000,000 copies. *Famiglia Cristiana* was the biggest selling magazine in Italy. In 1960 Italy could count on 64,000 priests, 172,000 monks and nuns and 360 bishops, see P. Allum, *Italy: Republic without Government?* (London: Norton, 1973), p. 53. The 'non-political' organization Catholic Action peaked at 3,000,000 members with 80,000 associations in the 1960s, before going into rapid decline. Of course, the Church could also count on an extensive network of schools, universities, nurseries, playgrounds and social centres, welfare services, charities and hospitals.

54. Cited in P. Allum, '"From Two into One": The Faces of the Italian Christian Democratic Party', *Party Politics*, 3, 1 (1997), pp. 23–52. See also L. Elia and G. Vassalli, *I quarant'anni della Costituzione* (Milan: Libri Scheiwiller, 1989). For the DC, see M. Einaudi and F. Goguel, *Christian Democracy in Italy and France* (Notre Dame, IL: University of Notre Dame Press, 1952); R. A. Webster, *Christian Democracy in Italy, 1860–1960* (London: Hollis and Carter, 1961); M. Calise, *Il sistema DC. Mediazione e conflitto nelle campagne democristiane* (Bari: De Donato, 1978); M. Follini, *C'era una volta la DC* (Bologna: Il Mulino, 1994); G. Galli, *Storia della Democrazia Cristiana* (Rome: Laterza, 1978); D. Hanley (ed.), *Christian Democracy in Europe: A Comparative Perspective* (London: Pinter, 1994); P. Furlong, *The Italian Christian Democrats: From Catholic Movement to Conservative Party* (Hull: Department of Politics, 1982); A. De Gasperi, *Idee sulla Democrazia Cristiana* (Rome: Edizioni

Cinque Lune, 1974); P. Scoppola, *Dal neoguelfismo alla Democrazia Cristiana* (Rome: Editrice Studium, 1963).

55. Others argue that the Albertine Statute survived the fascist period virtually intact; see, for example, L. Paladin, in *Enciclopedia del diritto* (Milan: Giuffre, 1967), vol. XVI. See also P. Pombeni, 'The Roots of the Italian Political Crisis: A View from History, 1918, 1945, 1989...and After', in C. Levy and M. Roseman (eds), *Three Postwar Eras in Comparison: Western Europe, 1918–1945–1989* (Basingstoke: Palgrave Macmillan, 2002), pp. 276–96.

56. P. Pombeni, *Demagogia e tirannide. Uno studio sulla forma partito del fascismo* (Bologna: Il Mulino, 1984), and P. Pombeni, 'Il partito fascista', in A. Del Boca, M. Legnani and M. Rossi (eds), *Il regime fascista. Storia e storiografia* (Bari: Laterza, 1995), pp. 203–19.

57. G. De Luna, *Le vicende politiche dal dopoguerra al centrosinistra* ('Storia dell'Italia repubblicana: dalla ricostruzione al boom economico', 15 dicembre 1997, Istituto per la storia della Resistenza e della società contemporanea di Asti).

58. See Gentile, *Storia del Partito Fascista*, and Pombeni, *Demagogia e tirannide*.

59. V. De Grazia, *How Fascism Ruled Women: Italy, 1922–1945* (Berkeley, CA: California University Press, 1992); see also P. Willson, *The Clockwork Factory: Women and Work in Fascist Italy* (Oxford: Clarendon Press, 1993).

60. M. Salvati, 'Da piccola borghesia a ceti medi', in Del Boca, Legnani and Rossi (eds), *Il regime fascista*, p. 467.

61. R. J. B. Bosworth, *Mussolini* (London: Arnold, 2002), p. 232.

62. Ibid., p. 181.

63. L. Ganapini, *La Repubblica delle camicie nere* (Milan: Garzanti, 1999).

64. Of minor interest were the various monarchist groupings, who continued to pick up votes and support right up to the 1970s, especially in the south. More important, if more short-lived, was the *Uomo Qualunque* movement set up by a charismatic journalist, Guglielmo Giannini, in 1946. This party gained significant numbers of votes, especially in Rome and the south, in the 1946 elections, winning 5.3 per cent of the national vote (with 20.7 per cent in Rome, 19.7 per cent in Naples, 46 per cent [with the Monarchists and Liberals] in Bari, and 47 per cent in Lecce), which revealed the deep distrust of the new state felt by many southerners, and their absence from the democratic movements of renewal who had organized the anti-fascist resistance, S. Setta, *L'Uomo Qualunque, 1944–1948* (Bari: Laterza [1975] 1995). With the formation of the MSI, the *Uomo Qualunque* lost most of its electorate and by 1948 was a spent force.

65. P. Ignazi and C. Ysmal, 'New and Old Extreme Right Parties', *European Journal of Political Research*, 22 (1992), p. 119.

66. For the *Lega Nord*, see Chapter 1. There is no space here to discuss the various other important regional parties which have campaigned in Italy since 1945 (and before) – from local organizations in the Valle d'Aosta, Trentino and Alto Adige, through to the separatist parties in Sicily after 1945 and the interesting experience of the Sardinian Action Party. Nor is there space to discuss the myriad of Catholic groups and parties which emerged from the decline of the DC and which eventually, in most cases, ended up on the centre–right or the centre–left.

67. R. Romanelli, *Il comando impossibile: Stato e società nell'Italia liberale* (Bologna: Il Mulino, 1995).

68. Romero-Maura, 'Caciquismo as a Political System', p. 54.

69. Cited in F. Andreucci, 'La norma e la prassi. Le elezioni irregolari nell'Italia liberale (1861–1880)', *Passato e Presente*, 34 (1995), pp. 39–78.

70. The relevant Articles are Article 56 [The Chamber of Deputies]: (1) The Chamber of Deputies shall be elected by universal and direct suffrage. (2) The number of deputies shall be six hundred and thirty. (3) All those voters who have reached the age of twenty-five years on the day of the election may be elected as deputies. Article 57 [The Senate of the Republic]: (1) The Senate of the Republic shall be elected on a regional basis. (2) Elected senators shall be three hundred and fifteen. No Region shall have less than seven senators; Molise shall have two senators and Valle d'Aosta one. Article 58 [Elections for the Senate]: (1) Senators shall be elected by universal and direct ballot by voters over twenty-five years of age. (2) All voters over forty years of age may be elected to the Senate. Article 61 [Elections]: (1) Elections for the new Chambers must take place within seventy days from the dissolution of the previous Chambers. The first sitting must be held not later than twenty days after the elections.

71. Italians abroad were also given votes in national elections via a 2000 law. Twelve constituencies were dedicated to these Italians (for the Lower House) and six in the Senate.

72. The only reform which Parliament was able to produce without the push of a referendum was that for the election of local mayors (a two-round system with extra seats for the winner, acknowledged by everyone as the best electoral system at work in Italy). Later, similar systems were introduced for the direct election of Provincial Presidents and Regional Presidents.

73. D. Gambetta and S. Warner, 'The Rhetoric of Reform Revealed (or: If you bite the ballot it may bite back)', *Journal of Modern Italian Studies*, 1, 3 (1996).

74. This 4 per cent applies to lists not connected to a coalition. The figure is reduced to 2 per cent for those within coalition lists which win more than 10 per cent of the overall vote.

75. The cut-off points for coalitions and parties were also different for the Senate.

76. Duggan, *Francesco Crispi*, p. 415.

77. There is far too little in general in this book concerning questions of gender and women's history and politics. For some indications, see P. Gabrielli, *Il 1946, la donna, la Repubblica* (Rome: Donzelli, 2009); P. Willson, *Women in Twentieth Century Italy* (London: Palgrave, 2010); Perry Willson (ed.), *Gender, Family and Sexuality: The Private Sphere in Italy, 1860–1945* (London: Palgrave, 2004).

78. G. E. Rusconi, *Se cessiamo di essere una nazione* (Bologna: Il Mulino, 1993).

79. See G. Nevola, 'A Constitutional Patriotism for Italian Democracy: the Contribution of President Napolitano', *Bulletin of Italian Politics*, 3, 1 (2011), pp. 159–84. The important role of various presidents in reinforcing or creating this 'constitutional patriotism' should be underlined here, in particular the tenures of Sandro Pertini (1978–85), Oscar Luigi Scalfaro (1992–99) and Carlo Azeglio Ciampi (1999–2006). See also G. Napolitano, *Il patto che ci lega. Per una coscienza repubblicana* (Bologna: Il Mulino, 2009) and M. Viroli, *For Love of Country: An Essay on Patriotism and Nationalism* (Oxford: Clarendon Press, 1995).

80. See J. Habermas, 'Staatsbürgerschaft und nationale Identität', in *Faktizität und Geltung* (Frankfurt: Suhrkamp, 1992), pp. 632–60.

81. G. Napolitano, *Una e indivisibile. Riflessioni sui 150 anni della nostra Italia* (Milan: Rizzoli, 2011), p. 140.
82. L. Passerini, 'Memories of Resistance, Resistances of Memory', in H. Peitsch et al. (eds), *European Memories of the Second World War* (New York and Oxford: Berghahn, 1999), p. 289.
83. Foot, *Italy's Divided Memory*, p. 1.

Bibliography and Further Reading

(This bibliography should be used in conjunction with the various chapters in the book and with the boxes.)

GENERAL AND REFERENCE WORKS

Allum, P., *State and Society in Western Europe* (Cambridge: Polity, 1995).
Baldoli, C., *A History of Italy* (London: Palgrave, 2009).
Baranski, Z. and R. J. West (eds), *The Cambridge Companion to Modern Italian Culture* (Cambridge: Cambridge University Press, 2001).
Candeloro, G., *Storia dell'Italia moderna*, 11 vols (Milan: Feltrinelli, 1970–86).
Cannistraro, P., *Historical Dictionary of Fascist Italy* (Westport, CT and London: Greenwood, 1982).
Carter, N., *Modern Italy in Historical Perspective* (London: Bloomsbury, 2010).
Castronovo, V., *Storia economica d'Italia: dall'Ottocento ai giorni nostri* (Turin: Einaudi, 1995).
Chabod, F., *L'Italia contemporanea (1919–1948)* (Turin: Einaudi, 1961).
Clark, M., *Modern Italy, 1871–1995*, 3rd edn (London: Pearson, 2008).
Colarizi, S., *Storia del Novecento italiano* (Milan: Rizzoli, 2013).
——, *Storia dei partiti nell'Italia repubblicana* (Bari: Laterza, 1996).
Coppa, F. (ed.), *Dictionary of Modern Italian History* (Westport, CT: Greenwood, 1985).
Crainz, G., *Storia del miracolo italiano. Culture, identità, trasformazioni fra anni cinquanta e sessanta* (Rome: Donzelli, 2003).
——, *Il paese mancato. Dal miracolo economico agli anni ottanta* (Rome: Donzelli, 2003).
——, *Autobiografia di una repubblica. Le radici dell'Italia attuale* (Rome: Donzelli, 2009).
——, *Il paese reale. Dall'assassinio di Moro all'Italia di oggi* (Rome: Donzelli, 2012).
Davis, J. (ed.), *Italy in the Nineteenth Century, 1796–1900* (Oxford: Oxford University Press, 2000).

——, 'Modern Italy – Changing Historical Perspectives since 1945', in M. Bentley (ed.), *Companion to Historiography* (London and New York: Routledge, 1997), pp. 591–619.

De Benardi, A. and L. Ganapini, *Storia d'Italia, 1860–1995* (Milan: Bruno Mondadori, 1996).

Deaglio, E., *Patria. 1978–2010* (Milan: Il Saggiatore, 2010).

Dizionario di storia (Milan: Bruno Mondadori, 1993).

Donovan, M., *Italy*, 2 vols (Dartmouth: Ashgate, 1998).

Duggan, C., *A Concise History of Italy*, 2nd edn (Cambridge: Cambridge University Press, 2013).

——, *The Force of Destiny: A History of Italy since 1796* (London: Harcourt, 2008).

Emmott, B., *Good Italy, Bad Italy: Why Italy Must Conquer its Demons to Face the Future* (New Haven: Yale University Press, 2013).

Gilmour, D., *The Pursuit of Italy: A History of a Land, its Regions and their Peoples* (London: Farrar, Straus and Giroux, 2012).

Ginsborg, P., *A History of Contemporary Italy: Society and Politics, 1943–1988* (London: Penguin, 1990).

——, *Italy and its Discontents: Family, Civil Society, State, 1980–2001* (London: Penguin, 2002).

——, '"Prologue" to *Salviamo l'Italia* (Turin: Einaudi, 2010)', *California Italian Studies*, 2, 1, http://escholarship.org/uc/item/1dz8v1nn (accessed 23 May 2013).

Gundle, S. and S. Parker (eds), *The New Italian Republic: From the Fall of the Berlin Wall to Berlusconi* (London: Routledge, 1996).

Hine, D., *Governing Italy* (Oxford: Oxford University Press, 1993).

Holmes, G. (ed.), *An Illustrated History of Italy* (Oxford: Oxford University Press, 2001).

I giorni della storia d'Italia: dal Risorgimento a oggi: cronaca quotidiana dal 1815 (Novara: De Agostini, 1997).

Lanaro, S., *Storia dell'Italia repubblicana. Dalla fine della guerra agli Anni Novanta* (Venice: Marsilio, 1992).

Lepre, A., *Storia della prima Repubblica. L'Italia dal 1942 al 1992* (Bologna: Il Mulino, 1999).

Lyttelton, A. (ed.), *Liberal and Fascist Italy, 1900–1945* (Oxford: Oxford University Press, 2002).

Mack Smith, D., *Modern Italy: a Political History* (New Haven, CT: Yale University Press, 1997).

Mammarella, G., *L'Italia di oggi* (Bologna: Il Mulino, 2012).

Moliterno, G. (ed.), *Encyclopedia of Contemporary Italian Culture* (London: Routledge, 2000).

Sassoon, D., *Contemporary Italy: Politics, Economy, and Society*, 2nd edn (London: Longman, 1996).

Schnapp, J., *Modernitalia* (ed. F. Santovetti; London: Peter Lang, 2012).

Seton-Watson, C., *Italy from Liberalism to Fascism, 1870–1925* (London: Methuen, 1967).

Zamagni, V., *The Economic History of Italy, 1860–1990* (Oxford: Clarendon, 1993).

Italian History Internet Link: http://sissco.iue.it/VL/hist.italy/index.html

Film:

From Garibaldi to Berlusconi, 150 years of Italian History (*Andante ma non Troppo. 150 anni di Storia d'Italia*) (E. Cerasuolo, 2011).

INTRODUCTION: STUDYING ITALY

Agnew, J., *Place and Politics: The Geographical Mediation of Space and Society* (London: Allen and Unwin, 1987).

——, *Place and Politics in Modern Italy* (Chicago: Chicago University Press, 2002).

Allum, P., *State and Society in Western Europe* (Cambridge: Polity, 1995).

Aprile, P., *Terroni. Tutto quello che è stato fatto perché gli italiani del Sud diventassero Meridionali* (Rome: Piemme, 2010).

Barzini, L., *The Italians* (London: Penguin, 1968).

Bidussa, D., 'Dalla storia alla prosodia? Il dibattito sui libri di testo', *I viaggi di Erodoto*, 41/42 (2000), pp. 68–73.

Bocca, G., *Il secolo sbagliato* (Milan: Mondadori, 2000).

Bosworth, R., *Italy: The Least of the Great Powers* (Cambridge: Cambridge University Press, 1979).

——, *Italy and the Wider World: 1860–1960* (London: Routledge, 1996).

——, *The Italian Dictatorship: Problems and Perspectives in the Interpretation of Mussolini and Fascism* (London: Arnold, 1998).

Braudel, F., *The Mediterranean* (London and New York, 1973).

Ciampi, Carlo Azeglio, *Discorso a Cefalonia* (1 March 2001; reprinted in *Diario della Settimana*, 4 May 2001).

Clark, M., *Modern Italy, 1871 to the Present*, 3rd edn (Harlow: Pearson, 2008).

Clough, S. and S. Saladino, *A History of Modern Italy: Documents, Readings and Commentary* (New York and London: Columbia University Press, 1968).

Colarizi, S., *Il novecento italiano* (Milan: Rizzoli, 2000).

Contini, G., *La memoria divisa* (Milan: Rizzoli, 1997).

Contini, G. (ed.), *Un'isola in terra ferma. Storia orale di una comunità mineraria dell'Amiata* (Siena: Il Leccio, 1995).

Cooke, P., *The Legacy of the Italian Resistance* (London: Palgrave, 2011).

Craveri, P., *La Repubblica dal 1958 al 1992* (Milan: TEA, 1992).

Crouch, C., *Post-Democracy* (Cambridge: Polity, 2004).

Dal Lago, E. and R. Halpern (eds), *The American South and the Italian Mezzogiorno: Essays in Comparative History* (Basingstoke: Palgrave, 2002).

Davis, J., *People of the Mediterranean: An Essay in Comparative Social Anthropology* (London: Routledge & Kegan Paul, 1977).

Davis, J. (ed.), *Italy in the Nineteenth Century, 1796–1900* (Oxford: Oxford University Press, 2000).

de Bernières, L., *Captain Corelli's Mandolin* (1994; translated into Italian with the title *Una vita in debito*). Republished as *Il mandolino del capitano Corelli* (2001).

De Felice, R., *Mussolini* (Turin: Einaudi, 1965–97).

——, *Fascism, an Informal Introduction to its Theory and Practice* (New Brunswick: Transaction, 1976).

——, *Il rosso e il nero* (Milan: Baldini and Castoldi, 1995).

De Grazia, V., *The Culture of Consent: Mass Organization of Leisure in Fascist Italy* (Cambridge: Cambridge University Press, 1981).

Duggan, C., *Fascist Voices: An Intimate History of Mussolini's Italy* (London: Bodley Head, 2011).

——, *A Concise History of Italy*, 2nd edn (Cambridge: Cambridge University Press, 2013).

Dunnage, J., *Twentieth Century Italy: a Social History* (London: Longman, 2002).

Focardi, F., *Il cattivo tedesco e il bravo italiano: La rimozione delle colpe della seconda guerra mondiale* (Bari: Laterza, 2013).

Foot, J., 'Divided Memories in Italy: Stories from the Twentieth and Twenty-first Centuries', in K. Hall and K. Jones (eds), *Transmitting Memories of the Past in European Historiography, Culture and Media* (Oxford: Peter Lang, 2011), pp. 204–21.

——, *Italy's Divided Memory* (New York: Palgrave, 2009).

Forgacs, D. and R. Lumley (eds), *Italian Cultural Studies* (Cambridge: Cambridge University Press, 1997).

Galli della Loggia, E., *La morte della patria: La crisi dell'idea di nazione tra Resistenza antifascismo e Repubblica* (Rome: Laterza, 1999).

Giner, S., 'Political Economy, Legitimation and the State in Southern Europe', in R. Hudson and J. Lewis (eds), *Uneven Development in Southern Europe: Studies of Accumulation, Class, Migration and the State* (London: Methuen, 1985), pp. 309–51.

Ginsborg, P., *A History of Contemporary Italy: Society and Politics, 1943–1988* (London: Penguin, 1990).

——, *Italy and its Discontents: Family, Civil Society, State, 1980–2001* (London: Penguin, 2002).

——, '"Prologue" to *Salviamo l'Italia* (Turin: Einaudi, 2010)', *California Italian Studies*, 2, 1, http://escholarship.org/uc/item/1dz8v1nn

Ginzburg, C., *Miti emblemi spie* (Turin: Einaudi, 1974).

——, *The Cheese and the Worms: The Cosmos of a Sixteenth-Century Miller* (London: Routledge, 1980).

Gobetti, E., *Alleati del nemico: L'occupazione italiana in Jugoslavia (1941–1943)* (Bari: Laterza, 2013).

Gribaudi, G., *Guerra totale: Tra bombe alleate e violenze naziste. Napoli e il fronte meridionale 1940–41* (Turin: Bollati Boringhieri, 2005).

Guarracino, S., 'Le periodizzazioni del Novecento', *I viaggi di Erodoto*, 41/42 (2000), pp. 151–8.

Gundle, S., *Death and the Dolce Vita: The Dark Side of Rome in the 1950s* (London: Canongate, 2012).

Gundle, S. and N. O'Sullivan, 'The Mass Media and the Political Crisis', in S. Gundle and S. Parker (eds), *The New Italian Republic: From the Fall of the Berlin Wall to Berlusconi* (London: Routledge, 1996).

Gundle, S. and S. Parker (eds), *The New Italian Republic: From the Fall of the Berlin Wall to Berlusconi* (London: Routledge, 1996).

Hine, D., *Governing Italy* (Oxford: Oxford University Press, 1993).

Hobsbawm, E., *Age of Extremes: The Short Twentieth Century, 1914–1991* (London: M. Joseph, 1994).

Holden, P. and N. Purcell, *The Corrupting Sea: A Study of Mediterranean History* (Oxford: Blackwell, 2000).

Hudson, R. and J. Lewis (eds), *Uneven Development in Southern Europe: Studies of Accumulation, Class, Migration and the State* (London: Methuen, 1985).

Katzenstein, P., T. Lowi and S. Tarrow (eds), *Comparative Theory and Political Experience: Mario Einaudi and the Liberal Tradition* (London and Ithaca: Cornell University Press, 1990),

Kurth, J. and J. Petras (eds), *Mediterranean Paradoxes* (Oxford: Berg, 1993).

Levi, G., 'Italy: Catholicism, Power, Democracy and the Failure of the Past', in P. Furtado (ed.), *Histories of Nations: How their Identities Were Forged* (London: Thames and Hudson, 2012), pp. 266–7.

Levy, C., '1918–1945–1989: The Making and Unmaking of Stable Societies in Western Europe', in C. Levy and M. Roseman (eds), *Three Postwar Eras in Comparison: Western Europe, 1918–1945–1989* (Basingstoke: Palgrave Macmillan, 2002), pp. 1–39.

—— and M. Roseman (eds), *Three Postwar Eras in Comparison: Western Europe, 1918–1945–1989* (Basingstoke: Palgrave Macmillan, 2002).

Liebert, U. and M. Cotta (eds), *Parliament and Democratic Consolidation in Southern Europe* (London and New York: Pinter, 1990).

Lyttelton, A. (ed.), *Liberal and Fascist Italy, 1900–1945* (Oxford: Oxford University Press, 2002).

Mack Smith, D., *The Making of Italy, 1796–1866* (London: Macmillan, 1988).

——, *Modern Italy: a Political History* (New Haven, CT: Yale University Press, 1997).

Mazower, M., *Dark Continent: Europe's Twentieth Century* (London: Allen Lane, 1998).

——, *Hitler's Greece: The Experience of Occupation, 1941–1944* (New Haven, CT: Yale University Press, 1993).

McCarthy, P. (ed.), *Italy since 1945* (Oxford: Oxford University Press, 2000).

Meny, Y., *Government and Politics in Western Europe* (Oxford: Oxford University Press, 1998).

Morlino, L., *Democracy between Consolidation and Crisis* (Oxford: Oxford University Press, 1998).

Paggi, L. (ed.), *L'eccidio del Duomo di San Miniato. La memoria e la ricerca storica (1944–2044)* (San Miniato: Comune di San Miniato, 2004).

——, *Il «popolo dei morti». La Repubblica Italiana nata dalla guerra (1940–1946)* (Bologna: Il Mulino, 2009).

Passerini, L., *Fascism in Popular Memory: The Cultural Experience of the Turin Working Class* (Cambridge: Cambridge University Press, 1987).

Pes, L., 'Descrivere il territorio: il punto di vista storico', *I viaggi di Erodoto*, 12, 34 (1998), pp. 50–1.

Portelli, A., *The Battle of Valle Giulia: Oral History and the Art of Dialogue* (Wisconsin: Wisconsin University Press, 1997).

——, *The Death of Luigi Trastulli and Other Stories: Form and Meaning in Oral History* (New York: State University of New York Press, 1991).

Preston, P., 'The Great Civil War: European Politics, 1914–1945', in T. Blanning (ed.), *The Oxford History of Contemporary Europe* (Oxford: Oxford University Press, 1995), pp. 148–81.

Pridham, G. (ed.), *Encouraging Democracy: The International Context of Regime Transition in Southern Europe* (New York: St Martin's Press, 1991).

——, *Transitions to Democracy: Comparative Perspectives from Southern Europe, Latin America and Eastern Europe* (Aldershot: Dartmouth, 1995).

Ranzato, G. (ed.), *Guerre fratricide. Le guerre civili in età contemporanea* (Turin: Bollati Boringhieri, 1994).

Rochat, G. and M. Venturi (eds), *La divisione Acqui a Cefalonia. Settembre 1943* (Milan: Mursia, 1993).

Sapelli, G., *Southern Europe since 1945: Tradition and Modernity in Portugal, Spain, Italy, Greece and Turkey* (London: Longman, 1995).

Sassoon, D., *Contemporary Italy: Politics, Economy, and Society*, 2nd edn (London: Longman, 1996).

Scwarz, G. *Tu mi devi seppellir. Riti funebri e culto nazionale alle origini della Repubblica* (Turin: UTET, 2010).

Seton-Watson, C., *Italy from Liberalism to Fascism, 1870–1925* (London: Methuen, 1967).

Spotts, F. and T. Weiser, *Italy: A Difficult Democracy* (Cambridge: Cambridge University Press, 1986).

Venturi, M., *Bandiera bianca a Cefalonia* (1963; 2nd edn 1972, with an introduction by Sandro Pertini). Republished in 1997; translated into English as *The White Flag* (1966).

Williams, A. (ed.), *Southern Europe Transformed: Political and Economic Change in Greece, Italy, Portugal and Spain* (London: Harper and Row, 1984).

CHAPTER 1: THE NATION

General Bibliography

Absalom, R., *A Strange Alliance: Aspects of Escape and Survival in Italy, 1943–1945* (Florence: Olschki, 1991).

Aga Rossi, E., *Una Nazione allo sbando: L'armistizio italiano del settembre 1943* (Bologna: Il Mulino, 1993).

'Alberto Banti's Interpretation of Risorgimento Nationalism: a Debate', in *Nations and Nationalism*, 15, 3 (2009), pp. 396–460.

Anderson, B., *Imagined Communities: Reflections on the Origin and Spread of Nationalism*, new edn (London: Verso, 1991).

Banfield, E., *The Moral Basis of a Backward Society* (Glencoe, IL: Free Press, 1958).

Banti, A. M., *L'onore della nazione. Identità sessuali e violenza nel nazionalismo europeo dal XVIII secolo alla Grande Guerra* (Turin: Einaudi, 2005).

——, *La nazione del Risorgimento. Parentela, santità e onore alle origini dell'Italia unita* (Turin: Einaudi, 2000).

—— and P. Ginsborg (eds), *Il Risorgimento* (Turin: Einaudi, 2007).

Belco, V., *War Massacre and Recovery in Central Italy, 1943–1948* (Toronto: Toronto University Press, 2010).

Bevilacqua, P., 'New and Old in the Southern Question', *Modern Italy*, 1, 2 (1996), pp. 81–92.

——, *Breve storia dell'Italia meridionale dall'Ottocento a oggi* (Rome: Donzelli, 1993).

Brice, C., '"The King was Pale": Italy's National–Popular Monarchy and the Construction of Disasters, 1882–1885', in J. Dickie, J. Foot and F. Snowden (eds), *Disastro! Disasters in Italy since 1860: Culture, Politics, Society* (New York: Palgrave, 2002), pp. 61–79.

Brunello, P., *Pionieri. Gli italiani in Brasile e il mito della frontiera* (Rome: Donzelli, 1994).

Dal Lago, E. and R. Halpern (eds), *The American South and the Italian Mezzogiorno: Essays in Comparative History* (Basingstoke: Palgrave, 2002).

d'Amico, R., *Burocrazia e ente Regione: L'appunto amministrativo della Regione siciliana* (Bologna: Il Mulino, 1978).

De Felice, R., *Il rosso e il nero* (Milan: Baldini and Castoldi, 1995).

De Mauro, T., *Storia linguistica dell'Italia Unita* (Bari: Laterza, 1963).

Dickie, J., 'Imagined Italies', in D. Forgacs and R. Lumley (eds), *Italian Cultural Studies* (Cambridge: Cambridge University Press, 1997), pp. 19–33.

——, *Darkest Italy: The Nation and Stereotypes of the Mezzogiorno, 1860–1900* (New York: St Martin's Press, 1999).

——, 'A Patriotic Disaster: the Messina-Reggio Calabria Earthquake of 1908', in G. Bedani and B. Haddock (eds), *The Politics of Italian National Identity* (Cardiff: University of Wales Press, 2000), pp. 50–71.

——, *Una catastrofe patriottica. 1908: il terremoto di Messina* (Bari: Laterza, 2008).

Foot, J., 'The Family and the "Economic Miracle": Social Transformation, Work, Leisure and Development at Bovisa and Comasina (Milan), 1950–1970', *Contemporary European History*, 4, 3 (1995), pp. 315–38.

——, *Calcio: A History of Italian Football* (London: Harper, 2007).

——, *Fratture d'Italia* (Milan: Rizzoli, 2009).

——, *Italy's Divided Memory* (New York: Palgrave, 2009).

——, *Pedalare! Pedalare!: A History of Italian Cycling* (London: Bloomsbury, 2012).

—— and S. Owen, 'Il centocinquantesimo anniversario dell'Unità d'Italia', in A. Bosco and D. McDonnell (eds), *Politica in Italia. I fatti dell'anno e le intepretazioni* (Bologna: Il Mulino, 2012), pp. 275–92.

Forcella, E. and A. Monticone, *Plotone di esecuzione. I processi della prima guerra mondiale* (Bari: Laterza, 1998).

Franzina, E., *Merica! Merica! Emigrazione e colonizzazione nelle lettere dei contadini veneti e friulani in America latina (1876–1902)* (Milan: Feltrinelli, 1979).

Franzinelli, M., 'L'8 settembre', in M. Isnenghi (ed.), *I luoghi della memoria* (Bari: Laterza, 1997), pp. 241–71.

Frye Jacobson, M., *Whiteness of a Different Colour: European Immigrants and the Alchemy of Race* (Cambridge and London: Harvard University Press, 1998).

Gabaccia, D., *Italy's Many Diasporas* (London: UCL Press, 2000).

Gallerano, M., *La nuova legge sulla cittadinanza italiana* (Rimini: Maggioli, 1994).

Galli della Loggia, E., *La morte della patria* (Bari: Laterza, 1999).

Gallino, L., *Dizionario di Sociologia* (Turin: UTET, 1993).

Gatti, F., *Bilal. Viaggiare, lavorare, morire da clandestini* (Milan: Rizzoli, 2008).

Gentile, E., *La Grande Italia: The Rise and Fall of the Myth of the Nation in the Twentieth Century* (Wisconsin: University of Wisconsin Press, 2008).

Ginsborg, P., *Salviamo l'Italia* (Turin: Einaudi, 2010).

Gooch, J., *Army, State and Society in Italy, 1870–1915* (London: Macmillan, 1989).

Horn, D., *Social Bodies: Science, Reproduction and Italian Modernity* (Princeton, NJ: Princeton University Press, 1994).

Ilari, V., 'Le forze armate', in G. Pasquino (ed.), *La politica italiana. Dizionario critico 1945–1995* (Bari: Laterza, 1995), pp. 47–59.

——, *Storia del servizio militare in Italia (1506–1870)*, vol. 1 (Rome: Centro militare di studi strategici, 1989).

Isnenghi, M., 'La Grande Guerra', in M. Isnenghi (ed.), *I luoghi della memoria* (Bari: Laterza, 1997), pp. 273–329.

——, *Le guerre degli italiani: Parole, immagini, ricordi, 1848–1945* (Milan: Mondadori, 1989).

——, *Gli Italiani in guerra. Conflitti, identità, memorie dal Risorgimento ai nostri giorni* (Turin: UTET, 2008).

—— and Eva Cecchinato (eds), *Fare l'Italia: unità e disunità nel Risorgimento* (Turin: UTET, 2008).

King, R. (ed.), *The Mediterranean Passage: Migration and New Cultural Encounters in Southern Europe* (Liverpool: Liverpool University Press, 2001).

—— and N. Mai, *Out of Albania: From Crisis Migration to Social Inclusion in Italy* (London: Berghahn Books, 2008).

Korner, A., *The Politics of Culture in Liberal Italy: From Unification to Fascism* (Routledge: London, 2008).

Lamont, W. (ed.), *Historical Controversies and Historians* (London: UCL Press, 1998).

Lazar, M., S. Romano and M. Canonica, *L'Italia disunita* (Milan: Longanesi, 2011).

Leed, E., *No Man's Land: Combat and Identity in World War One* (Cambridge: Cambridge University Press, 1979).

Lumley, R. and J. Morris (eds), *The New History of the Italian South: The Mezzogiorno Revisited* (Exeter: Exeter University Press, 1997).

Moe, N., *The View from Vesuvius: Italian Culture and the Southern Question* (Berkeley, CA: University of California Press, 2002).

Napolitano, G., *Il patto che ci lega. Per una coscienza repubblicana* (Bologna: Il Mulino, 2009).

——, *Una e indivisible. Riflessioni sui 150 anni della nostra Italia* (Milan: Rizzoli, 2011).

Oliva, G., 'La Naja', in M. Isnenghi (ed.), *I luoghi della memoria* (Bari: Laterza, 1997), pp. 95–109.

Passerini, L., *Fascism in Popular Memory: The Cultural Experience of the Turin Working Class* (Cambridge: Cambridge University Press, 1987).

Patriarca, S., *Italian Vices: Nation and Character from the Risorgimento to the Republic* (Cambridge: Cambridge University Press, 2010).

——, *Numbers and Nationhood: Writing Statistics in Nineteenth Century Italy* (Cambridge: Cambridge University Press, 2003).

Pavone, C., *Una guerra civile. Saggio storico sulla moralità della Resistenza* (Turin: Bollati Boringhieri, 1991).

Pecout, G., *Il lungo Risorgimento. La nascita dell'Italia contemporanea* (Milan: Bruno Mondadori, 2011).

Perlmutter, T., 'All Roads Lead to Rome: the Domestic and Geopolitics of "Enfranchising" Italians Abroad' (paper given to the Council for European Studies Conference, Chicago, April 2000).

Pezzino, P., *Memory and Massacre: Revisiting Sant'Anna di Stazzema* (London: Palgrave, 2012).

Pick, D., *Faces of Degeneration: A European Disorder, 1848–1918* (Cambridge: Cambridge University Press, 1989).

Procacci, G., 'The Disaster of Caporetto', in J. Dickie, J. Foot and F. Snowden (eds), *Disastro! Disasters in Italy since 1860: Culture, Politics, Society* (New York: Palgrave, 2002), pp. 141–61.

Putnam, R., with R. Leonardi and R. Y. Nanetti, *Making Democracy Work: Civic Traditions in Modern Italy* (Princeton, NJ: Princeton University Press, 1993).

Revelli, N., 'La ritirata di Russia', in M. Isnenghi (ed.), *I luoghi della memoria* (Bari: Laterza, 1997), pp. 365–80.

Rastello, L., *La frontiera addosso. Cosi si deportano i diritti umani* (Rome: Laterza, 2010).

Riall, L., *Sicily and the Unification of Italy: Liberal Politics and Local Power* (Oxford: Clarendon Press, 1998).

——, *Garibaldi: Invention of a Hero* (New Haven: Yale University Press, 2008).

——, *Risorgimento: The History of Italy from Napoleon to Nation State* (London: Palgrave, 2009),

——, *Under the Volcano: Empire and Revolution in a Sicilian Town* (Oxford: Oxford University Press, 2013).

—— and S. Patriarca (eds), *The Risorgimento Revisited: Nationalism and Culture in Nineteenth Century Italy* (London: Palgrave, 2012).

Rochat, G. and G. Massobrio, *Breve storia dell'esercito italiano dal 1861 al 1943* (Turin: Einaudi, 1978).

——, *L'esercito italiano in pace e in guerra: studi di storia militare* (Milan: RARA, 1992).

Rousso, H., *The Vichy Syndrome: History and Memory in France since 1944* (Boston: Harvard University Press, 1991).

Rusconi, G. E. (ed.), *Nazione, etnia, cittadinanza in Italia e in Europa: Per un discorso storico-culturale* (Brescia: Editrice La Scuola, 1993).

——, 'Will Italy Remain a Nation?', *Archives Européennes de Sociologie*, XXXIV (1993), pp. 309–21.

Sabbatucci, G., 'La vittoria mutilata', in G. Belardelli et al. (eds), *Miti e storia dell'Italia unita* (Bologna: Il Mulino, 1999), pp. 101–6.

Sales, I., 'Federalismo italiano', *Meridiana*, 43 (2002), pp. 238–52.

Salvemini, G., 'Fu L'Italia prefascista una democrazia?', *Il Ponte*, VIII, I (January 1952), pp. 11–23.

Salvietti, P., *Corda e sapone: Storie di linciaggi degli italiani negli Stati Uniti* (Rome: Donzelli, 2003).

Sapelli, G., *Southern Europe since 1945: Tradition and Modernity in Portugal, Spain, Italy, Greece and Turkey* (London: Longman, 1995).

Schneider, J. (ed.), *Italy's Southern Question: Orientalism in One Country?* (Oxford: Berg, 1998).

Smith, A., *National Identity* (London: Penguin, 1991).

Sullam, S. L., *L'apostolo a brandelli. L'eredità di Mazzini tra Risorgimento e fascismo* (Rome: Laterza, 2010).

Thompson, M., *The White War: Life and Death on the Italian Front, 1915–1919* (London: Faber and Faber, 2009).

Tocco, M., *Libro nero di Sicilia. Dietro le quinte della politica, degli affari e della cronaca della Regione Siciliana* (Milan: Sugarco editore, 1972).

Viroli, M., *For Love of Country: An Essay on Patriotism and Nationalism* (Oxford: Clarendon Press, 1995).

Whittam, J., *The Politics of the Italian Army, 1861–1918* (London: Croom Helm, 1977).

Box 1.1

Aprile, P., *Terroni. Tutto quello che e stato fatto perché gli italiani del sud diventassero "meridionali"* (Milan: Piemme, 2010).

Banti, A. M., *Sublime madre nostra. La nazione italiana dal Risorgimento al fascismo* (Bari: Laterza, 2011).

—— and P. Ginsborg (eds), *Il Risorgimento* (Turin: Einaudi, 2007).

Isabella, M., *Risorgimento in Exile: Italian Emigres and the Liberal International in the Post-Napoleonic Era* (Oxford: Oxford University Press, 2009).

Marwil, P., *Visiting Modern War in Risorgimento Italy* (London: Palgrave, 2010).

Riall, L., *Garibaldi: Invention of a Hero* (New Haven: Yale University Press, 2007).

Box 1.2

De Mauro, T. (ed.), *Come parlano gli italiani* (Florence: La Nuova Italia, 1994).

——, *Storia linguistica dell'Italia unita*, 8th edn (Bari: Laterza, 1998).

di Sparti, A., *Lingue a metà: plurilinguismo e emigrazione di ritorno in Sicilia* (Palermo: Centro studi filiologici, 1993).

Franzina, E., *Dall'Arcadia in America: attività letteraria ed emigrazione transoceanica in Italia (1850–1940)* (Turin: Fondazione Agnelli, 1996).

Lepschy, A. and G. Lepschy, *The Italian Language Today*, 2nd edn (London: Hutchinson, 1988).

Box 1.3

Alatri, P., *Nitti, D'Annunzio e la questione adriatica* (Milan: Feltrinelli, 1976).

Badoglio, P., *Rivelazioni su Fiume* (Rome: Donatello de Luigi, 1946).

De Ambris, A., *Dalla frode al fratricidio. Le responsabilità del governo italiano nella strage di Fiume, Novembre–Dicembre 1920* (Rome: La Fionda, 1921).

Hughes-Hallett, L., *The Pike: Gabriele D'Annunzio. Poet, Seducer and Preacher of War* (London: Fourth Estate, 2013).

Leeden, M., *The First Duce: D'Annunzio at Fiume* (Baltimore and London: Johns Hopkins University Press, 1977).

Woodhouse, J., *Gabriele D'Annunzio: Defiant Archangel* (Oxford: Oxford University Press, 1998).

Boxes 1.4–1.5

Baratieri, D., *Memories and Silences Haunted by Fascism: Italian Colonialism MCMXXX–MCMLX* (London: Peter Lang, 2010).

Bosworth, R. J. B. and P. Dogliani (eds), *Italian Fascism: History, Memory and Representation* (London: Macmillan, 1999), pp. 161–77.

De Felice, R., *Fascism: An Informal Introduction to its Theory and Practice* (New Jersey: Transaction Books, 1976).

Del Boca, A., *Gli italiani in Africa Orientale: Dall'Unità alla marcia su Roma*, 4 vols (Rome/Bari: Laterza, 1996, 1999).

——, *Gli italiani in Libia. Dal fascismo a Gheddafi*, 2 vols (Milan: Mondadori, 1997).

——, *L'Africa nella coscienza degli italiani. Miti, memorie, errori, sconfitte* (Bari: Laterza, 1992).

Dickie, J. and J. Foot, 'Introduction' to J. Dickie et al. (eds), *Disastro! Disasters in Italy since 1860: Culture, Politics, Society* (New York: Palgrave, 2002), pp. 3–51.

Doumanis, N., *Myth and Memory in the Mediterranean: Remembering Fascism's Empire* (Basingstoke: Macmillan, 1997).

——, 'The Italian Empire and Brava Gente: Oral History and the Dodecanese Islands', in G. Finaldi, 'Italy's Scramble for Africa from Dogali to Adowa', in Dickie et al. (eds), *Disastro!*, pp. 80–97.

Isnenghi, M. (ed.), *I luoghi dell'identità* (Bari: Laterza, 1997).

Kallis, A. A., *Fascist Ideology: Territory and Expansionism in Italy and Germany, 1922–1945* (London: Routledge, 2000).

Knox, M., *Common Destiny: Dictatorship, Foreign Policy and War in Fascist Italy and Nazi Germany* (Cambridge: Cambridge University Press, 2000).

Labanca, N., *Storia dell'Italia coloniale* (Milan: Fenice, 2000).

Lombardi-Diop, C. and C. Romeo (eds), *Postcolonial Italy: Challenging National Homogeneity* (New York: Palgrave, 2012).

Rodogno, D., *Fascism's European Empire: Italian Occupation during the Second World War* (Cambridge: Cambridge University Press, 2006).

Box 1.6

Ara, A. and E. Kolb (eds), *Regioni di frontiera nell'epoca dei nazionalismi: Alsazia e Lorena/ Trento e Trieste, 1870–1914*, Annali dell'Istituto storico italo-germanico, *Quaderno 41* (Bologna: Il Mulino, 1995).

de'Robertis, A. G., *La frontiera orientale italiana nella diplomazia della seconda guerra mondiale* (Naples: Edizioni scientifiche italiane, 1981).

Rabel, R. G., *Between East and West: Trieste, the United States and the Cold War, 1941–1954* (Durham, NC: Duke University Press, 1988).

Sapelli, G., *Trieste italiana: Mito e destino economico* (Milan: Franco Angeli, 1990).

Sluga, G., *The Problem of Trieste and the Italo-Yugoslav Border: Difference, Identity and Sovereignty in Twentieth-Century Europe* (Albany: State University of New York Press, 2001).

Box 1.7

Ambrosini, M., *Utili invasori: L'inserimento degli immigrati nel mercato del lavoro italiano* (Milan: Franco Angeli, 1999).

Andall, J. and D. Duncan (eds), *National Belongings Hybridity in Italian Colonial and Postcolonial Cultures* (London: Peter Lang, 2010).

Caniglia, B., *Italia e Albania (Ottobre 1914–Agosto 1920): Studio storico-politico-economico* (Rome: Fratelli Brocato, n.d.).

Dal Lago, A., *Non-persone: L'esclusione dei migranti in una società globale* (Milan: Feltrinelli, 1999).

Mai, N., '"Italy is Beautiful": the Role of Italian Television in Albanian Migration to Italy', in R. King and N. Woods (eds), *Media and Migration: Constructions of Mobility and Difference* (London and New York: Routledge, 2001), pp. 95–109.

Mannheimer, R. (ed.), *La Lega Lombarda* (Milan: Feltrinelli, 1991).

Maserati, E., *Momenti della questione adriatica (1896–1914): Albania e Montenegro tra Austria e Italia* (Verona: Del Bianco editore, 1981).

Parati, G., *Migration Italy: The Art of Talking Back in a Destination Culture* (Toronto: University of Toronto Press, 2005).

Stella, G. A., *Schei. Dal boom alla rivolta: il mitico nordest* (Milan: Mondadori, 2000).

Films:

G. Amelio, *Lamerica* (1994).

N. Moretti, *Aprile* (1996).

Box 1.8

Choate, M., *Emigrant Nation: The Making of Italy Abroad* (Boston: Harvard University Press, 2008).

Gabaccia, D., *From Sicily to Elizabeth Street: Housing and Social Change among Italian Immigrants, 1880–1930* (Albany: State University of New York Press, 1984).

Guglielmo, J. and S. Salerno, *Are Italians White? How Race Is Made in America* (London: Routledge, 2003).

Maffi, M., *Gateway to the Promised Land: Ethnic Cultures in New York's Lower East Side* (New York: New York University Press, 1995).

Riis, J., *How the Other Half Lives: Studies among the Tenements of New York* (London: Penguin, 1997).

Box 1.9

Agliani, T., G. Bigatti and U. Lucas (eds), *È un meridionale però ha voglia di lavorare* (Milan: Franco Angeli, 2011).

Alasia, F. and D. Montaldi, *Milano Corea: Inchiesta sugli immigrati* (Rome: Donzelli, 2010).

Cumoli, F., *Un tetto a chi lavora. Mondi operai e migrazioni italiane nell'Europa degli anni Cinquanta* (Milan: Guerini, 2012).

Foot, J., *Milan since the Miracle: City, Culture and Identity* (Oxford: Berg, 2001).

——, *Pero: città d'immigrazione* (Pero: Comune di Pero, 2002).

——, 'Southern Italian Immigrant Workers in Northern Italy: 1945–1975', in K. Bade, P. C. Emmer, L. Lucassen and J. Oltmer (eds), *The Encyclopedia of Migration and Minorities in Europe from the 17th Century to the Present* (Cambridge: Cambridge University Press, 2011), pp. 684–6.

Fofi, G., *L'immigrazione meridionale a Torino* (Milan: Feltrinelli, 1964).

——, 'Immigrants to Turin', in C. J. Jansen (ed.), *Readings in the Sociology of Migration* (Oxford: Pergamon, 1970).

King, R., 'Population Mobility: Emigration, Return Migration and Internal Migration', in A. Williams (ed.), *Southern Europe Transformed: Political and Economic Change in Greece, Italy, Portugal and Spain* (London: Harper and Row, 1984), pp. 145–78.

Sacchi, P. and P. P. Viazzo, *Più di un sud. Studi antropologici sull'immigrazione a Torino* (Milan: Franco Angeli, 2011).

Virciglio, G., *Milocca al nord: una comunità di immigrati siciliani ad Asti* (Milan: Franco Angeli, 1991).

Films:

L. Visconti, *Rocco and his Brothers* (1960).

G. Amelio, *Cosi ridevano* (1998).

Box 1.10

Andall, J., *Gender, Migration and Domestic Service: The Politics of Black Women in Italy* (Aldershot: Ashgate, 2000).

Cole, J., *The New Racism in Europe: A Sicilian Ethnography* (Cambridge: Cambridge University Press, 1998).

Foot, J., 'Immigration and the City: Milan and Mass Migration, 1950–1998', *Modern Italy*, 4, 2 (1999), pp. 159–72.

King, R. (ed.), Special Issue of *Modern Italy* on 'New Immigration to Italy' (1999).

——, *The Mediterranean Passage: Migration and New Cultural Encounters in Southern Europe* (Liverpool: Liverpool University Press, 2000).

Film: *L'orchestra di Piazza Vittorio* (A. Ferrante, 2006).

Box 1.11

Garlando, L. and M. Balotelli, *Buuuuu* (Turin: Einaudi, 2012).

Panizza, R., *Mario Balotelli negrazzurro. La vita difficile di un ragazzo impossibile* (Reggio Emilia: Aliberti, 2010).

Ravera, F., *Oro nero. Mario Balotelli e la sua generazione* (Arezzo: Limina, 2009).

Box 1.12

Gordon, R., *The Holocaust in Italian Culture, 1944–2010* (Stanford: Stanford University Press, 2012).

Kertzer, D., *Unholy War: The Vatican's Role in the Rise of Modern Anti-Semitism* (London: Palgrave, 2002).

Levi, P., *If This Is a Man* (London: Vintage, 1997).

——, *The Drowned and the Saved* (London: Joseph, 1988).

Levy, C., 'Fascism, National Socialism and Conservatives in Europe, 1914–1945: Issues for Comparativists', *Contemporary European History*, 8, 1 (1999), pp. 118–21.

Picciotto Fargon, L., *Il libro della memoria: Gli ebrei deportati dall'Italia 1943–1945* (Milan: Mursia, 1991).

Picciotto Fargion, L., *L'alba ci colse come un tradimento : gli ebrei nel campo di Fossoli, 1943–1944* (Milan: Mondadori, 2010).

Sarfatti, M., *Gli ebrei nell'Italia fascista* (Turin: Einaudi, 1999).

——, *The Jews in Mussolini's Italy: From Equality to Persecution* (Wisconsin: University of Wisconsin Press, 2006).

Schwarz, G., *After Mussolini: Jewish Life and Jewish Memories in Post-Fascist Italy* (London: Vallentine Mitchell, 2012).

Stille, A., *Benevolence and Betrayal: Five Italian Jewish Families under Fascism* (London: Vintage, 1993).

Zuccotti, S., *Italians and the Holocaust: Persecution, Rescue and Survival* (London: Halban, 1997).

——, *Under His Very Windows: The Vatican and the Holocaust in Italy* (New Haven, CT: Yale University Press, 2001).

Box 1.14

Baldoli, C., 'L'ossimoro cremonese. Storia e memoria di una comunità tra Bissolati e Farinacci', *Italia contemporanea*, 207 (1997), pp. 285–316.

Grimaldi, A., *Farinacci, il più fascista* (Milan: Bompiani, 1972).

Lussu, E., *Marcia su Roma e dintorni* (Turin: Einaudi, 1968).

Pieroni Bortolotti, F., *Francesco Misiano: vita di un internazionalista* (Rome: Riuniti, 1972).

Stajano, C., *Patrie smarrite: Racconto di un italiano* (Milan: Garzanti, 2001).

Box 1.15

Foot, J., *Italy's Divided Memory* (New York: Palgrave, 2009).

Lanz, O. and L. Klinkhammer (eds), *La morte per la patria. La celebrazione dei caduti dal Risorgimento alla Repubblica* (Rome: Donzelli, 2008).

Wittman, L., *The Tomb of the Unknown Soldier: Modern Mourning and the Reinvention of the Mystical Body* (Toronto: University of Toronto Press, 2011).

Box 1.16

Foot, J., *Italy's Divided Memory* (New York: Palgrave, 2009).
Paggi, L. (ed.), *L'eccidio del Duomo di San Miniato. La memoria e la ricerca storica (1944–2044)* (San Miniato: Comune di San Miniato, 2004).

Box 1.17

Ballinger, P., *History in Exile: Memory and Identity at the Borders of the Balkans* (Princeton: Princeton University Press).
Crainz, G., *Il dolore e l'esilio. L'Istria e le memorie divise d'Europa* (Rome: Donzelli, 2005).
——, *L'ombra della guerra. Il 1945, l'Italia* (Rome: Donzelli, 2007).
Franzinetti, G., 'The Rediscovery of the Istrian Foibe', *Jahrbücher für Geschichte und Kultur Südosteuropas*, 8 (2006), pp. 85–98.
Glynn, R. and Lombardi, G. (eds)., *Remembering Moro: The Cultural Legacy of the 1978 Kidnapping and Murder* (London: Legenda, 2012).
Gordon, R., *The Holocaust in Italian Culture, 1944–2010* (Stanford: Stanford University Press, 2012).
Pupo, R., *Il lungo esodo. Istria: le persecuzioni, le foibe, l'esilio* (Milan: Rizzoli, 2005).
—— and R. Spazzali, *Foibe* (Milan: Bruno Mondadori, 2003).

Box 1.18

Foot, J., *Calcio: A History of Italian Football* (London: Harper, 2007).
——, *Pedalare! Pedalare!: A History of Italian Cycling* (London: Bloomsbury, 2012).
Goldblatt, D., *The Ball Is Round: A Global History of Football* (London: Penguin, 2007).
Martin, S., *Football and Fascism. The National Game Under Mussolini* (Oxford: Berg, 2004).
——, *SportItalia: The Italian Love Affair with Sport* (London: IB Tauris, 2011).

CHAPTER 2: THE STATE

General Bibliography

Ainis, M., 'La chiarezza delle leggi', in L. Violante (ed.), *Storia d'Italia, Annali 14, Legge Diritto Giustizia* (Turin: Einaudi, 1998), pp. 909–39.
Allum, P., *Politics and Society in Post-war Naples* (Cambridge: Cambridge University Press, 1973).
Balsamo, G. and Lauro, R., *Il Prefetto della Repubblica* (Rimini: Maggioli, 1992).
Behan, T., *The Camorra* (London: Routledge, 1995).
Calamandrei, P., 'Sulla riforma dei codici' (1945), in *Piero Calamandrei, Scritti e discorsi politici*, ed. N. Bobbio, vol. 1 (Florence: La Nuova Italia, 1966), pp. 86–99.
——, 'In difesa di Danilo Dolci' (1956), now in *Piero Calamandrei, Scritti e discorsi politici*, ed. N. Bobbio, vol. 1 (Florence: La Nuova Italia, 1966), p. 163.
Canright Chiari, E., *Undoing Time: The Cultural Memory of an Italian Prison* (London: Legenda, 2012).

Cantarella, E., 'Homicides of Honor: the Development of Italian Adultery Law over Two Millennia', in D. Kertzer and R. Saller (eds), *The Family in Italy from Antiquity to the Present* (New Haven, CT: Yale University Press, 1991), pp. 229–46.

Codice di procedura penale per il Regno d'Italia (Naples: Giovanni Jovene, 1882).

Codice di procedura penale per il Regno d'Italia (Rome: Camera dei deputati, 1914).

Crespi, A., G. Zuccalà and F. Stella, *Commentario breve al Codice Penale* (Padova: CEDAM, 1998).

D'Agostino, F., *Reggio Calabria: I moti del luglio 1970–febbraio 1971* (Milan, 1972).

De Grand, A., *The Hunchback's Tailor: Giovanni Giolitti and Liberal Italy from the Challenge of Mass Politics to the Rise of Fascism, 1882–1922* (Westport, CT: Praeger, 2001).

Del Negro, P., *Esercito, Stato, Società: saggi di storia militare* (Bologna: Cappelli editore, 1979).

De Vito, C., *Camosci e girachiavi. Storia del carcere in Italia 1943–2007* (Bari: Laterza, 2009).

Dickie, J., *Cosa Nostra: A History of the Sicilian Mafia* (London: Hodder, 2007).

——, *Mafia Brotherhoods: Camorra, Mafia, 'Ndrangheta: the Rise of the Honoured Societies* (London: Sceptre, 2012).

——, *Mafia Republic: Italy's Criminal Curse. Cosa Nostra, 'Ndrangheta and Camorra from 1946 to the Present* (London: Sceptre, 2013).

Dines, N., *Tuff City: Urban Change and Contested Space in Central Naples* (New York: Berghahn, 2012).

Einaudi, L., *Il Buongoverno* (Bari: Laterza, 1955), pp. 52–9.

Femia, J., *Gramsci's Political Thought: Hegemony, Consciousness and the Revolutionary Process* (Oxford: Clarendon Press, 1987).

Finer, S. (ed.), *Five Constitutions* (London: Penguin, 1979).

Foa, V., *Il cavallo e la torre: Riflessioni su una vita* (Turin: Einaudi, 1991).

Francioni, F. (ed.), *Italy and EC Membership Evaluated* (London: Pinter, 1992).

Fraser, R., *1968: A Student Generation in Revolt* (London: Chatto and Windus, 1987).

Gambetta, D., *The Sicilian Mafia: the Business of Private Protection* (Cambridge, MA: Harvard University Press, 1993).

Gambetta, D., 'Mafia: the Price of Distrust', in D. Gambetta (ed.), *Trust: Making and Breaking Cooperative Relations* (electronic edition, Department of Sociology, University of Oxford), pp. 158–75.

Gardini, N., *I baroni. Come e perché sono fuggito dall'università italiana* (Milan: Feltrinelli, 2013).

Ginsborg, P., *A History of Contemporary Italy: Society and Politics, 1943–1988* (London: Penguin, 1990).

——, *Italy and its Discontents: Family, Civil Society, State, 1980–2001* (London: Penguin, 2002).

Ginzburg, C., *The Judge and the Historian: Marginal Notes on a Late Twentieth-Century Miscarriage of Justice* (London: Verso, 1999).

Girlando, R., *PAI. Polizia dell'Africa italiana* (Campobasso: Italia editrice, 1996).

Gorrieri, E., *La giungla retributiva* (Bologna: Il Mulino, 1972).

Gribaudi, G., *Mediatori: Antropologia del potere democristiano nel Mezzogiorno* (Turin: Rosenberg and Sellier, 1980).

Gustapane, E., 'Il sistema dei concorsi pubblici: Le origini, l'evoluzione', in A. Varni and G. Melis (eds), *Le fatiche di Monsò Travet: Per una stona del lavoro pubblico in Italia* (Turin: Rosenberg and Sellier, 1997).

Habermas, J., *Legitimation Crisis* (Cambridge: Polity, 1988).

Kivel Mazuy, P., 'L'orario di lavoro', in M. Rusciano and L. Zoppoli (eds), *Il lavoro pubblico* (Bologna: Il Mulino, 1993).

Lane, D., *Into the Heart of the Mafia: A Journey through the Italian South* (London: Profile, 2010).

Levi, G., 'Italy: Catholicism, Power, Democracy and the Failure of the Past', in P. Furtado (ed.), *Histories of Nations: How their Identities Were Forged* (London: Thames and Hudson, 2012), pp. 264–71.

Luciani, V., 'Le assunzioni nel pubblico impiego', in M. Rusciano and L. Zoppoli (eds), *Il lavoro pubblico* (Bologna: Il Mulino, 1993), pp. 35–92.

Machin, H., *The Prefect in the French Public Administration* (London: Croom Helm, 1977).

Mann, M., *Consciousness and Action amongst the Western Working Class* (London: Macmillan, 1973).

Mascambruno, M. C., *Il Prefetto*, I, *Dalle origini all'avvento delle regioni* (Milan: Giuffrè, 1988).

Melis, G., *Storia dell'amministrazione italiana (1861–1993)* (Bologna: Il Mulino, 1996).

—— (ed.), *Le fatiche di Monsù Travet: Per una storia del lavoro pubblico in Italia* (Turin: Rosenberg, 1997), pp. 21–43.

Missori, M., *Governi, Alte cariche dello Stato, Alti Magistrati e Prefetti del Regno d'Italia* (Rome: Ministero per i beni cultural e ambientali, 1989).

Oliva, G., 'La Naja', in M. Isnenghi (ed.), *I luoghi della memoria* (Bari: Laterza, 1997), pp. 95–109.

Padovani, T., 'I delitti nelle relazioni private', in L. Violante (ed.), *La criminalità, Storia d'Italia, Annali*, 12 (Turin: Einaudi, 1997), pp. 219–46.

Perotti, R., *L'università truccata* (Turin: Einaudi, 2008).

Pipitone, C., 'The Black Army: Survey on the Culture of the Italian Officer in East Africa' (unpublished paper delivered at the Italian Colonialism and Post-Colonial Legacies Conference, ASMI, London, 30 November–1 December 2001).

Pistone, S. (ed.), *L'Italia e l'unità europea* (Turin: Einaudi, 1982).

Polimeni, G., *La rivolta di Reggio Calabria del 1970. Politica, istituzioni, protagonisti* (Cosenza: Pellegrini, 1996).

Pombeni, P., 'The Roots of the Italian Political Crisis: A View from History, 1918, 1945, 1989… and After', in C. Levy and M. Roseman (eds), *Three Postwar Eras in Comparison: Western Europe, 1918–1945–1989* (Basingstoke: Palgrave, 2002).

Randeraad, N., *Authority in Search of Liberty: The Prefects of Liberal Italy* (Amsterdam, 1993).

Riall, L., *The Italian Risorgimento: State, Society and National Unification* (London: Routledge, 1994).

—— *Risorgimento: The History of Italy from Napoleon to Nation State* (London: Palgrave, 2009).

Rochat, G., 'L'esercito italiano negli ultimi cento anni', *Storia d'Italia*, vol. V, *I documenti*, 2 (Turin: Einaudi, 1973), pp. 1867–902.

Rochat, G. and G. Massobrio, *Breve storia dell'esercito italiano dal 1861 al 1943* (Turin: Einaudi, 1978).

Romanelli, R., *Il comando impossibile: Stato e società nell'Italia liberale* (Bologna: Il Mulino, 1995).

Romeo, R., *Risorgimento e capitalismo* (Bari: Laterza, 1959).

Rossi, E., *Abolire la miseria* (Bari: Laterza, 1977).

——, *Il Malgoverno* (Bari: Laterza, 1954).

Salvemini, G., *Opere*, V, *Scritti sulla scuola* (Milan: Feltrinelli, 1966), p. xiii.

Santoro, C., *Obiezioni di coscienza al servizio militare, all'aborto, al lavoro* (Salerno: Edizioni il sapere, 1995).

The Italian Penal Code (Littleton, CO: Fred Rothman, 1978).

Turati, F., *Rifare l'Italia* (Milan: Lega nazionale delle cooperative, 1920).

Venditti, R., *I reati contro il servizio militare e contro la disciplina militare* (Milan: Giuffrè, 1995).

Violante, L., 'La repressione del dissenso politico nell'Italia liberale: stati d'assedio e giustizia militare', *Rivista di storia contemporanea*, v (1976), pp. 481–524.

Zinn, D. L., *La raccomandazione: Clientelismo vecchio e nuovo* (Rome: Donzelli, 2001).

Box 2.1

Antonello, P. and A. O'Leary (eds), *Imagining Terrorism: The Rhetoric and Representation of Political Violence in Italy 1969–2009* (London: Legenda, 2009).

Boatti, G., *Piazza Fontana. 12 dicembre 1969: il giorno dell'innocenza perduta* (Turin: Einaudi, 1999).

Bull, A., *Italian Neofascism. The Strategy of Tension and the Politics of Nonreconciliation* (Oxford: Berghahn, 2007).

—— and P. Cooke, *Ending Terrorism in Italy* (London: Routledge, 2013).

—— and A. Giorgio (eds), *Speaking Out and Silencing: Culture, Society and Politics in Italy in the 1970s* (Leeds: Legenda, 2006).

Foot, J., 'The Massacre and the City: Milan and Piazza Fontana since 1969', in J. Dickie et al. (eds), *Disastro! Disasters in Italy since 1860: Culture, Politics, Society* (Basingstoke: Palgrave, 2002), pp. 256–80.

—— 'L'Italia degli ultimi trent'anni', in *1974 28 Maggio 2004. 30 Anniversario della strage di Piazza della Loggia. 'Brescia: La Memoria, La Storia'. Testimonianze, riflessioni, iniziative* (Brescia: Casa della Memoria, 2005), pp. 224–30.

—— 'The Death of Giuseppe Pinelli: Truth, Representation, Memory: 1969–2006', in S. Gundle and L. Rinaldi (eds), *Assassinations and Murder in Modern Italy: Transformations in Society and Culture* (New York and London: Palgrave, 2007), pp. 59–72.

—— 'Contested Memories: Milan and Piazza Fontana', in P. P. Antonello and A. O'Leary (eds), *Imagining Terrorism: The Rhetoric and Representation of Political Violence in Italy 1969–2009* (Oxford: Legenda, 2009), pp. 152–66.

—— 'Looking back on Italy's "Long '68'": Public, Private and Divided Memories', in I. Cornils and S. Waters (eds), *Memories of 1968: International Perspectives* (Oxford: Peter Lang, 2011), pp. 103–30.

Fraser, R., *1968: A Student Generation in Revolt* (London: Chatto and Windus, 1987).

Glynn, R., *Women, Terrorism and Trauma in Italian Culture* (London: Palgrave, 2013).

—— and G. Lombardi (eds), *Remembering Moro: The Cultural Legacy of the 1978 Kidnapping and Murder* (London: Legenda, 2012).

—— G. Lombardi and A. O'Leary (eds), *Terrorism, Italian Style: Representations of Political Violence in Contemporary Italian Cinema* (London: Igrs, 2012).

Moss, D., *The Politics of Left-Wing Violence in Italy, 1969–85* (Basingstoke: Macmillan, 1989).

O'Leary, A., *Tragedia All'Italiana: Italian Cinema and Italian Terrorisms, 1970–2010* (London: Peter Lang, 2011).

Passerini, L., *Autobiography of a Generation: Italy 1968* (London: University Press of New England, 1996).

Serenelli, S., '1968 in an Italian Province: Memory and the Everyday Life of a New Left Group in Macerata', in I. Cornils and S. Waters (eds), *Memories of 1968: International Perspectives* (Oxford: Peter Lang, 2010), pp. 345–75.

—— 'Il '68 e la "morte della famiglia". Storia di una comune nella provincia anconetana', in E. Asquer et al. (eds), *Famiglie del Novecento. Conflitti, culture e relazioni*, (Rome: Carocci, 2010).

—— 'Private 1968 and the Margins: the Vicolo Cassini's Community in the Macerata Province', in *Memory Studies*, 6, 1 (2013), pp. 91–104.

—— 'Il Sessantotto e la famiglia. Storia di una comune nella campagna marchigiana 1976–1987', *Italia Contemporanea*, 255 (2009), pp. 173–202.

Tarrow, S., *Democracy and Disorder: Protest and Politics in Italy, 1965–1975* (Oxford: Clarendon, 1989).

Tobagi, B., *Come mi batte forte il tuo cuore. Storia di mio padre* (Turin: Einaudi, 2011).

Willan, P., *Puppetmasters: The Political Use of Terrorism in Italy* (London: Constable, 1991).

Film:
Il romanzo di una strage (M. Tullio Giordana, 2012).

Box 2.2 (see also Box 2.1)

Foot, J., *Italy's Divided Memory* (New York: Palgrave, 2009).

—— 'Contested Memories: Milan and Piazza Fontana', in P. P. Antonello and A. O'Leary (eds), *Imagining Terrorism: The Rhetoric and Representation of Political Violence in Italy 1969–2009* (Oxford: Legenda, 2009), pp. 152–66.

Box 2.3

Jemolo, A., *Church and State in Italy, 1850–1950* (Oxford: Blackwell, 1960).

Luzzatto, S., *Padre Pio, Miracles and Politics in a Secular Age* (London: Picador, 2012).

Pollard, J., *Catholicism in Modern Italy: Religion, Society and Politics, 1861 to the Present* (London: Routledge, 2008).

Box 2.4

Dickie, J., *Cosa Nostra: A History of the Sicilian Mafia* (London: Hodder, 2007).

——, *Mafia Brotherhoods: Camorra, Mafia, 'Ndrangheta: the Rise of the Honoured Societies* (London: Sceptre, 2012).

——, *Mafia Republic: Italy's Criminal Curse. Cosa Nostra, 'Ndrangheta and Camorra from 1946 to the Present* (London: Sceptre, 2013).

Lane, D., *Into the Heart of the Mafia: A Journey through the Italian South* (London: Profile, 2010).

Lupo, S., *Storia della mafia. Dalle origini ai nostri giorni* (Rome: Donzelli, 2004).

Saviano, R., *Gomorrah: Italy's Other Mafia* (London: Pan, 2011).

Films:
Gomorra (M. Garrone, 2008).
The Hundred Steps (M. Tullio Giordana, 2000)

Box 2.5

Mack Smith, D., *The Making of Italy, 1796–1866* (Oxford: Macmillan, 1988).

Box 2.6

Finer, S. (ed.), *Five Constitutions* (London: Penguin, 1979).
The most recent text of the Constitution is available in English at: www.senato.it/
documenti/repository/istituzione/costituzione_inglese.pdf

Box 2.7

Floridia, G. C., 'La costituzione', in G. Pasquino (ed.), *La politica italiana: Dizionario
critico, 1945–95* (Bari: Laterza, 1995), pp. 5–31.

Box 2.8

Calamandrei, P., 'La Costituzione e le leggi per attuarla' (1955) and 'L'ostruzionismo
di maggioranza' (1953), in N. Bobbio (ed.), *Piero Calamandrei, Scritti e discorsi politici*
(Florence: La Nuova Italia, 1966), vol. II, pp. 467–577 and pp. 546–95.
Volcanesk, M. L., *Constitutional Politics in Italy: The Constitutional Court* (London:
Macmillan, 2000).

Box 2.9

Leroy Certoma, G., *The Italian Legal System* (London: Butterworths, 1985).
Nelken, D., 'A Legal Revolution? The Judges and Tangentopoli', in S. Gundle and
S. Parker (eds), *The New Italian Republic: From the Fall of the Berlin Wall to Berlusconi*
(London: Routledge, 1996), pp. 191–205.

Boxes 2.10–2.11

Andrews, G., *Not a Normal Country: Italy after Berlusconi* (London: Pluto Press, 2005).
Emmott, B., *Good Italy, Bad Italy: Why Italy Must Conquer its Demons to Face the Future*
(New Haven: Yale University Press, 2013).
Ginsborg, P., *Silvio Berlusconi: Television, Power and Patrimony* (London: Verso, 2005).
Jones, T., *The Dark Heart of Italy: Travels through Time and Space across Italy* (London:
Faber and Faber, 2007).
Lane, D., *Berlusconi's Shadow: Crime, Justice and the Pursuit of Power* (London: Allen
Lane, 2004).
Stille, A., *The Sack of Rome: Media + Money + Celebrity = Power = Silvio Berlusconi*
(London: Penguin, 2007).

Box 2.13

Corsieri, S., *La villeggiatura di Mussolini. Il confino da Bocchino a Berlusconi* (Milan: Dalai,
2005).
Dal Pont, A., *I lager di Mussolini. L'altra faccia del conflitto nei documenti della polizia fas-
cista* (Milano, 1975).
Ebner, M., *Ordinary Violence in Mussolini's Italy* (Cambridge: Cambridge University
Press, 2011).
Ghini, G. and A. Dal Pont, *Gli antifascisti al confino, 1926–1943* (Rome: Editori Riuniti, 1971).

Neppi Modona, G. and M. Pelissero, 'La politica criminale durante il fascismo', in L. Violante (ed.), *La criminalità, Storia d'Italia, Annali*, 12 (Turin: Einaudi, 1997), pp. 757–847.

Porta, G., 'Il confino', in M. Isenghi (ed.), *I luoghi della memoria* (Bari: Laterza, 1996), pp. 439–60.

Box 2.14

Cendon, P. (ed.), *Codice civile annotato con la giurisprudenza*, vol. 5: *Del Lavoro* (Turin: UTET, 1995), p. 2109.

Box 2.16

Fiorentino, F., *Ordine pubblico nell'Italia giolittiana* (Rome: Carecas, 1978).

Box 2.17

Neppi Modona, G., 'La giustizia penale degli anni novanta', and 'Dal sistema inquisitorio al modello accusatorio', both in P. Ginsborg (ed.), *Stato dell'Italia* (Milan: Il saggiatore, 1994), pp. 512–20.

Guarnieri, C., 'Prosecution in Two Civil Law Countries: France and Italy', in D. Nelken (ed.), *Comparing Legal Cultures* (Aldershot: Darmouth, 1997), pp. 183–93.

Box 2.18

Lupo, S., 'Usi e abusi del passato. Le radici dell'Italia di Putnam', *Meridiana*, 19 (1993), pp. 151–68.

Putnam, R. with R. Leonardi and R. Nanetti, *Making Democracy Work: Civic Traditions in Modern Italy* (Princeton: Princeton University Press, 1993), p. 130.

Specialized Bibliography (1): The *Lega Nord*

Biorcio, R., *La padania promessa* (Milan: Il Saggiatore, 1997).

Bull, A., *Social Identities and Political Cultures in Italy: Catholic, Communist and Leghist Communities between Civicness and Localism* (Oxford: Berghahn, 2001).

—— and M. Gilbert, *The Lega Nord and the Northern Question in Italian Politics* (London: Palgrave, 2001).

Diamanti, I., *La Lega: Geografia, storia e sociologia di un nuovo soggetto politico* (Rome: Donzelli, 1993).

——, 'The Northern League: from Regional Party to Party of Government', in S. Gundle and S. Parker (eds), *The New Italian Republic: From the Fall of the Berlin Wall to Berlusconi* (London: Routledge, 1996), pp. 113–30.

Dickie, J., 'The South as Other: from Liberal Italy to the Lega Nord', in A. C. Bull and G. Adalgisa (eds), *Culture and Society in Southern Italy: Past and Present*, supplement to *The Italianist*, 14 (1994), pp. 124–40.

Levy, C. (ed.), *Italian Regionalism: History, Identity and Politics* (Oxford: Berg, 1996).

Specialized Bibliography (2): Silvio Berlusconi and the 'Berlusconi era'

Albertazzi, D., C. Brook, C. Ross and N. Rothenberg (eds), *Resisting the Tide: Cultures of Opposition under Berlusconi (2001–2006)*, (London: Continuum, 2011).

Andrews, G., *Not a Normal Country: Italy after Berlusconi* (London: Pluto Press, 2005).

Ciofalo, G., *Infiniti anni Ottanta. Tv, cultura e società alle origini del nostro presente* (Milan: Mondadori, 2011).

Ginsborg, P., *Silvio Berlusconi: Television, Power and Patrimony* (London: Verso, 2005).

Gundle, S., 'Berlusconi, Sex and the Avoidance of a Media Scandal', in M. Giuliani and E. Jones (eds), *Italian Politics: Managing Uncertainty* (Oxford: Berghahn, 2010), pp. 59–75.

Jones, T., *The Dark Heart of Italy: Travels through Time and Space across Italy* (London: Faber and Faber, 2007).

Lane, D., *Berlusconi's Shadow: Crime, Justice and the Pursuit of Power* (London: Allen Lane, 2004).

Politi, M., *Il corpo del capo* (Milan: Guanda, 2011).

Rizzo, M., 'The Creation of Shared Space and the Definition of a "Light" Community in Italian Television in the 1980s', *Modern Italy*, 18, 1 (2013), pp. 55–73.

Severgnini, B., *Mamma Mia! Berlusconi's Legacy Explained for Posterity and for Friends Abroad* (Milan: Rizzoli, 2011).

Shin, M. and J. Agnew, *Berlusconi's Italy: Mapping Contemporary Italian Politics* (Philadelphia: Temple University Press, 2008).

Stille, A., *The Sack of Rome: Media + Money + Celebrity = Power = Silvio Berlusconi* (London: Penguin, 2007).

Viroli, M., *The Liberty of Servants: Berlusconi's Italy* (Princeton: Princeton University Press, 2011).

Films:
Aprile (N. Moretti, 1998).
Il Caimano (The Caiman) (N. Moretti, 2006).
Girlfriend in a Coma (A. Piras, 2012).
Quando c'era Silvio (E. Deaglio, 2005).
Videocracy (E. Gandini, 2009).

Specialized Bibliography (3): The Anti-fascist Resistance, 1943–1945

Colombara, F., *Vesti la giubba di battaglia. Miti, riti e simboli della guerra partigiana* (Rome: DeriveApprodi, 2009).

Cooke, P., *The Italian Resistance: An Anthology* (Manchester: Manchester University Press, 1998).

Dondi, M., *La resistenza tra unità e conflitto. Vicende parallele tra dimensione nazionale e realtà piacentina* (Milan: Bruno Mondadori, 2004).

Luzzatto, S., *Partigia. Una storia della resistenza* (Milan: Mondadori, 2013).

Pansa, G., *Il sangue dei vinti. Quello che accadde in Italia dopo il 25 Aprile* (Milan: Sperling and Kupfer, 2005).

Pavone, C., *A Civil War: A History Of The Italian Resistance* (London: Verso, 2013).

Peli, S., *Storia della Resistenza in Italia* (Turin: Einaudi, 2006).

Pugliese, S., *Fascism, Anti-Fascism, and the Resistance in Italy: 1919 to the Present* (New York: Rowman and Littlefield, 2003).

——, *Italian Fascism and Anti-Fascism: A Critical Anthology* (Manchester: Manchester University Press, 2001).

Storchi, M., *Il sangue dei vincitori. Saggio sui crimini fascisti e i processi del dopoguerra (1945–46)*, (Reggio Emilia: Aliberti, 2008).

—— 'Post-war Violence in Italy: A Struggle for Memory', *Modern Italy*, 12, 2 (2007), pp. 237–50.

CHAPTER 3: ECONOMY AND SOCIETY

General Bibliography

Accati, L., 'L'occupazione delle terre: lotte rivoluzionarie dei contadini siciliani e pugliesi nel 1919–1920', *Il Ponte* (1970), pp. 1263–93.

Agnew, J., 'The Myth of Backward Italy in Modern Europe', in B. Allen and M. Russo (eds), *Revisioning Italy. National Identity and Global Culture* (Minneapolis: University of Minnesota Press, 1997), pp. 23–42.

Amatori, F. and F. Brioschi, 'Le grandi imprese private: famiglie e coalizioni', in F. Barca (ed.), *Storia del capitalismo italiano dal dopoguerra a oggi* (Rome: Donzelli editore, 1997), pp. 117–53.

Ambrosi, L., *La rivolta di Reggio. Storia di territori, violenza e populismo 1970* (Soveria Mannelli: Rubettino, 2009).

Amin, A., 'Small Firms in Italy: Myths and Realities', in N. R. Gilbert, R. Burrows and A. Pollert (eds), *Fordism and Flexibility: Divisions and Change* (New York: St Martin's Press, 1992).

Andrews, R., *A Theatre of Community Memory: Tuscan Sharecropping and the Teatro Povero di Monticchiello*, The Society for Italian Studies, occasional papers, 4 (1998).

Arlacchi, P., *Mafia, Peasants and Great Estates: Society in Traditional Calabria* (Cambridge: Cambridge University Press, 1983).

Aymard, M., 'Nation-states and Interregional Disparities of Development', in G. Arrighi (ed.), *Semiperipheral Development: The Politics of Southern Europe in the Twentieth Century* (Beverly Hills, CA: Sage, 1985).

Bairati, P., *Valletta* (Turin: UTET, 1983).

Baldassari, M., *The Italian Economy: Heavan or Hell?* (London: Macmillan, 1994).

Barca, F. (ed.), *Storia del capitalismo italiano dal dopoguerra a oggi* (Rome: Donzelli editore, 1997).

Becattini, G., 'Dal "settore" industriale al "distretto" industriale. Alcune considerazioni sull'unità di indagine dell'economia industriale', *Rivista di Economia e Politica Industriale*, v (1979), pp. 7–21.

——, *L'industrializzazione leggera della Toscana* (Milan: Angeli, 1999).

Becchi, A., 'La questione meridionale', in G. Pasquino (ed.), *La politica italiana: Dizionario critico, 1945–95* (Bari: Laterza, 1995).

Belmonte, T., *The Broken Fountain* (New York: Columbia University Press, 1979).

Berta, G., *Fiat-Chrysler e la deriva dell'Italia industriale* (Bologna: Il Mulino, 2011).

Bessel, R. (ed.), *Fascist Italy and Nazi Germany: Comparisons and Contrasts* (Cambridge: Cambridge University Press, 1996).

Bevilacqua, P. (ed.), *Storia dell'agricoltura italiana in età contemporanea* (Venice: Marsilio, 1989–91), vols 1–3.

——, *Breve storia dell'Italia meridionale dall'Ottocento a oggi* (Rome: Donzelli, 1993).

—— and M. Rossi-Doria, *Le bonifiche in Italia dal '700 a oggi* (Bari: Laterza, 1984).

Bianchi, E., *Il tramonto della mezzadria toscana e i suoi riflessi geografici* (Milan: Unicopoli, 1983).

Bigazzi, D., 'Un inventario del progetto del saper fare', in A. Pansera (ed.), *L'anima dell'industria: un secolo di disegno industriale nel Milanese* (Milan: Skira, 1996), pp. 11–14.

Bogliari, F. (ed.), *Il movimento contadino in Italia. Dall'unità al fascismo* (Turin: Loescher, 1980).

Bonelli, F., 'Il capitalismo italiano. Linee generali d'interpretazione', in *Storia d'Italia, Annali 1, Dal feudalismo al capitalismo* (Turin: Einaudi, 1979), pp. 1193–256.

Bonomi, A., *Il capitalismo molecolare* (Turin: Einaudi, 1997).

Bosio, G., *Il trattore ad Acquanegra* (Bari: De Donato, 1981).

Bosworth, R. J. B. and P. Dogliani (eds), *Italian Fascism: History, Memory and Representation* (London: Macmillan, 1999).

Branzi, A., 'Italian Design and the Complexity of Modernity', in G. Celant (ed.), *The Italian Metamorphosis, 1943–1968* (New York: Guggenheim Museum, 1994), pp. 597–606.

Brusco, S. and S. Paba, 'Per una storia dei distretti industriali italiani dal secondo dopoguerra agli anni Novanta', in F. Barca (ed.), *Storia del capitalismo italiano dal dopoguerra a oggi* (Rome: Donzelli, 1997), pp. 265–334.

Bull, A., 'The Lombard Silk Workers in the Nineteenth Century: an Industrial Workforce in a Rural Setting', *The Italianist*, 7 (1987), pp. 104–9.

——and P. Corner, *From Peasant to Entrepreneur: The Survival of the Family Economy in Italy* (Oxford: Berg, 1993).

Byres, T. J. (ed.), *Sharecropping and Sharecroppers* (London: Frank Cass, 1983).

Cafagna, L., 'La industrializzazione ritardata tra Ottocento e Novecento', *La Storia*, vol. 6, *L'Età Contemporanea*, 1, 'I quadri generali' (Turin: UTET, 1988), pp. 27–70.

Cappelloto, I., 'La mozione agraria', *L'Italia*, 11 December 1920.

Caracciolo, A., *Il movimento contadino in Lazio, 1870–1922* (Rome: Bib. del Movimento Operaio, 1952).

Cardoza, A., *Agrarian Elites and Italian Fascism: The Province of Bologna, 1901–1926* (Princeton, NJ: Princeton University Press, 1983).

Carr, R., *Spain, 1808–1975* (Oxford: Clarendon, 1982).

Carter, N., 'Rethinking the Italian Liberal State', *Bulletin of Italian Politics*, 3, 2 (2011), pp. 225–45.

——, 'The Economy of Liberal Italy: a Roundtable Discussion with Brian A'Hearn, Nick Carter, Giovanni Federico and Vera Zamagni on Stefano Fenoaltea's The Reinterpretation of Italian Economic History: From Unification to the Great War. Cambridge, CUP, 2011', *Modern Italy*, 18, 1 (2013), pp. 81–94.

Castronovo, V., 'Lo sviluppo economico in Italia nel cinquantennio repubblicano. Problemi aperti', *Studi Storici*, 1, 36 (1995).

——, 'La storia economica', in *Storia d'Italia*, vol. 4 (Turin: Einaudi, 1973).

Cazzola, F., *Storia delle campagne padane dall'Ottocento a oggi* (Milan: Bruno Mondadori, 1996).

Clemente, P. et al., *Mezzadri, letterati e padroni nella Toscana dell'Ottocento* (Palermo: Sellerio, 1980).

Cohen, J. and G. Federico, *The Growth of the Italian Economy, 1820–1960* (Cambridge: Cambridge University Press, 2001).

Consonni, G., 'Dalla città alla metropoli. La classe invisibile', in M. Antonioli et al. (eds), *Milano operaia dall'800 a oggi*, vols I and II (Bari/Rome: Cariplo/Laterza, 1993), pp. 19–36.

—— and G. Tonon, 'Alle origini della metropoli contemporanea', in C. Pirovano, *Lombardia: il territorio, l'ambiente, il paesaggio*, vol. 4: *L'età delle manifatture e della rivoluzione industriale* (Milan: Electa, 1984), pp. 89–164.

Corner, P., 'Il contadino-operaio dell'Italia Padana', in P. Bevilacqua (ed.), *Storia dell' agricoltura italiana in età contemporanea* II (Venice: Marsilio, 1990), pp. 751–83.

——, *Contadini e industrializzazione: società rurale e impresa in Italia dal 1840 al 1940* (Bari: Laterza, 1993).

——, *Fascism in Ferrara, 1915–1925* (Oxford: Oxford University Press, 1975).

Crainz, G., 'La cascina padana', in P. Bevilacqua (ed.), *Storia dell'agricoltura italiana in età contemporanea*, vol. 1, *Spazi e paesaggi* (Venice: Marsilio, 1989), pp. 37–76.

—— 'La violenza postbellica in Emilia fra "guerra civile" e conflitti antichi', in P. Pezzino and G. Ranzato (eds), *Laboratorio di storia: Studi in onore di Claudio Pavone* (Milan: Franco Angeli, 1994), pp. 191–205.

——, *Padania. Il mondo dei braccianti dall'Ottocento alla fuga dalle campagne* (Rome: Donzelli, 1994).

——, *Storia del miracolo italiano: Culture, identità, trasformazioni fra anni cinquanta e sessanta* (Rome: Donzelli, 1996).

Cuzzola, F., *Reggio 1970. Storie e memorie della rivolta* (Rome: Donzelli, 2008).

Davis, J., *Conflict and Control: Law and Order in Nineteenth-Century Italy* (London: Macmillan, 1988).

D'Orsi, A., *La rivoluzione bolscevica: Fascismo, classi, ideologie (1917–1922)* (Milan: Franco Angeli, 1985).

De Cecco, M. and A. Pedone, 'Le istituzioni dell'economia', in R. Romanelli (ed.), *Storia dello Stato italiano dall'Unità a oggi* (Rome: Donzelli, 1995), pp. 253–300.

De Grand, A., *Fascist Italy and Nazi Germany: The 'Fascist' Style of Rule* (London: Routledge, 1995).

Delzell, C. (ed.), *Mediterranean Fascism, 1919–1945* (New York: Harper and Row, 1970).

Dines, N., 'Centri sociali. Occupazioni autogestite a Napoli negli anni novanta', *Quaderni di Sociologia*, XLIII, 21 (1999).

—— 'Urban Change and Contested Space in Contemporary Naples' (unpublished PhD thesis, Department of Italian, UCL, 2002).

Einaudi, L., *La condotta economica e gli effetti sociali della guerra italiana* (Bari: Laterza, 1933).

Federico, G. and G. Toniolo, 'Italy', in R. Sylla and G. Toniolo (eds), *Patterns of European Industrialization: The Nineteenth Century* (London: Routledge, 1991), pp. 197–214.

Federico, G. and R. Giannetti, 'Italy: Stalling and Surpassing', in J. Foreman-Peck and G. Federico (eds), *The Mediterranean Response to Globalisation before 1950* (London: Routledge, 2000), pp. 269–96.

Foot, J., 'Alliances and Socialist Theory: Milan and Lombardy, 1914–1921' (unpublished PhD thesis, Cambridge, 1991).

Galli della Loggia, E., 'La Fiat e l'Italia', in C. Annibaldi and G. Berta (eds), *Grande impresa e sviluppo italiano* (Bologna: Il Mulino, 1999), pp. 7–36.

Gerschenkron, A., *Economic Backwardness in Historical Perspective* (Cambridge, MA: Belknap Press, 1962).

Gianetti, R., *Tecnologia e sviluppo economico italiano, 1870–1990* (Bologna: Il Mulino, 1998).

Gianotti, L., *Gli operai della Fiat hanno cento anni* (Rome: Riuniti, 1999).

Gill, D., 'Tuscan Sharecropping in United Italy: The Myth of Class Collaboration Destroyed', in T. J. Byres (ed.) *Sharecropping and Sharecroppers* (London: Frank Cass, 1983), pp. 146–69.

Ginsborg, P., 'The Communist Party and the Agrarian Question in Southern Italy, 1943–1948', *History Workshop Journal*, 17 (1984), pp. 81–101.

——, *Italy and its Discontents: Family, Civil Society, State, 1980–2001* (London: Penguin, 2002).

Gramsci, A., *L'ordine nuovo*, 3:1 (1920), now in *Selections from Political Writings, 1910–1920* (London: Lawrence and Wishart, 1977).

Gribaudi, G., 'Familismo e famiglia a Napoli e nel Mezzogiorno', *Meridiana*, 17 (1993), pp. 13–42.

Gribaudi, G., *A Eboli. Il mondo meridionale in cent'anni di trasformazioni* (Venice: Marsilio, 1990).

Gribaudi, M., *Mondo operaio e mito operaio: Spazi e percorso sociali a Torino nel primo Novecento* (Turin: Einaudi, 1987).

Griffin, R. (ed.), *International Fascism, Theories, Causes and the New Consensus* (London: Arnold, 1998).

Kertzer, D., *Family Life in Central Italy, 1880–1910: Sharecropping, Wage Labor and Coresidence* (New Brunswick: Rutgers University Press, 1984).

Lange, P., 'Semiperiphery and Core in the European Context: Reflections on the Postwar Italian Experience', in G. Arrighi (ed.), *Semiperipheral Development: The Politics of Southern Europe in the Twentieth Century* (Beverly Hills, CA: Sage, 1985).

Lerner, G., *Operai. Viaggio all'interno della Fiat. La vita, le case, le fabbriche di una classe che non c'è più* (Milan: Feltrinelli, 1988).

Levy, C., 'Fascism, National Socialism and Conservatives in Europe, 1914–1945: Issues for Comparativists', *Contemporary European History*, 8, 1 (1999), pp. 97–126.

Lorenzoni, G., *Inchiesta Parlamentare sulls Condizioni dei Contadini nelle Provincie Meridionali e nella Sicilia*, vol. 6 (Rome: Tipografia Nazionale di Giovanni Bertero, 1910).

Lumley, R. and J. Morris (eds), *A New History of the Italian South: The Mezzogiorno Revisited* (Exeter: Exeter University Press, 1997).

Marino, G. C., *Socialismo nel latifondo: Sebastiano Cammareri Scurti nel movimento contadino della sicilia occidentale (1896–1912)* (Palermo: ESA, 1972).

Mason, T., 'The Turin Strikes of March 1943', in T. Mason, *Nazism, Fascism and the Working Class: Essays by Tim Mason* (Cambridge: Cambridge University Press, 1995), pp. 274–95.

Mazzoni, G., *Un uomo, una città: Giuseppe Massarenti a Molinella* (Bologna: Coop Il Nove, 1990).

Mazzoni, N., *Il problema della terra e il socialismo* (Milan: PSI, 1920).

Meriggi, M., *Storia dell'Italia settentrionale dall'Ottocento a oggi* (Rome: Donzelli, 1996).

Monti, A., *I braccianti* (Bologna: Il Mulino, 1998).

Oglethorpe, S., *Change and Memory: the Central Italian Countryside, 1945–1970* (PhD thesis, UCL, 2009).

Pasolini, P. P., *Scritti corsari* (Milan: Garzanti, 1975).

Pazzagli, C., 'Dal paternalismo alla democrazia: il mondo dei mezzadri e la lotta politica in Italia', *Passato e Presente*, January–April 1987, pp. 156–78.

Petrusewicz, M., 'The Demise of Latifondismo', in R. Lumley and J. Morris (eds), *A New History of the Italian South: The Mezzogiorno Revisited* (Exeter: Exeter University Press, 1997), pp. 20–41.

——, *Latifundium: Moral Economy and Material Life in a European Periphery* (Ann Arbor, MI: University of Michigan Press, 1996).

Piccone Stella, S., *La prima generazione. Ragazze e ragazzi nel miracolo economico italiano* (Milan: Franco Angeli, 1993).

Piore, M. J. and C. F. Sabel, *The Second Industrial Divide* (New York: Basic Books, 1984).

Preston, P., *The Politics of Revenge: Fascism and the Military in Twentieth-century Spain* (London: Routledge, 1995).

Revelli, M., *Lavorare in Fiat* (Milan: Garzanti, 1989).

Rogger, H. and E. Weber (eds), *The European Right: A Historical Profile* (Berkeley: University of California Press, 1965).

Romeo, R., *Risorgimento e capitalismo* (Bari: Laterza, 1959).

Rossi, R., *Inchiesta sulla piccola proprietà coltivatrice formatasi nel dopoguerra*, III, *Lombardia* (Rome, 1931).

Rossi-Doria, A., *Il ministro e i contadini: Decreti Gullo e lotte nel Mezzogiorno (1944–1949)* (Rome: Bulzoni, 1983).

Saltini, A., *L'agricoltura modenese dalla mezzadria allo sviluppo agroindustriale* (Milan: Franco Angeli, 1998).

Salvadori, M., *Gaetano Salvemini* (Turin: Einaudi, 1963).

Salvemini, G., 'Un Comune dell'Italia meridionale: Molfetta', pp. 3–23, *Critica Sociale*, 1 and 16 March and 1 April 1897.

——, *The Fascist Dictatorship in Italy*, vol. 1 (New York: H. Holt, 1928).

——, *Scritti sulla questione meridionale, 1896–1955* (Turin: Einaudi, 1955).

Sapelli, G., *Southern Europe since 1945: Tradition and Modernity in Portugal, Spain, Italy, Greece and Turkey* (London: Longman, 1995).

——, 'Dalla periferia all'integrazione europea', in R. Romano (ed.), *Storia dell'economia italiana*, vol. III: *L'età contemporanea: un paese nuovo* (Turin: Einaudi, 1991), pp. 59–141.

Schneider, J. and P. Schneider, *Culture and Political Economy in Western Sicily* (New York: Academic Press, 1976).

——, *Festival of the Poor: Fertility Decline and the Ideology of Class in Sicily, 1860–1980* (Tucson: University of Arizona Press, 1996).

Sereni, E., *Il capitalismo nelle campagne, 1860–1900* (Turin: Einaudi, 1975).

Serpieri, A., *La guerra e le classi rurali italiane* (Bari: Laterza, 1930).

Sione, P., 'From Home to Factory: Women in the Nineteenth-Century Italian Silk Industry', in D. M. Hafter, *European Women and Pre-Industrial Craft* (Bloomington, IN: Indiana University Press, 1995), pp. 137–52.

Snowden, F., 'From Triumph to Disaster: Fascism and Malaria in the Pontine Marshes, 1928–1946', in J. Dickie et al., *Disastro! Disasters in Italy since 1860: Culture, Politics, Society* (New York: Palgrave, 2002), pp. 113–40.

——, *The Fascist Revolution in Tuscany, 1919–1922* (Cambridge: Cambridge University Press, 1989).

——, *Violence and the Great Estates in the South of Italy: Apulia, 1900–1922* (Cambridge: Cambridge University Press, 1986).

Toniolo, G., *An Economic History of Liberal Italy, 1850–1918* (London: Routledge, 1990).

Villari, P., *La Sicilia e il socialismo* (Milan: Treves, 1896).

Wallerstein, I., 'The Relevance of the Concept of Semiperiphery to Southern Europe', in G. Arrighi (ed.), *Semiperipheral Development: The Politics of Southern Europe in the Twentieth Century* (Beverly Hills, CA: Sage, 1985).

Willson, P. (ed.), *Gender, Family and Sexuality: The Private Sphere in Italy, 1860–1945* (London: Palgrave, 2004).

Zamagni, V., *Lo stato italiano e l'economia. Storia dell'intervento pubblico dall'unificazione ai giorni nostri* (Florence: Le Monnier, 1981).

——, *The Economic History of Italy, 1860–1990* (Oxford: Oxford University Press, 1993).

——, 'Alcune tesi sull'intervento dello stato in una prospettiva di lungo periodo', in P. L. Ciocca (ed.), *Il progresso economico in Italia* (Bologna: Il Mulino, 1994), pp. 151–60.

Zanardelli, G., 'Discorso pronunciato a Potenza il 29 Settembre 1902', now in P. Corti (ed.), *Inchiesta Zanardelli sulla Basilicata* (Turin: Einaudi, 1976).

Ziino, N., *Latifondo e latifondismo. Studio di economia rurale* (Palermo: Orazio Fiorenza, 1911).

Box 3.1

Arlacchi, P., *Mafia, Peasants and Great Estates: Society in Traditional Calabria* (Cambridge: Cambridge University Press, 1983), p. 143.

Mack Smith, D., 'The Latifundia in Modern Sicilian History', *Proceedings of the British Academy*, 51, 81 (1965), pp. 85–124.

Sereni, E., *Il capitalismo nelle campagne, 1860–1900* (Turin: Einaudi, new edition, 1975), p. 153.

Snowden, F., '"Fields of Death": Malaria in Italy, 1861–1962', *Modern Italy*, 4, 1 (1999), pp. 25–47.

Box 3.5

Banti, A., *Storia della borghesia italiana. L'età liberale* (Rome: Donzelli, 1996).

Bonelli, F., *Lo sviluppo di una grande impresa in Italia. La Terni dal 1884 al 1962* (Turin: Einaudi, 1975).

Portelli, A., 'The Death of Luigi Trastulli: Memory and the Event', *The Death of Luigi Trastulli and Other Stories: Form and Meaning in Oral History* (New York: State University of New York Press, 1991), pp. 1–26.

—— *Acciai speciali. Terni, la ThyssenKrupp, la globalizzazione* (Rome: Donzelli, 2008).

Box 3.6

Accornero, A., *Fiat confino. La storia dell'Ors* (Milan: Avanti, 1959).

Bigazzi, D., 'Management Strategies in the Italian Car Industry, 1906–1945: Fiat and Alfa Romeo', in S. Tolliday and J. Zeitlin (eds), *The Automobile Industry and its Workers: between Fordism and Flexibility* (Cambridge: Polity, 1986).

Franzosi, R., *The Puzzle of Strikes: Class and State Strategies in Postwar Italy* (Cambridge: Cambridge University Press, 1995).

Box 3.8

Emmott, B., *Good Italy, Bad Italy: Why Italy Must Conquer its Demons to Face the Future* (New Haven: Yale University Press, 2013).

Peston, R., *How Do We Fix this Mess? The Economic Price of Having it All and the Route to Lasting Prosperity* (London: Hodder, 2013).

Box 3.9

Del Parigi, A. and R. Demetrio, *Antropologia di un labirinto urbano. I Sassi di Matera* (Matera: Osanna, 1994).

Levi, C., *Christ Stopped at Eboli*, 10th edn (Turin: Einaudi, 1972).

Musatti, R., 'Viaggio ai "Sassi" di Matera', *Comunità*, 9 (1950).

Mutual Security Agency Mission to Italy, *Il villaggio La Martella a Matera* (Rome, 1953).

Nitti, F., *Una città del Sud* (Rome: Unrra Casas prima giunta, 1956).

Parmly Toxey, A., *Materan Contradictions. Architecture, Preservation and Politics* (London: Ashgate, 2012).

Quaroni, L., 'L'esperienza di Matera', in M. Fabbri and A. Greco (eds), *La Comunità concreta: progetto e immagine* (Rome: Fondazione Adriano Olivetti, 1998).

Talamona, M., 'Dieci anni di politica dell'Unrra Casas: dalle case ai senzatetto ai borghi rurali nel Mezzogiorno d'Italia (1945–1955). Il ruolo di Adriano Olivetti', in C. Olmo (ed.), *Costruire la città dell'uomo. Adriano Olivetti e l'urbanistica* (Turin: Edizioni di Comunita, 2001), pp. 173–204.

Tentori, T., *Il sistema di vita della comunità materana* (Rome: Unrra Casas prima giunta, 1956), vol. III.

Film:
The Passion of Christ (Mel Gibson, 2004).

Box 3.10

Di Vittorio, G., Secretary of the Cgil, 4 October 1949, *Il Congress of the Cgil.* Extracts from speech illustrating the Cgil's *Piano del lavoro* (Plan of Work).

CHAPTER 4: POLITICS

General Bibliography

Accornero, A., R. Mannheimer and C. Sebastiani (eds), *L'identità comunista. I militanti, le strutture, la cultura del Pci* (Rome: Riuniti, 1983).

Albertazzi, D. and D. McDonnell (eds), *Twenty-First Century Populism: The Spectre of Western European Democracy* (London: Palgrave, 2007).

Allum, P., *Italy: Republic without Government?* (London: Norton, 1973).

——, *Politics and Society in Post-war Naples* (Cambridge: Cambridge University Press, 1973).

——, *Potere e società a Napoli nel dopoguerra* (Turin: Einaudi, 1975).

——, '"From Two into One": the Faces of the Italian Christian Democratic Party', *Party Politics*, 3, 1 (1997), pp. 23–52.

Anderson, P. and P. Camiller (eds), *Mapping the West European Left* (London: Verso, 1994).

Andreucci, F., 'La norma e la prassi. Le elezioni irregolari nell'Italia liberale (1861–1880)', *Passato e Presente*, 34 (1995), pp. 39–78.

Acquarone, A., *L'organizzazione dello stato totalitario* (Turin: Einaudi, 1973).

Ballini, P. L., *Le elezioni nella storia d'Italia dall'Unità al fascismo. Profilo storico-statistico* (Bologna: Il Mulino, 1988).

Behan, T., *The Long Awaited Moment: The Working Class and the Italian Communist Party in Milan, 1943–1948* (New York: Peter Lang, 1997).

Blackburn, R. (ed.), *After the Fall: The Failure of Communism and the Future of Socialism* (London: Verso, 1991).

Blackmer, D. and S. Tarrow (eds), *Communism in Italy and France* (Princeton, NJ: Princeton University Press, 1977).

Bobbio, L., *Lotta Continua. Storia di un organizzazione rivoluzionaria* (Rome: Savelli, 1979).

Bongiovanni, B., *Storia della guerra fredda* (Bari: Laterza, 2001).

Bosworth, R. J. B., *The Italian Dictatorship: Problems and Perspectives in the Interpretation of Mussolini and Fascism* (London: Arnold, 1998).

——, *Mussolini* (London: Arnold, 2002).

——, *Mussolini's Italy: Life under the Fascist Dictatorship, 1915–1945* (London: Penguin, 2007).

——, *Whispering City: Modern Rome and its Histories* (New Haven: Yale University Press, 2011).

Boxhoorn, A., *The Cold War and the Rift in the Governments of National Unity: Belgium, France and Italy in the Spring of 1947, a Comparison* (Amsterdam: Historisch Seminarium, van de Universiteit Van Amsterdam, 1993).

Bufacchi, V. and S. Burgess, *L'Italia contesa. Dieci anni di lotta politica da Mani Pulite a Berlusconi* (Rome: Carocci, 2002).

Bull, M. J. and P. Heywood, *West European Communist Parties After the Revolutions of 1989* (Basingstoke: Macmillan, 1994).

Bull, M. and J. Newell, *Italian Politics: Adjustment under Duress* (Cambridge: Cambridge University Press, 2005).

Calise, M., *Il sistema DC. Mediazione e conflitto nelle campagne democristiane* (Bari: De Donato, 1978).

——, 'The Italian Particracy: Beyond President and Parliament', *Political Science Quarterly*, 109, 3 (1994; now in M. Donovan, *Italy*, 2 vols (Dartmouth: Ashgate, 1998), vol. 2, pp. 441–66).

Carocci, G. (ed.), *Il trasformismo dall'Unità a oggi* (Milan: Unicopli, 1992).

Carr, R., *Spain, 1808–1975* (Oxford: Clarendon, 1982).

Chiarini, R., 'The "Movimento Sociale Italiano": A Historical Profile', in L. Cheles et al. (eds), *Neo-fascism in Europe* (London: Longman, 1991), pp. 19–42.

Chubb, J., *Patronage, Power and Poverty in Southern Italy: A Tale of Two Cities* (Cambridge: Cambridge University Press, 1982).

Conway, M., *Catholic Politics in Europe, 1918–1945* (London: Routledge, 1997).

Corner, P., *The Fascist Party and Popular Opinion in Mussolini's Italy* (Oxford: Oxford University Press, 2012).

De Gasperi, A., *Idee sulla Democrazia Cristiana* (Rome: Edizioni Cinque Lune, 1974).

De Grand, A., *Italian Fascism: its Origins and Development* (Lincoln, NE: University of Nebraska Press, 2000).

——, *Fascist Italy and Nazi Germany: The 'Fascist' Style of Rule* (London: Routledge, 1995).

De Grazia, V., *How Fascism Ruled Women: Italy, 1922–1945* (Berkeley, CA: California University Press, 1992).

De Luna, G., *Storia del Partito d'Azione (1942–1947)* (Rome: Riuniti, 1997).

Del Pero, M., *La guerra fredda* (Rome: Carocci, 2001).

Della Porta, D., 'Political Parties and Corruption: Reflections on the Italian Case', *Modern Italy*, 1, 1 (1995), pp. 97–114.

——, *La politica locale* (Bologna: Il Mulino, 1999).

Di Palma, G., 'Eurocommunism?' *Comparative Politics*, IX (April 1977), pp. 357–75.

Donovan, M., 'Political Leadership in Italy: Towards a Plebiscitary Democracy?' *Modern Italy*, 3, 2 (1998), pp. 281–94.

Duggan, C., *Francesco Crispi, 1818–1901: From Nation to Nationalism* (Oxford: Oxford University Press, 2002).

Duggan, C. and Gundle, S. (eds), 'The Cult of Mussolini in Twentieth-Century Italy' (special issue of *Modern Italy*, 18, 2, 2013).

Duggan, C. et al eds., *The Cult of the Duce: Mussolini and the Italians* (Manchester: MUP, 2013).

Duggan, C. and C. Wagstaff (eds), *Italy in the Cold War, Politics, Culture and Society* (Oxford: Berg, 1995).

Dunphy, R., *From Eurocommunism to Eurosocialism: The Search for a Post-Communist European Left* (Dundee: Department of Political Science, 1993).

Einaudi, M. and F. Goguel, *Christian Democracy in Italy and France* (Notre Dame, IL: University of Notre Dame Press, 1952).

Elia, L., 'Forme di governo', in *Enciclopedia del Diritto*, vol. XIX (Milan: Giuffré, 1960), pp. 634–75.

—— and G. Vassalli, *I quarant'anni della Costituzione* (Milan: Libri Scheiwiller, 1989).

Farneti, P., *The Italian Party System (1945–1980)* (London: Pinter, 1985).

Femia, J., *Gramsci's Political Thought: Hegemony, Consciousness and the Revolutionary Process* (Oxford: Clarendon Press, 1987).

Ferrara, M., 'The Rise and Fall of Democratic Universalism: Health Care Reform in Italy, 1978–1994', *Journal of Health Politics, Policy and Law*, 20, 2 (1996), in M. Donovan (ed.), *Italy*, 2 vols (Dartmouth: Ashgate, 1998), vol. II, pp. 355–68.

Fiori, G., *Il venditore* (Milan: Garzanti, 1995).

Flores, M., 'Il Pds', *Linea d'ombra*, 72 (1992), pp. 6–7.

—— and N. Gallerano, *Sul PCI: Un'interpretazione storica* (Bologna: Il Mulino, 1992).

Follini, M., *C'era una volta la DC* (Bologna: Il Mulino, 1994).

Fontana, S., 'Towards a History of Transformism (1883–1983)', in M. Donovan (ed.), *Italy*, vol. II (Dartmouth: Ashgate, 1998), pp. 305–21.

Foot, J., 'The Left Opposition and the Crisis: Rifondazione Comunista and La Rete, 1989–1994', in S. Gundle and S. Parker (eds), *The New Italian Republic: From the Fall of the Berlin Wall to Berlusconi* (London: Routledge, 1996), pp. 173–88.

——, '"White Bolsheviks"? The Catholic Left and the Socialists in Italy – 1919–1920', *Historical Journal*, 40, 2 (1997), pp. 415–33.

——, *Milan since the Miracle: City, Culture and Identity* (Oxford: Berg, 2001).

——, *Italy's Divided Memory* (New York and London: Palgrave, 2010).

Forgacs, D., *Rethinking Italian Fascism: Capitalism, Populism and Culture* (London: Lawrence and Wishart, 1986).

Furlong, P., *The Italian Christian Democrats: From Catholic Movement to Conservative Party* (Hull: Department of Politics, 1982).

Gabrielli, P., *Il 1946, la donna, la Repubblica* (Rome: Donzelli, 2009).

Galli, G., *Storia della Democrazia Cristiana* (Rome: Laterza, 1978).

——, *Storia del Pci. Il Partito Comunista Italiano: Livorno 1921, Rimini 1991* (Milan: Kaos, 1993).

Gambetta, D. and S. Warner, 'The Rhetoric of Reform Revealed (or: If you bite the ballot it may bite back)', *Journal of Modern Italian Studies*, 1, 3 (1996).

Ganapini, L., *La Repubblica delle camicie nere* (Milan: Garzanti, 1999).

Gentile, E., 'Mussolini's Charisma', *Modern Italy*, 3, 2 (1998), pp. 219–35.

——, *Storia del Partito Fascista, 1919–1922: Movimento e milizia* (Bari: Laterza, 1989).

——, *The Sacralization of Politics in Fascist Italy* (Cambridge, MA: Harvard University Press, 1996).

——, 'Fascism as Political Religion', *Journal of Contemporary History*, 25, 3 (1990), pp. 229–51.

Ginsborg, P., 'Italian Political Culture in Historical Perspective', *Modern Italy*, 1, 1 (1995), pp. 3–17.

Graziano, L., 'Compromesso storico e democrazia consociativa: verso una "nuova democrazia"', in L. Graziano and S. Tarrow (eds), *La crisi italiana* (Turin: Einaudi, 1979), vol. II, pp. 719–63.

Graziano, L., 'Patron–Client Relationships in Southern Italy', *European Journal of Political Research*, I, 1 (1973), pp. 3–34.

——, *Clientelismo e sistema politico. Il caso dell'Italia* (Milan: Franco Angeli, 1980).

——, 'Center–periphery Relations and the Italian Crisis: the Problem of Clientelism', in L. Graziano, P. Katzenstein and S. Tarrow (eds), *Territorial Politics in Industrial Nations* (New York: Praeger, 1978), pp. 290–326.

Gundle, S., *Between Hollywood and Moscow: The Italian Communists and the Challenge of Mass Culture, 1943–1991* (Durham, NC: Duke University Press, 2000).

Habermas, J., 'Staatsbürgerschaft und nationale Identität', in *Faktizität und Geltung* (Frankfurt: Suhrkamp, 1992).

Hanley, D. (ed.), *Christian Democracy in Europe: A Comparative Perspective* (London: Pinter, 1994).

Hine, D., 'Social Democracy in Italy', in W. Paterson and A. Thomas (eds), *Social Democratic Parties in Western Europe* (London: Croom Helm, 1977).

Ignazi, P. and C. Ysmal, 'New and Old Extreme Right Parties: the French Front National and the Italian Movimento Sociale', *European Journal of Political Research*, 22 (1992), pp. 101–21.

Kertzer, D., *Comrades and Christians: Religion and Political Struggle in Communist Italy* (Cambridge: Cambridge University Press, 1980).

——, 'The 19th Congress of the PCI: the Role of Symbolism in the Communist Crisis', in R. Leonardi and F. Anderlini (eds), *Italian Politics: A Review*, vol. 6 (London: Pinter, 1992), pp. 69–82.

——, *Politics and Symbols: The Italian Communist Party and the Fall of Communism* (New Haven, CT: Yale University Press, 1996).

Kurth, J., 'A Tale of Four Countries: Parallel Politics in Southern Europe, 1815–1990', in J. Kurth and J. Petras (eds), *Mediterranean Paradoxes* (Oxford: Berg, 1993).

Levy, C., 'From Fascism to "Post-fascism": Italian Roads to Modernity', in R. Bessel (ed.), *Fascist Italy and Nazi Germany: Comparisons and Contrasts* (Cambridge: Cambridge University Press, 1996), pp. 165–96.

——, 'Currents of Italian Syndicalism before 1926', *International Review of Social History*, 45 (2000), pp. 209–50.

—, 'Historians and the "First Republic": Italy Fifty Years after 1945', in S. Berger et al. (eds), *Writing National Histories: Western Europe since 1800* (London: Routledge, 1999), pp. 88–106.

Lovett, C., *The Democratic Movement in Italy, 1830–1876* (Cambridge, MA: Harvard University Press, 1982).

Luzzatto, S., *Il corpo del duce. Un cadavere tra immaginazione, storia e memoria* (Turin: Einaudi, 1998).

—, 'The Political Culture of Fascist Italy', *Contemporary European History*, 8, 2 (1999), pp. 317–34.

—— *The Body of Il Duce: Mussolini's Corpse and the Fortunes of Italy* (New York: Metropolitan Books, 2006).

Lyttelton, A., *The Seizure of Power: Fascism in S. Italy, 1919–1929* (London: Weidenfeld and Nicolson, 1973).

Mammone, A. and G. Veltri (eds), *Italy Today: The Sick Man of Europe* (London: Routledge, 2010).

Manzella, A., 'Il percorso delle istituzioni', in S. Cassese (ed.), *Ritratto dell'Italia* (Bari: Laterza, 2001), pp. 33–59.

Marino, G. C., *Autoritratto del Pci staliniano, 1946–1953* (Rome: Riuniti, 1991).

McCarthy, P., *La crisi dello Stato italiano. Costume e vita politica nell'Italia contemporanea* (Rome: Riuniti, 1996).

Morgan, P., *Italian Fascism, 1919–1945* (Basingstoke: Macmillan, 1995).

Musella, L., *Individui, amici, clienti. Relazioni personali e circuiti politici in Italia meridionale tra Otto e Novecento* (Bologna: Il Mulino, 1994).

Napolitano, G., *Il patto che ci lega. Per una coscienza repubblicana* (Bologna: Il Mulino, 2009).

—— *Una e indivisibile. Riflessioni sui 150 anni della nostra Italia* (Milan: Rizzoli, 2011).

Nevola, G. 'A Constitutional Patriotism for Italian Democracy: The Contribution of President Napolitano', *Bulletin of Italian Politics*, 3, 1 (2011), pp. 159–84.

Newell, J., *The Politics of Italy: Governance in a Normal Country* (Cambridge: Cambridge University Press, 2010).

Paladin, L., in *Enciclopedia del diritto* (Milan: Giuffrè, 1967), vol. XVI.

Pansa, G., *Bisaglia. Una carriera democristiana* (Milan: Sugarco, 1975).

Pappalardo, A., 'Consociational Politics and Italian Democracy' (1980), now in M. Donovan (ed.), *Italy*, vol. 2 (Dartmouth: Ashgate, 1998), pp. 271–394.

Parker, S., 'The End of Italian Exceptionalism? Assessing the Transition to the Second Republic', *The Italianist*, 19 (1999), pp. 251–83.

—, 'The Government of the Ulivo', in R. D'Alimonte and D. Nelken (eds), *Italian Politics: The Center–Left in Power* (Oxford: Istituto Cattaneo, 1997).

Pasquino, G., 'Sources of Stability and Instability in the Italian Party System', *West European Politics*, 6 (1983), pp. 93–110.

Passerini, L., *Mussolini immaginario. Storia di una biografia, 1915–1939* (Bari: Laterza, 1991).

—, 'Memories of Resistance, Resistances of Memory', in H. Peitsch et al. (eds), *European Memories of the Second World War* (New York and Oxford: Berghahn, 1999).

Pizzorno, A., 'Le difficoltà del consociativismo', in A. Pizzorno, *Le radici della politica assoluta* (Milan: Feltrinelli, 1993), pp. 285–313.

Poli, E., *Forza Italia. Strutture, leadership e radicamento territoriale* (Bologna: Il Mulino, 2001).

Pollard, J., *The Fascist Experience in Italy* (London: Routledge, 1998).

Pombeni, P., *Demagogia e tirannide. Uno studio sulla forma partito del fascismo* (Bologna: Il Mulino, 1984).

——, *Partiti e sistemi politici nella storia contemporanea (1830–1968)* (Bologna: Il Mulino, 1985).

——, 'Il partito fascista', in A. Del Boca, M. Legnani and M. Rossi (eds), *Il regime fascista. Storia e storiografia* (Bari: Laterza, 1995), pp. 203–19.

——, 'The Roots of the Italian Political Crisis: A View from History, 1918, 1945, 1989… and After', in C. Levy and M. Roseman (eds), *Three Postwar Eras in Comparison: Western Europe, 1918–1945–1989* (Basingstoke: Palgrave Macmillan, 2002), pp. 276–96.

Pridham, G., *Political Parties and Coalitional Behaviour in Italy* (London: Routledge, 1988).

Putnam, R., 'Bowling Alone: America's Declining Social Capital', *Journal of Democracy*, 6, 1 (1995), pp. 65–78.

Ricci, A. G., *La Repubblica* (Bologna: Il Mulino, 2001).

Ridolfi, M., *Il circolo virtuoso. Sociabilità democratica, associazionismo e rappresentanza politicale nell'Ottocento* (Florence: Centro editoriale Toscano, 1990).

——, *Il partito della repubblica. I repubblicani in Romagna e le origini del Pri nell'Italia liberale (1972–1895)* (Milan: Franco Angeli, 1990).

——, *Il PSI e la nascita del partito di massa, 1892–1922* (Bari: Laterza, 1992).

Romanelli, R., *Il comando impossibile: Stato e società nell'Italia liberale* (Bologna: Il Mulino, 1988).

——, 'Electoral Systems and Social Structures: a Comparative Perspective', in R. Romonelli (ed.), *How Did They Become Voters? The History of Franchise in Modern European Representation* (The Hague: Kluwer Law International, 1998), pp. 1–37.

Romero-Maura, J., 'Caciquismo as a Political System', in E. Gellner and J. Waterbury, *Patrons and Clients in Mediterranean Societies* (London: Duckworth, 1977).

Rusconi, G. E., *Se cessiamo di essere una nazione* (Bologna: Il Mulino, 1993).

Salomone, A. W., *Italian Democracy in the Making* (Philadelphia: University of Pennsylvania Press, 1945).

Salvadori, M., *Storia d'Italia e crisi di regime. Alle radici della politica italiana* (Bologna: Il Mulino, 1994).

Salvati, M., 'Da piccola borghesia a ceti medi', in A. Del Boca, M. Legnani and M. Rossi (eds), *Il regime fascista. Storia e storiografia* (Bari: Laterza, 1995), pp. 446–75.

Salvemini, G., 'Un sarto pei gobbi', *Il Ponte*, VIII, 3 (1952), pp. 281–97.

Sapelli, G., *Cleptocrazia: Il meccanismo unico della corruzione tra economia e politica* (Milan: Feltrinelli, 1994).

——, 'The Italian Crisis and Capitalism', *Modern Italy*, 1, 1 (1995).

——, *Southern Europe since 1945: Tradition and Modernity in Portugal, Spain, Italy, Greece and Turkey* (London: Longman, 1995).

Sartori, G., *Parties and Party Systems: A Framework for Analysis* (Cambridge: Cambridge University Press, 1976).

Sassoon, D., *One Hundred Years of Socialism: the West European Left in the Twentieth Century* (London: Tauris, 1996).

Scarpellini, E., *Material Nation: A Consumer's History of Modern Italy* (Oxford: Oxford University Press, 2011).

Scoppola, P., *Dal neoguelfismo alla Democrazia Cristiana* (Rome: Editrice Studium, 1963).

Segrestani, M., *Un collegio elettorale nell'età Giolittiana: Correggio* (Bologna: Li Causi editore, 1984).

Setta, S., *L'Uomo Qualunque, 1944–1948* (Bari: Laterza, [1975] 1995).

Signorelli, A., *Chi può e chi aspetta. Giovani e clientelismo in un'area interna del Mezzogiorno* (Naples: Liguori editore, 1983).

Spriano, P., *Intervista sulla storia del PCI* (Bari: Laterza, 1979).

Togliatti, P., *Lectures on Fascism* (London: Lawrence and Wishart, 1976).

Tranfaglia, N., 'Trasformismo', in P. Ginsborg (ed.), *Stato dell'Italia* (Milan: Bruno Mondadori, 1994), pp. 95–8.

Ullrich, H., 'L'organizzazione politica dei liberali italiani nel Parlamento e nel Paese (1870–1914)', in R. Lill and N. Matteucci, *Il liberalismo in Italia e in Germania dalla rivoluzione del '48 alla prima guerra mondiale* (Bologna: Il Mulino, 1980), pp. 403–51.

Van Loenen, G., 'Weimar or Byzantium: Two Opposing Approaches to the Italian Party System', *European Journal of Political Research*, 18 (1990), pp. 241–56.

Vandelli, L., 'The New Local Government Law', in R. Leonardi and F. Anderlini (eds), *Italian Politics: A Review*, vol. 6 (London: Pinter, 1992), pp. 25–40.

Viroli, M., *For Love of Country: An Essay on Patriotism and Nationalism* (Oxford: Clarendon, 1995).

Walker, M., *The Cold War and the Making of the Modern World* (London: Fourth Estate, 1993).

Webster, R. A., *Christian Democracy in Italy, 1860–1960* (London: Hollis and Carter, 1961).

Whittam, J., *Fascist Italy* (Manchester: Manchester University Press, 1995).

Willson, P., *The Clockwork Factory: Women and Work in Fascist Italy* (Oxford: Clarendon Press, 1993).

—— (ed.), *Gender, Family and Sexuality: The Private Sphere in Italy, 1860–1945* (London: Palgrave, 2004).

——, *Women in Twentieth Century Italy* (London: Palgrave, 2010).

Zinn, D. L., *La Raccomandazione. Clientelismo vecchio e nuovo* (Rome: Donzelli, 2001).

Zuckerman, A., *On the Institutionalization of Political Clienteles: Party Factions and Cabinet Coalitions in Italy* (Beverly Hills, CA, 1974).

Box 4.1

Venditti, R., *Il manuale Cencelli. Il prontuario della lottizzazione democristiana. Un documento sulla gestione del potere* (Rome: Riuniti, 1981), p. 16.

Film:
Il Divo (2008, P. Sorrentino).

Box 4.2

Etnasi, F., *2 Giugno 1946* (Rome: Dies, 1966).

Gabrielli, P., *Il 1946, le donne, la Repubblica* (Rome: Donzelli, 2010).

Giovana, M., *Dalla parte del re. Conservazione, 'piemontesità' e 'sabaudismo' nel voto referendario del 2 giugno 1946* (Milan: Franco Angeli, 1996).

Katz, R., *La fine dei Savoia* (Rome: Riuniti, 1975).

Mack Smith, D., *Italy and its Monarchy* (New Haven, CT: Yale University Press, 1989).

Piretti, M. S., *Le elezioni politiche in Italia dal 1848 a oggi* (Bari: Laterza, 1995).

Ricci, A., *La Repubblica* (Bologna: Il Mulino, 2011).
Rusconi, G., *Patria e repubblica* (Bologna: Il Mulino, 1997).

Box 4.3

Caferra, V. M., *Il sistema della corruzione. Le ragioni, i soggetti, i luoghi* (Bari: Laterza, 1992).

Box 4.4

Foot, J., *Calcio: A History of Italian Football* (London: Harper, 2007).

Jones, T., *The Dark Heart of Italy: Travels through Time and Space across Italy* (London: Faber and Faber, 2007).

Sapelli, G., *Cleptocrazia: Il meccanismo unico della corruzione tra economia e politica* (Milan: Feltrinelli, 1994).

Stella, G. A. and S. Rizzo, *La casta. Così i politici italiani sono diventati intoccabili* (Milan: Rizzoli, 2007).

Box 4.5

Corner, P., *Fascism in Ferrara, 1915–1925* (Oxford: Oxford University Press, 1975).

De Grand, A., *Italian Fascism: Its Origins and Development* (Lincoln, NE: University of Nebraska Press, 2000).

Gentile, E., *Storia del Partito Fascista 1919–1922. Movimento e milizia* (Bari: Laterza, 1989) (from where the example in the box is taken).

Snowden, F., *The Fascist Revolution in Tuscany, 1919–1922* (Cambridge: Cambridge University Press, 1989).

Tasca, A., *The Rise of Italian Fascism* (pseud. A. Rossi) (London, 1938).

Box 4.9

Capurso, A., *I discorsi che hanno cambiato l'Italia. Da Garibaldi e Cavour a Berlusconi e Veltroni* (Milan: Mondadori, 2008).

Fiori, G., *Il venditore* (Milan: Garzanti, 1995).

Ginsborg, P., *Italy and its Discontents: Family, Civil Society, State, 1980–2001* (London: Penguin, 2002).

——, *Silvio Berlusconi: Television, Power and Patrimony* (London: Verso, 2005).

Box 4.10

Fiori, G., *Il venditore* (Milan: Garzanti, 1995).

Ginsborg, P., *Italy and its Discontents: Family, Civil Society, State, 1980–2001* (London: Penguin, 2002).

——, *Silvio Berlusconi: Television, Power and Patrimony* (London: Verso, 2005).

Box 4.11

Amadori, A., *Mi consenta. Come Berlusconi ha conquistato l'Italia* (Milan: Scheiwiller, 2002).

Berlusconi, S., *Discorsi per la democrazia* (Milan: Mondadori, 2001).

—— *Discorsi per la libertà* (Milan: Mondadori, 2013).

Bolasco, S. et al., *Parole in libertà. Un'analisi statistica e linguistica dei discorsi di Berlusconi* (Rome: Manifestolibri, 2006).

Box 4.13

Setta, S., *L'uomo qualunque. 1944–1948* (Bari-Roma: Laterza, 2004).

Box 4.14

Stella, G. A. and S. Rizzo, *La casta. Così i politici italiani sono diventati intoccabili* (Milan: Rizzoli, 2007).

——, *La deriva: Perché l'Italia rischia il naufragio* (Milan: Rizzoli, 2010).

——, *Licenziare i padreterni: L'Italia tradita dalla casta* (Milan: Rizzoli, 2011).

Box 4.15

Natale, P. and R. Biorcio, *Politica a 5 stelle: Idee, storia e strategie del movimento di Grillo* (Milan: Feltrinelli, 2013).

Santoro, G., *Un Grillo qualunque: Il Movimento 5 Stelle e il populismo digitale nella crisi dei partiti italiani* (Rome: Castelvecchi, 2013).

Stella, G. A. and S. Rizzo, *La casta. Così i politici italiani sono diventati intoccabili* (Milan: Rizzoli, 2007).

Index